Design for
Sustainability

Design for Sustainability

A Sourcebook of Integrated Eco-logical Solutions

Dr Janis Birkeland

EARTHSCAN

Earthscan Publications Limited
London • Sterling, VA

First published in the UK and USA in 2002 by
Earthscan Publications Ltd

ISBN: 1 85383 897 7 paperback
       1 85383 900 0 hardback

Background image: 'Snowy Gudgenby Trees' © Terry Woollcott
Printed and bound by The Bath Press, Bath
Cover design by Susanne Harris

The individual authors remain responsible for the content of their chapters

For a full list of publications please contact:

Earthscan Publications Ltd
120 Pentonville Road
London, N1 9JN, UK
Tel: +44 (0)20 7278 0433
Fax: +44 (0)20 7278 1142
Email: earthinfo@earthscan.co.uk
http://www.earthscan.co.uk

22883 Quicksilver Drive, Sterling, VA 20166–2012, USA

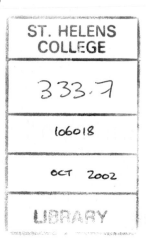

A catalogue record for this book is available from the British Library

Library of Congress Cataloging-in-Publication Data

Birkeland, Janis.
Design for sustainability : a sourcebook of integrated ecological solutions / Janis Birkeland.
     p. cm.
  Includes bibliographical references and index.
  ISBN 1-85383-897-7 (paperback) – ISBN 1-85383-900-0 (hardback)
   1. Ecological engineering. 2. Sustainable development. I. Title.

GE350 .B57 2000
363.7–dc21

                              2002000385

Earthscan is an editorially independent subsidiary of Kogan Page Ltd and publishes in association with WWF-UK and the
International Institute for Environment and Development

This book is printed on elemental chlorine-free paper

Contents

List of Illustrations

Boxes

Figures, Tables, Boxes

List of Acronyms and Abbreviations

ABS	Australian Bureau of Statistics
AHC	Australian Heritage Commission
ATM	automatic teller machine
ATSIC	Aboriginal and Torres Strait Islander Commission
BCSD	Business Council for Sustainable Development
BES Index	building material ecological sustainability index (previously BMAS: building material assessment system)
BIA	Building Industry Authority (NZ)
BOMA	Building Owners and Managers Association (US)
CERF	Engineering Research Foundation
CIB	Conseil International du Batiment (Fr)
CSD	Council for Sustainable Development
CSTB	Scientific and Technical Centre for Building (Fr)
DEST	Department of the Environment, Sport and Territories (now Environment Australia)
DfE	Design for Environment
EMS	environment management systems
EPA	Environment Protection Authority
EQI	environmental quality indicators
ERDC	Energy and Development Research Centre (SA)
ERP	electronic road pricing
ESD	ecological sustainable development
FSC	Forest Stewardship Council
GDP	gross domestic product
GIS	geographic information system
GNP	gross national product
GPI	genuine process indicator
HVAC	heating, ventilating and air conditioning
IAQ	indoor air quality
ICLEI	International Council for Local Environmental Initiatives
ICOMOS	International Council on Monuments and Sites
IPCC	Intergovernmental Panel on Climate Change
ISO	International Standardisation Organisation
LCA	life cycle analysis or assessment
LSL	laminated strand lumber beams
LVL	laminated veneer beams
MAI	multi-lateral agreement on investment
MCS	multiple chemical sensitivity
MTR	minimum termite risk
NAFI	National Association of Forest Industries
NAS	National Academy of Sciences (US)
NPI	national pollution inventories
OEL	occupational exposure limits
PBC	performance-based contracting
PV	photovoltaic
R&D	research and development
RH	relative humidity
RMI	Rocky Mountain Institute (US)
RMIT	Royal Melbourne Institute of Technology
SAA	Standards Association of Australia
SBS	sick building syndrome
SEAC	State of the Environment Advisory Council
SFM	sustainable forest management
SWOT	strengths, weaknesses, opportunities, threats (analysis of)
UEA	Urban Ecology Australia
ULEV	ultra-low-emission vehicle
UN	United Nations
UNCED	United Nations Conference on Environment and Development
UNCHS	United Nations Centre for Human Settlement
UNEP	United Nations Environment Programme
UNESCO	United Nations Educational, Scientific and Cultural Organisation
UWRA	Urban Water Research Association of Australia
VOC	volatile organic compound
WBCSD	World Business Council for Sustainable Development
WCED	World Commission on Environment and Development
WI	Worldwatch Institute
WRI	World Resources Institute (US)
WWF	World Wide Fund for Nature

Chapter Outlines

Section 1: Designing Eco-solutions

The first two chapters explain the centrality of the built environment in ecological and social sustainability and suggest that ecological design is a new paradigm for addressing the challenges of the 21st Century.

1.1 Education for Eco-innovation: Research and Development (R&D) for innovation and commercialisation needs to be targeted at eco-efficiency and radical resource reduction to be relevant to 21st Century needs.

Box 1: Environmental Education Principles.

1.2 The Centrality of Design: Built environment design and construction is central in environmental problems; however, design has not been appreciated as a form of environmental management.

Box 2: Conventional and Ecodesign Compared.

The second two chapters show links between eco-logical design and ecophilosophy, and defines eco-logical design as both an ethic and a method to help society move towards ecological rationality.

1.3 Green Philosophy: A truly green architecture has not yet been achieved, but ecophilosophy can provide insights for developing eco-logical design principles.

Box 3: Eco-logical Design Principles.

1.4 Responsible Design: Eco-logical design is a way of thinking and doing, and can contribute to any field of social and environmental problem solving.

Box 4: Paradigm Quiz.

Section 2: The Concepts of Growth and Waste

The first two chapters argue that most environmental designers have largely ignored the need to face the realities of population growth and resource distribution, and to supplant the goal of industrial growth with that of personal development and life quality.

2.1 Limits to Growth and Design of Settlements: The ecological 'bottom line' (the physical limits to population and consumption) needs to be integrated into basic principles of planning and design.

Box 5: Exponential Growth.

2.2 Redefining Progress: The idea of 'progress' must be redefined so that design solutions enhance life quality rather than promote only economic growth and materialism.

Box 6: Genuine Progress Indicators.

The second two chapters explain that the design of eco-solutions which reduce waste over the life of the building or product requires that designers acquire ecological literacy and systems design thinking.

2.3 Designing Waste: Designers need to be mindful that the present design paradigm is inherently wasteful, in that new products turn existing products into waste.

2.4 Designing for Durability: Built environment planning, design and management must be reconceived to value heritage and prioritise life cycle costing.

Box 7: Waste Reduction Checklist.

Many students in the Division of Science and Design at the University of Canberra contributed to this book with their comments and chapter assessments as it evolved over three years.

Section 3: Industrial, Urban and Construction Ecology

The first two chapters show that our present linear, sequential and competitive systems of production (factories and transport, cities and infrastructure, or the building industry itself) have created waste and inefficiency on a large scale.

3.1 **Industrial Ecology**: Basic principles of ecology can be applied to industrial structures and processes to create efficiencies in material and energy use.

3.2 **Urban Ecology**: Cities should be analysed and redesigned as interactive systems involving the interrelationship of humans with their environments, and cities with their hinterland.

Box 8: Eco-efficiency Checklist.

The second two chapters suggest that our regulatory, economic or managerial approaches to environmental problem-solving have neglected the built environment and construction industry, and often compound problems.

3.3 **Construction Ecology**: The organisation of the construction industry, and our understanding of it, reinforces an inherently wasteful paradigm of development.

3.4 **Pollution Prevention by Design**: Systems design approaches offer an alternative to conventional (bureaucratic) regulatory controls or (linear) economic incentives to pollution control.

Box 9: Eco-footprints and Eco-logical Design.

Section 4: Design Within Complex Social Systems

The first two chapters explore the potential of 'complexity' theories to promote better understanding of problems, inspire new design methods and/or guide the appropriate application of older methods.

4.1 **Complexity and the Urban Environment**: Research in self-organising systems from science offers concepts for analysing issues of urban form, management, government and community action in cities.

4.2 **Unified Human Community Ecology**: Theories from human ecology fields can be integrated to develop a useful set of design checklists and guidelines.

Box 10: Human Ecology Design Checklist.

The second two chapters suggest design and organisational processes must change, yet designers may in fact revert to old processes if new concepts or metaphors from the sciences are merely transposed as ecological principles and goals.

4.3 **The Bionic Method in Industrial Design**: Natural evolution and the resulting life-forms are useful precedents for exploring sustainable product design – if not superficially applied.

4.4 **Green Theory in the Construction Fields**: The integration of ecological design and project management principles is necessary to realise eco-efficiency in the construction industry.

Box 11: Ecodesign Considerations for Urban Buildings.

Section 5: Permaculture and Landscape Design

The first two chapters suggest that permaculture can help to improve the education of environmental designers, while 'permaculture buildings', edible landscapes and integrated site planning are elements of sustainable environments.

5.1 **Permaculture and Design Education**: Permaculture offers a model for design education because it promotes living environments that are designed to evolve and grow with building use.

5.2 **The Sustainable Landscape**: Urban rooftop greening illustrates how buildings can provide edible landscapes and reduce the impacts of transportation.

Box 12: Permaculture: 'Functional Analysis of the Chicken'.

The second two chapters suggest that built environments will be more successful if they meet the psychological and cultural needs of the users and challenge the conceptual design barrier between the built and natural environment.

5.3 Place, Community Values and Planning: Conserving places of meaning and value (ie cultural landscapes) requires more integration of community values through participatory planning.

5.4 Playgardens and Community Development: Traditional playground design reflects dated social values, while playgardens have the potential to influence children's attitudes towards nature.

Box 13: Pros and Cons of Design Charrettes.

Section 6: Values Embodied in and Reinforced by Design

The first two chapters show how the bias towards linear reductionist (as opposed to systems design) thinking is reflected in the built environment itself. Without new theory construction, designers may be influenced by biased concepts.

6.1 Urban Forms and the Dominant Paradigm: The basic values and premises of the dominant paradigm of development remain embodied and concretised in the built environment.

6.2 Models of Ecological Housing: Models of ecological housing are legitimised by reference to environmental metaphors, but do not yet challenge conventional housing patterns.

Box 14: Adaptable Housing.

The second two chapters look at examples of how dated conceptions among designers (eg about nature, architecture and user groups) are reflected in product design concepts.

6.3 Marketing-led Design: The design of mass-produced products are market driven and can reinforce stereotyping, consumerism and even anti-social behaviour.

Box 15: The Rebound Effect.

6.4 Gender and Product Semantics: Unconscious gender biases can influence environmental design education adversely, unless they are recognised by designers and educators.

Box 16: Ergonomics or Human-Centred Design.

Section 7: Design for Community Building and Health

The first two chapters examine the need for designers to scrutinise their own values and to accommodate differing preferences and cultural diversity, especially in addressing the needs of disenfranchised groups (eg elderly, immigrants.

7.1 ESD and 'Sense of Community': Community design can counteract social alienation and build the community allegiance necessary to foster greater care for the environment.

7.2 Sustainability and Aboriginal Housing: Communities have differing design needs partly because cultures evolved in response to surrounding environments, as in the case of Aboriginal Australians.

Box 17: Aboriginal Dwellings.

The second two chapters suggest that conventional design has not adequately taken into account some of the basic *physical* needs of building users, let alone the building's impact on the environment, leading to problems like sick building syndrome.

7.3 Indoor Air Quality in Housing: Increased indoor air pollution and other environmental hazards correspond with the growing use of synthetic building materials and 'modern' forms of construction.

7.4 Beyond the Chemical Barrier: Where building longevity and human health requires eliminating pests, chemical-based insect controls can be.avoided by design.

Box 18: Air Quality Problems in Buildings.

Section 8: Productivity, Land and Transport Efficiency

The first two chapters show that eco-logical design can reverse the serious health, safety, comfort and productivity issues that have resulted from poor design and lack of enlightened consumer demand.

8.1 Greening the Work Place: Design for human health and comfort benefits business, as it coincides with cost savings through energy efficiency and worker productivity.

8.2 Sustainable Personal Urban Transport: Given the demand for private transport and inadequacy of public transport to meet activity patterns, car design can be more safe, efficient and low impact.

Box 19: The Hypercar Concept.

The second two chapters suggest that debates over land use planning – specifically urban consolidation versus decentralisation – must take into account the realities of differing preferences, while seeking to enlighten and change public values.

8.3 From Sub-urbanism to Eco-cities: The suburbs – as presently designed – waste space, resources and energy, and contribute to the alienation of people from both nature and community.

8.4 Density, Environment and the City: The existing social context and physical infrastructure impede radical change to cities, yet minor changes could make them far more ecologically sound.

Box 20: ESD and Urban Transport Infrastructure.

Section 9: Design with less Energy, Materials and Waste

The first two chapters look at how resource and energy loops can be closed at the household and neighbourhood level, to create environments that approach self-sufficiency.

9.1 Living Technologies: 'Living Machines', (solar powered microbe-based ecosystems) purify water and recycle waste, without the problems associated with conventional machines.

Box 21: Principles for Designing Living Machines.

9.2 Housing Wastewater Solutions: Existing or new homes should be made 'autonomous'; that is, able to collect all their fresh water and treat household waste and pollution on site.

The second two chapters show how the careful design and selection of materials (eg 'woodless timber' products) and passive energy systems, could greatly reduce greenhouse emissions and other impacts of construction.

9.3 Autonomous Servicing: Houses can be designed or retrofitted so that they do not need to draw upon the energy grid, with a short and sometimes immediate pay-back period.

Box 22: Implementing Design for Environment.

9.4 Timber Waste Minimisation by Design: Designers can reduce the environmental impacts of buildings and the depletion of forests through the selection of eco-efficient timber products.

Box 23: Timber Certification and Labelling.

Section 10: Low-impact Housing Design and Materials

The first two chapters dispel some of the myths about 'alternative' construction materials (eg earth, strawbale, bamboo and hemp), which have the potential to house the world's poor (and wealthy) with low-impact natural materials.

10.1 Earth Buildings: Among the benefits of earth wall construction is that people without formal qualifications can easily be taught the skills to build their own homes.

10.2 Strawbale Construction: Strawbale construction has a long and successful track record, and by overcoming legislative barriers, is beginning to have a revival in many places.

Box 24: A Carbohydrate Economy.

The second two chapters show that if the global warming and energy crises usher in a 'carbohydrate economy' construction materials already exist which could revolutionise the construction industry.

10.3 Bamboo as a Building Resource: Bamboo, the fastest growing 'timber', can be grown in many places and turned into many different, relatively low-impact construction materials.

10.4 Hemp Architecture: Hemp fibre could contribute to a carbohydrate-based economy by providing many low-impact construction materials.

Box 25: Carbon Storage.

Section 11: Construction and Environmental Regulation

The first two chapters suggest that many legislative or economic instruments currently used by government authorities to protect the environment focus on internalising environmental costs, rather than on promoting direct design solutions.

11.1 Legislative Environmental Controls: Traditional regulatory approaches to pollution control have led to end-of-pipe solutions, and discourage no-pipe or closed loop design solutions.

11.2 Market-based Regulation: Approaches to pollution control that use economic instruments and incentives to try to shape the behaviour of business and industry are indirect and inefficient.

Box 26: Environmental Taxes.

The second two chapters discuss the many legislative parameters within which environmental designers must work, such as planning and building codes, and pollution controls, which can operate against environmental protection.

11.3 Building Codes and Sustainability: Professionals must develop new kinds of building codes that promote whole-systems life cycle analysis and eco-logical design solutions.

Box 27: Environmental Quality Indicators.

11.4 Assessing Building Materials: Due to time constraints, designers need to develop simplified and practical tools for quantifying the ecological costs of building materials.

Box 28: Design Criteria and Indicators.

Section 12: Planning and Project Assessment

The first two chapters look at planning strategies for addressing a range of environmental problems (eg pollution, waste, urban expansion, homogenisation and social alienation).

12.1 Planning for Ecological Sustainability: Planning systems need to be redirected toward achieving ecological restoration, not just mitigating the public costs of private development.

Box 29: The Earth Charter.

12.2 Bioregional Planning: Bioregional planning reverses traditional planning methods by conforming human activities to the region's ecology, culture and resources.

Box 30: Beyond Biological Boundaries.

The second two chapters suggest that if designers are to become ecologically responsible as a profession, they will need to develop design tools and technologies for assessing the wider impacts of development in detail.

12.3 Environmental Management Tools: Designers need to recognise that decision aids, such as life cycle analysis, environmental audits and EIAs, are now indispensable tools of design.

Box 31: Regional Sustainability Audits.

12.4 Limits of Environmental Impact Assessment: Environmental impact assessment has improved government decision making, but its limitations need to be appreciated by environmental design consultants and their clients .

Box 32: Mini Debates on EIAs.

Some decades ago it was obvious to many that society, in its present form, was not ecologically sustainable. Today, some still debate whether we have 10 years, or 100, before we must change course dramatically and transform society to correspond more closely with ecological systems. Yet the dominant Western model of development does not sustain the (roughly) 40,000 people dying each day as a consequence of the destruction of natural systems, and the resultant lack of clean air, water, fertile soils, wetlands or biodiverse forests, which once provided for their sustenance and health. Nor does it sustain the 1 billion people now living in extreme poverty and hunger without clean water or reliable energy supplies, often amidst warfare over land and resources. The notion that ecological sustainability is a future problem denies their existence.

A conception of progress that prioritises industrial growth and economic expansion has led to inappropriate technologies and systems of manufacturing and construction that cause acid rain, ozone depletion, global warming, and toxic overload on human and **ecosystem** immune systems, to name a few. These so-called **externalities** are in fact intrinsic to a model of development that is still colonising the world's cultures and environments. This form of industrial development is reliant on non-renewable resource 'capital' (eg forests and fossil fuels) rather than solar 'income' (eg biomass and solar energy). It has created unnecessary demands for non-renewable resources and energy, as well as excessive waste and pollution downstream. This is simply poor systems design.

The design, construction and management of the built environment (cities, buildings, landscapes and products) is central to this industrial system because it largely determines the amount of resources, space and energy consumed by development. Apart from damaging our health and life quality, economic forces and development interests are transforming our cityscapes into inhumane environments. The built environment has derived from design 'of, for and by' the industrial order, rather than 'of, for and by' its inhabitants. Even where urban designers create isolated pockets for people to enjoy natural landscapes or public spaces, the quality of these experiences are being cumulatively destroyed by over-development, with its congestion, noise, pollution and other stresses.

Nonetheless, there are many countervailing examples of building, product and landscape design that dramatically reduce resource and energy usage while achieving the same functions, and even improving life quality – at less cost. The moral imperatives, practical exigencies, eco-solutions and fiscal resources already exist. What is required is a move from traditional 'remedial' approaches to preventative 'systems design' solutions that restore the ecology, foster human health and prioritise universal well-being over private wealth accumulation. Designers in all fields and walks of life have a crucial role to play in this transformation. It is now possible to design products, buildings, and landscapes that purify the air and water, generate electricity, treat sewage and produce food. The following chapters explore many areas and roles in which citizens, people in business, government and professions – as co-designers – can contribute to community building, social justice and ecological sustainability, while enjoying the unique satisfaction of the design process. Saving the planet is fun, and good for us too.

The structure of the book

Systems design is an exceptionally transdisciplinary process. Therefore, design professionals must learn to:

- Work across the boundaries of academic disciplines (social, ecological, psychological, economic, political).
- Communicate in many 'languages' (legal, numerical, conceptual, aesthetic) with clients, collaborators and decision makers from different perspectives and backgrounds.
- Avoid or reduce negative impacts of projects on all levels – site specific, regional and global.
- Understand how philosophical underpinnings of design influence their decisions.
- Integrate different practical parameters: functional and ecological requirements, social needs, cultural values and economic constraints.

- Work to achieve new social goals, while dislodging existing social, economic and political impediments to sustainability.
- Think simultaneously on different scales – from the design of product components to complex urban developments.
- Develop an ability to deal with uncertainty and uncharted territory – the future.

Eco-solutions involve not just technical but social, cultural, economic and political dimensions. Therefore, this book introduces an array of ethical concepts, epistemologies, and public policy issues that designers, environmental professionals or environmentalists need to consider in their professional practice or activist roles. Any selection of readings, no matter how many themes are canvassed, could not begin to touch on all the issues or information that designers need. To cover this diversity of requirements, the material in this book is organised as 'windows' onto a range of issues, methods, perspectives and dimensions within eco-logical design, varying from the practical to the theoretical.

Eco-logical design, as an approach to social and environmental problem solving, deals with complex open systems, so it would be inappropriate to specify a fixed set of solutions. In fact, the 'solutions' of the past have been a major cause of our current ecological problems and social dislocation. Further, many texts are available on the specifics of climatic and energy efficient design, so there is no reason to duplicate that material here. Designers need to do far more than calculate sun angles; they must invent new systems which improve the quality of life and human experience, while simultaneously restoring the environment,

rebuilding community and creating a sense of place.

While specific principles and facts are contained in the chapters, then, the emphasis is on contestable concepts and ideas. This is not to reject abstract, quantitative methods; these should serve subsidiary roles in support of social and environmental aims but each problem requires the design or selection of suitable ends and means. Therefore, instead of applying generalised analyses, goals, criteria, techniques and indicators to any situation (as did 'modernism' in architecture) the design of appropriate case-specific, problem solving tools should form a fundamental part of the design process.

Although there is a clear value system underlying this book, that of 'responsible design', it tries to avoid telling readers what to think. To encourage debate, the chapters are arranged in pairs to facilitate the comparison of ideas and approaches. The arguments or proposals offered in the readings should be reflected upon critically, not taken at face value. The range of positions and theories, as well as the focus on group discussion and action research exercises, are intended to encourage lateral thinking and foster the self-reflection, inquisitiveness and critical thinking that builds flexible 'design muscles'.

The reader will hopefully synthesise this jigsaw of multi-dimensional problems, parameters and potentials in their own unique, creative way, and move on to contribute original theories, concepts, practices and methods in the many different environmental planning, design and management fields that affect the quality of life on this planet.

Keys used in the book

Words that are in the glossary are bold the first time used in the text. **[Numbers in brackets]** refer to another chapter in this book.

Eco-logical design as environmental management

In the last four decades, dozens of books and articles have emerged that unravel and articulate the many systemic reasons for the environmental crisis from various 'green' perspectives. Essentially, these analyses have maintained that the necessary change to a sustainable society has been impeded by cultural, religious, intellectual and economic traditions that (while dating further back) co-evolved with industrialisation, upon the premise that humans could and should transcend nature.

A common, but usually tacit, thread in critiques of industrialised development is that its monumental waste, environmental degradation and social dislocation is a manifestation of poor systems design. These systems have been perpetuated by academic and professional ideologies. Consequently 'green' critiques, from both outside and within academia, have challenged the mainstream professional disciplines and germinated new fields of intellectual inquiry. 'Environmental' or 'eco-' has been prefixed to new branches of most academic subjects: planning, policy, law, politics, education, economics and so on.

These new hybrid fields share a recognition of the fundamentally ethical nature of environmental problems and social solutions, and the need to question the underlying premises of traditional academic theories and methods. However, these theorists have largely overlooked the significance of designed objects, structures, settlement patterns and spaces in the creation of virtually all environmental problems. Thus, the role of the **built environment** (cities, infrastructure, buildings, products, landscapes and public spaces) in implementing sustainability has also been overlooked.

While the rhetoric of systems thinking has been commonplace for years, the intellectual frameworks of the fields most directly concerned with environmental quality have tended to remain **linear** and **reductionist**, more process-focused than outcome-oriented, and wedded to methods, tools and strategies that developed within the dominant (economic) paradigm. Ironically, among the least progressive of fields concerning the environment – from a systems perspective – have been the environmental management and design fields themselves. Many of the impediments to sustainable development are embedded in the paradigms and processes of the planning, design and construction fields, and even reform proposals often reflect the premises that they purport to challenge.

Among the reasons for this, addressed by this book, is the failure to understand the design process as a problem-preventing/solving method, and the marginalisation of both design and the built environment in environmental policy and health sciences. Paradigms, decision-making processes and analytical methods need to incorporate design thinking. At the same time, the environment design fields will also require a total rethink if we are to foster the new values that 'green' perspectives seek to inculcate.

Social goals are gradually evolving from economic 'growth' to **sustainable development**, health and well-being. However, our environmental management processes remain geared towards predicting and accommodating growth and controlling nature, rather than working with natural processes. Further, the environmental management fields still tend to treat environmental issues narrowly. For example, they usually divide professionally and academically into those concerned with either wilderness protection or industrial pollution. Due in part to linear–reductionist thinking, they have largely overlooked the demands created by the urban and built environment upon both wilderness and industry, as shown in the following diagram.

In fact, industrial designers, landscape/building architects, and urban planners have not been seen as environmental managers – although their decisions directly impact the environment (eg Wilson and Bryant 1997; Barrow 1995). In marginalising the design of the built environment and focusing instead on conventional policy science approaches, environmental management has tended to preclude preventative design solutions.

Dualistic approach to environmental management

Systems approach to environmental management

Dualistic approach to problem solving

Systems approach to problem solving

Health sciences: The health fields tend to downplay the physical and psychological impacts of the built environment. Because humans have been seen as separate from nature, the health and well-being of ecosystems and human systems are still usually treated as separate issues for separate disciplines (see diagram below). Thus, while the impacts of building materials and mechanical systems on air quality is now recognised as a factor in many health problems, it receives relatively little research investment [7.3]. Preventative health care requires the redesign of the built environment at all scales from products to agriculture and urban/regional transport systems. For example, building components can be produced from organic materials (rather than materials to off-gas toxins) and natural ventilation systems can replace mechanical ones.

Dualistic approach to health and well-being

Systems approach to health and well-being

Design fields: Finally, the design fields remain apolitical and unconcerned with the distributional impacts of design as they affect the health of humans and ecosystems. This reflects the separation of the social and physical sciences (see following diagram). Relatively few designers as yet have explored the transformative potential of eco-logical design, let alone addressed ecological issues. The idea of design as a method of social and environmental problem-prevention/solving and of creating sustainable systems is still largely dormant in the design professions, as well as in other fields.

Eco-logical design as politics

The planning, organisation and design of the built environment has enormous geo-political implications that can cancel out both environmental policy and advances in ecological literacy and citizenship. With over half the world's population soon to be living in cities, global urbanisation is becoming a hotbed of political as well as environmental problems. Moreover, the scarcity of natural resources, such as timber, oil and water (in large part due to built environment design), creates threats to international security and peace, and reduces our ability to solve social problems. Until recently, however, the physical aspects of development have been largely left out of mainstream socio-political research, social change, and even the literature of development studies.

The readings in this text suggest that designers are potential change agents, whose decisions can constrain, alter, guide or enhance the future decisions of others.

Designers have the (largely untapped) capacity to design healthy habitats that reduce demands upon nature and enhance life quality – more effectively than those tweaking policy levers and weighting pulleys. Nonetheless, even today in environmental design courses, ecodesign is often taken less seriously than design that reveals an arrogant disdain for environmental and social responsibility. In much of environmental design, 'natural conditions are represented rather than sustained' (Ingersoll 1991, p. 139).

As a profession, designers have largely accepted the passive, a-political role that accompanies conventional design practice. Design theories often legitimise this passivity, tending to consider the aesthetic, poetic, and sensory effects of design on users, but seldom their relational and political impacts. Many designers rely on intuition and/or historical design precedents because they lack the conceptual tools for real world problem-solving. The few that theorise how built environment design effects/reflects our values and sense of place often focus on our sensual experiences of built environments. Literature that concerns itself more with values and attitudes or 'nature appreciation' than with redesigning systems, can implicitly endorse acceptance of the built environment 'as is' (Seamon 1993; Spirn 1984).

Some designers even take the position that environmental design cannot significantly influence human attitudes and behaviours. While **physical determinism** (the belief that the built environment influences social behaviour) is overly simplistic, so is the view that it has no discernable effect. This latter view also conveniently absolves designers of responsibility for even presenting their public or private clients with the wider social and ecological implications of their proposed projects or investments. Just like physical determinism, its critique is based on the misconception that the causes of values and behaviours are singular, separate or sequential. In a complex reality, however, everything effects everything else.

The built environment constrains or enhances social and personal relationships and, as a social construction, both reflects and influences our attitudes toward nature and society. In *Discrimination by Design*, Weisman (1992) has shown how the spatial configuration of buildings and communities influence gender, race and class relations. While the effect of design on people's attitudes, feelings and relationships cannot be isolated in a laboratory and measured, there is plenty of evidence that design influences how we feel, emotionally and physically. Australia's issue of 'Aboriginal deaths in custody' – an extraordinarily high rate of suicide among incarcerated Aboriginals – provides a grizzly example.

A view of design that does not consider the political nature of designed environments and objects is a very partial analysis, neither integrated nor **holistic** – and is therefore not compatible with systems design. In concept, though not yet in practice, eco-logical design holds the promise of a comprehensive and viable alternative to the traditional (linear–reductionist, dualistic) approach to development and environmental management. It can help us to leapfrog the barriers created by the **dominant paradigm** – the entrenched philosophical underpinnings of Western development that underlie and perpetuate our environmental problems.

Design for consumption

Ironically, though many designers take the view that design

is apolitical and not accountable for its social impacts, they readily use design to influence consumption. Design is practised self-consciously to segregate consumers and differentiate products to induce consumers to spend more. This contradiction may be partially explained by the belief that designers follow, rather than lead, consumer demand. 'Market choice' is sustained by the myth that consumer demand is a given or part of the natural order of things – even though there was no demand for 'pet rocks', electronic pets or myriad 'barbie dolls' until they were designed and marketed.

Realistically, consumers can only exercise choice over what is put on the shelf before them. The choice between McDonald's and Burger King, packaging styles, appliances with different door handles, or many TV channels all showing sports at once is not substantive choice. Market choice cannot provide genuine alternatives unless better plans, buildings and products exist in the market. Thus when people are given a choice between conventional petrochemical-based heating appliances or *nothing*, they must 'choose' the former. It is therefore incumbent upon designers to make the market work for the environment. For example, designers could sway the apparent preference for 'conspicuous consumption' towards a desire for low-impact dwellings and/or products as new status symbols. Even now, the demand for eco-efficient homes drives up their price beyond the means of most homebuyers, although they are often less expensive to build in real terms. Yet conventional homes in conventional suburbs remain the norm.

Designers can also have a dramatic impact on reducing the material content of consumption and hence aggregate demand on the environment. For example, in poorer countries, people may demand the capital and resource intensive drainage, sewer and water lines seen in wealthy nations – but this could only be achieved by external financial 'aid' which would increase their national debt. Ecodesigners would redefine the problem as 'a need for better sanitation', rather than a need for conventional infrastructure and, in this way, demand can be met at a far lower economic and environmental cost.

For design to become relevant to social and environmental problem solving, however, design education and the design process itself must be dramatically transformed. First, it needs to be recognised that eco-logical design is a highly intellectual activity: any technology, building or product must function within an existing context of anachronistic social, political and institutional structures, as well as within its natural environment. And yet it must also function to transform those very systems, as these militate against life quality, social justice and healthy, **symbiotic** relationships. Second, design needs to shift from a paradigm of 'transforming nature' to one of 'transforming society' towards sustainability by improving the life quality of, and relationships between, all living things, communities and the natural/built environment. This means designers in all fields need to:

- Re-examine human needs, and set appropriate goals which prioritise ecological sustainability and social equity.
- Rethink the basic nature, methods, and goals of the design process itself.
- Integrate knowledge from other fields concerned with human and ecosystem health.
- Promote new technologies, systems of production, and construction methods that do not rely on natural capital, fossil fuels and harmful chemicals.

The following chapters expand this list by examining design problems, parameters, principles and priorities.

References

Barrow, C.J. 1995, *Developing the Environment: Problems and Management*, Longman, London.

Ingersoll, R. 1991, 'Second Nature: on the Social Bond of Ecology and Architecture', in T.A. Dutton and L.H. Mann, eds, *Reconstructing Architecture: Critical Discourses and Social Practices* 5, University of Minnesota Press, Minneapolis, KS, pp. 119–157.

Lyle, J.T. 1999, *Design for Human Ecosystems: Landscape, Land Use, and Natural Resources*, Island Press, Washington, DC.

Seamon, D. ed, 1993, *Dwelling, Seeing, and Designing: Toward a Phenomenological Ecology*, State University of New York Press, Albany, NY.

Spirn, A.W. 1984, *The Granite Garden*, Basic Books, New York.

Spirn, A.W. 1998, *The Language of Landscape*, Yale University Press, New Haven, CN.

Smith, M., Whitelegg, J. and Williams, N. 1998, *Greening the Built Environment*, Earthscan, London.

Weisman, L.K. 1992, *Discrimination by Design: A Feminist Critique of the Man-Made Environment*, University of Illinois Press, Chicago, IL.

Williams K., Burton, E. and Jenks, M. eds. 2000, *Achieving Sustainable Urban Form*, Spon Press, London and Melbourne.

Wilson, G.A., and Bryant, R.L. 1997, *Environmental Management: New Directions for the 21st Century*, UCL Press, London.

Sustainability

Some of the basic requirements for a sustainable urban environment are :

Carrying capacity: Functioning within the natural and human carrying capacities of its bioregion; that is, living off the environmental interest rather than capital (for example, tailoring systems of production to local resources to increase regional resource autonomy).

Thresholds: Not breaching critical environmental thresholds for any specific substances or amenities, and ensuring the elimination of toxins or non-recyclable waste, produced locally or imported into the urban area.

Biodiversity: Preserving the health of both ecosystems and individual species, restoring indigenous ecosystems, and promoting diversity in human-made landscapes.

Health: Using buildings and landscapes to generate clean air, water and food; providing access to 'green' open spaces, opportunities for walking and cycling, etc.

User-friendly: Providing an enriching environment – an easy, safe and stimulating environment for all its inhabitants.

Equity: Promoting equity in access to facilities and services, environmental quality and 'social justice' (eg ensuring all neighbourhoods have relatively equal standards of living).

Governance: Providing inclusive development assessment procedures for all parties affected that protect the public interest in sustainability.

This list draws from Smith et al (1998) and Williams, Burton and Jenks (2000).

Section 1: Designing Eco-solutions

1.1 Education for Eco-innovation

Janis Birkeland

Many developed countries are currently debating how much to invest in research and development (R&D) funding in order to foster innovation in industry. This debate is occurring largely within the rhetoric of becoming more 'internationally competitive' in the face of rapid globalisation, through more production and consumption – rather than through resource and energy savings. This chapter argues that the innovation agenda must prioritise 'eco-innovation': that which addresses social and environmental needs while greatly reducing net resource and energy consumption. Innovation that lacks positive social, economic and environmental spin-offs can no longer be afforded.

Radical resource reduction

Independent experts have concluded that, in order to achieve sustainable consumption levels, it will be necessary to reduce resource and energy usage tenfold – an imperative sometimes called 'Factor 10'. In other words, material and energy consumption will need to be reduced by as much as 90% in the next 40 years if we are to meet human needs equitably within the Earth's **carrying capacity** (Schmidt-Bleek et al 1997; WBCSD 1997, p.6). It will be physically impossible for developing nations to achieve Western material living standards with existing 'industrial age' technologies, as the **ecological footprint** [the equivalent land and water area required to produce a given population's material standard, including resources appropriated from other places] already greatly exceeds the carrying capacity of the planet [**Box 9**]. Also, the **rebound effect** will continue to reduce net efficiency gains, as a portion of the income saved through more efficient production will be spent on increased material consumption [**Box 15**].

In recent years, innovations have increased the **eco-efficiency** of industry significantly. However, net resource and energy flows have increased at a faster rate, due to increasing production and consumption. In the next 50 years, global economic activity is expected to increase roughly fivefold, while global manufacturing activity, energy consumption, and the throughput of materials are likely to rise threefold (Lash et al 2000). The dramatic reduction in material and energy consumption required is still theoretically possible to achieve through **dematerialisation** [the reduction in the resource and **energy intensity** of products and processes]. For example, carbon fibres support about ten times the weight as the same quantity of metal did in 1800. However, this dematerialisation can only occur on a large enough scale if our systems of production, construction and distribution are fundamentally *redesigned*. The transformation of human designed systems – industry, built environment, urban form and land use systems – is essential (though not sufficient) to bring society within the limits to growth [**2.1**].

There are some grounds for optimism. The inherent economic advantages and competitive forces for becoming more eco-efficient mean that business, industry and construction could greatly reduce waste of their own accord. Companies are learning that waste and pollution increase the firm's occupational health and safety liabilities, enforcement and litigation costs, and insurance premiums – while damaging their public relations and corporate image (Schmidheiny 1992; Romm 1999). It is these factors that erode profits in an increasingly competitive global economy, not the lack of consumers. Thus, a key challenge for the new design professions of the 21st Century is to assist business and industry to move beyond 'reduce, reuse and recycle', to the 'three Rs' of radical resource reduction.

Of course, despite inbuilt competitive drivers, the redesign of whole systems cannot occur on an adequate scale without the removal of what are often referred to as **perverse subsidies**. This term refers to the fact that society seldom pays the full cost of natural resources and energy, because the public costs of poorly designed development (pollution, deforestation, global warming) are not 'internalised' by industry (see OECD 1996; Myers and Kent 2001). The focus of this book, however, is on the role of design in the shift to ecologically sustainable development, not on the incentives for making the shift. Education in the 21st Century, and particularly design education, will need to be of a new order that encourages 'systems design thinking' to achieve eco-solutions.

Traditional R&D

The bulk of practising professionals, managers and technicians that are in positions to implement systems change were trained to approach problems with linear–reductionist intellectual methods. Thus, education for innovation is still marginalised in relatively obscure ecodesign courses. It is not surprising, therefore, that the public debates on how to foster innovation emphasise the promotion of inventions through government subsidies at either end of what is regarded as a linear production line (Figure 1.1.1).

Figure 1.1.1: Targets for R&D funding

Some call for more investment in R&D, research centres and research infrastructure in universities (the front end of this imaginary conveyor belt). Others call for more assistance to business for commercialising R&D, more mobility between research, industry and commercialisation roles, and/or more scientists at the managerial level or on company boards to encourage technological innovation – investment at the tail end of the conveyor belt (see, for example, www.isr.gov.au/science/review).

Some recurring patterns emerge from the backcloth of these positions on R&D funding: innovation is assumed to occur within the constraints of a linear industrial system, with incentives geared toward inputs (subsidies) rather than outcomes, and little or no emphasis on education for a paradigm shift to **eco-innovation**. These thought patterns are explored and contrasted below with more modern views under the following headings: 1) industrial growth versus 'natural capitalism'; 2) supply-side versus demand-side incentives; 3) stimulating commerce versus eco-innovation.

Industrial growth versus natural capitalism

The industrial growth model

R&D is often regarded as an end in itself – rather than as a means to solve or prevent social and environmental problems. The function of R&D investment within the traditional business framework, is to spur economic growth through resource exploitation and consumption. In this outmoded 20th Century conceptual framework, cheaper access to natural resources, transport and labour, or more consumers and/or consumption per capita is assumed to be good for the economy because it increases the throughput of resources [3.3]. However, this 'lowest price' model has led to policies that often increase the amount of materials and energy used to achieve productive outcomes, which is costly in terms of waste and pollution. Further, this limited vision does not take into account the environmental and social context, or **externalities**.

When sustainability is introduced into the R&D debate, it is still treated as an added cost or a regulatory issue – rather than as an economic opportunity, social necessity or spur to innovation. Sustainability is seldom the ultimate goal of competition policies. This goal would require a 'least cost' as opposed to 'lowest market price' approach. Further, commercialisation is considered the last stage in the innovation process, or the 'ends', when it should be a 'means' to meeting *human needs*, such as:

- clean air and water (health);
- productive soil, uncontaminated food;
- affordable (resource efficient) housing;
- peace and secure social relationships;
- ecological sustainability.

Even when innovation is linked to eco-efficiency, its value appears to lie in the survival of business, rather than human health and well-being (not to mention that of other species) – as if ecological and economic sustainability were separate things. This older view of R&D conforms with research indicating that enthusiasm among senior business managers for a leadership role in this area is limited (despite promises of long-term commercial success for those who take up the green business challenge). A common perception among managers is that their only role is to respond to customer demand and government regulations (Foster and Green 1999).

The 'natural capitalism' model

Because the R&D debate has been embedded in the traditional industrial growth paradigm that ignores natural and social resources or 'capital', the centrality of ecological sustainability to the economy is overlooked. While the world's annual GDP is about $39 trillion, the Earth's natural capital [services to humans provided directly by nature, such as water purification] has been calculated at roughly $36 trillion –most of which is wasted (Costanza et al 1997). This $36 trillion is like 'interest' flowing from the Earth's natural capital stocks which would amount to about $500 trillion (Hawken, Lovins and Lovins 1999, p. 5). Similarly, the World Bank has found the value of 'human capital' (intelligence, organisational ability, culture, labour) to be three times greater than all financial and manufactured capital reflected on global balance sheets (World Bank 1995, pp. 57–66).

In *Natural Capitalism* (1999) Paul Hawken and Amory and Hunter Lovins note that most environmental and social harm is caused by the wasteful (and toxic) use of human and natural resources. They put forward four key strategies for an 'industrial revolution' that could save the economy and planet from the economic, social and ecological costs of an exorbitant industrial system. These are quoted below:

- radical resource productivity – a 90% reduction in energy and material intensity;
- biomimicry – redesigning industrial systems on biological lines to eliminate waste and toxicity [similar to industrial ecology and urban ecology];
- service and flow economy – life cycle product stewardship focused on meeting customer needs rather than the acquisition of goods;
- investing in natural capital – restoring the health of natural systems so the **biosphere** can continue to produce **ecosystem services** and natural resources.

All four strategies both inspire and require eco-innovation through systems design thinking, and offer a strategic framework for converting business and industry to becoming part of the solution. While these strategies would lead to profits, they would also lead to socially and environmentally beneficial outcomes. But ecodesign can go further than engineering approaches, because it can influence such things as the quality of social interaction and human interaction with nature.

Supply-side versus demand-side incentives

The supply-side model

It is widely acknowledged that money invested in R&D has not always been well targeted. This is partly because project evaluation has usually been based on criteria other than social outcomes or investment returns (eg political jurisdictions). But not all innovations are equal. For example, a recent innovation – landmines that move so that they are virtually impossible to decommission (*New Scientist*

30 September 2000) – reminds us that technology is never value neutral. If we really want innovation, we need education systems that foster the ability to create and innovate, and strategies to maximise the social benefits accruing from public investments in R&D.

The dominant innovation strategy could be described as a 'supply-side' model (Figure 1.1.2). In this model, innovation is assumed to flow automatically from increased R&D. Arguments for subsidies for 'innovation and commercialisation' – as opposed to 'education for innovation' – assume that commercial applications and markets are to be generated after the fact.

Figure 1.1.2: 'Supply-side' model of innovation

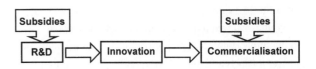

The demand-side model

In the demand-side model proposed here (Figure 1.1.3), incentives would be designed to encourage eco-solutions that address the sustainability imperative. This would not replace the funding of basic scientific research. However, instead of only funding R&D to create knowledge for which applications are then sought, priority would could be given to basic research in areas likely to address critical areas of need in terms of sustainability. Creating markets for non-essential consumer items requires expensive advertising, whereas eco-efficiencies largely pay their own way through resource savings (von Weizsäcker et al 1997; Romm 1999). There is a potentially endless demand for life-quality improvements through eco-innovation, because basic needs are provided at a cost saving (eg pollution prevention technologies and processes, low-cost housing, indoor air quality through natural materials, and preventative medicine).

At a minimum, priority should be given to innovations that target wasteful or polluting processes and products, or reduce material and energy flows, while innovations that encourage consumerism or non-essential services should be actively discouraged. The very idea of linking research priorities to social benefits is often taboo, as if it were an imposition on freedom of expression. Yet, ironically, many government grant schemes have prioritised primary industry sectors that are seen as pivotal within an 'industrial growth' paradigm, which generally increase resource and energy exploitation and throughput.

Figure 1.1.3: 'Demand-side' model of innovation

It should be remembered that while basic R&D is a social good that should be supported, not all R&D assists long-term global competitiveness. To be competitive in price in a global economy that accesses cheap labour, the resource and energy intensity of production and development must be radically reduced. International competitiveness can be realised through the rapidly expanding markets for eco-efficient, low-impact products and materials, or materials derived from sustainable processes (such as timber from forests certified as sustainably managed). Further, appropriate technologies are essential to capture new markets in developing nations, where the standard of living must be raised within extremely limited means (see Wallace 1996).

Funding that targets innovation to enhance life quality and meet basic needs should not entail a net increase over any other investment strategy, as it should require less investment in commercialisation. Some subsidies could of course shift from private business to public education as this is consistent with the tenets of a market economy – where business is meant to pay its own way.

Stimulating commerce versus eco-innovation

Innovation as a black box

Another theme in the debate over how to increase economic competitiveness is the need to strengthen the nexus between science and its commercial applications. But while the nexus is innovation (which derives from systems thinking as opposed to knowledge production), precisely how innovation will be fostered by increased investment in science inputs and business outputs is never explained. The issue should be how to generate eco-innovation, which is what translates scientific inputs into good social outcomes. Instead, what should be the primary target of public investment – innovation itself – is treated as a 'black box'.

It would appear that no one knows how to foster innovation itself, perhaps because innovation – the sudden cessation of stupidity – involves a flash of creative intelligence (Edwin Land, quoted in Hawken et al 1999). This requires more than pump priming: it requires a paradigm shift in both the education system and the organisational culture of business and industry.

'Before any organisation can develop or build an innovation system it has to be able to articulate the numerous ways and means that it squashes innovation and forces conformity. Without being conscious about the habitual practices used to deny individuality, to stop changes to existing systems, and to enforce and reward deference to the status quo at all levels, then all we are doing with an innovation system is building it on top of a sausage factory. All you will ever get are acceptable improvements to the same old sausages.' (anonymous education specialist quoted in *Australian Energy News,* 15 March 2000)

Radical resource reduction usually equals profitability. A paradigm shift in industry from 'innovation and commercialisation' to 'eco-innovation for sustainability' requires building capacity for systems thinking through education. As the quote suggests, to do so will require a critical examination of existing educational principles and practices. Formal and informal education itself needs a new approach: one that fosters ecodesign [Box 2]. Until this occurs, students – whether in school or in professional practice – will have to act as their own mentors.

References

Department of Industry, Energy and Resources, *Australian Energy News,* 2000, Canberra, ACT, March 15.

Costanza R. et al 1997, 'The Value of the World's Ecosystem Services and Natural Capital', *Nature* 387, pp. 253–260, May 15.

Foster C. and Green, K. 1999, 'Greening the Innovation Process', in *Greening of Industry Network Conference: Best Paper Proceedings*, UK.

Hawken, P., Lovins, H. and Lovins, A. 1999, *Natural Capitalism: Creating the Next Industrial Revolution*, Earthscan, London.

Lash J. et al 2000, *The Weight of Nations*, World Resources Institute, Washington, DC.

Myers, N. and Kent, J. 2001, *Perverse Subsidies: How Tax Dollars can Undercut the Environment and the Economy*, Island Press, Washington, DC.

New Scientist, 30 September 2000.

OECD 1996, *Subsidies and Environment: Exploring the Linkages,* OECD Publications and Information Center, Washington, DC.

Romm J. 1999, *Cool Companies: How the Best Businesses Boost Profits and Productivity by Cutting Greenhouse-Gas Emissions,* Island Press, Washington, DC.

Schmidheiny, S. with the BCSD 1992, *Changing Course: A Global Business Perspective on Development and the Environment,* MIT Press, Cambridge, MA.

Schmidt-Bleek F. et al 1997, *Statement to Government and Business Leaders,* Wuppertal Institute, Wuppertal, Germany.

Wallace D. 1996, *Sustainable Industrialization,* The Royal Institute of International Affairs, Earthscan, London.

WBCSD, DeSimone, L. and Popoff, F. 1997, *Eco-efficiency: The Business Link to Sustainable Development,* MIT Press, Cambridge, MA.

Weizsäcker, E. von, Lovins, A. and Lovins, H. 1997, *Factor 4: Doubling Wealth – Halving Resource Use,* Allen and Unwin, NSW.

Wheeler, K.A. and Perraca A., eds, 2000, *Education for a Sustainable Future: a Paradigm of Hope for the 21st Century,* Kluwer Academic, Plenum, New York.

World Bank 1995, *Monitoring Environmental Progress: A Report on Work in Progress,* Ecologically Sustainable Development, World Bank, Washington, DC.

Questions

1. There will always be an important place for 'pure research' in the sciences. To what extent does/should this apply to design fields?

2. Given that we are presently using resources at a rate beyond the Earth's capacity to replace, and that global economic activity and net material and energy use is expected to increase many fold, even reducing resource consumption by up to 90% cannot be a permanent answer. What are some other essential elements of social change? Can design affect these other factors? Discuss.

3. Despite a significant number of success stories about companies making impressive profits through radical resource reduction in the last decade or so, only a small percentage of businesses and industries are exploiting this opportunity so far. Why?

4. Debate: 'Public funding of R&D should give priority to research directed towards solving social or environmental problems.'

5. If the culture of large companies is geared towards encouraging more consumption through consumer diversification and market segregation, can a change in goals as dramatic as discouraging consumption be possible? Some successful companies are moving towards providing 'services' (eg thermal comfort) as opposed to products (eg electric heaters). How can this redefinition of goals help?

6. Do you agree that 'students – whether in school or in professional practice – will need to act as their own mentors'? If so, how should students proceed to teach themselves? What can they do to improve their school's capacity for educating for sustainability?

Projects

1. Do a search of newspapers for editorials or commentaries on innovation or science and technology, and/or using websites or other sources, examine the mission statements of several 'science and technology' professional organisations. Share the results and compare. Then analyse the materials to see how well they fit into the above models illustrated in the diagrams in this chapter. Do they emphasise environmental responsibility and accountability? Do they emphasise knowledge production over ecological problem solving? Do they assume that inventions precede their applications? Do they suggest commercial applications without social value should be rejected? Discuss.

2. There has been a notable effort on the part of some students and staff to green their university's campus and curriculum. Conduct a search of organisations, networks and key individuals involved in this effort. Ask them what they think are the greatest impediments to change in their university. Outline common themes or problems that emerge from this informal survey. Discuss solutions.

Box 1   Education for Sustainability Principles

Janis Birkeland

Education principles: The capacity to design and innovate must be fostered through an educational process. The first question is, what educational principles support capacity building for eco-innovation? Simply more environmental education is not the answer, as it has had a traditional science bias which centres on studying the impacts of existing systems, not how to transform them. Traditional education systems have shaped an approach to problem solving that often works against system-wide solutions. In contrast, themes in environmental education literature include an emphasis on, or re-alignment of:

- 'action learning' over environmental activities;

- participatory over top-down processes;

- multi-sector and transdisciplinary over specialist research only;

- holistic over reductionist frameworks;

- lifelong, inclusive and continuous learning over formal education structures only;

- critical thinking over knowledge production only;

- value explicitness over claims of value neutrality;

- multi-dimensional over linear analyses;

- quality of life outcomes over information outputs;

- empowerment over awareness raising;

- focusing on causal relationships over symptoms;

- systems change over monitoring and mitigating impacts;

- institutionalising ecodesign solutions over end-of-pipe regulations;

- developing partnerships over balancing competing interests;

- stewardship over control of resources; and

- respect for **indigenous design** knowledge.

Environmental education strategies: The above list forms guiding principles for education systems that encourage innovative thinking, but it does not provide a strategy for transforming the education system towards those ends. The second question, then, is what are the most efficient educational targets and strategies to facilitate innovation?

Given the urgency for education for sustainability, the priority needs to shift to the training and professional development of present and future decision makers. Boardrooms and branch managers generally do not design systems, but they determine who does. Managers (whether trained in science, technology, business, economics, planning or engineering) make decisions and instruct staff in matters of technology and production choices that can have long-term environmental consequences. Further, managers are in a better position to set systems in place that reduce environmental impacts through management tools such as purchasing practices, product stewardship and leasing arrangements, environmental management plans, energy audits, and so on.

A key problem, however, is that managers have typically been drawn from the ranks of the 'end-of-pipe professions' (such as mainstream lawyers, economists or accountants). These professions tend to perpetuate old systems and impose old tools regardless of the issues and consequences, as is evident by the resistance of neo-classical economists to ecological realities. Managers should have training in fields that affect 'upstream' decision making with the greatest 'downstream' impacts. These are the professions that shape systems design, such as engineering, science, landscape and building architecture and city and regional planning. If more managers were drawn from these 'upstream professions', it could also assist the modernisation of environmental policy from strategies that are downstream and *indirect* (such as accountancy-oriented 'levers and pulleys'), to upstream and *direct* systems design solutions [11.1, 11.2].

Janis Birkeland

The design of the built environment (along with other crucial issues such as population, militarism, globalisation and urbanisation), has held a minor position in the literature of environmental management and sustainability. Yet inappropriate design determines most of the avoidable environmental impacts which environmental protection laws, policies and programs can only mitigate. Because environmental professionals and academics have failed to appreciate the centrality of environmental design to sustainability, they have underestimated its potential as a method for environmental management and problem prevention/ solving.

Introduction

Virtually everything we make – whether as a result of conscious planning or by default – involves a design process that is constrained by complex social, economic and physical parameters. The present configuration of factories, city infrastructure, buildings, machines and tools, energy grids and road networks – and even policies and regulations – all bear the imprint of a particular form of thinking that has co-evolved within the context of an **industrial model of development**. This is characterised by the intensive use of fossil fuels and other forms of natural capital (resources, energy and space). This model is inherently non-sustainable. The underlying logic of our environmental planning, design, and management systems corresponds with this model of development.

Many of the pressures on rural populations and remnant natural ecosystems stem from urban development, as urban regions occupy an 'ecological footprint' far in excess of what is sustainable. Approximately half the world's population now live in cities, and in the developing nations roughly half of city dwellers lack adequate sanitation, and a quarter lack safe drinking water. Material and energy consumption – as well as environmental degradation – will need to be reduced drmatically within decades if we are to meet human needs equitably within the limits of the Earth's carrying capacity [1.1]. This can only occur through the redesign of cities,

buildings, transport systems, products and landscapes. Even with presently available environmental technologies, however, the resources and energy consumed by the built environment could be dramatically reduced through ecodesign, while generating employment and sound economic return on investment (Romm 1999).

Impacts of construction

Current patterns of design are wasteful of non-renewable resources, create toxic materials and by-products, require excessive energy for production, harm biodiversity at the source of extraction, and often involve energy-intensive long-distance transport. The construction industry is organised in a manner that is wasteful of energy, resources, land and, increasingly, human skills and talent [3.3]. Some estimates of the largely avoidable adverse impacts that built environment design has on land, materials and energy consumption are as follows:

- **Forests:** The Earth's surface has lost 50% of its forest cover (Brown et al 1996). Buildings alone account for one quarter of the world's wood harvest and (in the US at least) over 50% of wood is used in the building industry (Roodman and Lenssen 1995, p. 24).

- **Water:** Fresh water may be the most scarce resource in the next century. Buildings consume one sixth of fresh water supplies (Brown 1996). The US EPA has identified over 700 regular pollutants in drinking water, 20 of which are known carcinogens (Zeiher 1996, p. 8).

- **Carbon Dioxide:** In the past 100 years, the level of carbon dioxide in the atmosphere has risen 27%. One quarter of this is attributable to burning fossil fuels to provide energy for existing buildings. Energy use in buildings in the UK, for example, is 48% of total CO_2 emissions (Pout 1994).

- **Greenhouse:** Buildings account for one third to one half of total **greenhouse gases** emitted by industrialised countries each year (Roodman and Lenssen 1995).

- **Energy:** The energy used in construction alone is approximately 20 % of annual energy consumption (Tucker 1994). The total energy consumed in building operation, construction and services in the UK is 66% of annual energy consumption (Vale and Vale 1994).

- **Resources:** Buildings account for over 40% of the world's annual energy and raw materials consumption (Roodman and Lenssen 1995).

- **Landfill:** Building waste accounts for 44% of landfill and 50% of packaging waste in industrial nations.

Of even more significance is that inefficiencies in the planning, design, management and use of the built environment lead to pollution, waste and resource depletion that are attributed to other economic sectors (eg mining, forestry and transport).

Pyramidal design

The industrial model of development could be described as 'pyramidal', as it is supported by the exploitation of a huge base of resources. Pyramidal forms of development correspond with pyramidal social structures, where the benefits of development are enjoyed by the few, and the costs are passed on to others and to nature. The relatively poor in society, as well as future generations, are left to bear the social costs of extraction, conversion, distribution of resources and energy, and of the accumulation of land and capital (Figure 1.2.1).

Figure 1.2.1: Pyramidal systems

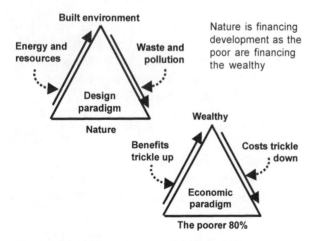

The US, with less than 6% of the world's population, is said to consume a third of the world's energy and a third of its natural resources. Further, 6% of Americans own 60% of American wealth, while the top 50% of Australian have 90%

of the wealth. The consequences of poor systems design are catching up with the world's wealthier citizens, however, as people spend far more in **defensive expenditure** to achieve the same levels of health, safety, security and life quality.

In the long run, pyramidal development is bad for a country's economy. The design of the built environment creates ongoing and unnecessary expenses for business and industry, even after construction and occupancy. Petrochemical-based heating, cooling and ventilating has been called 'an economic tapeworm' which is draining the economies of nations (Wann 1996, p. 69). Forty per cent of commercial energy in the developed world is to run heating, air conditioning and lighting systems, derived mostly from fossil fuels (Flood 1993). Around 30% of new buildings in the developed world attract complaints of **sick building syndrome**, caused by chemicals in materials and by mechanical ventilation, both of which are linked to fossil fuel use [7.4].

Nonetheless, designers do little to reduce the negative social and environmental impacts of development through the improved design of systems, products and buildings. Even everyday products are designed to trap consumers into buying related items, such as products designed for throwaway batteries rather than rechargeable ones. Most appliances are designed to use excessive amounts of operating energy and ecologically costly materials (Gertsakis et al 1997). Landscape designs often demand wasteful watering systems, and introduce feral plants while failing to provide local food sources for people or indigenous birds and mammals. At the end of product life, more costs are incurred in landfills that consume valuable space and leach toxins into diminishing ground water supplies.

Economies of eco-logical design

Eco-logical design can be cheaper, cleaner and more equitable, because it works with – rather than against – natural systems. Some buildings have been designed to create a fraction of the energy demand of similar buildings at little or no extra cost (Mackenzie 1997). Well-designed buildings can generally retrieve any extra costs incurred for energy conservation measures within eight to ten years, in those cases where extra costs cannot be avoided altogether (Edwards 1998, p. 2). Further, office building facades or roofs can be clad with photovoltaic cells to produce energy, as demonstrated by the '4 Times Square' building in New York. Advances are rapidly being made despite the fact that eco-solutions and organic materials seldom compete on an 'even playing field', due to the range of indirect subsidies enjoyed by petrochemical-based fuels and materials.

Residential: At a domestic scale, relatively simple, cost-effective changes to design and construction practices for new construction, such as passive solar design, can reduce the operating energy demands of housing up to 90%. This is because the mechanical systems and operational energy requirements of buildings – which are costly in dollars, energy and resources to manufacture, distribute and operate – can be reduced or eliminated altogether. Simply retrofitting existing housing with basic off-the-shelf measures (such as insulation and smart windows), can reduce the annual cost of electricity to householders by more than half. The payback time on residential properties can be just a few months or years, making what Richard Heede calls 'home made money' (Heede et al 1995). In fact, a study conducted for the US Environmental Protection Authority (EPA) in 1998 showed that, on average, homeowners recover their investments in upgrades regardless of how long they stay in the home. The property value increases immediately to around three times the builder's upgrade costs (Nevin and Watson 1998).

On a national level, eco-logical improvements to the existing housing stock with simple design technology (insulation, solar heating, better windows) could make a 50% dent in a country's annual energy bill. For example, New Zealand's 1.27 million households spend an average of NZ$734 a year on energy, or over $900 million in total. By retrofitting for energy efficiency, a feasible 50% reduction in energy consumption could mean $450 million in savings and a boom in employment.

Commercial: Eco-logical design in commercial buildings has meant profits for business [8.1]. For example, the well-known ING Bank in Amsterdam uses 90% less energy per square metre than its predecessor. It cost $0.7 million extra to build, but has saved $2.4 million a year, plus another $1 million annually through reduced employee absenteeism, due to a more pleasant work environment (see Wilson et al 1998). Hence, the one-off investment of $0.7 million has meant over US$3.5 million extra income a year.

Likewise, the green design or retrofitting of office buildings pays dividends through increased worker health and productivity, as well as through significantly reduced operational costs (see Tuluca 1997). For example, by improving the lighting in a post office, which cost

US$300,000, worker productivity increased by US$500,000 a year and another US$50,000 is now saved annually in energy costs. That is, a one-off investment of US$300,000 has meant over half a million a year extra income. See von Weizsäcker et al 1997 and Romm 1999 for more examples.

The building refurbishment industry is growing at a rate ahead of new construction (Property Council 1997; Dickinson 1994, p. 89), and much refurbishing is unnecessary and wasteful [2.4]. Growth is likely to continue in this area, due to the increasing supply of aged or unused buildings and those in need of maintenance in the business districts of most cities. Those buildings that remain structurally sound are likely to be redeveloped, either with an internal fit-out or a completely new development within the existing structural frame. The prevalence of proprietary office layouts and modular building systems (enabling complete demolition and reconstruction of interiors) often lead to the total refurbishment option being chosen, with significant environmental consequences.

Property investors, who usually determine how funds are spent, are generally unaware of the economic benefits of eco-logical design (as are builders). Most comprehensive refurbishments are more often than not exclusively market driven through a desire to attract new tenants, follow corporate interior design trends, and/or outclass business competitors (Bolotin 1994, p. 92). Proceeding solely on the basis of short-term financial analysis, owners and managers usually consider only the price of the materials and associated labour. The cost to society, in terms of lost natural resources, amenities and future options, is not reflected in these prices.

The easiest way to increase profits from redevelopment is to reduce the initial cost; the consequential losses in terms of quality are not obvious until after the project has been occupied. A component that looks good but needs replacement after a short time will meet the requirements of salability and/or lease. In fact, at the project planning stage (before a building has been constructed), allowance will typically be made for a partial refurbishment every five to eight years and a full refurbishment including all services after 15. Once refurbishments are accounted for at the project planning stage, they become almost inevitable, and will usually be written into tenancy agreements, increasing their likelihood. Because of short-term and speculative investment practices, of course, further refurbishments soon become necessary due to deterioration of the internal fit-out and finishes. Often these deteriorated conditions limit worker productivity, contribute to health problems and, in extreme cases, can become a safety issue. On the other hand, every refurbishment project also offers the potential for eco-logical retrofitting, where improvements can achieve efficiency in energy consumption, healthier workplaces, and sustainable use of renewable materials.

Conclusion

Social conflict, exploitation and environmental destruction occur almost inevitably as a long-term consequence of pyramidal systems. The US imports 53% of its energy and Australia imports 60%, when they could be energy self-sufficient by using appropriate technologies. Smart investments in eco-technologies could increase national security in many developed nations by reducing reliance on external sources of water, oil and minerals that are presently secured by aggressive corporate or military strategies. Eco-investments could also increase personal security in poorer nations, and reduce the pressure on the world's poor to have more children as a form of old age insurance. Eco-logical design, which seeks more social and environmental value for less resources and energy, can reduce many of the side-effects – if not some of the causes – of inequitable wealth transfers. Yet designers still often serve to enhance the social divisions between their clients and average citizens through design symbolism and conspicuous consumption (eg imported materials).

References and further readings

Bolotin, R. 1994, 'The Secrets of Shopping Centre Refurbishment: Maintenance or Marketing?', *Building Owner and Manager* 8(6) March, pp. 92–96.

Brown, L.R., Flavin, C. and Kane, H. 1996, *Vital Signs 1996*, W.W. Norton and Co, New York.

Dickinson, D. 1994, 'Waiting for Better Signals', *Building Owner and Manager* 8(6) March, p. 89.

Edwards, B., ed, 1998, *Green Buildings Pay*, Spon Press, London.

Flood, M. 1993, *Power to Change – Case Studies in Energy Efficiency and Renewable Energy*, Greenpeace International, London.

Gertakis, J., Lewis, H. and Ryan, C. 1997, *A Guide to EcoReDesign*, Centre for Design at RMIT, Melbourne.

Heede, R. et al 1995, *Homemade Money*, Rocky Mountain Institute with Brick House Publishing Company, NH.

Mackenzie, D. 1997, *Green Design: Design for the Environment*, Laurence King Publishing, London.

Nevin R. and Watson, G., 1998, 'Evidence of Rational Market Values for Home Energy Efficiency', *The Appraisal Journal* conducted for EPA by ICF Inc, October. See also EPA 1998, *Market Values for Home Energy Efficiency*, Washington, DC.

Pout, C. 1994, 'Relating CO_2 Emissions to End-Uses of Energy in the UK', *1st International Conference on Buildings and Environment CIB and BRE*, Watford.

Property Council of Australia 1997, *Australian Office Market Report*, Property Council of Australia, Sydney, January.

Romm, J. 1999, *Cool Companies: How the Best Businesses Boost Profits and Productivity by Cutting Greenhouse-Gas Emissions*, Island Press, Washington, DC.

Roodman D.M. and Lenssen, N., 1995, *A Building Revolution: How Ecology and Health Concerns Are Transforming Construction – Worldwatch Paper 124*, Worldwatch Institute, Washington, DC.

Tucker, S.N. 1994, 'Energy Embodied in Construction and Refurbishment of Buildings', *1st International Conference on Buildngs and Environment CIB and BRE*, Watford.

Tuluca, A. and Steven Winter Associates, Inc 1997, *Energy Efficient Design and Construction for Commercial Buildings*, McGraw-Hill, New York.

Vale, R. and Vale, B. 1994, *Towards a Green Architecture*, RIBA Publications, London.

Weizsäcker, E. von, Lovins, A. and Lovins, H., 1977, *Factor 4: Doubling Wealth – Halving Resource Use*, Allen and Unwin, NSW.

WBCSD (World Business Council for Sustainable Development), DeSimone, L. and Popoff, F., 1997, *Eco-Efficiency: The Business Link to Sustainable Development*, MIT Press, Cambridge, MA.

Wann, D. 1996, *Deep Design: Pathways to a Livable Future*, Island Press, Washington, DC.

Wilson, A., Uncapher, J., McManigal, L., Lovins, L.H., Cureton, M. and Browning, W. 1998, *Green Development: Integrating Ecology and Real Estate*, John Wiley, New York.

Zeiher, L.C. 1996, *The Ecology of Architecture*, Whitney Library of Design, New York.

Questions

1. Debate: 'The demand for energy and resources is a function of design, not a function of population.'

2. Why is it cheaper to create energy by saving energy instead of producing it? Why have some electricity utilities insulated homes and provided low-wattage light bulbs to their customers at no cost?

3. In some places, people move houses on an average of about five years. Therefore, they often do not want to spend money on insulation or solar heating if it takes over five years to recoup the investment. What can governments or industry do to ease the short-term burden of such investments in ecological retrofits?

4. In one column, list examples of 'anti-ecological design' (eg flush toilets). For each example, list in another column ways that eco-logical design can reduce these ecological costs.

5. List ways in which ecodesign can reduce some of the causes and impacts of ecologically harmful forms of urbanisation (eg reduce transport of materials, goods and people).

6. How can design reduce the causes of militarism (hint: need to secure access to oil and water)?

Projects

1. Organise a seminar on 'Globalisation and Eco-logical Design'. Have each presenter deliver a short paper followed by group discussion and written summary of conclusions. What are some of the negative environmental impacts of globalisation (hint: what about the international style in architecture)? How is built environment design affected by globalisation? How can design help to reduce those negative impacts? What is the role of ecodesign in an age of globalisation, and what should be its role?

2. Refer to Box 2 below. Design a poster that communicates the essential difference between conventional and eco-logical design. Select the best one for purposes of increasing public awareness, then produce a professional-quality version and display it.

Box 2 Conventional and Eco-logical Design Compared

From Sim van der Ryn and Stuart Cowan, 1996, *Ecological Design*, Island Press, Washington, DC.

Issue	Conventional Design	Eco-logical Design
	Usually non-renewable and destructive, relying on fossil fuels or nuclear power; the design consumes natural capital	Renewable, whenever feasible: solar, wind, small-scale hydro, or biomass; the design lives off solar income
Materials use	High-quality materials are used clumsily, and resulting toxic and low-quality materials are discarded in soil, air, and water	Restorative materials cycles in which waste for one process becomes food for the next; designed-in reuse, recycling, flexibility, ease of repair, and durability
Pollution	Copious and endemic	Minimised; scale and composition of wastes conform to the ability of ecosystems to absorb them
Toxic substances	Common and destructive, ranging from pesticides to points	Used extremely sparingly in very special circumstances
Ecological accounting	Limited to compliance with mandatory requirements like environmental impact reports	Sophisticated and built in; covers a wide range of ecological impacts over the entire life cycle of the project, from extraction of materials to final recycling of components
Ecology and economics	Perceived as in opposition; short-run view	Perceived as compatible; long-run view
Design criteria	Economics, custom, and convenience	Human and ecosystem health, ecological economics
Sensitivity to ecological context	Standard templates are replicated all over the planet with little regard to culture or place; skyscrapers look the same for New York to Cairo	Responds to bioregion: the design is integrated with local soils, vegetation materials, culture, climate, topography; the solutions grow from place
Sensitivity to cultural context	Tends to build a homogeneous global culture; destroys local commons	Respects and nurtures traditional knowledge of place and local materials and technologies; fosters commons
Biological, cultural, and economic diversity	Respects and nurtures traditional knowledge of place and local materials and technologies; fosters commons	Maintains biodiversity and the locally adapted cultures and economies that support it

Box 2 continued

Issue	Conventional Design	Eco-logical Design
Knowledge base	Narrow disciplinary focus	Integrates multiple design disciplines and wide range of sciences; comprehensive
Spatial scales	Tends to work at one scale at a time	Integrates design across multiple scales, reflecting the influence of larger scales on smaller scales and smaller on larger
Whole systems	Divides systems along boundaries that do not reflect the underlying natural processes	Works with whole systems; produces designs that provide the greatest possible degree of internal integrity and coherence
Role of nature	Design must be imposed on nature to provide control and predictability and meet narrowly defined human needs	Includes nature as a partner: whenever possible, substitutes nature's own design intelligence for a heavy reliance on materials and energy
Underlying metaphors	Machine, product, part	Cell, organism, ecosystem
Level of participation	Reliance on jargon and experts who are unwilling to communicate with public, limits community involvement in critical design decisions	A commitment to clear discussion and debate; everyone is empowered to join the design process
Type of learning	Nature and technology are hidden; the design does not teach use over time	Nature and technology are made visible; the design draws us closer to the systems that ultimately sustain us

Janis Birkeland

The dominant paradigm of development is supported by a construction of reality that legitimises environmental exploitation. Green theories have challenged the basic premises of this paradigm, and have sought to replace it with a new environmental ethic. Some basic tenets of this evolving 'green' value system provides a foundation upon which to construct principles, methods and processes for the practice of eco-logical design.

Introduction

As noted earlier, the built environment has had unnecessary adverse impacts on the natural environment and human health and well-being due to inappropriate design. But it also situates people in an oppositional relationship with nature. Eco-logical design can play a part in restoring a sense of interconnectedness with nature. In fact, it can play a part in social 'healing', in the way that well-designed gardens associated with hospitals have been shown to do (Ulrich 1993; Kellert 1999). If this healing process were to occur on a larger scale, however, we would need a whole new language of form: an architecture that assists people in reconceiving their relationships to each other, the community and life as a whole.

It is not adequate to apply new principles to old practices; the design process needs to be reconstructed upon new foundations. Can new eco-logical design goals, criteria and practices be derived from work in the field of environmental ethics or eco-philosophy? The following outlines some key concepts of eco-philosophy that may assist in developing new approaches to design.

Green philosophies

While many voices have called for sustainable development in one sense or another, until recent decades the concern was mainly about the 'sustainable yield' of forest, river or soil resources (see Wall 1994). Few expressed an understanding that human well-being relies on the integrity of the biosphere and our sense of connection with nature. One such writer was Aldo Leopold, who wrote *A Sand County Almanac*

(1949). This work articulated a 'land ethic' based on the idea of nature having **inherent value**, or a right to exist apart from its usefulness to humans. Leopold's work later became a foundation text for many eco-philosophers and green activists who argued that the environmental crisis was one of human character and culture, not just inappropriate technology.

Perhaps the defining insight of green thought is that sustainability requires more than eco-efficiency, or the minimising of energy, resources and waste; it also requires fundamental personal, social and institutional transformation. This view was expressed as early as the 1960s (Marcuse 1964; Bookchin 1962 [as Lewis Herber]). By the 1980s, it had become apparent to a burgeoning green movement that more environmental education, public policies and conservation practices, while important, were not enough to bring about social change. Taking a systems view, greens recognised that the over-exploitation of nature could not end while *underlying* belief structures, institutions and decision-making processes worked to preserve pyramidal social structures. Social justice and non-violence, biological and cultural diversity, democracy and participatory decision making, and non-competitive and non-hierarchical forms of social organisation, became broadly accepted by the green movement as essential 'preconditions' of a sustainable society (Diesendorf and Hamilton 1997).

Green theorists began to construct analyses of the many systemic pathologies that work against these preconditions, such as industrialism, colonialism, capitalism, sexism, classism, consumerism, racism and militarism. A range of green schools of thought were developed which – although appreciating the interconnections – focused on different dimensions of these social pathologies [Table 1.3.1]. One element that all these pathologies have in common (though often unstated) is the *abuse of power*. Seeking power to obtain and maintain control over others involves acquiring and/or exploiting human and natural resources. Because power involves unequal access to resources, relationships of power (sometimes called 'patriarchy') are incompatible with sustainability in the long term, as they eventually lead to social repression and conflict, or even war. The above-listed pathologies can be seen then, not just as causes of the modern crisis but, as means through which power is sought and maintained (Birkeland 1993).

While social ecologists linked social hierarchies to the domination of nature (Bookchin 1982), the pendulum swung towards spirituality in the 1980s (Nollman 1990; Spretnak 1991). Many green theorists avoided the issue of power by developing transcendent philosophies, such as spiritual ecology and **deep ecology** (Devall 1988). However, the movement gradually broadened its analyses to integrate left-wing theories (Pepper 1993) and **environmental justice** more generally (Camacho 1998). From another direction, feminism had been primarily concerned with how power operates and is abused on personal and political levels within society, but **ecofeminism** expanded the analysis to show the

hotbed of intellectual debate, and has expanded to include environmental issues as diverse as genetic engineering, vegetarianism and world trade. While each green theory and theorist has introduced different concepts, there are a number of elements in common which constitute the groundwork of an eco-logical ethic, upon which a new approach to design theory, method and practice could possibly be grafted. A few of these underlying concepts are suggested below.

'Rational Man' v a relational view of humans

Old paradigm: Philosophies start from a conception of what it is to be human. The theories and methods of the traditional professions having most impact on the environment (eg economics, management) derive from a 'model of man' or archetypal human that is individualistic, independent, goal seeking, action-oriented, calculating and

Table 1.3.1: Table of some major green philosophies

	Problem Definitions	Major Concern	Means of Change	Desired Ends
Greens (general)	Industrial growth	Government policy	Ecological understanding	Sustainable practices
Social ecologists	Hierarchies	Institutional forces	Social organisation	Anarchism
Deep ecologists	Anthropocentrism	Perception of world	Expanded identification	Biocentrism
Eco-socialists	Individualism	Economic forces	Political reform	Commuitarian
Eco-Marxists	Class society (capitalism)	Forces of production	Class struggle	Socialist or classless society
Ecofeminists	Abuse of power Androcentrism and Hierarchical dualism	Patriarchy, ie power-based order and culture	De-linking power and masculinity Social redesign	Beyond power

See glossary for definitions. *Source*: Birkeland 1993

links between human oppression and environmental exploitation (Mies and Shiva 1993; Salleh 1997). Thus, there has been a gradual convergence of the ecology, feminism and socialism in green thought (Mellor 1997).

Eco-logical ethics

Collectively, these schools of thought within eco-philosophy resuscitated the previously moribund field of ethics. Ethics had become anachronistic because it did not adequately address our responsibility to the planet, future generations and other species. Environmental ethics has since become a

'rational' (meaning self-interested). This 'rational man' of Western thought is one who makes decisions by weighing up the costs and benefits to himself. As a result, self-serving behaviour is validated and accepted as normal – in fact, to be altruistic is often considered 'irrational' in our society. Given this conception of humanity, power-based relationships and hierarchies are logical ways to ensure social order and security (at least for the powerful). The 'rational man' also personifies the denial of interdependency with others and the rest of nature. Moreover, it has meant a rejection of those aspects of human nature that have been defined as 'feminine' in Western culture (attached, passive, emotional); these traits are associated with a lower order of being that does not achieve the ideals of independence and rationality.

New paradigm: In contrast, a 'relational' conception of humanity is one where individuals are seen as intimately and inseparably connected to community and nature, such that the well-being of each depends on the well-being of the whole. A relational or systems view of humans suggests that people are capable of altruism, empathy and caring, in addition to dispassionate reason. Hence, it challenges the idea of a (selfish) 'human nature' that is so often used to rationalise unethical and exploitative behaviour. It instead validates the possibility of **symbiotic** relations with nature, and egalitarian social systems. This more optimistic conception of human nature would encourage people to re-invest in humanity. Moving from a social order based on hierarchies and power relations to systems of social justice and equity, however, requires the deliberate design and construction of new ways of thinking, designing and living. The design disciplines must pay more attention to how design and spatial organisation affects social relationships, attitudes and behaviour.

Rights-based ethic v ethic of care

Old paradigm: If the human is an autonomous and competitive individual, society is by definition less a whole than a collection of individuals. In such a society, people can only relate to others in terms of 'rights' or power. This is why the ethic upon which decision-making structures and processes are constructed in a liberal society is 'rights-based'. The problem is that in a rights-based social structure, those who have more power have more rights. Moreover, equal rights cannot be an adequate basis for preserving ecosystems and wilderness areas. Bushes and bugs will never obtain rights (see Stone 1974). In practice, a rights-based ethic leads, at best, to 'balancing the interests'. An interest-balancing approach, for example, can mean periodically allocating a portion of native forests to development to meet conflicting demands as they arise, with the inevitable result of no native forests. Thus we have rights-based, utilitarian decision-making tools and processes that are designed to make trade-offs.

New paradigm: A relational view that sees the individual as integral to society and nature, begins from a feeling of care (as in a family) rather than rights (as in a business). Thus, equity (ie fairness, but not necessarily equality) takes precedence. Instead of trade-offs (wherein the poor and

nature will inevitably lose out over time), systems could be designed to accommodate basic needs and foster natural and cultural diversity. The design disciplines should therefore prioritise basic social needs such as the shortage of world housing, sanitation and clean water, and the distribution of environmental benefits and burdens. In practice, this would mean that when we must take from nature, we would give something back – not just compensate monetarily for some of the impacts. Creative design thinking can avoid trade-offs between rich and poor, or nature and society. The relational view would therefore foster proactive 'systems design thinking' and problem solving methods geared toward restoring the health of human and natural systems.

The market v citizenship

Old paradigm: The limited view of society as a collection of individuals corresponds with a basis for decision making that underlies not only economics, but also influences the environmental management fields: **utilitarianism**. Utilitarianism is the belief that decisions over resource use should be made by comparing the 'utilities' (ie measures of satisfaction) of the individuals affected by the decisions. It is an underlying 'ethic' of market economies. Economics treats people primarily as 'consumers', and therefore 'willingness to pay' is seen as the measure of the satisfaction they obtain from consuming. Social responsibility has thus been abdicated to the 'invisible hand' of the market. This market ideology also provides a convenient excuse for avoiding professional responsibility just as economists blame consumers and politicians blame voters, designers blame clients for the inadequacies of the built environment – as if it were due to lack of 'demand' or 'willingness to pay', rather than poor economic, political and physical systems design.

New paradigm: A relational view of humans would demand a wide range of values and considerations in decision-making processes, not primarily consumer demand [4.2]. Humans are more than consumers; they are ethically concerned family members and citizens (Daly and Cobb 1989; Hamilton 1994). As such, they are capable of deciding their own destinies, rather than leaving things to the invisible hand of world markets. While current patterns of development sustain pyramidal social structures, an environmental ethic would require the redesign of economic and planning systems so that they foster social justice and equity. While economists seek solutions that make individuals or firms better off without making others worse off (**Pareto Optimum**), planning for sustainability would mean designing for the health and well-being of the whole system in ways that do not make people worse off, or less equal (we can call this the **Green Optimum**). Systems of governance, planning and design would need to be devised to enable genuine democracy, ethical discourse, learning and participation.

Linear v an ecological view

Old paradigm: There is a tendency to look for problems that existing professional techniques and processes can be applied to. Despite the rhetoric about systems, therefore, the mainstream professions inculcate linear-reductionist forms of analysis, instrumentalist goals, utilitarian methods, mechanistic processes, and narrow economic indicators. For example, environmental management has traditionally concerned itself with issues that lend themselves to 'hard', measurable, dispassionate methodologies; hence, our solutions are geared towards predicting, controlling, monitoring and mitigating 'outputs', rather than creating life quality outcomes. This has led to measurements of welfare using crude monetary measures like **Gross Domestic Product** (GDP) or abstract concepts like 'willingness to pay'. For example, GDP is increased by bombs and landmines, even though they destroy humans and nature, because there are monetary transactions involved.

New paradigm: Because our indicators of welfare do not distinguish expenditures that are ultimately destructive or wasteful from those that improve human conditions, these measures have distorted decision making [2.2]. A relational view of the human suggests that abstract economic constructs are inadequate to deal with the complexity of social, environmental and life quality issues. The development of sustainable systems of resource allocation and economics require tools that can measure life quality outcomes. There has been increasing attention to developing **life quality indicators** that look at outcomes, rather than outputs that are measurable only in monetary terms) [Box 6]. Instead of being prioritised, narrow economic tools should be subsumed within a more eco-logical, relational view. Environmental designers are beginning to modify tools such as **life cycle assessment** and **embodied energy analysis**, to better serve the specific needs of designers [12.3].

Conclusion

The above shows some of the ways that an ethic derived from a relational view of the human can provide a basis for:

- Modifying environments to facilitate social justice and equity and to restore public health.

- Seeking symbiotic, 'win–win' decision-making methods that avoid trade-offs.

- Utilising participatory democratic design processes rather than following consumer demand.

- Developing indicators and analytical tools that focus on life quality outcomes instead of material outputs.

To implement these things, planning and design must be re-oriented to attempt to enable healthy and diverse communities to co-exist and co-evolve in symbiotic relationships with biotic communities. Some principles to help reorient the design process towards a more integrated, holistic perspective are provided [Box 3].

References and further reading

Birkeland, J. 1993, 'Some Pitfalls of "Mainstream" Environmental Theory and Practice', *The Environmentalist* 13(4), pp. 263–275.

Bookchin, M. 1982, *The Ecology of Freedom: The Emergence and Dissolution of Hierarchy*, Cheshire Books, Palo Alto, CA.

Bookchin, M. [Lewis Herber] 1962, *Our Synthetic Environment*, Albert A. Knopf, New York.

Camacho, D. 1998, *Environmental Injustices, Political Struggles: Race, Class, and the Environment*, Duke University Press, Durham and London.

Daly, H. and Cobb, J. 1989, *For the Common Good: Redirecting the Economy toward Community, the Environment, and a Sustainable Future*, Beacon Press, Boston, MA.

Devall, B. 1988, *Simple in Means, Rich in Ends: Practicing Deep Ecology*, Gibbs-Smith Publisher, Utah.

Diesendorf M. and Hamilton, C. 1997, *Human Ecology, Human Economy: Ideas for an Ecologically Sustainable Future*, Allen and Unwin, Sydney, NSW.

Hamilton, C. 1994, *The Mystic Economist*, Willow Park Press, Fyshwick, ACT.

Kellert, S. 1999, 'Ecological Challenge, Human Values of Nature, and Sustainability in the Built Environment', in C. Kibert, ed, *Reshaping the Built Environment: Ecology, Ethics, and Economics*, Island Press, Washington, DC.

Leopold A. 1949, *A Sand County Almanac*, Oxford University Press, Oxford.

Marcuse, H. 1964, *One-Dimensional Man*, Beacon Press, Boston, MA.

Mellor, M. 1997, *Feminism and Ecology*, NY University Press, New York.

Mies, M. and Shiva, V. 1993, *Ecofeminism*, Zed Books, London.

Nollman, J. 1990, *Spiritual Ecology: A Guide to Reconnecting with Nature*, Bantam Books, London.

Pepper, D. 1993, *Eco-Socialism: From Deep Ecology to Social Justice*, Routledge, New York.

Salleh, A. 1997, *Ecofeminism as Politics: Nature, Marx and the Postmodern*, Zed Books, New York.

Spretnak, C. 1991, *States of Grace: Recovery of Meaning in the Postmodern Age*, HarperCollins, New York.

Stone, C. 1974, *Should Trees have Standing? Toward Legal Rights for Natural Objects*, W. Kaufmann, Los Altos, CA.

Ulrich, R. 1993, 'Biophilia, Biophobia, and Natural Landscapes', in *The Biophilia Hypothesis*, S.R. Kellert and E.O. Wilson, eds, Island Press, Washington, DC.

Wall, D. 1994, *Green History: A Reader in Environmental Literature, Philosophy and Politics*, Routledge, London.

Questions

1. Name examples of how designers could actually implement the concept in practice that 'when we must take from nature, we must give something back'. Is, for example, planting two trees for every one used in a building or product enough to satisfy this criterion?

2. Do you consider yourself a citizen or a consumer? Do you contribute as much to society as you take? Are some developers 'unjustly enriched' by development? How? Can this be avoided?

3. What are rights? Should animals have rights? Should trees have rights?

4. Debate: 'The acceptance of eco-logical design has been impeded by "soft" principles, that lack hard science validation.'

5. Do designers have a special capacity to act as social change agents? Discuss.

6. Should we live in a society based on equality or equity? What would be some of the differences?

Projects

1. Articulate specific design concepts to implement each of the principles cited in van der Ryn and Cowans principles and McDonough's Hannover Principles [**Box 3**]. Can you think of any new ecodesign principles that do not fit logically under these principles?

2. Reflect for a few minutes on the idea of society as an ecological system and how this could be used to justify certain ethical positions. Does it suggest that people should: Look for a safe eco-logical niche to occupy? Claw their way to the top in a Darwinian struggle or cooperate? Manipulate the system to work for their own self-interest, or to redesign the system to work better for everyone? Share your ideas with the group. Can you explain these different perspectives in terms of the evolution of scientific thinking? Do you see these perspectives reflected in different attitudes toward design practice?

Box 3   Eco-logical Design Principles

A number of well-known architects who derive their design concepts and practices from ecological principles have developed their own ethical frameworks to guide the design process.

Design Principles: Sim van der Ryn and Stuart Cowan

From van der Ryn, S. and Cowan, S. 1996, *Ecological Design*, Island Press, Washington, DC.

1. **Solutions grow from place:** Ecological design begins with the intimate knowledge of a particular place. Therefore, it is small-scale and direct, responsive to both local conditions and local people. If we are sensitive to the nuances of place, we can inhabit without destroying.

2. **Ecological accounting informs design:** Trace the environmental impacts of existing or proposed designs. Use this information to determine the most ecologically sound design possibility.

3. **Design with nature:** By working with living processes we respect the needs of all species while meeting our own. Engaging in processes that regenerate rather than deplete, we become more alive.

4. **Everyone is a designer:** Listen to every voice in the design process. No one is participant only or designer only: everyone is a participant-designer. Hone the special knowledge that each person brings. As people work together to heal their places, they also heal themselves.

5. **Make nature visible:** De-natured environments ignore our need and our potential for learning. Making natural cycles and processes visible brings the designed environment back to life. Effective design helps inform us of our place within nature.

The 'Hannover Principles': William McDonough

Provided by William McDonough

1. **Insist on rights of humanity and nature to co-exist in a healthy, supportive, diverse and sustainable condition.**

2. **Recognise interdependence.** The elements of human design interact with and depend upon the natural world, with broad and diverse implications at every scale. Expand design considerations to recognising even distant effects.

3. **Respect relationships between spirit and matter.** Consider all aspects of human settlement including community, dwelling, industry and trade in terms of existing and evolving connections between spiritual and material consciousness.

4. **Accept responsibility for the consequences of design decisions upon human well-being, the viability of natural systems and their right to co-exist.**

5. **Create safe objects of long-term value.** Do not burden future generations with requirements for maintenance or vigilant administration of potential danger due to the careless creation of products, processes or standards.

6. **Eliminate the concept of waste.** Evaluate and optimise the full life cycle of products and processes, to approach the state of natural systems, in which there is no waste.

7. **Rely on natural energy flows.** Human designs should, like the living world, derive their creative forces from perpetual solar income. Incorporate this energy efficiently and safely for responsible use.

8. **Understand the limitations of design.** No human creation lasts forever and design does not solve all problems. Those who create and plan should practice humility in the face of nature. Treat nature as a model and mentor, not as an inconvenience to be evaded or controlled.

9. **Seek constant improvement by the sharing of knowledge**. Encourage direct and open communication between colleagues, patrons, manufacturers and users to link long-term sustainable considerations with ethical responsibility, and re-establish the integral relationship between natural processes and human activity.

The Hannover Principles should be seen as a living document committed to the transformation and growth in the understanding of our interdependence with nature, so that they may adapt as our knowledge of the world evolves.

Janis Birkeland

Despite the occasional rhetoric about ecological interdependency, the response by environmental designers, architects and builders to the ecological crisis has been, on the whole, superficial. Dysfunctional human society–nature relationships remain largely unchallenged in built environment design. Eco-logical design should be as fundamental to building as structural logic is to engineering; however, this is not yet the case. Eco-logical design can be viewed as an ethic and method for achieving social transformation.

Introduction

Design decisions, conscious or not, are fundamental to the social, environmental and economic impacts of development on all scales. As such, designers only have one choice: to remain part of the problem or become part of the solution. But design in general has been marginalised or overlooked entirely as a means of **social transformation**. If poor design is the problem, perhaps designers have a special responsibility to act as change agents. If building upon the foundations of eco-philosophy is the first step [1.3], redefining 'design' is the second step towards making design relevant to sustainability. There are many alternative ways of defining eco-logical design; the pivotal point in the following description is professional responsibility – to users, society, future generations, other species, ecosystems, bioregions and the planet.

Eco-logical design

What is eco-logical design? Rigid definitions of eco-logical design would be problematic, as design should be a fluid, adaptive and self-generating way of thinking. It is therefore described here simply by using a set of adjectives.

Responsible: Eco-logical design redefines project goals around issues of basic needs, social equity, environmental justice and ecological sustainability.

Eco-logical design involves reconsidering the end uses which products, buildings, landscapes and other designed systems serve, and how these ends impact on different user groups,

distributional issues and environmental protection goals. At the very least, designers should ensure that the long-term social and ecological costs of products or developments are internalised, rather than passed on to third parties, the poor or future generations. But every design problem is also an opportunity to create or restore natural ecosystems. Thus, for example, a design brief for low-income housing can be an opportunity to regenerate indigenous flora and fauna, restore buried streams, or otherwise revitalise the local ecology on the site (Register 1997). Such biological design elements can be designed to pay for themselves by providing environmental services that would otherwise come at a cost, such as flood protection, water purification, 'organic' sewage treatment, biodiversity values and recreation (see Daily 1997). For example, New York intends to invest US$1.4 billion in a watershed protection strategy which will save US$3–8 billion that would otherwise be needed for a new filtration system (O'Meara 1999).

Synergistic: Eco-logical design creates positive feedback loops and symbioses between different functional elements to create systems change.

Whereas 'pyramidal' design creates negative externalities, eco-logical design creates positive **synergies**. Eco-logical design not only solves specific problems, but seeds opportunities for reciprocities and symbioses on other dimensions that are beyond the specific design 'problem'. As put by David Orr, 'when people fail to design with ecological competence, unwanted side effects and disasters multiply', but 'where good design becomes part of the social fabric at all levels, unanticipated positive side effects (synergies) multiply'. Thus, for example, urban design that reduces car numbers and usage also reduces greenhouse emissions and toxins; makes it easier for people to bike to work and breath clean air; cuts down on health bills, accidents and insurance costs; and reduces petrol and oil spills, and so on (see Orr 1992). Green design can also create employment through new 'green' products (with net positive impacts), by utilising heat and materials that would otherwise become waste (Romm 1999).

Contextual: Eco-logical design involves re-evaluating design conventions and concepts (in the context of changing socio-political, economic systems) to contribute to social transformation.

'Contextual' design usually just refers to buildings that blend in with the existing urban fabric or complement existing facades, building heights or setbacks. It usually conforms to, and hence reinforces, the existing urban infrastructure. But while a design must always be considered within the broader context of aesthetic, cultural and political conventions, it also needs to contribute to their transformation. For example, urban developments should always reduce demand for conventional infrastructure systems (transport, sewage, water and food supply). Although consumer preferences must be considered, eco-logical designers should not merely target existing markets, but try to shape consumer demand toward less materialistic aims (eg design objects worthy of keeping forever). But eco-logical designers must do more than increase life quality with reduced resource and energy throughput. Their responsibilities also include working for reforms in their respective professions, which requires undertaking a broader education than design alone.

Holistic: Eco-logical design takes a life cycle perspective to ensure that products are low-impact, low-cost and multi-functional on as many levels as possible.

Many of the methods and processes already practised in the design fields are well suited for addressing complex environmental issues that require collaborative and interdisciplinary work processes, lateral and holistic thinking, and the integration of economic, social and environmental parameters. However, traditional design has tended to be reductionist, focusing on isolated issues and limited criteria (eg aesthetics or image) within a limited time horizon (often backward looking). Eco-logical design is, in contrast, an integrative, multilateral problem-solving method that seeks to reduce ecological, economic and social impacts over the life of the product or structure. Such design strategies include **design for disassembly**, design for reuse and design for long life. Another example of whole systems design criteria is adaptable housing that accommodates changing family sizes, composition and life stages over time [Box 14]. A multitude of software is now available to help designers estimate the life cycle impacts of design decisions.

Empowering: Eco-logical design fosters human potential, self-reliance and ecological understanding through the use of appropriate technologies and environments for living.

Pyramidal design has distributed the burdens of production primarily onto the poor, creating dependency and distancing them from access to healthy, clean environments. It also makes invisibile these transfers of resources and environmental quality impacts. Many well-off people do not know where their food, water, energy and other resources or products come from, or the effects their consumption patterns have on their life support systems. Eco-logical design can instead create environments that promote ecological awareness and self-reliance by integrating food production into the community through permaculture, urban agriculture or similar practices [5.2]. Likewise, on-site solar heating and ventilation, waste treatment and water recycling, when made visible and comprehensible by design, makes people more aware of natural processes. It also gives people more control over their personal space, because visible technologies enhance the ability of users to interact with, repair and modify their own environments.

Restorative: Eco-logical design nurtures and strengthens human and natural health and 'immune systems', and can contribute to psychological well-being.

Eco-logical design can help improve the health of humans and other flora and fauna. This is partly a technical matter which can be achieved, for example, by replacing toxic chemicals with natural materials or incorporating more air purifying plants into the building envelope and floor plan. In this way, design can strengthen resilience to stress and resistance to illness. But restoration also implies a 'spiritual' element, acknowledging that our built environments influence our sense of being, belonging and place, and our attitudes towards other species, community and nature [5.3]. Conventional architecture usually creates a barrier between humans and nature [6.1]. Eco-logical design can help re-integrate the social and natural world, restoring physical and psychological health and recultivating a sense of wonder.

Eco-efficient: Eco-logical design takes eco-effectiveness as true economics; it minimises inputs of materials and energy and outputs of pollution and waste.

Given that a design brief or assignment is ecologically and socially sound to begin with, eco-logical design entails a pro-active effort to increase eco-efficiency (ie economy of energy, materials and costs). This involves re-examining materials, industrial processes, construction methods, building forms and/or urban systems to find opportunities to further reduce ecological costs where they cannot be eliminated altogether. Resource and energy loops can be closed at both site specific and regional levels such that any unavoidable 'waste' from one process becomes the raw material for another. Ecodesigners should not just reduce impacts of their own projects, but consider the regional economy. For example, they can initiate: collaborative efforts among different industries and sectors to implement principles of **industrial ecology [3.1]**; **urban metabolism** studies to improve urban policy and planning [Box 31]; or the development of useful products for waste resources.

Creative: Eco-logical design represents a new paradigm that can transcend the intellectual necrophilia and entrenched hierarchies of academia.

Eco-logical design, as a method, has the potential to overcome many of the problems created by the legacy of an over-emphasis on history, aesthetic theory and linear–reductionist thinking in design education. As a way of thinking and doing, eco-logical design also has much to offer 'green' academics in other non-design fields concerned with bringing about institutional change and social transformation. Because design occupies a different sphere, it is not burdened with the need to justify itself by either building upon or debunking anachronistic theories in order to be accepted or validated (an impediment faced by eco-politics and eco-philosophy). As a method, then, design can leapfrog over the tribal disciplines and academic protection racket that are now impeding the introduction of ecological literacy in many universities.

Visionary: Eco-logical design focuses on visions or desired outcomes and then selects or invents appropriate methods, tools and processes to achieve them.

Eco-logical design is directed toward a vision for a better future. Determining ways of making decisions about the future that suit the nature of the specific problems at hand is part of the design process. This means that design requires critical reflection upon existing systems and tools in terms of real world outcomes. This process involves determining needs and priorities through participatory planning and design processes, and encouraging clients and relevant communities to rethink the end uses, functions or services required to meet their needs. Second, processes and methods need to be created or regeared to better conform to those priorities, so that the means are designed to achieve the ends. This way, the designer can find the best low-impact processes, components and materials that will produce the desired

outcome. This sometimes requires working with manufacturers to invent better processes and materials.

Multi-dimensional: Eco-logical design is a multi-layered, multi-dimensional process that accommodates different cultures and personal preferences simultaneously.

Eco-logical design can be 'hard tech', or 'nuts and bolts', such as the Hypercar (which among other things uses advanced materials to reduce car weight and hence its power requirements) [Box 19]; or polyvalent reactive building envelopes where the different surfaces of the building form an active living skin that responds to changing diurnal climatic conditions. Eco-logical design can also be 'soft tech' or 'nuts and berries', such as permaculture [5.1], or living technologies, which are biological, self-generating systems that digest pollution and grow food [9.1].

Scales of eco-logical design

Work in eco-logical design has been branching out to operate in every stage and scale of development ranging from termite control technologies to **bioregional planning**, as illustrated in Figure 1.4.1.

Figure 1.4.1: Eco-logical design fields exist at all scales

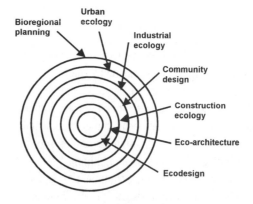

- **Ecodesign**: At the product scale, eco-logical designers are reducing the amount of toxic materials and energy used in industries and homes, facilitating disassembly, reuse and recycling, and working to reduce status-seeking and waste by consumers [6.3].

- **Eco-architecture**: At the building scale, eco-logical designers are reducing both up-front and ongoing operating impacts of structures (through methods like solar design and healthy materials specification, or on-site waste and water recycling) [9.2, 9.3] and working to improve human productivity, health and well-being through design [8.1].

- **Construction ecology**: At the project development scale, eco-logical designers are reducing construction impacts, including materials transport, through strategies such as ecological facilities management [3.3, 4.4], green building products, co-generation and construction waste management processes [Box 7].

- **Community design**: At the neighbourhood scale, eco-logical designers are reducing the environmental impacts of buildings and settlements through principles of ecodesign, eco-architecture, construction ecology, ecological site planning, permaculture [5.1], co-housing [7.1], and so on.

- **Industrial ecology**: At the industrial scale, eco-logical designers are seeking economies in production processes by facilitating industry food webs and principles of green engineering and eco-design, that add value while reducing resource and energy requirements [3.1].

- **Urban ecology**: At the city scale, eco-logical designers are reducing transport, energy and infrastructure requirements through planning strategies and multi-use residential developments [8.2, 3.2], while helping to create a sense of place, community and social well-being [8.3].

- **Bioregional planning**: At the regional scale, eco-logical designers are shaping lifestyles, systems of production and governance to the unique ecological attributes and carrying capacity of ecosystems and bioregions, to improve social relationships and economies while reducing ecological disturbance [12.2].

Conclusion

Because design is a social activity, the built environment in many ways mirrors, or is a projection of, the culture. The existing built environment is an outcome of conventions, technologies and construction practices that evolved out of a particular industrial order and contra-ecological way of thinking, often called the dominant paradigm. Even new 'green' technologies have generally been incorporated within the same design syntax. Urban areas should no longer be seen as separate and independent of the bioregion. Buildings, landscapes and urban areas as a whole should provide their own ecosystem services (biodiversity, food production, air and water purification etc), use only renewable or reusable materials, and supply their own energy and water on site (ie be resource autonomous).

References and further reading

Crosbie, M. 1994, *Green Architecture: A Guide to Sustainable Design*, Rockport Publishers, Rockport, MA.

Daily, G.C. 1997, *Nature's Services: Societal Dependence on Natural Ecosystems*, Island Press, Washington, DC.

Jones, D.L. 1998, *Architecture and the Environment: Bioclimatic Building Design*, The Overlook Press, New York.

Kibert, C.J. 1999, *Reshaping the Built Environment: Ecology, Ethics and Economics*, Island Press, Washington, DC.

Lyle, J.T. 1994, *Regenerative Design for Sustainable Development*, John Wiley, New York.

O'Meara, M. 1999, 'Exploring a New Vision for Cities' in L.R. Brown et al, *State of the World*, W.W. Norton and Co, New York, pp. 133–150.

Orr, D.W. 1992, *Ecological Literacy: Education and the Transition to a Postmodern World*, State University of New York, New York.

Papanek, V. 1995, *The Green Imperative: Ecology and Ethics in Design and Architecture*, Thames and Hudson, London.

Register, R. 1997, 'Strategies and Tools for Building and Ecological Civilisation', in J. Birkeland, ed, 1998, *Designing Eco-Solutions: Proceedings of Catalyst '97*, University of Canberra, ACT.

Romm, J. 1999, *Cool Companies: How the Best Businesses Boost Profits and Productivity by Cutting Greenhouse-Gas Emissions*, Island Press, Washington, DC.

Vale, R. and Vale, B. 1994, *Towards a Green Architecture*, RIBA Publications, London.

Van der Ryn, S., and Cowan, S. 1996, *Ecological Design*, Island Press, Washington, DC.

Hinte, E. and Bakker, C. 1999, *Trespassers: Inspirations for Eco-efficient Design*, Netherlands Design Institute, Amsterdam.

White, R. 1994, *Urban Environmental Management: Environmental Change and Urban Design*, John Wiley, New York.

Questions

1. Develop an alternative typology to that of the scales of eco-logical design set out in Figure 1.4.1.

2. If you were offered a commission to design a project that would destroy a remnant ecosystem, would you reject the job? Accept the job, but try to re-educate the client? Role play to try persuading a hypothetical client to reconsider the use of the site.

3. How many landscape, building or industrial designers can you name? How many of them are known for eco-logical design? Did you hear about them in school, TV, or workplace? Will designers of ecologically insensitive buildings be glorified in the 21st Century?

4. Do you think design is an 'intellectual activity', or is it reliant on natural talent? Are the required knowledge and skills taught at your school or workplace?

5. Think of examples of how design has hidden the social and environmental costs of development (eg water, electricity, sewage, food).

6. Assume that you have already had a career as an eco-logical designer. Write your epitaph. Put it in a safe place and revisit it later in your career.

Projects

1. It could be said that there are two stylistic traditions in environmental design: hard and technical (nuts and bolts), and soft and organic (nuts and berries). Find examples of both in design journals and prepare a poster.

2. In separate groups, collect scrap materials (cardboard, cans, twigs, styrofoam, sand, etc). Then design an ideal environment for a mouse, in an escape-proof container. As a group, decide which mouse house is 'best' and which you think a mouse would be most happy in. Test and compare these designs with a live pet mouse, borrowed for the occasion. What can be learned by designing for another species?

Box 4   Paradigm Quiz

Ariel Salleh

'How Green is My Paradigm Shift?'

Instructions:

* Do not turn page over until you have performed this exercise.

* Read the CHECKLIST and circle the number by any words which regularly feature in your writing.

* Try to circle at least 4 numbers in each group.

Group 1	Group 2	Group 3	Group 4
1 biophysical systems	1 social organisation	1 government	1 objectivity
2 process thinking	2 distribution	2 workers	2 subjectivity
3 species	3 pricing	3 professionals	3 behavioural change
4 biodiversity	4 social change	4 children & aged	4 discourse
5 human population	5 ownership	5 markets	5 central planning
6 interconnection	6 use values	6 women	6 critical insight
7 either/or	7 contract	7 consumers	7 consultation
8 chaos theory	8 alienation	8 disabled	8 distress
9 natural resources	9 licences	9 management	9 risk assessment
10 sustainability	10 cooperation	10 indigenous people	10 participatory learning
11 labour resources	11 rights-based ethic	11 pharmo-nuclear	11 survey
12 nature–human continuum	12 needs	complex	12 empowerment
13 sexual resources	13 social issue	12 homeless	13 degradation
14 power relations	14 social obligation	13 farmers	14 bioregionalism
		14 animals & plants	

1. Add totals of positive (+) and negative (-) numbers for each columns below

Group 1 totals		Group 2 totals		Group 3 totals		Group 4 totals	
+	-	+	-	+	-	+	-

2. Add totals of positive (+) and negative (-) numbers for all columns

Totals for all groups	
+	-

... see overleaf for answers

Key to Scoring

Group 1 Ontology: If you have circled 4 or more of any odd numbers, your underlying ontology is very likely a conservative functionalist one, treating societies and environments as mechanical systems. If you have circled 4 or more of any even numbers, you share more in common with social ecology and the radical face of the green spectrum.

Group 2 Values: If you have circled 4 or more of any odd numbers, your political values are consistent with the economic individualism which prevails in ruling-class circles. If you have circled 4 or more of any even numbers, you are moving with the alternative post-materialist generation.

Group 3 Agency: If you have circled 4 or more of any odd numbers, you probably emphasise the role of government and professionals as the movers and shakers of social change. If you have circled 4 or more of any even numbers, you want to see community-based initiatives for change.

Group 4 Process: If you have circled 4 or more of any odd numbers, your attitude to problem solving might be rather instrumentalist or manipulative. If you have circled 4 or more even numbers, your approach is deep and grounded in democratic processes.

TOTALS: Count up the odd number circles you have across Groups 1–4, then tally the even numbers. A greater frequency of odd-numbered circles indicates a tendency toward piecemeal reforms that could be incompatible with the longer-term green vision. A greater frequency of even-numbered circles suggests that you understand how ecological sustainability and social equity are interrelated.

Paradigm 1 Status quo		Paradigm 2 Shift to green	
Ontology			
functional analysis		**social ecology**	
biophysical system	natural resources	chaos theory	nature–human continuum
species	labour resources	biodiversity	power relations
human population	sexual resources	interconnection	sustainability
either/or		process thinking	
Values			
economic individualism		**post-materialism**	
social organisation	licences	alienation	social obligation
contract	rights-based ethic	needs	equsl distribution
ownership	social issues	use values	social change
pricing		cooperation	
Agency			
ruling elites		**community**	
government	professionals	indigenous people	children and aged
pharmo-nuclear complex	farmers	women	homeless
markets	consumers	workers	plants and animals
management		disabled	
Process			
instrumental		**experiential**	
central planning	risk assessment	bioregionalism	critical insight
objectivity	consultation	subjectivity	participatory learning
survey	behavioural change	discourse	empowerment
degradation		distress	

Section 2: The Concepts of Growth and Waste

2.1   Limits to Growth and Design of Settlements

Ted Trainer

Current settlement design discourages productive local self-sufficiency, and maximises the volume of goods that must be transported in and wastes that must be transported out. The 'greening' of cities, architecture and products alone make little contribution to the development of self-sufficient economies or to the shift to a zero-growth economy. This chapter argues that conventional architecture, planning, industrial and urban design must recognise the limits to growth, and design for simpler lifestyles, local economic sufficiency, and a steady-state economy.

The basic 'limits to growth' case

Eleven billion people are expected to be living on earth soon after 2060 AD (UN median estimate). If each were to consume minerals and energy at the present Rich World per capita rate, world annual output of these items would have to increase to about eight times their present level. For about one third of the basic list of 35 mineral items, all potentially recoverable resources would probably be exhausted in under 40 years (Trainer 1995a). All potentially recoverable oil, gas, shale oil, and coal (assuming 2000 billion tonnes) and uranium (via burner reactors) would be exhausted in about the same time span. It would require approximately 700 times the world's present nuclear capacity to produce the required amount of energy from breeder reactors, given that fusion power is not likely to be available on the necessary scale for many decades, if ever. This would mean that, at any one time, approximately three quarters of a million tonnes of plutonium would be in use.

It requires 2ha of crop and grazing land per person to produce the average North American diet. If 11 billion people were to have such a diet, 22 billion ha would be needed. However, there are only 13 billion ha of land on the planet (world crop land is not likely to increase beyond the present 1.5 billion ha). Thus, present Rich World diets would be impossible for all to share. It takes about 1.4ha to provide a typical North American per capita annual timber consumption. For 11 billion people to rise to this level of consumption would require four times the world's forest area.

These points suggest that it would be impossible for all the people likely to inhabit the world by 2060 to have anywhere near the lifestyles and resource use rates presently taken for granted in the rich countries. Indeed, it would not be possible for the present 6 billion to rise to these levels. The 1 billion who enjoy 'high material living standards' today do so essentially because they are taking far more than their fair share of the planet's resource capital – most of which will have been consumed in one generation.

The same general conclusion is evident when aspects of the environment problem are considered. The 1990s appear to be the decade in which a number of critical agricultural and biological indices will reach their limits. The Worldwatch Institute has documented slower growth, plateauing or falling trends for world crop land, grain production, meat production, fish catch, irrigated land, fertiliser consumption and wool production (Brown 1992). The biological resources of the planet currently provide well for only 1 billion and are likely to decline rapidly. The 'biological productivity of the planet is falling now' (Brown 1990, p. 7). Is it reasonable to expect these to support 11 billion people?

A glance at the greenhouse problem indicates the severity of the limits to growth and their drastic implications. The Intergovernmental Panel on Climate Change has stated that total world fossil fuel consumption must be reduced by 60–80%. If it were cut by 60% and spread equally among 11 billion people, per capita use would have to fall to 1/18 of the present Rich World per capita average.

In short, the limits to growth analysis indicates that a sustainable world order cannot be achieved unless social systems are developed in which a satisfactory quality of life can be achieved on average per capita resource use rates and aggregate GNP levels that are a small fraction of present levels. Indeed, in some key areas, reductions of the order of 90% would seem to be required. Yet the goal of industrial economies remains to increase the GNP and 'living standards' as fast as possible.

The absurdity of this goal is easily demonstrated. In the 1980s, Australia's average **economic growth** rate was 3.2%

33

per annum, yet poverty increased, unemployment almost doubled and the foreign debt multiplied by more than ten. If we assume that the Australian economy will maintain 4% growth in GNP until 2060, it will be producing 16 times as much each year as it does now. If all people likely to live on earth were to enjoy Australian living standards by 2060, total world output would be 220 times as great as it is now.

Not only is the quest for growth failing to solve our problems, it is the basic cause of the most serious global problems surrounding us. Resource depletion, environmental destruction, the deprivation of billions of people in the Third World, and social breakdown in even the richest countries are in large part due to the determination to increase already unsustainable levels of production and consumption. Yet while resources are being depleted at an accelerating rate, inequality is also rapidly increasing. Resources are drawn into production in the interests of the relatively rich. This is especially evident in the Third World (Trainer 1989). The poorest third or more in a typical poor country are actually seeing the productive capacity they once had, especially land, taken from them to produce mostly for the benefit of distant corporations, countries and consumers.

The living standards we have in rich countries could not be as high as they are if the global economy did not work in these unjust ways. Its market mechanism delivers to us most of the world's resource output simply because we can pay more for the oil and timber – but usually far less than the real costs. Appropriate development in the Third World will not occur until the rich countries start living on their fair share of world resources and until Third World people are able to devote their resources to meet their own needs.

Implications for sustainable settlement design

The limits to growth analysis has a number of implications for the nature of a sustainable society. Given that per capita resource use and environmental impact must be a small fraction of their current Rich World rates, we need:

- Much simpler lifestyles, based on acceptance of material sufficiency.

- A high level of economic self-sufficiency, within household, national and especially local areas.

- More cooperative ways of working and sharing of resources.

- A zero-growth or steady-state economy, achieved after a long period of negative growth. That is, a large-scale reduction in *unnecessary* production and consumption.

Living simply does not mean deprivation. Life quality can improve if unnecessary production and consumption is reduced. Adequate material living standards can be easily achieved on very low cash incomes, if acceptance of simpler lifestyles is combined with intensive use of eco-design strategies such as earth building and permaculture. An essential theme in the rapidly increasing eco-design literature is the development of small-scale, highly self-sufficient economies, especially at the town, suburban and regional level. These are crucial if, for example, present high rates of transport are to be cut (9000km per person per annum for road transport alone in Australia).

In small localised economies nutrients can be recycled to soils, resource intensive methods of production can be avoided through, for example, increased craft production, and the non-cash sectors of the real economy can be fostered (mutual aid, giving of surpluses, community working bees, free produce from community commons). Many presently resource-expensive services (welfare, care of disabled, care of aged) can be performed spontaneously in small self-sufficient economies with less professional input or fewer specially built facilities. Further, employment can be guaranteed to all, and social breakdown can be greatly reduced.

These sorts of changes are not just essential to achieve sustainability; they would ensure a higher quality of life than most people experience now. These changes imply no reduction in the high-tech systems we need, such as modern dentistry, hospitals or solar panel research. They simply involve the reorganisation of our suburban and town geographies, the remaking of our values, and the reconstruction of our economy; changes that would eliminate unnecessary production, work, transport and consumption. The 'eco-village' movement is gathering momentum worldwide, going beyond theorising to building new settlements based on the sorts of principles indicated above (See Trainer 1995b).

There has been a recent surge of interest in increasing density in order to reduce the costs associated with urban sprawl (eg in extending water, phone and electricity supplies to ever more distant suburbs). The problem with this view is that it has only taken into account consumption issues. Increasing density will undoubtedly reduce some of the per capita costs associated with providing goods and services for households consumption. However, sustainable settlements must be highly self-sufficient in production, and this requires space. The more that cities increase their density, the more they reduce their capacity to provide for themselves and must increasingly transport goods in and transport wastes out [3.2].

Box 2.1.1: Some elements of sustainable settlements

- **Urban decentralisation** of many small firms producing largely for local consumption, using local resources, labour and capital.

- Far less transporting, packaging and trade, far fewer roads and cars, therefore much scope for digging up roads and increasing gardening within cities.

- Market gardens and **edible landscapes** of free food trees throughout our suburbs.

- Being able to get to work on a bike.

- Much home, craft and hobby production, much less factory production.

- Small local markets.

- **Commons**: neighbourhood wood lots, ponds, orchards, clay sources and facilities for all to use.

- Neighbourhood workshops, for shared tools, recycling, repairing, leisure.

- Local voluntary committees, working bees and rosters to carry out many tasks presently performed by highly paid professionals and bureaucrats.

- Leisure-rich neighbourhoods in which it is possible to spend time without consuming resources.

- Recycling of all food nutrients back to local soils.

- Participation in the governing of our town or locality, through town meetings, referenda and public discussion.

- Town banks which make savings available for investment in ventures which will enrich the town.

- The possibility of working for money only one or two days a week.

- A large non-cash sector of the real economy, including gifts, mutual aid, barter, **LETS systems**, working bees, and free goods.

- Local collection and allocation of most tax revenue, partly payable in non-cash forms (eg contributions to working bees).

Thus, there should be few, if any, big cities and few buildings requiring lifts. Big cities are highly unsustainable and most, if not all, of their social and cultural merits can be provided by cities that are relatively small. Kirkpatrick Sale (1980) has argued in detail that cities need be no bigger than 10,000 in population. The basic settlement units should be small towns surrounded by natural landscapes linked by good public transport systems to big towns and small cities. The ideal balance is most likely to involve a mixture of small, relatively dense centres surrounded by low-density settlements and areas that are made up of farms, forests, commons, and nature reserves.

Conclusion

A limits to growth perspective entails a paradigm shift in several design fields. At present, most architects, planners and industrial designers take for granted resource-expensive externalities, such as access by car, long-distance delivery of food, dependence on experts for maintenance, and short lifetimes for products and structures. Design for sustainability needs to be based on a global perspective which values simplicity, frugality, durability, reparability, distributive justice, smallness of scale, avoidance of luxurious and affluent styles, and easy maintenance. The rich must live more simply so that the poor may simply live.

Whether or not we will make the transition from a consumer to **conserver society** will depend on how well we raise public awareness about the unsustainable nature of industrial growth and affluence, and the existence of viable and attractive alternatives. Few professions are in a better position to contribute to this educational task as are architects, designers and planners. But how many architects presently devote themselves to the design of US$5,000 houses?

References and further reading

Brown, L.R. 1990, 1992, *The State of the World*, Worldwatch Institute, Washington, DC.

Daly, H. and Cobb, J. 1989, *For the Common Good*, Greenprint, London.

Douthwaite, R. 1992, *The Growth Illusion*, Green Books, Devon.

Harrison, P. 1992, *The Third Revolution: Environment, Population and a Sustainable World*, World Wide Fund for Nature, London.

Meadows, D. et al 1983, *The Limits to Growth*, Pan, London.

Sale, K. 1980, *Human Scale*, Secker and Warburg, London.

Trainer, F.E. 1989, *Developed to Death*, Greenprint, London.

Trainer, F.E. 1995a, *Towards a Sustainable Economy*, Envirobooks, Sydney, NSW.

Trainer, F.E. 1995b, *The Conserver Society: Alternatives for Sustainability*, Zed Books, London.

Questions

1. This chapter suggests that major global problems are basically due to global market capitalism, growth and production for profit. Is change to a fundamentally different economic system desirable? Possible?

2. List the countervailing arguments to this limits to growth analysis. What assumptions underlie these positions?

3. List some technical advances that might eliminate the need for radical change in lifestyles, social organisation, values and systems. Will they improve the quality of life? Could they be implemented and/or distributed in time?

4. If under-development in the Third World is due to the over-development of the rich world, what does this suggest about the links between built environment design and ethics? Is it feasible to convince the rich to reduce consumption? Can eco-design replace status-seeking through conspicuous consumption?

5. Is the alternative sketched in this chapter feasible in the context of globalisation? What strategies can be undertaken to move society in this direction?

6. List some benefits and problems of both urban consolidation and decentralisation. To what extent do these benefits depend on good design to be successful?

Projects

1. In groups, take a typical urban neighbourhood plan and redesign it to maximise local economic and social self-sufficiency along the lines indicated in the chapter. Consider the necessary quantities and location of the community workshops, community gardens, wood lots, small businesses, sources of materials, animals, ponds and lakes, alternative energy sources, common areas, leisure resources, small farms, wilderness, recycling centres, wastewater and nutrient recycling systems. What existing structures could be demolished or converted? Consider alternative uses for roads, warehouses, supermarkets, parking lots, concrete drains and so on. Display and compare plans in the following tutorial or class session.

2. Each member of the class will receive confidential notes indicating an income they are to imagine they have received. One-fifth of the class members will get US$35, half will get US$1 and the rest will get US$10. Now conduct an auction to sell lunch. Write on the board several possibilities: from US$1 for yesterday's sandwiches up to a roast dinner with dessert and wine for US$25. Write down the numbers wanting each offering. The auctioneer will make the most money supplying the more expensive meals, so those who only ask for sandwiches will have to go without lunch, because more expensive meals will be made as these are more profitable. Is this distribution mechanism just, efficient? How well does this game represent the way markets function (ie scarce things go to the rich). One-fifth of the world's people get 70 times the average for the poorest half.

Box 5   Exponential Growth

David Marsden-Ballard

There are limits to the growth of individuals and species, and to the carrying capacity of ecosystems and the biosphere. Many ecologists believe that we are beyond sustainable limits. Some of the planet is already irretrievably damaged. It has been estimated that humans now consume over 40% of the available photosynthetic energy of the planet. This fact, combined with continuing over-development, significantly contributes to the increasing rate of extinctions of other species, all of which are part of the global ecosystem that supports human life.

The J curve

Sometimes called the 'J' curve, exponential growth is growth of growth. The current global population growth rate is somewhere between 1.3 and 1.5 %. This means a population increase of 80 to 90 million extra people per year. At 90 million, the world population grows by 246,406 every day, or 10,267 every hour, or 171 every minute. If we concentrated global population growth in one city, it would be like Sydney, having 4 million people, doubling every 16 days, 5 hours and 36 minutes.

There is a formula for calculating the years until the doubling of any exponential growth:

70/n% = doubling time in years.

If the government's goal for the economy is 5% growth, this means: 70/5% = 14 years. It means that if a country does not reduce energy consumption and pollution, then the economy will be consuming twice the energy and producing twice the pollution in approximately 14 years' time. What are the consequences for the environment?

Example: death in a lily pond

Imagine you are an environmental manager of a small river catchment, which includes a pristine natural lily pond. You know that phosphate is the essential element in shortest supply. Upstream from the lily pond a new housing development and entertainment complex is being constructed. The artificially bright green lawns and golfing greens indicate that a lot of phosphate fertiliser is being used. Phosphate-based detergents, dog droppings and lawn clippings are being washed into the stormwater system. Adding phosphate causes exponential growth of algae and water plants until this chokes the lily pond (a few years ago, it caused over 1000km of toxic algal bloom in the Darling River). If it takes 30 days of exponential growth for the lily pond to overgrow with algae and choke to death; on what day is the pond half full of algae?

Answer:

The 29th day.

You try to negotiate with the developers to reduce the nutrient pollution on the 23rd day, and they respond: 'No worries, the weeds are only covering 1% of the pond'.

Day	30th	29th	28th	27th	26th	25th	24th	23rd
% of weeds	100%	50%	25%	12.5%	7.25%	3.6%	1.8%	0.9%

Richard Eckersley

Is life getting better – healthier, wealthier, and more satisfying and interesting? If the answer is 'no', then fundamental assumptions about our way of life, long taken for granted, need reassessing. This chapter suggests that the task we face goes far beyond the adjustment of policy levers by government: we need a more open and spirited debate about how we are to live and what really matters, or should matter, in our lives.

Introduction

The notion of 'progress' has been a cornerstone of Western culture for centuries. But is this conception of progress delivering real benefits? Some commentators believe that if we continue resolutely on our present path of economic and technological development, humanity can overcome the obstacles and threats it faces and enter a new age of peace, prosperity and happiness. Others foresee an accelerating deterioration in the human condition leading to a major perturbation in human history, even the extinction of our species – along with many others. Every relevant issue is contested: economic prospects, the state of the environment, population carrying capacity, technological change, social justice and equity, war and peace.

The question of whether life is getting better is difficult to answer objectively because the data are incomplete, or open to differing interpretations. We lack agreement on what constitutes 'a better life'; we do not have good measures, or **indicators**, of many aspects of life. Furthermore, most analysts view the question through the prism of their particular expertise, giving a distorted or incomplete picture. To the economist, we are consumers making rational choices to maximise our utility, or personal satisfaction; to the ecologist, we are one of millions of species whose fate hangs on the quality of our interactions with other species and the physical environment.

Essentially, we are seeing a clash of paradigms, a confrontation between beliefs and world views to which people are deeply committed. Increasingly, the paradigm of material progress is being challenged by that of social

transformation: which holds that economic, social and environmental problems are systemic and require whole-system change.

Defining progress

In developed nations, we have defined progress in mainly material terms and measured it as economic growth; that is, a rising per capita GDP (**Gross Domestic Product**). The equation of more with better – of **standard of living** with **quality of life** – remains largely unquestioned in mainstream political debate. The fundamental assumptions about economic growth as currently defined and derived – that it enhances well-being (or welfare) and is environmentally sustainable – are rarely highlighted or explored. Let us consider each of these two assumptions.

Does economic growth enhance welfare?

In the late 1980s, the Chilean economist, Manfred Max-Neef, and his colleagues undertook a study of 19 countries, both rich and poor, to assess the things that inhibited people from improving their well-being. They detected among people in rich countries a growing feeling that they were part of a deteriorating system that affected them at both the personal and collective level. This led them to propose a threshold hypothesis, which states that for every society there seems to be a period in which economic growth (as conventionally measured) brings about an improvement in quality of life, but only up to threshold point – beyond which, quality of life may begin to deteriorate with more economic growth (Max-Neef 1995).

This possibility has been supported in recent years by the development of indicators, such as the **Genuine Progress Indicator** (GPI), that adjust GDP for a wide range of social and environmental factors **[Box 6]**. These 'GDP analogues' show that trends in GDP and social well-being, once moving together, have diverged since about the mid-1970s in all countries for which they have been constructed – including Australia.

Public opinion surveys also support the view that growth has diminishing benefits and escalating costs. Even the new alternative measures to GDP do not come close to reflecting the negativity expressed in surveys of public perceptions about the state of society and the future of humanity. For example, in a 1997 national poll, we asked people whether – taking into account social, economic and environmental conditions and trends – they thought overall quality of life in Australia was getting better, worse or staying about the same (Eckersley 1998). 52% believed life was getting worse, and only 13% that it was getting better. The rest, 33%, said quality of life was staying about the same.

Sociologist Michael Pusey's 'Middle Australia Project' indicates that 'too much greed and consumerism' and 'the breakdown of traditional values' are the main reasons Australians give for what most see as a declining quality of life and adverse changes in family life (Pusey 1998). Social researcher Hugh Mackay said his qualitative research reveals growing community concern in Australia about the gap between our values and the way we live. We crave greater simplicity in our lives, yet continue to complicate them. We would like to be less materialistic, but seem to acquire more and more. Mackay says people are concerned that they do not 'seem to know where to stop' (Mackay 1998).

Research shows that in rich, developed nations, health seems to be influenced more by income distribution than by average income levels. This research suggests that what is important to health is not the physical effects of poverty and material deprivation, but the psychological and social consequences of relative deprivation, of living in an unequal society. These may relate to qualities such as hostility, stress, hopefulness and a sense of control or mastery over our lives. The British medical researcher, Richard Wilkinson (1994), says that what seems to matter are the social meanings attached to inferior material conditions and how people feel about their circumstances and about themselves. The health data suggests, he says, that the quality of the social fabric, rather than increases in average wealth, may now be the prime determinant of the quality of human life.

Is economic growth sustainable?

Advocates of economic growth argue that it is good for the environment: as countries grow richer, they will invest more in environmental improvements, consumer preferences and the structure of the economy will change, and technology will become more efficient and cleaner. This proposition has been supported by empirical evidence of an 'inverted U'

relationship between per capita income and some measures of environmental quality. That is, environmental degradation and pollution increase with income up to a point, after which they decrease with increasing income.

In late 1994, a small international group of ecologists and economists met in Sweden to consider the relationship between economic growth and the environment. Their report, published in the journal *Science* (Arrow et al 1995), states that the inverted U-shaped curves need to be interpreted cautiously. So far, they have been shown to apply only to a selected set of pollutants with local, short-term costs (for example, urban air and water pollution). The curves do not apply to the accumulation of waste, or to pollutants such as carbon dioxide which involve long-term and more dispersed costs.

The relationship is less likely to hold for resource stocks such as soils and forests, and it ignores issues such as the transfer of polluting industries to other countries. Further, where emissions have declined with rising income, the reductions have been due to local institutional reforms such as environmental legislation. Where environmental costs are borne by the poor, by future generations, or by other countries, the report says, the incentives to correct the problem are likely to be weak.

Even if the premise is accepted, economic growth will worsen rather than improve environmental conditions at the global level, because countries with a large majority of the world's population will have average incomes below the estimated turning points for some time to come.

An industrial economy requires a huge amount of natural resources, excluding air and water, to produce its flow of goods and services – totalling 45–85 tonnes per person per year. Much of this activity is not captured in national economic accounts partly because the resources involved do not become commodities that are bought and sold. These 'hidden flows' are associated with mineral extraction, crop harvesting and infrastructure development. For example, estimates of the material flows for Sydney between 1970 and 1990 show increases in per capita resource inputs and waste outputs across the board: water, food, energy, sewage, solid wastes and air pollution.

Environmental indicators suggest that, globally, there is an overall trend away from sustainability, not towards it. The final statement of the 1997 United Nations Earth Summit noted that participants were deeply concerned that overall trends for sustainable development were worse than they were in 1992, the year of the previous Summit.

The World Wide Fund for Nature (WWF) has developed a *Living Planet Index* based on an assessment of forest, freshwater and marine ecosystems (WWF 1998). The index has declined by about 30% between 1970 and 1995, it says, 'meaning that the world has lost nearly a third of its natural wealth in that time'. WWF also says that, globally, consumption pressure, a measure of the impact of people on natural ecosystems based on resource consumption and pollution data, is increasing by about 5% a year. At this rate, consumption pressure will double in about 15 years.

The need to question prevailing assumptions about economic growth, quality of life and ecological sustainability is also demonstrated by the trends in five indicators of Australia's development over the past 100–150 years – per capita GDP, life expectancy, unemployment, per capita energy consumption and population (Eckersley 1998). Australians are, on average, almost five times richer (in real terms) now than at the beginning of the 20th Century. Per capita energy use, a broad measure of resource consumption and waste production, has increased correspondingly. The population has also increased about fivefold, so that total economic activity and energy use are about 25 times greater now than 100 years ago.

While Australians are materially much better off than ever before, some of the improvements in well-being are less directly linked to economic growth than is widely believed. Growth was stagnant before the Second World War, but life got better for most people because public policy initiatives improved education, health, housing and working conditions and, for some of this time, wealth and income were becoming more evenly distributed. Reflecting these changes, life expectancy, which has increased by about 30 years or 60% since the 1880s, was rising steadily when per capita GDP was not. With employment, the nature of the relationship with economic growth appears to be shifting; despite relatively strong growth, unemployment in the 1990s is at its highest level outside the depressions of the 1890s and 1930s.

Conclusion

The crux of the debate about progress is the direction of change. Both expert analysis and public opinion suggest the need to canvass more openly the possibility and feasibility of new directions, towards new personal and social goals.

The rationale for continuing economic growth in rich countries seems flawed in several important respects:

- It overestimates the extent to which past improvements in well-being are attributable to growth.

- It reflects too narrow a view of human well-being, and fails to explain why, after 50 years of rapid growth, so many people today appear to believe life is getting worse.

- It underestimates the gulf between the magnitude of the environmental challenges we face and the scale of our responses.

The issue in contention is not simply a question of growth versus no-growth. The main political justification for promoting growth is jobs. Economic expansion may be better than contraction in increasing employment, but it is also now creating more over-work and under-work, more job insecurity, and a widening income gap. All these things, like unemployment, put pressure on individuals, families and the whole fabric of society.

We need to focus not just on wealth creation but also on the distribution and conservation of wealth, not just on the rate of growth but also on the content of growth. We need to look much more closely at what is growing, what effects this growth is having, and what alternatives might exist. Improving both our current personal well-being and the long-term quality and sustainability of life require the same shift: from an economy characterised by high growth, increasing inequality and conspicuous consumption, to one directed towards safeguarding the natural environment, increasing social cohesion and equity, and enriching human life.

The task, then, is not simply to abandon growth; it is to move beyond growth. To suggest this is not necessarily to be 'anti' the economy, business or technological innovation, but to argue that these activities need to be driven by different values towards different ends.

References and further reading

Arrow, K., Bolin, B. et al 1995, 'Economic Growth, Carrying Capacity, and the Environment', *Science* 268, April, pp. 520–521.

Eckersley, R. 1998, 'Perspectives on Progress: Economic Growth, Quality of Life and Ecological Sustainability', in R. Eckersley, ed, *Measuring Progress: Is Life Getting Better?*, CSIRO Publishing, Collingwood, Victoria.

Mackay, H. 1998, 'Mind & Mood', *The Mackay Report*, June.

Max-Neef, M. 1995, 'Economic Growth and Quality of Life: A Threshold Hypthesis', *Ecological Economics* 15, pp. 115–118.

Pusey, M. 1998, 'The Impact of Economic Restructuring on Women and Families: Preliminary Findings from the Middle Australia Project', *Australian Quarterly*, July–August , pp. 18–27; personal communication.

Wilkinson, R. 1994, 'The Epidemiological Transition: From Material Scarcity to Social Disadvantage', *Daedalus* 123(4) Fall, pp. 61–77.

WWF (World Wide Fund for Nature) 1998, *Living Planet Report 1998*, WWF, Gland, Switzerland.

Questions

1. What built environment policies would you propose to enhance quality of life that do not require net economic costs (often called 'no regrets' options)?

2. It is often said that people in certain poor countries seem 'happy'. It this a false stereotype? Does wealth produce happiness? If true, how might this relate to the built environment?

3. 'Our environmental, social and economic problems are just glitches we can fix without fundamental change.' Do you agree? Is your view on this changing over time?

4. What evidence is there for and against the 'threshold hypothesis' about economic growth and quality of life?

5. It has been said that two major causes of global environmental damage are extreme poverty and excessive wealth. Why is this so?

6. Debate: 'What is important to health is the psychological and social consequences of relative deprivation, of living in an unequal society, not poverty in itself'.

Projects

1. Design a survey to evaluate people's perceptions about the quality of the urban environment, whether it is improving or not, what they think are the most important factors, and what they anticipate future life quality will be. Based on the survey, develop a policy proposal for integrating indicators of life quality into local council policies. Compare with actual council policies.

2. What are current design criteria and indicators? What fundamental changes to conventional design indicators need to be made to accommodate the increased life span of the population? Remember to consider industrial design, landscape architecture, architecture and other fields of design.

Box 6   Genuine Progress Indicators

Clive Hamilton

	Column name		Description of indicator
A	Personal consumption	+	Private final consumption expenditure from the national accounts.
B	Income distribution	+/	Share of lowest quintile in total income. A new index constructed from taxation statistics.
C	Weighted personal consumption	+/	Personal consumption weighted by index of changing income distribution.
D	Public consumption expenditure (non-defensive)	+	Value of non-defensive government consumption spending. Includes portions of spending on defence, public order, social security, education, health and general government.
E	Value of household and community work	+	Hours of household and community work performed each year valued by the housekeeper replacement method. Some components of household work (including some childcare, gardening and shopping) are valued for the process rather than the product.
F	Costs of unemployment	-	Value of hours of idleness of the unemployed.
G	Costs of under-employment	-	Value of hours of idleness of part-time employees who want to work full-time.
H	Costs of overwork	-	Value of hours of work done involuntarily.
I	Private defensive spending on health and education	-	Health and education spending that offsets declining conditions (assessed as half of health spending and half of tertiary education costs).
J	Services of public capital	+	Contribution of public investment in non-defensive works (eg roads), valued annually by a depreciation rate.
K	Costs of commuting	-	Time spent commuting valued at opportunity cost.
L	Costs of noise pollution	-	Excess noise levels valued by cost of reducing noise to acceptable level.
M	Costs of transport accidents	-	Costs of repairs and pain and suffering (but excluding medical costs and lost earnings counted elsewhere).
N	Costs of industrial accidents	-	Costs of pain and suffering (but excluding medical costs and lost earnings counted elsewhere).
O	Costs of irrigation water use	-	Damage to environment estimated by the opportunity cost of environmental flows (for example, 30% of current diversions in the Murray-Darling).
P	Costs of urban water pollution	-	Damage to environment estimated by the control cost of improving water quality.
Q	Costs of air pollution	-	Damage to humans and environment from noxious emissions measured mainly by health costs.
R	Costs of land degradation	-	Costs to current and future generations from soil erosion etc measured by forgone output and ecological damage.
S	Costs of loss of old-growth forests	-	Environmental values denied to future generations measured by willingness to pay to retain environmental values.
T	Costs of depletion of non-renewable energy	-	Costs of shifting from petroleum and natural gas to renewables using US replacement cost estimate.
U	Costs of climate change	-	Annual greenhouse gas emissions valued by the expected cost of emission abatement using taxes or permits.
V	Costs of ozone depletion	-	Annual emissions valued by future impacts on human health and environment.
W	Costs of crime	-	Measured by property losses and household spending on crime prevention.
X	Net capital growth	+	Growth in value of stock of built capital net of depreciation adjusted for growth in the labour force.
Y	Net foreign lending	-	Change in net foreign liabilities (the current account deficit).

Glen Hill

*Products of design are often turned into waste long before
the end of their expected life span. This is the result of
complex cultural forces which create a desire for new
design products and thereby cause the obsolescence of
existing design products. The waste created by 'the desire
for the new' has significant environmental costs. This
chapter examines how designers are implicated in the
generation and maintenance of the desire for new design
products, and asks: if designers are central in creating
'cultural' waste, is it possible for them to contribute to its
solution?*

What is waste?

Waste is generally considered to be a straight forward
concept: the 'surplus' or 'discard' arising from any system of
production and use. In this view, waste is either the unusable
by-product of a process, or the products of a process which
are produced in excess of what can be used. When examined
more closely, however, waste is not so easy to define or
categorise. All biological systems produce waste, but the
waste from one system may become a valuable resource for
another system. A leaf that falls from a deciduous tree in
autumn, for example, is no longer necessary to the biological
functioning of the tree. Yet the fallen leaf becomes an
essential resource for innumerable other biological systems.
Even human excrement may be a valuable resource for other
biological systems: soil fertilised by excrement may support
photosynthetic plant systems and eventually return as a
human food resource.

Thus waste is never simply waste. In reality, whether
something is waste or a resource is determined by the
perspective of the cultural system from which it is viewed.
Because of our **anthropocentric** perspective, if something
has no utility to humans (or its utility to humans is not
understood), it is seen as 'waste'.

Waste and fashion

Discussing waste as a human cultural phenomenon is,
however, more complex; here waste is not simply about
'utility', but also about 'value'. We probably all have many

items of clothing of various ages and styles stored in our
wardrobes. Considered in **utilitarian** terms, most would
quite adequately fulfil their function. Nevertheless, there are
probably many items that we would not dare to wear because
their designs are so 'out of date' as to be embarrassing. These
clothes have been transformed into 'waste', not because they
have worn out and lost their functionality, but because they
have been made valueless by compelling cultural forces to
which we often succumb without even noticing.

Not only clothing, but every product of design is subject to the
same forces. We may at some stage have noticed that our
computer is annoyingly slow in performing some function;
that the image produced by our office photocopier lacks
sharpness; that the sound reproduction of our cassette player
is rather poor; that our kitchen cupboards are out of date; or
that the office building we are working in fails to convey the
progressive image of our firm. While these products of design
might be functioning adequately and be in sound physical
condition, this dissatisfaction – which shows up as the desire
for something different – has already initiated the
devaluation that will transform these artefacts into waste. In
other words, these items have been transformed into 'waste',
not because they have worn out or stopped functioning, but
because they have been made valueless by cultural processes.

In a witty book entitled *Rubbish Theory* (1979) Michael
Thompson draws some fascinating conclusions about the
way things in our human cultural world accrue and lose
value. He notes that things may either have a positive value,
or they may have zero value and therefore be categorised as
waste. Thompson uses examples such as inner city Victorian
terraced housing and items of bric-a-brac to demonstrate
how a thing's value may fluctuate dramatically. A curio piece
might, for example, deteriorate from its initial value at the
time of purchase to the point of being categorised as waste. It
may later be deemed a 'collectable' or an 'antique' and
increase sharply in value to a level many times its original
value (though only relatively few artefacts actually do regain
their value and utility in everyday life). In a human cultural
context, therefore, an object's value can never simply be
reduced to quantifiable properties such as the quality of its

material constituents, its functionality, its location, its age, or its physical condition.

The process by which a product is transformed into waste has significant ecological costs. The resources embodied in the obsolete product are no longer productive, and further resources are consumed creating the products which replace it. Some people who assume design is a rational process and should not be subject to the whims of fashion, advocate functional solutions to this problem. For example, texts about ecological design often encourage designers to increase the life span of artefacts by making them functionally adaptable or by using durable materials. A cathedral that has life span of 500 years will, for example, consume far less building resources over that time period than buildings replaced or remodelled every few decades [2.4]. Technologies exist to enable the design of artefacts that would be highly durable: buildings could be designed to last for centuries, clothing could be designed from fabric that would not readily rip, wear or perish. Yet, the time cycles within which designed products are replaced or renovated appear to be getting ever shorter.

The contemporary economic system does not encourage longevity in designed artefacts. Indeed, if the products of design did have significantly longer in-service life spans, the very fabric of our consumer society would be placed in jeopardy. The whole economic infrastructure in its present form – the industries producing the consumer goods, the retail outlets selling the consumer goods, the institutions financing and marketing the consumer goods, and so on – would be threatened with collapse. Our economies and industries have become dependent upon short life span consumer goods – on disposability. In this context the possibility of employing design to minimise waste appears remote. Indeed, designers presently have the exact opposite role of maintaining the flow of desirable new products, thus devaluing and transforming what already exists into waste.

What makes us desire the new?

While the economic system fosters a consumerist orientation, the desire for the new cannot simply be attributed to a commitment to a particular economic ideology. We do not desire a faster computer, a smaller mobile telephone, a higher resolution photocopier, the latest digital sound reproduction, a new-look kitchen, or a face-lift for our office building, in order to lend support to the market economy. Indeed, it is the desire for the new that maintains the modes of production and consumption upon which our market economy depends.

All products of design can be seen to be 'technologies'. And all aspects of life – work, leisure, travel, even something as apparently 'natural' as sex – are in some way mediated by technologies which are products of design. Vast sets of interwoven technologies and practices constitute the different, but sometimes overlapping, 'worlds' in which we are involved: the world of business, sport, academia, fashion design, or that of urban street gangs. The technologies and practices which constitute each world can be seen to 'care' for (support) the well-being of those who participate in it. (Heidegger uses the term 'care' to describe a complex concept which is grounded in the temporality of human understanding; for an explanation of this concept see Hill 1997).

In the world of business, for example, practices involving computers can be seen to take 'care' of assembling accounts, economic forecasts, letters to clients and so on. In the world of sport, practices involving tracksuit use can be seen to take care of keeping an athlete's body warm before and after intense activity. Even the aesthetics of technologies can be seen to play a role as part of the 'caring' practices of that world. The clothing fashions of business executives or the dress codes of street gangs can, for example, be seen to illicit a powerful sense of identity, affiliation and hence 'care' from within the particular group.

It is evident, however, that the care provided by our 'technologised' practices is imperfect. There are points where care breaks down – where the computer is not fast enough, where a public phone is out of service, or where the widespread adoption of a once 'elite' fashion style (the baseball cap for example) means that it no longer serves as a unique identifier for the group. It is in these situations that design comes into play, bringing into being new technologies which overcome these points of breakdown.

With the appearance of the new product of design, however, something very significant occurs. The new **technology** does *not* simply slot into some pre-existing space in the weave of technologies and practices that constitute a world. Rather, the new technology gathers a new world of technologies and practices around it which subtly or substantially transforms the previous world. Stephen Boyden (1992, p. 173) describes this profound process as '**techno-addiction**'. As an outcome of this process, the technologies which were integral to the old world but are no longer integral to the new world are devalued and begin their transformation into 'waste'.

To illustrate this process, consider the effect of the transformation of copying technology on the world of teaching. A generation ago a slow hand-cranked 'gestetner' stencil duplicator was commonly used to copy student handouts. The introduction of faster, high volume sorting and stapling photocopiers enabled handouts to be produced ever more quickly. As less time was necessary, less time was allowed for producing ever more voluminous handouts. A new world of time allocation and student expectations 'gathered' around the new technology. If reintroduced, the old 'gestetner' would no longer meet the expectations of this new world. In this new world, the preceding technology has been tangibly devalued – transformed into 'waste.' The same story could be told for any successful technology.

The desire for new technologies is thus the desire to meet the new expectations of our ever changing worlds. But as our ever changing worlds are themselves driven by the adoption of new technologies, the desire for the new operates within a dangerously self-perpetuating circle.

Conclusion

There is no easy way for designers to resist the cultural forces described in this chapter. Well-intentioned solutions aimed at minimising the ecological impact of techno-addiction – such as design for adaptability, reuse and recyclability – have the reverse effect, as they both facilitate and normalise the process of techno-addiction. Perhaps the most important thing designers can do is remain constantly aware that the 'progress' brought about by design is always double edged:

- each new design we create will inevitably distribute its 'care' unevenly, benefiting some and disadvantaging others; and

- every new design we create participates in turning a network of existing designs into waste.

References and further readings

Borgmann, A. 1984, *Technology and the Character of Contemporary Life*, University of Chicago Press, Chicago.

Boyden, S. 1992, *Biohistory: The Interplay Between Human Society and the Biosphere*, UNESCO, Paris.

Heidegger, M. 1977, *The Question Concerning Technology and Other Essays*, Harper and Row, New York.

Hill, G. 1997, 'The Architecture of Circularity: Design', *Heidegger and the Earth*, University of Sydney, Sydney, NSW.

Ihde, D. 1990, *Technology and the Lifeworld: From Garden to Earth*, Indiana University Press, Bloomington, IN.

Thompson, M. 1979, *Rubbish Theory: The Creation and Destruction of Value*, Oxford University Press, New York.

Winner, L. 1986, *The Whale and the Reactor*, University of Chicago Press, Chicago.

Questions

1. Which stages of a design and production process usually generate the most waste? Can 'thinking' create waste? How?

2. Is it possible to design products that do not generate waste? Think of some examples of 'design for ecological restoration' which would generate a net resource gain or income.

3. List examples where waste from one culture becomes (or could become) a 'resource' for another culture (eg water canteens made from tyre inner tubes).

4. List examples where the waste from human societies becomes a resource for non-human entities or ecosystems (eg mosquitoes or snakes making homes in old tyres).

5. Should we favour waste that eventually returns to benefit human populations over waste that supports other non-human populations (eg algae) but that may be detrimental to human populations? How should such decisions be made?

6. If people could adopt a truly whole systems view, would the idea of anthropocentrism become irrelevant?

Projects

1. In groups, develop a list of ways that environmental design courses can integrate waste reduction principles into the curriculum. Compare, revise and consolidate these proposals with others; then circulate the results to the teaching and administrative staff and management. Check back in six months to see what became of the proposal.

2. You have designed a nuclear-powered dishwasher that functions as a table, cupboard and waiter, that serves, gathers the dirty crockery from the table, and puts them away clean in the cupboard. It uses very few resources and is very cheap. Compile a list of all of the existing equipment, products, skills and everyday practices that this new product will turn into waste. Think laterally about all of the stages of production and use of the new product. Do the benefits of this invention outweigh the costs? Why or why not?

John B. Storey

Over the last 50 years, Western economic theories have been increasingly adopted as a model for worldwide development. The urbanisation that accompanied this development has resulted in many buildings being constructed to last only a short period before being demolished and replaced, which requires prodigious amounts of materials and energy at every phase of their life cycle. However, supplies of many materials in common use today are predicted to run out. Ideas such as fashion replacement, built-in obsolescence and disposability have infiltrated the building industry.

Short-life buildings

The current average life of buildings in New Zealand (BIA 1995), Australia (SAA 1988) and Britain (Brand 1994) is 50–60 years; in the US it is about 35 years (Brand 1994) and in some parts of Japan an astonishing 20 years (Coates 1990). Even during their relatively short lives, many of these buildings undergo major reconstruction. For instance, in the new retail and commercial business centres built around the edge of many American cities, it is common practice to replace the entire outer wall of a building – simply to attract a different class of tenant. Developers expect their buildings to become stylistically passé every 15 years or so and plan accordingly (Garreau 1991).

In US commercial buildings, the average life of the building skin is only 20 years. Other elements are replaced at even more frequent intervals in these buildings: services every 7–15 years and interior space defining elements every 3–5 years (Brand 1994). Vast amounts of resources are expended on maintenance. In effect, many commercial buildings have been virtually rebuilt during their brief lives. Average life-span figures also obscure the fact that pre-1940 buildings tend to be more durable than their more modern counterparts. Furthermore, institutional and residential buildings generally have a longer life expectancy than commercial buildings, although average life spans are falling in these areas too, as the same materials and construction processes used in commercial buildings are also being applied to these building types.

These attitudes are pervasive and are often institutionalised. In Australia, AS 3880-1988 suggests a 40–60 year life span for all normal buildings. In the New Zealand Building Code, the section on 'Durability' defines three categories of durability, the highest of 50 years being for structure and elements which are difficult to replace or where failures would be difficult to detect, 5 years for materials which are easily accessible and where failures are easy to detect, and 15 years for the rest.

Moreover, maintenance and other operating costs are usually not taxable. This means that it is the community that pays for their upkeep, rather than the perpetrators of these minimalist designs. US tax laws require a residential building to be depreciated over 27.5 years, a commercial building over 31.5 years. In other words, the value of the building has supposedly arrived at zero after three decades. Small wonder buildings are often constructed to last only that long in the US.

These low durability norms are now so well established that they are seldom even questioned by building providers. Yet this limited life concept is a 20th Century phenomenon and is very much at odds with the perception the public have of buildings as permanent artefacts which, with proper maintenance, will last indefinitely.

Consequences

As a direct consequence of the concentration on minimising first cost and maximising short-term financial return, there has been a decline in building standards and the creation of universally banal, minimalist urban architecture which is disliked by the public and often hated by its occupants. In some extreme cases, apartment buildings built in the 1960s and 1970s have been so abused by their occupants that they have been demolished. Significant numbers of office buildings built to these minimal standards have never been, and may never be, occupied. The waste of resources involved is intolerable. The visual and experiential degeneracy of our cities is just as real, though harder to quantify.

At least 3 billion tonnes of material, which amounts to 40% of the total global material flow, is used in buildings each year (See Table 2.4.1). A similar proportion of the world's total energy output is also devoted to constructing and operating buildings. In most industrialised countries, building material waste constitutes over 50% of municipal solid waste generation (Roodman and Lenssen 1995). All but a tiny fraction of the materials used in construction are taken from virgin sources. A conservative estimate is that we will require between three and four times the amount of building materials we currently use by the year 2020 due to rapidly increasing population, urbanisation and lifestyle expectancy (Corson 1990).

a particular amount of accommodation instead of several times, the potential resource savings would be tremendous. Owners gain by having an investment which continues to generate income for very long periods of time. If they incorporate perdurable, low-maintenance materials, operational costs would be minimised. The incorporation of natural environmental systems would also minimise operating costs, help to create healthy living environments and reduce energy use. The community would benefit by a reduced need to subsidise the wasteful use of resources through tax breaks. It would make sense to create beautiful buildings once more, to maximise their long-term viability,

Table 2.4.1: Impacts of modern buildings on people and the environment

Problem	% Used for Buildings	Environmental Effects
Use of virgin minerals	40% of raw stone, gravel, and sand; comparable share of other processed materials such as steel	Landscape destruction, toxic run-off from mines and tailings, deforestation, air and water pollution from processing
Use of virgin wood	25% for construction	Deforestation, flooding, siltation, biological and cultural diversity losses
Use of energy resources	40% of total energy use	Local air pollution, acid rain, damming of rivers, nuclear waste, risk of global warming
Use of water	16% of total water withdrawals	Water pollution; competes with agriculture and ecosystems for water
Production of waste	Comparable in industrial countries to municipal solid waste generation	Landfill problems, such as leaching of heavy metals and water pollution
Unhealthy indoor	Poor air quality in 30% of new and renovated buildings	Higher incidence of sickness – lost productivity in tens of billions annually

Source: Roodman and Lennsen, 1995

At the same time, material resources are coming to an end. For example, in 1990 it was estimated that there was a 50–100 years supply of aluminium ore, at then current production figures. But between 1950 and 1987 production rose tenfold (Corson 1990): an extrapolation of these figures suggests that we could run out of aluminium ore somewhere between 2010 and 2020.

Long-life buildings

Perdurable or long-life buildings are buildings whose life spans are measured in centuries rather than decades. The arithmetic is obvious: if we could build only once, to provide

create visual assets for the community and achieve and retain a high level of user satisfaction.

Most buildings in the commercial sector are commissioned by developers whose prime motivation is to maximise short-term profits in order to satisfy their investors. Owner occupiers might be expected to take a different stance. There are many examples of more responsible attitudes coming into play in continental Europe, where owner-occupier development is more common than in Australasia. Institutional and governmental organisations might also be expected to take a much more enlightened, longer term view, but few such organisations seem prepared to pay, up front, for the materials or construction strategies which would deliver long-term operating and resource savings. Changing such ingrained attitudes will not be easy.

There are, however, some signs of change. A growing number of organisations can observe a direct relationship between the quality of working environments and productivity, and users are demanding more stimulating, healthier and generous workplaces. Some building developers are already responding to this message. In Europe, and to a lesser extent in the US, user-friendly workplaces are becoming more widespread.

Governments have a responsibility to ensure the long-term viability and well-being of their nation, but few national governments have begun to consider long-term resource issues related to the built environment. Governmental organisations could lead by example and remove existing financial incentives that encourage such things as minimisation of initial building cost, high operating and maintenance costs, low durability, low final recovery design. Some European governments have begun this process, but in Australasia and the US, where responsibility lies with local and state authorities, there has been little success.

Adaptable buildings

A long-life building must be useful during the whole period of its existence. It is not difficult to design a long-life building. The real challenge is to design buildings that can be adaptable to many uses over the whole period of their lives. Factors which significantly affect a building's life span fall roughly into four categories: planning, form/space, materials/construction and user satisfaction.

Change is inevitable and growth is likely in long-life buildings; therefore the initial design must facilitate these factors [Box 14]. For long-term viability it is worth considering as many different uses for a building as possible, however unlikely, and trying to design to accommodate as many of these scenarios as possible. This is termed **scenario planning**.

Parts of buildings such as exterior cladding and interior partitions change at different rates, so it is wise to avoid physically interdependent parts. Simple forms are easier to adapt than complex forms. Generic space is usually more useful than space specifically tailored to one activity. A generous proportion of initially unallocated space and

loading allowances beyond code minimas also greatly facilitate future adaptability.

Both materials and construction should be durable and low maintenance. Most traditional and many modern materials can be both, if properly detailed and utilised in suitable ways and locations. Frequently it is not the materials themselves, but rather the way in which they are combined, which reduces their durability. For instance, mechanical joints have now been largely replaced by sealants, which are quicker and initially cheaper, but are very difficult and expensive to maintain over the building's life.

Designs which facilitate user adaptation and personalisation of the building, encourage occupants to carry out their own incremental changes and give them as much control of their immediate physical environment as possible, tend to engender long-term user satisfaction, well-being and a caring attitude towards the building. Similarly, buildings which are individualised and have crafted elements often develop their own personality and tend to generate pride of place among the users. Buildings which are cherished in these ways are much more likely to survive and remain in use than those which users simply tolerate.

Conclusion

We are coming to the end of virgin resource availability on our small planet and must find ways to reduce our resource use. Designers could make a dramatic difference by designing long-life, adaptable buildings and products. Short-life, specialised, minimalist building design and construction is so embedded in our consumer culture that it will not be easy to create the necessary attitudinal shift towards sustainability among building providers. But there is a growing groundswell of public antipathy towards our current unsustainable practices. By selectively utilising modern technologies, we should be able to generate a long-life, loose-fit, low-energy architecture which will be cherished by users and the public, and make a significant contribution to ecological sustainability.

References and further reading

BIA (Building Industry Authority) 1995, *New Zealand Building Code Clause B2*, BIA, Wellington, New Zealand.

Brand S. 1994, *How Buildings Learn: What Happens After They're Built,* Viking Penguin, New York.

Coates N. 1990, *Architecture Design Profile 86*, Second Architecture Forum Conference, Tokyo.

Corson W.H. 1990, *The Global Ecology Handbook*, Beacon Press, Boston, MA.

Garreau J. 1991, *Edge City*, Doubleday, New York.

Lawson, B. 1996, *Building Materials, Energy and the Environment: Towards Ecological Sustainability*, RAIA, ACT.

Roodman D.M. and Lenssen N. 1995, *A Building Revolution: How Ecology and Health Concerns Are Transforming Construction – Worldwatch Paper 124*, Worldwatch Institute, Washington, DC.

SAA (Standards Association of Australia) 1988, *Australian Standard AS 3800: 1988*, Standards Association of Australia, Canberra, ACT.

Questions

1. Reasons are given in this chapter for the shift to ephemeral (short-life) buildings, such as consumer expectations and urbanisation. List these and other reasons, and then try to rank the reasons in order of significance. How can designers influence these factors?

2. Are there any potentially negative outcomes of adopting long-life, loose-fit, low-energy buildings as an environmental design strategy? Explain.

3. What policies could federal, state and local governments adopt to minimise the use of resources in construction? How can these actions be encouraged? What are some existing examples? [Box 7]

4. What lessons can we learn from the past with respect to the sustainable use of resources? Why, for instance, have 17th, 18th and 19th Century townhouses proved to be so useful, popular and adaptable to such a range of functions?

5. What measures would help to create an attitudinal shift towards the sustainable use of resources in our built environment among building developers, building owners, building users, and the general public? [Box 27]

6. Changing transport systems have one of the biggest causes of building demolition or deterioration of once popular neighbourhoods. Describe changes in shipping, road transport and air travel, and how these have affected the building and housing stock. [Box 20]

Projects

1. Trace the development of a street, part of a street or an individual building site, from its earliest origins to the present day (using archival drawings, photographs, direct observation and so forth). Establish the materials and construction methods used as far as possible. How did the buildings from different eras perform in terms of their use of resources? How and why were the buildings replaced and/or repaired? Were the more recent changes more wasteful in terms of energy and resources?

2. The public perception of the durability of building is rather different to actuality. Develop and conduct a survey to check the accuracy of this statement in your school or city. For example, people might be asked to estimate the life spans of different types of buildings (eg factories, government offices, small and large commercial buildings, bridges, roads and medium-density housing). Disseminate the results in the school newsletter or local paper (after being vetted by relevant authorities or parties).

Box 7   Waste Reduction Checklist

Nigel Bell

We pay for wastes three times over: the cost of the materials now wasted; waste disposal costs; and the cost of the lost opportunity to fully use that material. Fees for disposal are increasing, and fines are increasing for illegal disposal or land clearance, or allowing earth to be washed into stormwater drains. However, designers can affect each stage below in a positive way. Questions for individuals and/or companies are provided below to assist in waste reduction.

Waste minimisation plans

- Have you and/or your company committed in writing to best practice waste minimisation?

- Has a culture of resource efficiency been developed in your operation?

- Are subcontractors and suppliers aware and involved in your waste minimisation plan?

- Have you set realistic waste reduction targets?

- Have you developed waste minimisation manuals?

- Do you have a reward system that benefits waste-smart staff?

- Do you celebrate waste reduction achievements (eg through promotion and marketing)?

Waste audits

- Have you assessed the different waste contributors (eg office, estimating, purchasing, site, trades)?

- Have you developed waste minimisation performance indicators?

- Do you have baseline performance figures from elsewhere for comparison?

- Do you have a suitable record-keeping system to monitor and assess performance?

Personnel

- Are all key office and site personnel involved in your waste reduction planning (even before construction commences)?

- Do you involve subcontractors and site operators in waste training appropriate to their role?

- Have all on-site personnel been instructed in correct disposal procedures?

- Do suppliers and subcontractors know what is required of them?

- Is someone responsible appointed to oversee implementation of the waste minimisation plan?

Site arrangements

- Have you developed policies and procedures for separating waste materials on site? Is your construction site planned for work efficiency and waste minimisation (access, deliveries, stockpiles, etc)?

- Do you adopt consistent disposal procedures (eg types of containers, appropriate signage, suitable location for bins)?

- Do your waste/reuse/recycling containers have lids for clean and dry storage and collection?

- Are trees and native vegetation retained to the fullest possible extent? Is the development site landscaped/ rehabilitated before handover?

- Do you minimise the potential for your building site to pollute the air (eg dust, chemical usage)?

- Do you minimise the potential for construction noise on yourself, workers and neighbours?

- Do you retain topsoil for reuse on the site? Do you protect sand and soil stockpiles with sediment controls? Do you prevent vehicles tracking sediment and other pollutants onto sealed roads?

- Are erosion and sedimentation controls in place before excavation? Are these controls checked regularly and after heavy storms to ensure they remain effective?

- Do you wash paintbrushes and concrete tools in a protected area away from surface drainage?

Materials

- Are leftover solvents, cleaners and paints kept for the next job, or taken to waste collection centres where available?

- Do you use materials produced locally within your region whenever possible?

- Do you avoid or minimise the use of materials that off-gas (eg containing volatile organic compounds)?

- Does your project use durable materials and construction techniques to maximise the life of the building?

Contracts and purchasing

- Have you developed waste-smart contracts for material reuse and/or recycling?

- Do you have waste reduction/removal clauses in contracts with subcontractors?

- Are all materials ordered to size and deliveries scheduled to minimise wastes?

- Do you require minimal packaging from suppliers (eg metal strapping, reuseable pallets)?

Design

- Do you maximise prefabrication (which significantly reduces on-site waste)?

- Do you specify and/or purchase recycled products where possible?

A 'futures wheel' shows the effects of a single action with wider interactions, and how effects can become causes.

Section 3: Industrial, Urban and Construction Ecology

3.1 Industrial Ecology

Hardin Tibbs

Industrial ecology is an emerging field of research and practice based on a set of global principles for framing the design of technology and the deployment of industrial infrastructure. The principles are designed to eliminate (not just reduce) the environmental impact of industry. The industrial ecology framework is based on an analysis of ecosystems and industrial infrastructure in terms of flows of materials. Over the longer term it is expected that this approach will dominate the environmental management of technology and industry.

The global scale of industry

The industrial production system has now reached planetary scale. The volume of materials flowing through the industrial system and the human economy worldwide is now impacting on all flows of materials occurring naturally as part of global bio-geochemical processes.

In the case of some materials, industry is already larger than nature. The anthropogenic (human-caused) flow of lead into the atmosphere is 11.9 times greater than the amount of lead naturally mobilised into the biosphere through geological processes such as the weathering of rock. When materials are released by industry, they disperse into the biosphere – for example 13 million pounds of mercury (a neurotoxin) falls in rain every year.

Table 3.1.1: Toxic heavy metals – worldwide emissions to the atmosphere (thousands of tonnes per year)

	Artificial flows	Natural flow	Ratio
Lead	332.0	28.0	11.9: 1
Zinc	132.0	45.0	2.9:1
Copper	35.0	6.1	5.7:1
Arsenic	19.0	12.0	1.6:1
Antimony	3.5	2.6	1.3: 1
Cadmium	7.6	1.4	5.4:1

Source: Nriagu 1990, pp. 7–32

Another example is the release of carbon dioxide. By the early 1990s the burning of fossil fuels and deforestation were releasing roughly eight billion tonnes of carbon into the atmosphere every year (in the form of 30 billion tonnes of carbon dioxide). This anthropogenic flow of carbon is equal to about a sixth of the natural background flow.

Why are these global-scale flows a problem? One concern is that industrial flows of materials are now so large that they can destabilise natural global systems because of their sheer scale compared to natural flows. Climatologists believe that the increasing (but non-toxic) level of atmospheric carbon dioxide is changing the world's climate. Another concern is that global-scale flows of pollution will lead to chronic toxification of the entire biosphere.

Also, the flows are not only large but are growing exponentially **[Box 5]**. The doubling period for world population growth is now 40 years but the doubling period for materials consumption by industry is only 20 years – twice as fast. Anthropogenic carbon dioxide released into the atmosphere every year has doubled twice-over since 1950. Total materials use in the US alone has ballooned from 140 million metric tonnes a year in 1900 to 2.8 billion metric tonnes a year in 1990, up from about 1.6 tonnes a person to 10.6 tonnes a person.

On average, overall consumption of materials in the US has doubled every 20 years during the 20th Century. The exponential growth of industry is now reaching levels that risk a global ecosystem breakdown. According to an estimate in 1986 (Vitousek 1986), the human economy was then using 40% of the entire annual growth of land-surface biomass. Since this percentage is increasing in line with growth in the use of materials – doubling every 20 years – it could reach the 80% level by 2006. Increasing the human share this much is inherently risky as it means that much less than half the total natural ecological processes and habitat will remain, which may compromise their viability as a planetary life-support system (Baskin 1997). The so-called 'ecosystem services' provided by the natural environment include water and air purification, and their contribution to the world economy has been valued at over US$33 trillion a year (Daily 1997).

Figure 3.1.2: Consumption of materials in the US, 1900–1989

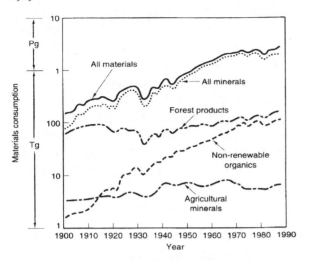

Source: Graedel, T. E. and Allenby, B. R. 1995, p. 147

Steps to an ecology of industry

The global scale of industry implies that the existing architecture of the industrial system is obsolete, as it will not be able to support environmentally sustainable development into the future. Industrial ecology is the emerging response to this challenge (National Academy of Sciences 1992; Allenby and Deanna 1994). It sets out systemic design principles for harmonious co-existence of the industrial system and the natural system. Two of the most important foundation concepts are the 'cyclic economy' and the 'industrial ecosystem'.

At the moment, the industrial 'system' is less a system than a collection of linear flows. Industry draws materials from the Earth's crust and the biosphere, processes them with fossil energy to derive transient economic value, and dumps the residue back into nature. For every 1kg of finished goods we buy, about 20kg of waste have been created during production, and within six months, 1/2kg of our average purchase is already waste. This 'extract and dump' pattern is at the root of our current environmental difficulties.

The biosphere works very differently. From its early non-cyclic origins, it has evolved into a truly cyclic system, endlessly circulating and transforming materials, and managing to run almost entirely on solar energy (Lovelock 1988). There is no reason why the international economy could not be redesigned along these lines as a continuous cyclic flow of materials. Such a '**cyclic economy**' (Box 3.1.3) would not be limited in terms of the economic activity and

prosperity it could generate, but it would be limited in terms of the input of new materials and energy it required. Pollution would be reduced close to zero.

At the time of writing this paper, Germany is the first country to begin seriously experimenting with the legislation needed to create a cyclic economy.

Box 3.1.3: Cyclic economies and natural ecosystems

Characteristics of a cyclic economy

- Industrial system seen as a dependent subsystem of the biosphere.
- Economic flows decoupled from materials flows.
- Environmental costs fully internalised into the market domain.
- Cyclic flow of materials.
- Virgin materials use minimised.
- Information substitutes for mass.
- System **entropy** kept as low as possible.

Characteristics of natural ecosystems

There are many features of natural ecosystems that could be emulated by industry:

- In natural systems there is no such thing as 'waste' in the sense of something that cannot be absorbed constructively somewhere else in the system.
- Nutrients for one species are derived from the death and decay of another.
- Concentrated toxins are not stored or transported in bulk at the systems level, but are synthesised and used as needed only by individual species.
- Materials and energy are continually circulated and transformed in extremely elegant ways. The system runs entirely on ambient solar energy, and over time has actually managed to store energy in the form of fossil fuel.
- The natural system is dynamic and information-driven, and the identity of ecosystem players is defined in terms of processes.
- The system permits independent activity on the part of each individual of a species, yet cooperatively meshes the activity patterns of all species. Cooperation and competition are interlinked, held in balance.

At a more detailed level, the design principles embedded in natural ecosystems (Box 3.1.3) have given rise to the idea of the '**industrial ecosystem**'. This involves more than simple recycling of a single material or product. In effect, industrial ecosystems are complex 'food webs' between companies and industries to optimise the use of materials and embedded energy. They involve 'closing loops' by recycling, making maximum use of recycled materials in new production, conserving embedded energy in materials, minimising waste generation, and re-evaluating 'wastes' as raw material for other processes. They also imply more than simple 'one-dimensional' recycling of a single material or product – as with, for example, aluminium beverage can recycling. In effect, they represent 'multi-dimensional' recycling, or the creation of 'food webs' between companies and industries. A complex of industrial producers applying these principles has been referred to as an **eco-industrial** park.

The best-known example of an eco-industrial park is in Denmark (Tibbs 1992). A network of independent companies in the town of Kalundborg created, over time, a permanent waste exchange system in an area about ten miles across (Figure 3.1.4). The waste transfers are across industries, so that the by-product of one company becomes the raw material for another. The cooperation involves an electric power generating plant, an oil refinery, a biotechnology production plant, a plasterboard factory, a sulphuric acid producer, cement producers, local agriculture and horticulture, and district heating. Among the 'wastes' that are traded, some by direct pipeline, are water at various levels of heat and purity, sulphur, natural gas, industrial gypsum, and fly ash.

Figure 3.1.4: Industrial ecosystem at Kalundborg

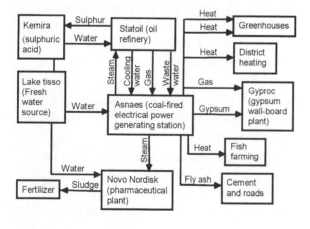

Source: Novo Nordisk

This cooperation was not required by regulation; the earliest deals were purely economic. Recent initiatives have been made for environmental reasons, yet have also paid off financially. In some cases mandated cleanliness levels, such as the requirement for reduced nitrogen in waste water, or the removal of sulphur from flue gas, have permitted or stimulated the reuse of wastes, and helped make such cooperation feasible. Most of the exchanges are between geographically close participants since the cost of infrastructure, such as pipelines, is a factor. But proximity is not essential; the sulphur and fly ash are supplied to distant buyers. Ultimately, this kind of industrial ecosystem could be extended into a large-scale network that might include the entire industrial system (Frosch and Gallopoulos 1989).

Dematerialisation, decarbonisation and industrial metabolism

If large-scale industrial ecosystems are established, resulting in a continuous cyclic flow and reuse of materials, this would largely eliminate the direct environmental impact of industry. But to be fully effective, additional steps would be needed.

Dematerialisation

The amount of materials in the closed loop, or web, can either be increased over time, kept stable, or decreased. Keeping it the same would avoid use of virgin non-renewable resources. But the system needs energy to run and leaks are possible (see below), and minimising these means reducing the volume of material in the loop over time.

If the global population doubles and becomes more affluent during the time the closed loop is established (within the next 20 to 40 years), reducing or just holding the amount of material steady will require accelerated dematerialisation.

Dematerialisation refers to a decline in the materials and energy intensity of industrial production – a trend in industrially developed economies. Both materials and energy use (measured as quantity per constant dollar of GNP) have been falling since the 1970s (Larsen et al 1986). This is because the market for basic products has been saturated, while the weight and size of many other products has fallen. Information technology increasingly allows embedded information to reduce product bulk. New technologies such as nanotechnology – assembling materials atom by atom – promise to accelerate dematerialisation.

Industrial ecology would aim for miniaturised, lower-mass products with longer life. This would decouple economic growth from growth in materials use, enabling a fixed flow of materials in the cyclic loop to provide goods for many more people.

Industrial metabolism

The efficiency of materials use is a key focus of industrial ecology. **Industrial metabolism** refers to the type and pattern of chemical reactions and materials flows in the industrial system. Potential improvements could yield significant environmental benefits. Compared with the elegance and economy of biological metabolic processes, such as photosynthesis and the citric acid cycle, most industrial processes are far from their potential ultimate efficiency in terms of basic chemical and energy pathways.

Similarly, the cyclic flow of materials, like any engineered system, would suffer from leaks. But the most serious 'leaks' come from design, not by accident. Many materials are 'dissipated' or dispersed into the environment as they are used, with no hope of recovery for recycling. This problem can be overcome by designing differently. For instance, car brake pads leave a finely distributed powder on our highways as they wear down. This can be avoided with frictionless electrically regenerative braking, as in the latest hybrid-electric cars like the 1998 Toyota Prius.

Decarbonisation

Energy would be required to move materials through the cyclic loop and periodically reprocess them for reuse. To minimise its environmental impact, this energy will need to be progressively **decarbonised** – contain less carbon over time. Energy sources have been decarbonising for more than 150 years, as industrialised countries move away from high carbon fuel sources such as firewood and coal, to oil and low carbon sources such as natural gas (Ausubel and Sladovich 1989).

Because carbon dioxide from industry is a major dissipative flow of material, industrial ecology would aim for the decarbonisation of energy. A completely carbon-free energy supply could be provided using pure hydrogen gas. A possible future hydrogen-electric economy would combine hydrogen (the lightest element) to provide a clean, low-mass carbon-free store of renewable energy, and electricity to provide precision and control in energy delivery.

Conclusion

Industrial ecology addresses the global scale and environmental impacts of industry with a new approach focused on material flows. By taking a systemic perspective, the environmental footprint of industry can be reduced almost to zero. But the changes needed will take time to accomplish because the existing base of installed industrial capacity locks in huge linear-pattern throughputs of material. Even with accelerated depreciation and scrappage, the widespread installation of completely new production equipment designed to form part of an industrial ecosystem would take many years. Changes of environmental policy will also be needed to remove impediments – for example to allow certain chemicals currently classed as hazardous waste to be reclassified as acceptable secondary materials for production use. Nevertheless, it is expected that in the long term the superior engineering logic of this approach will dominate and industrial ecology will become the technical core of global sustainable development.

References and further reading

Allenby, B. and Deanna R., eds, 1994, *The Greening of Industrial Ecosystems*, National Academy Press, Washington, DC.

Ausubel, J. and Sladovich, H. 1989, *Technology and Environment*, National Academy Press, Washington, DC.

Ayres, R.U. and Simonis, U.E., eds, 1994, *Industrial Metabolism: Restructuring for Sustainable Development*, UN University Press, Tokyo and New York.

Baskin, Y. 1997, *The Work of Nature*, Island Press, Washington, DC.

Daily, G. 1997, *Nature's Services*, Island Press, Washington, DC.

Frosch, R. and Gallopoulos, N. 1989, 'Strategies for Manufacturing', *Scientific American*, September.

Graedel, T.E., and Allenby, B.R. 1995, *Industrial Ecology*, Prentice Hall, Englewood Cliffs, NJ.

Larson, E., Ross, M. and Williams, R. 1986, 'Beyond the Era of Materials', *Scientific American*, June.

Lovelock, J. 1988, *The Ages of Gaia: A Biography of Our Living Earth*, Norton, New York.

National Academy of Sciences of the USA, 1992, *Proceedings* 89(3).

Nriagu, J.O. 1990, 'Global Metal Pollution', *Environment* 32 (7), pp. 7–32.

Tibbs, H.B.C. 1992, 'Industrial Ecology: An Agenda for Environmental Management', *Pollution Prevention Review*, Spring, pp. 167–180. (Erratum: page 169, line 18; replace 'remain' with 'be eliminated'.)

Vitousek, P.M. et al 1986, 'Human Appropriation of the Products of Photosynthesis', *Bioscience* 36, June, pp. 368–373.

Questions

1. Faced with the prospect of a cyclic economy, how would you expect mining companies to react? What recommendations would you make to them for their future business based on the principles and aims of industrial ecology?

2. In some countries, electric utilities have been able to make money by selling less of their product. How does this work? What has been the impact of a free market in electric power generation?

3. In what ways do environmental regulations sometimes prevent or inhibit the reuse of industrial materials? What other factors influence the priority that an industrial producer gives to materials reuse?

4. Industrial 'food webs' between companies and industries can optimise the use of materials and embodied energy. What are some examples that could be created by cooperation between local industries, and/or new industries?

5. Can the idea of a bioregion be usefully translated into the idea of an 'industrial catchment area'? Would this provide an appropriate scale of assessment for industrial ecology?

6. Debate: 'The principles of industrial ecology will be furthered by the globalisation of the economy.'

Projects

1. Determine which government agencies, industry associations and business organisations are responsible for, or capable of, bringing about systems change in industry. Develop some recommendations for your (bio)region based on principles of industrial ecology and, once assessed, present them to the relevant organisations.

2. If there is no secondary materials exchange in your area, draw up a proposal for creating one as a new business enterprise.

Meg Keen

While modern urban life masks our biological origins, people still remain dependent on ecological systems to meet basic needs, such as food, oxygen and water. Urban ecology studies the complex systems of relationships and interactions between people, culture, and resource use within urban environments. The purpose of urban ecology is to develop a better understanding of the urban environment as an integrated whole and to use this knowledge to create sustainable human settlements.

What is urban ecology?

Urban ecology is concerned with the complex systems of relationships and interactions between people and their living and non-living environments in the urban context.

Although urban areas occupy only 2% of the world's land surface, they use 75% of the world's resources and release a similar percentage of global wastes (Girardet 1996b). Sometime shortly in the 21st Century, more than 50% of people will be living in these urban areas and contributing to this huge consumption of global resources (UNCHS 1996). Urban ecology studies how these flows of resources in and out of the cities change over time in relation to human activities, and the affect this has on human well-being and urban sustainability.

Modern urban systems can be complex to study because they are **open systems**. That is, cities are not self-contained, they rely on the exchanges of materials, energy and information with areas external to them. For example, agricultural production for urban consumption, and associated land degradation, occurs in rural, not urban centres; air pollution from urban activities affects regions well beyond the urban environment. The significant impact on surrounding regions was illustrated in a study by Rees (1992) which found that the land required for the population of the fertile Lower Fraser Valley of British Columbia, Canada (which includes the city of Vancouver and surrounds) is 20 times the area of land that the valley occupies.

Box 3.2.1   Urban ecology

Processes of **urbanisation** within modern industrial society are characterised by:

- Increased fossil fuel consumption and associated greenhouse gases and pollutants.
- Increased production of synthetic chemicals used to create products which are not easily broken down by natural ecological processes such as pesticides and plastics.
- New forms of human organisation which are not directly engaged with food production and associated ecosystem functions.
- Exponential growth in human populations.

The ecology of a city encompasses a complex array of interactions and resource uses:

- The flows of energy and materials in and out of the urban area.
- The interrelationships between energy/material use and human activities.
- The responses of social and ecological systems to these human activities (Boyden et al 1981).

More recently a World Resources Institute study (Matthews et al 2000) analysed the material flows and the environmental impacts of five industrialised countries. Two major findings were: a) numerous resource flows remain undocumented despite the hazards they present to human and environmental health; and b) technological advances and economic restructuring have not achieved any overall reduction in resource use or waste volumes.

In order to achieve the long-term sustainability of our cities, and thus safeguard our own well-being, the study of urban ecology emphasises the need to reconsider our use of resources, our neglect of ecological systems within the city, and our human responses to the resulting ecological and social stresses. As noted by Newman (1999, p. 22) 'By looking at the city as a whole and by analysing the pathways along which energy and materials including pollutants move, it is possible to begin to conceive of management systems and technologies which allow for the reintegration of natural processes, increasing the efficiency of resource use, the recycling of wastes as valuable materials and the conservation of (and even production of) energy.'

Urban metabolism

The metabolism concept, as applied to people, simply refers to the processes which we use to produce food and energy to conduct our daily activities. Urban metabolism refers to the material and energy inputs needed to meet the demands of living and non-living components of urban systems. For example, in an average urban day, inputs would include food for humans and other animals, water for drinking and industrial processes, petrol for transportation systems, electricity for lighting, and so on. When we have used these inputs, we have what is commonly referred to as waste [2.3]. In natural ecosystems there are no wastes except heat energy. Instead, the wastes of one process become the inputs for other processes (for example, animal droppings are nutrients for plants).

Figure 3.2.2: Urban metabolism

Linear metabolism

Circular metabolism

Source: Giradet 1996

Many industrial societies simply deposit wastes in landfill sites. The garbage going to landfill sites is increasing in many countries (McKinney and Schoch 1998, p. 527). As this practice continues, landfill sites fill up and many useful resources are wasted. The result is that resource consumption continues to grow. This wasteful process is referred to as **linear metabolism** because inputs are used once and disposed. Fortunately, there is an alternative.

Circular metabolism mimics natural systems, ensuring that waste products are re-integrated into the wider ecosystem (see

Giradet 1996, pp. 22–23). In Australia's capital, Canberra, there is now a policy of reducing waste to zero by the year 2010. Canberra has been able to achieve a significant reduction in resources going to landfill by treating waste as a resource for further input into the wider urban system. From 1993 to 1997 waste going to Canberra's landfills decreased by 43% (from 415,798 to 237,981 tonnes).

This has been achieved through:

- Education campaigns which encourage curbside recycling. Ninety-eight percent of Canberrans assist in the recovery of 24,000 tonnes of recyclables annually.

- Development of new industries which use what was once waste as raw materials (eg production of road bed from building waste).

- Development of new systems for reprocessing organic waste (eg composting and worm farming).

- Establishment of a resource recovery information network where waste products can be offered for use by others (ACT Waste 1998).

These are just small examples of the large gains which can be made if we start to think of 'wastes' as resources, and to enhance the ecosystems and human systems which function within urban environments. When materials cannot be easily re-integrated into human and natural systems without serious disruption to, or degradation of, living environments, restrictions may have to be placed on their production. However, in many cases, the circular metabolism of natural ecosystems can be successfully mimicked through human interventions and sound urban management. In the future, the concept of waste (ie unused materials) may be something from the past.

Urban ecological systems

Cities have functioning ecological systems. A good example is the urban water cycle. The failure to recycle urban water by using stormwater and household **greywater** for urban irrigation means that the demand for water supply is excessive, leading to the unnecessary damming of natural waterways and the accompanying loss of land and biodiversity. In Canberra, a series of urban lakes (water retention basins) and wetlands are used to store and cleanse urban stormwater run-off. They also provide an attractive area for recreation and relaxation. Large reeds (macrophytes) assist to take up excess nutrients and to settle out water-borne sediments, while simultaneously providing wildlife habitats. The water held in the lakes is used for watering city parks and lawns, as well as for urban recreational purposes.

A key issue is the current treatment of mainstream household waste water. Whether the water is used for washing an apple or flushing the toilet, it is all transported to, and treated at, sewage treatment plants. In many urban centres this process results in the loss of vital nutrients such as nitrogen, phosphorus and calcium from agricultural areas. The sewage sludge is incinerated and the waste (now insoluble) is deposited in landfill sites where nutrients are lost to the ecosystem. In a large number of other cities, the treated water and its nutrients are flushed out to sea. More ecologically advanced treatment processes use micro-organisms and plants to detoxify the sewage, eliminating chemical inputs and producing an end product which can be returned to agricultural lands as a fertiliser. At Cornell University in the US, experiments have found that this type of biological sewage treatment is not only cheaper, but also less land and energy intensive than conventional sewage plants (McKinney and Schoch 1998, pp. 458–59).

By gaining a better understanding of ecological processes and their applicability to the ecological functions of cities, adverse environmental impacts can be minimised. Ecological design is of interest to urban ecology studies because it promotes design which 'minimises environmentally destructive impacts by integrating itself with living processes' (Van der Ryn and Cowan 1996, p. 18). This is well illustrated by Corbett's residential development in Davis, California, which maximises its use of natural drainage ways, vegetation for food production and shade, and solar energy in order to create an economically successful development which meets the needs of social and ecological systems (Basiago 1996). Design ideas which integrate ecological systems with social and economic priorities are not new to urban design, as articulated by earlier writers such as Ebenezer Howard (1902) in his promotion of garden cities and Ian McHarg (1969) in *Design with Nature*. Urban ecology gives added importance to these ideas because it documents the benefits of such design to the attainment of low urban metabolism and healthy ecosystems.

The human dimension

Globally, the conferences and conventions concerning sustainable development (WCED 1987; UNCED 1992) have signalled an acceptance that current practices of urban industrial society are inflicting unacceptably high ecological and social costs (Folk et al 1997). Urban areas are human

creations, and people are responsible for their sustainability. The challenge is to develop the analytical frameworks and human organisations which allow us to meet this challenge.

To achieve sustainable cities, our human management systems and organisations need to become more sensitive to the ecological demands of urban environments. This is in part being achieved by the transformation of planning and economics to ensure that the ecological costs of urban activities are taken into account in decision making. Examples range from the specific to the systemic, such as legislation requiring that new suburbs have properly insulated and solar oriented houses, to land-use systems which are integrated with public transport systems [Box 20]. The latter can achieve significant energy savings by ensuring that new developments are on pre-existing public transportation routes (or extensions), and that urban population growth occurs within corridors well serviced by an energy efficient infrastructure (Newman 1995).

Citizens are also being encouraged to consider the impacts of their behaviour and consumption patterns. National Pollution Inventories (NPI), State of the Environment Reports, and various international and national eco-labelling programs are being used to affect consumer behaviour and encourage **green consumerism**, or consumption by urban and rural populations which minimises ecological and social impacts. Increasingly, industries are being made legally responsible for the disposal of their wastes and the costs of their pollution. This shift in responsibility has resulted globally in changes to industrial processes which reduce pollutants and energy use, as well as costs of production (Brandon and Ramankutty 1993). Because much industrial production occurs in urban areas, the benefits to urban ecology are large.

People's attitudes, values and behaviour patterns are fundamental to any study of urban ecology. In trying to achieve sustainable urban systems, human responses to the state of urban systems will be dependent on our ability to:

- Perceive the problems.
- Develop the knowledge and technology needed to solve the problems.
- Establish the cultural and organisational arrangements necessary to support a systemic, rather than fragmented, response.
- Sustain the political will to act.

Urban ecology helps us to generate information relevant to

the functioning of ecological and human systems, and to create responses which are holistic. Increasingly, there is an understanding that human well-being in cities depends upon its integration with ecosystem health, and to achieve that integration, greater civic engagement is required (Mega 1999; Smith et al 1998).

Conclusion

Cities are already the dominant form of human settlements, but this will only be a useful human adaptation to deal with our increasing population numbers if the forms and functions of cities are sustainable. Urban ecology provides a framework within which we can critically consider cities as living places for ourselves, and those living and non-living entities on which people depend. In particular, it is important to assess the flows of materials and energy in and out of cities. If these flows stretch renewable resources beyond their ability to replenish supplies, or if these flows generate wastes which adversely affect the functions of our life support systems, then people need to respond rapidly. The human responses must incorporate a sound understanding of the functions of ecosystems, because ultimately these systems are the ones which support human life.

References and further reading

ACT Waste 1998, *Earth Works*, Participants Notes for ACT Earth Workers, Canberra, ACT.

Basiago, A.D. 1996, 'The Search for the Sustainable City in 20th Century Urban Planning', *The Environmentalist* 16(2), pp. 135–155.

Boyden, S., Millar, S., Newcombe, K. and O'Neill, B. 1981, *The Ecology of a City and its People: The Case of Hong Kong*, Australian National University Press, Canberra, ACT.

Brandon, C. and Ramankutty, R 1993, *Toward an Environmental Strategy for Asia*, The World Bank, World Bank Discussion Paper 224, Washington, DC.

Folk, C., Jansson, A., Larsson, J. and Costanza, R. 1997, 'Ecosystem Appropriation by Cities', *Ambio* 26, pp. 167–172.

Girardet, H. 1996a, *The Gaia Atlas of Cities: New directions for Sustainable Urban Living*, Gaia Books, 2nd edn, London.

Girardet, H. 1996b, 'Giant Footprints', *Human Settlements – UNEP Newsletter*, June (http://www.ourplanet.com/imgversn/81/girardet.html).

Howard, E. 1902, *Garden Cities of Tomorrow*, 1946 edn, Faber and Faber, London.

Matthews, E. et al 2000, *The Weight of Nations: Material Outflows from Industrial Economies*, World Resources Institute, Washington, DC.

McHarg, I. 1969, *Design with Nature*, Natural History Press, Philadelphia, PA.

McKinney, M. and Schoch, R. 1998, *Environmental Science: Systems and Solutions*, Jones and Bartlett, London.

Mega, V. 1999, 'The Concept and Civilization of an Eco-Society: Dilemmas, Innovations, and Urban Dramas', in T. Inoguchi, E. Newman and G. Paoletto, eds, *Cities and the Environment: New Approaches for Eco-Societies*, United Nations Press, New York.

Newman, P. 1995, 'Roads, Cargo Cults and the Post-Industrial City', *Urban Futures* 20, pp. 17–24.

Newman, P. 1999, 'Sustainability and Cities: Extending the Metabolism Model', *Landscape and Urban Planning* 44, pp. 219–226.

Rees, W. 1992, 'Ecological Footprints and Appropriate Carrying Capacity: What Urban Economics Leaves Out', *Environment and Urbanization* 4(2), pp.121–129.

Smith, M., Whitelegg, J. and Williams, N. 1998, *Greening the Built Environment*, Earthscan, London.

UNCED 1992, *Earth Summit 1992: United Nations Conference on Environment and Development, Rio de Janeiro*, The Regency Press, London.

UNCHS (United Nations Centre for Human Settlements) 1996, *An Urbanizing World – Global Report on Human Settlements*, Oxford University Press, Oxford.

Van der Ryn, S. and Cowan, S. 1996, *Ecological Design*, Island Press, Washington, DC.

WCED (World Commission on Environment and Development) 1987, *Our Common Future*, Oxford University Press, Oxford.

1. What are examples of ecosystems on which humans in urban areas rely? Which of these are independent of technology? Do you think technology will ever replace these ecosystems?

2. In your own living environment make a list of the type of relationships with which urban ecology would be concerned. How could you measure and study these relationships?

3. In an urban area that is familiar to you, what types of energy sources are used? If these are not renewable forms of energy, think of some alternatives that may be used in the future. Where obvious alternatives exist (eg solar energy, geothermal energy, etc), identify the barriers to their use.

4. Is the collection and disposal of solid wastes in your area most closely exemplified by the concept of circular or linear metabolism? What types of waste disposal could be used to encourage greater energy efficiency, reuse and recycling (eg worm farms)? Why are these practices not currently in place?

5. What types of human responses have occurred as a result of negative impacts on urban ecology in your area? What are the impediments to systems solutions? If planning authorities, environmental protection agencies, or even the length of the term of governments were different, would the responses be different? Discuss what the ideal structure would be for the key agencies affecting urban ecology.

6. Can cities, as a form of human settlement, ever be sustainable? If so, under what conditions could cities be sustainable? Do you think there might be a maximum population for a city? [Box 31].

1. Draw a couple of ecological cycles which occur in your urban environment. Use one colour to draw the parts of the cycles which result in positive benefits to people, and another colour to represent parts of the cycles which produce negative impacts. When there are negative impacts (such as the leaching of polluted water from landfill sites, or the emissions of heavy metals from factories), consider how human interventions could encourage a better use of these potential resources/inputs. What should be done about the negative impacts that seem to be unsolvable or unavoidable? Present findings as a poster.

2. Think of examples where urban pollution has caused a problem and government or private organisations have responded in a positive way. Try and produce a table of four columns which lists: (a) an urban problem, (b) the response, (c) positive aspects of the response, (d) negative aspects of the response. Can the concepts of urban ecology help to explain the patterns which arise? Why or why not?

Box 8   Eco-efficiency Checklist

Reduce material intensity of goods and services

- Can the product or service be redesigned to make less use of material inputs?

- Are there less material-intensive raw materials?

- Can existing raw materials be produced or processed in less materially intense ways?

- Would higher quality materials create less waste in later stages?

- Can water consumption be reduced?

- Can water, wastewater treatment, or waste disposal costs be allocated to budgets to encourage greater control?

- Can yields be increased by better maintenance, control or other means'

- Can wastes be utilised?

- Can products be made of smaller size, or a different shape, to minimise material and packaging requirements?

- Can the product or service be combined with others to reduce overall material intensity?

- Can packaging be eliminated or reduced?

- Can the product be reused, remanufactured, or recycled?

Reduce energy intensity of goods and services

- Can raw materials be produced or dried with less or renewable energy?

- Would substitute materials or components reduce overall energy intensity?

- Can energy costs be directly allocated to budgets to encourage better control?

- Can energy be exchanged between processes?

- Can waste heat be utilised?

- Can processes be integrated to create energy savings?

- Can processes or building energy consumption be better monitored and controlled?

- Could better maintenance of boilers and other equipment improve energy efficiency?

- Can processes of buildings be insulated more effectively?

- Can more energy-efficient lighting be installed?

- Is there scope for better energy housekeeping?

- Can the energy efficiency of products in use be improved?

- Can the product or services be combined with others to reduce overall energy intensity?

- Can wastes and end-of-life products be reused, remanufactured, recycled, or incinerated?

- Can products be made biodegradable or harmless so that less energy is required for disposal?

- Can transport be reduced or greater use made of energy-efficient transport such as rail?

- Are there incentives for employees to cycle, walk, use public transportation or car-pool?

Reduce toxic dispersion

- Can toxic dispersion be reduced or eliminated by using alternative raw materials or producing them differently?

- Are products designed to ensure safe distribution, use, and disposal?

- Can harmful substances be eliminated from production processes?

- Can harmful substances generated in use be reduced or eliminated?

- Can any remaining harmful substances be recycled or incinerated?

- Are remaining harmful substances properly handled during production and disposal?

- Are equipment and vehicles properly maintained so that emissions are kept to a minimum?

Enhance material recyclability

- Can wastes from raw material production be reused or recycled?

- Can process wastes be remanufactured, reused, or recycled?

- Would separation of solid and liquid waste streams make recycling easier or reduce treatment costs?

- Can product specifications be amended to enable greater use of recycled materials and components?

- Can products be made of fewer or marked and easily recyclable materials?

- Can products be designed to facilitate customer use or revalorisation?

- Can products be designed for easy disassembly?

- Can product packaging be made more recyclable?

- Can old products and components be remanufactured or reused?

- Are there any opportunities to participate in waste exchange schemes?

- Can energy be recovered from end-of-life products?

Maximise sustainable use of renewable resources

- Can renewable or abundant materials be substituted for scarce, nonrenewable, ones?

- Can more use be made of resources that are certified as being sustainably produced?

- Can more use be made of renewable energy in production or processing?

- Are new buildings and refurbishments maximising use of passive heating and cooling?

- Can products be designed to utilise renewable or abundant materials in use?

Extend product durability

- Can materials or processes be altered in order to improve longevity?

- Can products or components be made more modular to allow easy upgrading?

- Can whatever aspects of the product that limit durability be redesigned?

- Can maintenance of the product be improved?

- Can customers be informed or educated about ways of extending product durability?

Increase the service intensity of goods and services

- What services are customers really getting from your product? Can this be provided more effectively or in completely different ways?

- What services will customers need in the future? Can you design new or develop existing products to meet them?

- Is your product providing other services as well as the most obvious one? Can these be accentuated or enhanced?

- Can the product or service be integrated or synchronised with others to provide multi-functionality?

- Can customer's disposal problems be eliminated by providing a take-back service?

- Can the properties of the product be accentuated or developed for greater customer value?

- Can products be designed to facilitate customer reuse or revalorisation?

- Can products be redesigned to make distribution and logistics easier?

- Can the product be made easier to customers to dispose of?

- Can production be localised to both enhance service and reduce transport needs?

- Can products be transported or distributed by alternative means to enhance customer value and reduce environmental impacts?

Source: World Business Council on Sustainable Development (WBCSD) with DeSimone, L.D. and Popoff, F. 1997, *Eco-Efficiency: The Business Link to Sustainable Development,* The MIT Press, Cambridge, MA, pp. 885–888.

Janis Birkeland

The tenacity of inefficient, polluting and wasteful systems of development and construction owe in part to entrenched ways of thinking that co-evolved with these systems of production in the first place. This chapter suggests that many environmental managers and academics, as well as society at large, still view the development process and construction industry through a linear, dualistic and hierarchical framework that obscures many of the sources of problems and thus prevents systems solutions.

Introduction

We are increasingly taking a 'systems approach' to understanding environmental problems:

- Analysing relationships and 'stepping outside the box' of traditional problem definitions.

- Looking for better questions, not just looking for new places to use old methods.

- Seeking prevention, not just monitoring and measuring environmental degradation.

It is suggested here, however, that our mental constructs have contributed to built environment design and construction systems that create waste, transfer wealth, and conceal the environmental costs of development. Some of these 'visors' (discussed below) are:

1. Our linear view of construction as a segmented and sequential process.

2. Our view of industry as a 'black box' (rather than a designed system).

3. Our dualistic view of 'supply and demand' as it applies to development.

4. Our hierarchical view of development as being driven by primary industry.

5. Our conception of the place of design in this intellectual framework.

Decisions taken throughout the spectrum of development – siting, structural systems, building configuration, materials specification and construction methods – greatly influence resource and energy consumption in extraction and manufacturing upstream, as well as the consumption of land, resources and energy downstream. There are many missed opportunities to create **symbiotic** relationships between the processes of extraction, distribution and construction, and to recapture resources and energy that are presently wasted. To create more quality of life with less materials and energy, however, we need to redesign not only the built environment, but the nature of development itself.

Our linear view of construction as a segmented and sequential process

Industrialised development has been both organised and understood as a linear, sequential and competitive process. Resources are extracted from nature and transported to factories to be converted to items of consumption for distribution to suppliers and construction sites. This occurs through a series of separate, often competitive operations instead of networks organised to achieve the most efficient resource and energy use.

Where the economy is believed to be driven by consumption and development, it appears logical that more development would occur if access to natural resources, transport and labour were cheaper, and/or there were more consumers or more consumption per capita. Development interests in government and industry have therefore pressured for an ever increasing supply of raw materials, or promoted increased demand or consumption. This has resulted in a growing throughput of materials and energy, when development should instead be geared to optimise life quality at the least economic, social and environmental cost (ie eco-effectiveness). The concept of efficiency has largely been linked to profit instead of reduced resource input. In fact, pollution and the wasteful use of resources and energy has been partly a result of cutting labour costs by replacing labour with energy- and materials-intensive processes in transport (von Weizsäcker et al 1997).

Our view of industry as a 'black box'

This linear framework of analysis has also led to a **black box analysis**, where industry itself has not been scrutinised for means by which it could become more efficient. The focus of environmental management has been on reducing the inputs (resource extraction) and outputs (pollution and waste) of industry, rather than encouraging eco-efficiency *within* an industry's plants and operations. In fact, the push for industrial ecology began largely with enlightened elements in business (Frankel 1998; Hawken 1993; WBCSD 1997) – rather than from within the environment fields [3.1].

Figure 3.3.1: Two views of efficiency

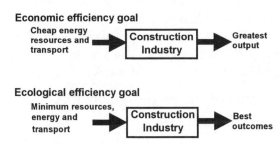

The failure to look at the design of industry itself (especially the construction industry) has contributed to **end-of-pipe controls**, or environmental regulations that filter or mitigate pollution, but do not prevent it [3.4]. This traditional approach – trying to tax, set caps on, or slow the rate of resource and energy use by regulation – is difficult to implement in a capitalist democracy, as producers, decision makers, consumers and voters generally oppose limits on consumption.

More recently, governments have initiated 'cleaner production' or 'pollution prevention' programs that use various forms of persuasion and partnerships to move firms away from end-of-pipe controls towards cleaner fuels and recycling programs. Governments have also begun to place more emphasis on encouraging recycling by consumers consumers and households. While the trend toward cleaner production and recycling is encouraging, however, it does not adequately counter traditional consumption patterns. For example, the US has one of the highest volumes of recycling per capita, yet Americans still produce far more than their share of waste. The trend toward cleaner

industrial production and domestic waste reduction does not look at the basic design of cities, industries and households, but simply regards these as users (black boxes) of fuel and sources of waste (Figure 3.3.1).

Our dualistic view of 'supply and demand' as it applies to development

The economists' dualistic notion of 'supply and demand' also impedes whole-systems analyses. The materials and energy produced by industry are generally regarded as 'supply', while consumers are seen as generating 'demand'. Nature, the real source of supply, is made invisible by this conception. In fact, nature is often regarded as creating demands upon society for protection, rehabilitation, maintenance. Thus, for example, we tend to think of the construction industry as part of the supply side of the equation, though its inefficiencies create unnecessary demands upon nature (Figure 3.3.2).

Figure 3.3.2: Conventional view – 'industry creates supply, consumers create demand'

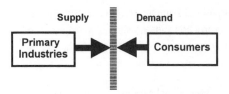

Demand for buildings and products is seen as coming from consumers, as a function of inherent needs, preferences and/ or affluence. Yet reducing demand on **primary industry**, and hence nature, through structures, materials and products that generate less embodied energy, pollution and waste is a function of design. Demand for resources and energy is always mediated by the design of cities, buildings, transport and infrastructure systems (Figure 3.3.3). Consumer accountability is an important issue, but consumers have little impact where choices are limited to inherently wasteful products.

Figure 3.3.3: Nature creates supply, the built environment creates demand

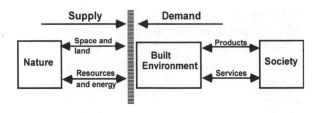

Our hierarchical view of development as driven by 'primary' industry

Since resource extraction and production processes entail concentrated volumes of materials and energy, the focus of environmental management has been on primary industries, such as forestry, mining, agriculture, energy production and metal works.

They are called 'primary' because they use raw materials, but they do not necessarily determine the total flow-through of materials and energy. In this hierarchical conception of economic development, the construction industry is deemed 'secondary', as if it were a product of the primary industries. But if we consider the development process in a systems framework, the built environment would not be seen as 'secondary'. The construction industry is central to land, resource and energy consumption, as virtually all primary industries are tributaries of the construction industry (Figure 3.3.4). Indeed, poor built environment design creates enormous demands on 'primary' industries and, in turn, nature. For purposes of reducing resource consumption, therefore, the construction industry should be seen as primary or central (of course, photosynthesis is the true primary industry).

To take a case in point, global warming is seen as largely a function of the production of energy. Roughly 50% of CO_2 emissions within Australia results from the generation of electricity, whereas only about 25% of CO_2 emissions is directly attributable to the burning of fossil fuels to heat buildings. Government regulations and incentives have therefore targeted electricity production plants and other coal-based energy producers, and negotiated voluntary agreements with energy plants to reduce their emissions. This is important, as most electricity in Australia still comes from coal, and coal produces toxic chemicals and radiation. However, the construction industry creates demand on the other main sources of CO_2 (eg metal works, forestry, transport, energy production). The scale and nature of environmental impacts attributable to CO_2 emissions in primary industries depends on how the construction sector is organised, the form of urban settlements, and the materials and energy sources used by buildings. Reducing CO_2 emissions per unit in electricity generation would mean little if overall demand for energy and materials, hence gross CO_2 production, continued to increase.

Figure 3.3.4: Primary industries are all linked with the built environment

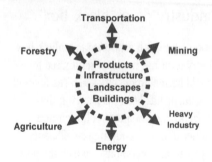

Of course, a more eco-effective construction industry and built environment would not reduce the consumption of materials and energy in itself, as industry would still push for the increased extraction, manufacture and provision of construction products. Nonetheless, it would at least enable the diversion of some materials and energy towards meeting the need for low-cost housing for the homeless or ill-housed, who presently do not generate enough 'demand' (in terms of money). Further, employment would be increased in ecological construction and retrofitting work.

Our conception of design in this linear framework

Another impediment to redesigning the construction sector is the conception of 'design' itself in this linear framework. Building, landscape, and product design are seen as coming at the end of the development sequence – cosmetics intended to 'sell' speculative development ventures or product lines. Ecological design and construction are often viewed as the private concern of the clients of 'alternative' architects/ designers – not the concern of academics or policy makers. For example, as in many other countries, only about 5% of buildings in Australia involve architects, and this limited role is being eroded by other emerging professions, such as 'project managers'. In this context, then, it is not surprising that architecture is sometimes called a 'boutique industry'.

Similarly, industrial designers are expected to enhance building fixtures and appliances to create a competitive advantage through appearance, rather than through technical innovation [6.4]. In fact, many appliances and equipment with different brand names are manufactured at the same factory and have essentially the same design with different details or exteriors. Landscape designers are often hired after construction to enhance the visual backdrop of a building, and sculptors are commissioned to add symbols of prestige to a development. That is, design is still conceived of as an 'add on', and will only work if the original planning is environmentally sound.

Design conceals resource transfers

Urban planning and design has treated the impacts of cities on the hinterland and environments as mere externalities, and has often disconnected beneficiaries from those who bear the burdens [Box 31]. The cost to society, in terms of lost natural resources and amenities, are often transferred to other environments and communities with less political clout [12.2].

Conventional design has also concealed these resource transfers. Trucks carry away refuse to the country before we awake, whereas worm farms in each garden would reduce these costs and make people more conscious of natural cycles. Stands of trees along roads conceal forest clearfelling to reduce public outrage, whereas planting hemp and bamboo on eroded farmland would raise consciousness about the availability of alternative 'woodless' timbers or other carbohydrate alternatives to fossil fuel-based processes and products [Section 10]. Highly capital and resource intensive stormwater systems transport water underground from building roofs and lawns to distant treatment plants. The water is then transported back in pipes to water the same lawns, whereas on-site recycling would make people more aware of their own water consumption [9.2]. Consumers would feel more accountable if they could see, hear, smell and touch the impacts of their individual behaviour.

Conclusion

The ways in which development is conceived tends to make our dependency on nature invisible, while the way in which development is designed conceals the impacts and distribution of resource transfers. Due partly to these latent intellectual constructs, both industry and government policy largely ignores the role of the construction industry and built environment design. But even within this difficult backdrop, designers can make a difference. They can:

- Reduce consumerism and promote consumer accountability by actively pursuing and promoting green alternatives.
- Facilitate public education by making environmental systems visible, so people know where resources come from and where wastes go (whether linear or circular).
- Physically internalise the costs of development by closing

loops so that no pollution and waste is generated (or else none leaves the site).

- Help the transition from a fossil fuel-based economy to a carbohydrate-based human ecology (through, for example, exploring the use of new veggie-fuels and veggie-materials in construction).

References and further reading

Ayres, R.U. and Simonis, U.E., eds, 1994, *Industrial Metabolism: Restructuring for Sustainable Development*, UN University Press, Tokyo and New York.

Baggs, S. and Baggs, J. 1996, *The Healthy House*, HarperCollins, Sydney, NSW.

Edwards, B., ed, 1998, *Green Buildings Pay*, Spon Press, London.

Frankel, C. 1998, *In Earth's Company: Business, Environment and the Challenge of Sustainability*, New Society Publishers, British Columbia, Canada.

Hawken, P. 1993, *The Ecology of Commerce*, HarperCollins, New York.

Heede, R. et al 1995, *Homemade Money*, Rocky Mountain Institute, Colorado, and Brick House Publishing Company, New Hampshire.

Hough, M. 1995, *Cities and Natural Process*, Routledge, London.

Platt, R., Rowntree, R. and Muick, P., eds, 1994, *The Ecological City: Preserving and Restoring Urban Biodiversity*, University of MA Press, Amherst, Nova Scotia, Canada.

Rudlin, D. and Falk, N. 1999, *Building the 21st Century Home: the Sustainable Urban Neighbourhood*, Architectural Press, Auckland, NZ.

Todd, N.J. and Todd, J. 1994, *From Eco-Cities to Living Machines*, Berkeley, N. Atlantic Books, Berkley, CA.

Van der Ryn, S. and Cowan, S. 1996, *Ecological Design*, Island Press, Washington, DC.

Wann, D. 1996, *Deep Design: Pathways to a Livable Future*, Island Press, Washington, DC.

WBCSD, DeSimone, L.D. and Popoff, F. 1997, *Eco-Efficiency: the Business Link to Sustainable Development*, MIT Press, Cambridge, MA.

Weizsäcker, E. von, Lovins, A. and Lovins, H. 1977, *Factor 4: Doubling Wealth – Halving Resource Use*, Allen and Unwin, NSW.

Young, J.E., Ayres, E. and Sachs, A.J., eds, 1994, *The Next Efficiency Revolution: Creating a Sustainable Materials Economy*, Worldwatch paper 121, Washington, DC.

Zeiher, L. 1996, *The Ecology of Architecture*, Whitney Library of Design, New York.

1. When you hear the term 'supply and demand', do you think of demand as being the demand of consumers upon industry for the supply of more products, or the demand of industry upon the environment for the supply of more resources and energy? Discuss how this could affect one's understanding of sustainable development.

2. Construct an argument for the position that the construction industry is a 'primary' industry because it determines the demand for natural resources in major economic sectors.

3. Debate: 'The design of the built environment is not the business of government. Individuals should be able to live any way they want.'

4. Why does the 'invisible hand' of the market not respond to consumer demand for environmental protection, when polls consistently indicate that this is what people demand?

5. How can environmental systems be made more visible (sewage, water supply, electricity generation)? How can these be made into 'closed loop' systems? List the advantages that this would offer.

6. Do you feel excessive consumerism is part of 'human nature'? If so, is it futile for designers to try to overcome the problem of (addictive) over-consumption? Explain.

1. Visit your local housing authority and ascertain if and why they use high-embodied energy materials (such as conventional brick construction). Ask what research has been undertaken into the use of alternative building materials, such as stabilised earth.

2. You are part of a design team hired to provide water and sanitation to a village in a 'developing' Third World community. The community leaders want conventional capital and resource intensive piped water and sewerage systems, but they cannot afford it. Outline a strategy for dealing with this situation and then 'role play' a discussion with the community.

Janis Birkeland

Once produced, pollution gets into the environment eventually. Pollution prevention therefore requires not only the redesign of industrial processes, but of products, buildings, landscapes, and the materials and methods used to produce them. As resources become more scarce and the cost of pollution clean-up escalates, the least costly pollution prevention program is the one that is fastest. The most efficient deployment of talent and capital may therefore be publicly coordinated, interdisciplinary eco-design teams to assist industry in the direct and immediate conversion to ecologically sustainable materials, methods and products, using cost neutral performance-based contracting.

The need for new approaches

Even were society able to achieve 'Factor 10' efficiencies as required for sustainability, the quality of the human and natural environment could not be guaranteed by conventional approaches to pollution control alone, such as market-based or legislative 'regulations' [11.1, 11.2]. Policies such as ecological tax reform are important components of change, but the costs are initially borne by industry, so they are difficult to enact [Box 26]. More importantly, they are not 'solutions' in themselves. They do not improve the quality of our environmental and social relationships; they only reduce certain impacts and provide incentives for producers and consumers to act in more ecologically rational ways.

Reducing pollution effectively, economically and without red tape means changing our industrial and construction processes, urban form and regional land use to conform to ecological principles. This is a design problem, not an economic one – although economy is always a key factor in design. Designers could do much more to create products and structures that use fewer toxic materials, less destructive manufacturing processes, and more (ecologically) efficient systems of production, if empowered by a (cost neutral) program that simultaneously builds eco-design capacity.

Different approaches to pollution control

Most regulatory frameworks in the Western democracies are really a mix of legal and fiscal 'incentives'. Contrary to the conventional view, both regulations and economic instruments are really incentives schemes, although regulations are seen as negative (coercive), while economic instruments are seen as positive (voluntary). Both legislative and economic instruments create financial incentives or disincentives for developers, producers or citizens to reduce and recycle, whether in the form of taxes on environmentally harmful products, charges on resources, or fees for waste disposal.

Both forms of incentives are largely *indirect*. That is, they are reliant on business and industry to solve ecological problems through their interest in profits. These managers must target pollution prevention as a cost reduction or profit maximising strategy, and hire the right experts – those that will find eco-solutions. *Indirect* tools, such as pricing/taxing, regulations, policies and litigation – do little to reduce the amount of resources and the impacts of production through more 'eco-effective' products, landscapes, buildings and systems of construction. Environmental management systems need to move towards *direct* solutions that change the design and construction systems that create demands on industry and wilderness in the first place.

[The conventional approaches are explained in Chapters 11.1 and 11.2, in the context of a proposed new framework for conceptualising environmental control.]

A design-based approach

Design-based measures do more than encourage managers to 'internalise' some of the monetary costs of pollution – they internalise pollution physically. For example, if water from a mill's outlet were piped back into its water supply, rather than downstream, the industry would not need lobbyists and lawyers, but would engage eco-logical designers and engineers to prevent pollution, as has been demonstrated when green activists have literally plugged refinery pipes. A simple example of a 'closed loop system' is where all waste water is collected and purified on site for reuse through wetlands, reed ponds or 'living machines' [9.1], which also produce healthy fish.

At the scale and level of mobilisation required, however, it has proven unrealistic to expect most firms to direct their own human and financial resources towards discovering better materials, manufacturing processes, construction methods, fuels, components, and/or end products. Some responsibly innovative producers and developers have shown that redesigning their industrial, management and construction processes can be very profitable (Romm 1999, von Weizsäcker et al 1997). Nonetheless, far too few managers are following these examples. While the involvement of managers is essential, they know little, as a group, about industrial, environmental or building design – let alone ecology – and management cultures are slow to change.

Environmental economists argue that this is due to 'perverse subsidies' that promote the destruction of the environment, as opposed to management failure. For example, on the global level, governments sell off public forests at a net economic loss (subsidised by US$40 billion a year); pay for the destruction of fish stocks (subsidised by US$54 billion a year); and prop up fossil fuel and nuclear energy production (subsidised by US$300 billion a year). Norman Myers has estimated that these perverse subsidies total US$850 billion worldwide each year (see Myers and Kent 2001).

But apart from perverse subsidies, business and industry do not always exhibit profit maximizing behaviour. For example, the Australian timber industry could make much more profit per tonne by value adding, but they continue to woodchip native forests for paper pulp. In fact, New South Wales in Australia recently legislated to allow the use of woodchips from native forests to fuel energy production facilities.

The World Business Council for Sustainable Development (WBCSD) has actively promoted a paradigm shift in business (Schmidheiny 1992; WBCSD 1997). However, the goals appear largely directed at sustaining development through increased productivity. The idea of bringing about an absolute reduction in resource use by lowering consumption still gets little mention in the industrial ecology literature.

Eco-design teams

Creating government programs to persuade and assist industries to solve ecological problems at industry's own cost may be a relatively expensive form of environmental education. To make change happen fast, we need a campaign that galvanises public attention, perhaps along the lines of the mechanics institutes or health centres in the late 19th Century. Some states in the US have tried to promote eco-design by making arrangements for grants and low-interest loans for industries to take the opportunity and initiative to hire environmental management firms on a performance-based contracting (PBC) basis. Nonetheless, the uptake is slow, because only progressive firms with environmentally literate management tend to participate.

However, government-managed eco-design teams (Birkeland 1995) could operate proactively on a PBC basis at a wider level. These would be interdisciplinary teams that could draw upon expertise among (or partner with) existing environmental management firms and consultants. This would generate work for these firms to avoid the public sector competing against private businesses and consultancies. The teams could include a targeted apprenticeship program to improve green technology transfer and the adoption of eco-design solutions in buildings. PBC would enable the teams to recoup costs from the savings accrued to industries through eco-solutions (eg lower energy, materials and disposal costs). Industries would not have to organise themselves to invest in a research and re-engineering program, they would only need to 'just say yes'.

While there are organisational and administrative costs, the program could eventually operate on a cost-neutral basis – *just as PBC contractors conduct similar operations at a profit now.*

There are many advantages of government coordination. It would help to overcome one of the perpetual biases against public investment in environmental quality – the fact that the economic benefits of public expenditure are hidden, while the costs of environmental control programs are only too apparent. The 'measurability' of resource and energy savings is one of the key advantages of the eco-logical design approach. Given that the program would recoup many costs for the government, it would be able to subsidise more intractable pollution/waste cases with long pay-back periods that might otherwise remain in the too hard basket. Government coordination or oversight would ensure the direct and immediate conversion to ecologically sustainable materials, methods and products at a profit to the parties and the general public.

A government coordinated Eco-Design Corps could also take a wider regional perspective in developing recommendations than would environmental consultants that are commissioned by private firms. Environmental management plans are being developed now (guided by ISO standards), but these generally only look at efficiencies within the firm – not the inadequacies of existing service systems or a whole product range across different firms. An Eco-Design Corps could be positioned to develop environmental plans for industrial networks and urban systems – as well as individual businesses. These plans would take into account ecology, energy and economy, but could also look at networks of industries or projects, to implement broader regional or industrial ecology strategies.

In consultation with a firm's management and staff, interdisciplinary teams would determine the best and most economically sound changes in product design, management systems and production processes from a '**least-cost planning**' perspective (as opposed to lowest market price), including product substitution to encourage products that create more employment for less throughput of materials and energy. They might also recommend changes in delivery systems, find re-uses for functionally obsolete facilities, or the conversion of industries dealing in toxic products/processes (such as tobacco, weapons or coal-fired energy plants).

Should the public sector pay?

The political debate is usually confined to *who* should pay – the public or private sector. (It is worth remembering that money itself is not the real problem: in a world where 255 individuals have as much wealth as 50% of the world's population, by merely diverting a fraction of the world's military budget to the restoration of our degraded soil, air, water and forests, society could provide for basic human needs, while eliminating some of the causes of warfare in the bargain.) In reality, regardless of who bears the initial cost of conversion to sustainable processes and products, it is still the public that pays for everything in the end: higher prices for safer, cleaner products, higher health insurance premiums, higher taxes for government regulatory bureaucracies, and

for cleaning up toxic sites along with other environmental damage from past market failure.

Assuming it were fair to expect industries to have to pick up the tab for eco-innovation or to seek government R&D grants or loans (a big investment in itself), this may be counter-productive for several reasons including the following:

1. It may be in the public interest that inventions or advances in green technologies or information made by private businesses be shared. Where the expertise and intellectual property (eg computer tools) are privatised, technology transfer can be impeded or delayed.

2. Corporate investments in design research and development could place industries at a competitive disadvantage with less ecologically responsible industries – whether local or overseas.

3. The public sector has the capacity to accumulate and collate information in a manner that is accessible to the general public and other eco-designers. It is important for data and information collected to be in the public domain. Data are not readily available on the ecological impacts of decisions that depend upon site specific and temporal factors, such as:

   - the relative scarcity and distance of the sources of materials;
   - the effects of materials extraction on the flora and fauna; and
   - the ecological integrity of the source area (eg whether from native forests or plantations).

This information could be compiled in expert systems, and material flows analyses, and regional sustainability audits [Box 31]. This requires centralised, ongoing organisation and databases that can be updated on a regular basis.

Conclusion

It has been argued here that the creation of government programs to persuade and assist industries to solve eco-logical design problems at industries' own expense, while appearing cost-effective, may actually represent a relatively slow, costly and inefficient form of pollution control – as well as of environmental education and social change. Direct assistance to the construction, industrial and commercial sectors to convert to sustainable materials, processes and products immediately on a cost recovery basis is a 'no regrets' approach that should find support among industrialists, developers and greens alike.

References and further reading

Beder, S. 1996, *The Nature of Sustainable Development*, Scribe Publications, Carlton North, VIC.

Birkeland J. 1993, *Planning for a Sustainable Society: Institutional Reform and Social Transformation*, University of Tasmania (thesis), Hobart, Tasmania.

Birkeland, J. 1995, 'Priorities for Environmental Professionals', Linking and Prioritising Environmental Criteria, CIB TG-8 Workshop, Ontario, 25–26 November, pp. 27–34.

Cairncross, F. 1995, *Green, Inc: A Guide to Business and the Environment*, Island Press, Washington, DC.

Myers, N. 1996, *The Ultimate Security: The Environmental Basis of Political Stability*, Island Press, Washington, DC.

Myers, N. and Kent, J., 2001, *Perverse Subsidies: How Tax Dollars can Undercut the Environment and the Economy*, Island Press, Washington, DC.

Romm, J. 1999, *Cool Companies: How the Best Businesses Boost Profits and Productivity by Cutting Geenhouse-Gas Emissions,* Island Press, Washington, DC.

Schmidheiny, S. with the BCSD 1992, *Changing Course: A Global Business Perspective on Development and the Environment*, MIT Press, Cambridge, MA.

Weizsäcker, E. von, Lovins, A. and Lovins, H. 1997, *Factor 4: Doubling Wealth – Halving Resource Use*, Allen and Unwin, NSW.

Wackernagel, M. and Rees, W.E. 1996, *Our Ecological Footprint: Reducing the Human Impact on the Earth*, New Society Publishers, Gabriola Island, BC and New Haven, CT.

Wackernagel, M., Onisto, L., Linares, A.C., Falzon, I.S.L., Barcia, J.M., Guerrero, A.I.S. and Guerrero, M.G.S. 1997, *Ecological Footprints of Nations*, Report to the Earth Council, Costa Rica.

WBCSD, with DeSimone, L. D. and Popoff, F. 1997, *Eco-Efficiency: the Business Link to Sustainable Development*, MIT Press, Cambridge, MA.

Young, J. and Sachs, A. 1994, *The Next Efficiency Revolution: Creating a Sustainable Materials Economy*, Worldwatch Paper 121, Worldwatch Institute for Environmental Studies, Washington, DC.

Questions

1. How does the 'polluter pays' principle differ from a 'consumer pays' principle? Does their implementation guarantee pollution prevention? Why or why not?

2. When an industry is required by law to retrieve its products after their use, it is called 'cradle to *grave*' legislation. How would 'cradle to *cradle*' legislation differ? Can you think of examples?

3. Debate: 'Corporate managers or developers should be personally liable for environmental crimes such as illegal waste disposal, even if they did not tell their staff to dump the waste (provided that a responsible manager should have known).'

4. Why are fines for illegal environmental damage usually less than the environmental damage itself (eg the Exxon Valdez and Bhopal disasters)? Produce a table which lists social, cultural, political, historical, ideological reasons for these low fines.

5. In recent years, the tobacco industry has invested in large new factories for making cigarettes. Could this industry diversify and develop other products instead? Think of some alternative products that could utilise these facilities or materials?

6. Debate: 'Regulating pollution emissions is a better use of public funds than supporting an eco-logical design corps.'

Projects

1. Corporations have allegedly bought the rights to energy and/or resource efficient inventions that would otherwise compete with their products. Then, instead of manufacturing these new products, they have continued to manufacture the old model. How can this practice be avoided?

2. Compare life cycle costs of reusable (glass) milk bottles and recyclable (card) milk cartoons. What factors need to be considered?

Box 9   Eco-footprints and Eco-logical Design

William Rees

Modern cities are the essence of civilisation: seats of government, intense nodes of economic activity, and centres of learning and culture. However, cities are also biophysical entities. From this perspective, cities resemble entropic black holes, sweeping up the resources of whole regions vastly larger than themselves. 'Great cities are planned and grow without any regard for the fact that they are parasites on the countryside which must somehow supply food, water, air and degrade huge quantities of waste' (Odum 1971). As much as 70% of the resource consumption and waste generation by the human population takes place in high-income cities around the world.

Ecological footprint analysis: Just how much of the biophysical output of the ecosphere is appropriated to satisfy human demand can be determined by ecological footprint analysis.

The ecological footprint of a specified population is the area of productive land and water (ecosystems),which is required on a continuous basis to produce the resources consumed, and to assimilate the wastes produced by that population, wherever on Earth that land may be located.

Studies show that each resident of high-income countries needs between 5-9ha (10,000 m²) of ecosystems per capita to support their consumer lifestyles (Rees and Wackernagel 1996). This means that wealthy cities impose ecological footprints on the Earth between several hundred to 1000 times larger than the political and geographic areas they physically occupy. To raise the present world population of six billion to European or North American [urban industrial] material standards, using prevailing technology, would require up to four additional Earth-like planets.

Built environment design: Improved design at all spatial scales is essential to reducing the total 'human load' on the Earth. Fortunately, cities can also generate enormous leverage in reducing humanity's total eco-footprint. In particular, urban economies of scale result in:

- Lower material costs per capita of providing piped treated water, sewer systems, waste collection, and most other forms of infrastructure and public amenities.
- Greater possibilities for electricity co-generation, and the use of waste process heat from industry or power plants, to reduce the per capita use of fossil fuel for space heating.
- Numerous opportunities to implement the principles of low throughput industrial ecology (where the waste energy or materials of some firms are the feed-stocks for others)[3.1].
- Great potential for reducing (mostly fossil) energy consumption by motor vehicles through walking, cycling, and public transit.

These factors present challenges and opportunities for urban, building, and industrial designers, as there is so much potential for improvement.

Whole systems planning: Planners and designers must redefine the 'city-as-system' to include the productive land upon which the city is dependent, and re-integrate the geography of living and employment, of production and consumption, of city and hinterland. Such a transformed 'homeplace, rather than being merely the site of consumption, might, through its very design, produce some of its own food and energy, as well as become the locus of work for its residents' (Van der Ryn and Calthorpe 1986, xiii). Following all such eco-logical design principles, urban regions can gradually become less a burden on the life-support functions of the ecosphere, and greatly reduce their respective eco-footprints.

Odum, H.T. 1971, *Environment, Power and Society*, Wiley Interscience, New York.

Van der Ryn, S. and Calthorpe, P. 1986, *Sustainable Communities*, Sierra Club Books, San Francisco, CA.

Rees, W. and Wackernagel, M. 1996, *Our Ecological Footprint: Reducing Human Impact on the Earth*, New Society Publishers, Gabriola Island, BC.

Kath Wellman

Changes in fundamental concepts from science on order, organisation, adaptability and complexity are changing the way we think about the dynamic nature of cities, our popular culture and the design of our environments. This chapter examines what this change in perception may have on the role of the professional, government and the community in urban planning, and argues for an integration of government and community action in dealing with the physical design and management of cities.

Introduction

The rate of urbanisation over the past decades, coupled with an ageing physical infrastructure in many of our cities, have placed overwhelming demands on the social, financial and environmental capital of cities and surrounding areas. Traditional Western construction technology, management, urban design and planning processes are still being imported to rapidly growing regions in developing nations. However, they are increasingly being put under scrutiny (not only by environmentalists but) by urban authorities who cannot meet the construction costs or maintain this capital and resource intensive infrastructure.

The urban planning and design professions have tried to direct change in accordance with traditional norms and standards. Despite an understanding that planning is dealing with a dynamic process, there appears to be an implicit belief that we can end up with a steady-state, sustainable system if only we knew the combinations of knobs and pulleys to adjust. This approach to planning was generated by the view that the world is ordered, predictable, capable of being reduced to its component parts, examined, understood and then managed. The result has been a plethora of urban specialists, each dealing with its own particular part of the system, examining it in isolation, then endeavouring to optimise its performance within a messy and highly interconnected world.

Changes in the fundamental concepts of order

Underlying the traditional approaches to planning and urban design is the perception that order emanates from two major sources, one being 'natural selection', or the efficiency of the marketplace, the other imposed from above by planners with foresight, a view of the rights of individuals in relation to society, and an understanding of the dynamics upon which the plan rests. These ideas of organisation came primarily from a 19th Century view of the world promulgated by Darwin and Newton respectively.

The questioning of these ideas of organisation in the late 20th Century gave us the opportunity to see our world and our cities in a different way. The idea of the world as a mechanism – where the whole could be understood by the properties of the parts, and the whole is made up of structures, forces and mechanisms through which these parts interact, where knowledge is objective and can be built on – has now changed. We are perceiving the world as more fluid, some would say 'alive', where the properties of the parts can only be understood from the dynamics of the whole, and where structure is seen as a manifestation of underlying process, with the entire web of relationships being intrinsically dynamic.

The shift in our understanding of order was inherent in Einstein's work, but brought to the forefront for many people through Benoit Mandlebrot's work with discontinuous equations and his discovery of **fractal** behaviour. Since then there has been increasing interest and research into the dynamics of seemingly chaotic and complex systems, such as the weather, the neural networks of the brain, stock market fluctuations, genetics and, to a more limited extent, cities. The fascination with these mathematical systems pertains to the ability they have for spontaneous self-organisation, not explainable by natural selection. The systems that have the capacity to do this are not characterised by top-down structures, but by a network of many agents working in parallel, reacting to their local environmental conditions.

Those working in the field of complex systems have found that this capacity for self-organisation only occurs at a particular level of information flow. Too little information flow and the system is too ordered and the information is frozen. No new information emerges. If there is too much interaction in the system, information moves very freely and chaotically and is difficult to retain. Between these two states there is a certain area where information changes, but not so rapidly that it loses all connection to where it had just been previously. It is in this region that the system can support the kind of complexity that is the mark of living systems (Langton in Levi 1992).

These mathematically derived systems of analysis have been taken up by theorists in other fields because they seem to explain things that thus far have no explanation. Sturt Kauffman in his book *The Origins of Order* (1993) postulates that within these systems and in particular the genetic system, there are two ordering mechanisms: natural selection and self-organisation, the latter being an intrinsic part of a complex system. These mechanisms work in a type of collaborative balance, with natural selection pushing the system towards a degree of complexity in which self-organisation can occur, at the edge of chaos.

Complexity and community

Theories about the nature of complexity suggest a fine line between order and chaos. If there is too much (or too little) change, a system will either precipitate into chaos or petrify into stasis. This concept has been applied to human societies at various levels of social organisation. It provides a heuristic tool for those looking at urban planning, management and design.

It is evident to many who have been involved in living in, researching or managing the growing urban places of the world, that we are in a time of very rapid and complex change. The circular, cumulative effect of increased concentrations of populations, services and industries in cities has accelerated the rate of urbanisation in developing regions. In many cases rural populations have been left with infrastructure burdens they can no longer support. These changes in urbanisation have placed stresses on the natural systems of cities, hinterlands and city management systems. These stresses have caused many to question whether the environmental and social costs of our present form of development are sustainable.

Coupled with this, there has been an information explosion facilitated by increased communication technology over the past 30 years, and particularly over the last decade with the introduction of the internet. Here, information is transferred in bits and bytes. On the internet, icons of culture are transferred across cultural barriers, primarily because of their overt visual simplicity and the viewer's ability to recognise the more complex meaning that underlies them. Cultures and cities are shown worldwide in a succession of images. Time no longer seems to progress in a linear fashion.

When we first see an icon we need to interpret its meaning and context. The second time, we recognise it for what it stands for. The unique design of buildings such as the Sydney Opera House and Canberra Parliament House are as readily transferable on tee shirts as McDonald's golden arches. Images begin to define architecture, and architecture begins to define images in a type of co-evolutionary dance. This popularisation of our cultural heritage and its marketing makes one wonder what is authentic and what is not.

The ready transferability of images, their effect not only on designers but also on the marketplace, and the ability of new construction technology and management systems to create them, have been disheartening for many who see 'place' as strongly rooted in the location, culture or ecosystem [5.3]. If we look dispassionately at many of the new resort or hotel developments, we can see a common set of symbols or icons used. These eventually become icons for a particular developer or design firm. Large firms, such as McDonald's, realise the commercial value of this community understanding. Perhaps these designs are rooted as strongly in our popular culture as site-sensitive, place-centred designs are to their physical locations.

Happily, our cultures, our abilities to finance and our values are much more diverse and complex than our built environment would indicate. In many cities of the world, communities are finding ways to structure their local physical environments to make them work more efficiently or effectively. This happens informally in squatter settlements, or more formally in citizens' forums to address specific local government issues. These local interventions in the environment have the potential not only to make our cities more livable, but also to add that diversity and richness which may become a well-spring of creativity and adaptability in the future.

The role of designers, government and community

The role of physical designers is to optimise a fit between cultural and functional goals and the natural processes and ecosystems upon which we depend for the long-term health of our cities. Design professionals have a fascination with the origins of creativity, innovation and adaptability. Makoto Kikuchi, a physicist, suggests that there are two modes of creativity: one well-suited to creating breakthroughs and setting a technological framework; the other flourishing within an already established technological framework, a type of adaptive creativity (Castells and Hall 1994). If Kikuchi is correct, then it is of interest to explore where the source of each of these types of creativity might be found.

The breakthroughs in setting a technological framework for the support of urban development is likely to come through gifted individuals, universities, research organisations, and through meetings or conferences that tackle such issues. This may be catalysed through improved technologies and expanded communication across discipline and sector boundaries. The second source of creativity may have greater potential for improving urban life quality immediately; it is more likely to flourish in collaborative partnerships between professionals, government agencies, private institutions and local communities.

It is evident that most urban areas in the world cannot be sustained on a top-down management structure without a huge injection of government finance and/or control. Therefore, most cities will increasingly depend on collaboration between community, private institutions and governments to deal with growing urban environmental and social problems.

Responsibility for infrastructure supply, and management of inter-regional resources (such as transport, water management and waste management), are going to require the combined capabilities of government and large institutions, as well as more effective utilisation and management, informed by critical citizen comment at the local level. A working collaboration between the community, government and private institutions, that can safeguard the health of these systems and their natural resource base, requires that the community understands the operation of these supply systems and the consequences of local action.

At a local scale, the potential gains from community tenure in decision making are great. Here local knowledge and expertise, craft skills and community labour all have the potential to augment and fine-tune the built environment to benefit local conditions and cultures. More flexible approval processes for buildings will allow for a diversity of building structures, which have the potential to supply housing for a broader segment of the community. This would also allow more innovation in dealing with local conditions.

Many bureaucratic structures are not adapting to this shift from government initiated management to community driven change. There is also a fundamental lack of confidence in giving control of these issues to community forums or trusts. Many government and non-government authorities are not structured to be able to manage the liabilities and risks that giving tenure to community groups entails, particularly if the perception is that these changes are not controlled. This results in a system of checks or resistance, which subtly or overtly withholds tenure from community organisations, impeding change.

Hierarchical structures have a different set of rules and norms which can create confusion. In collaborative relationships, there is the potential for ideas to compete or cooperate and mutate as they are passed across the collaborative matrix. In an equal relationship, this has the potential to create synergistic effects, but in a hierarchical structure this may result in mis-communication and a lack of trust between parties.

Conclusions

Recent technological change and a new understanding of the dynamic behaviour of complex systems, have combined to create a context in which we need to re-evaluate our roles and decision-making systems in the urban realm. We need to discern the discontinuities and leverage points within the urban system that have the potential to shift processes to those that are both socially and environmentally sustainable, while fostering the richness of both the cultural and urban fabric.

Unique 'high design' can co-exist with the informality and apparent chaos of informal economies and local citizen intervention in the built environment. Formal infrastructure provision can allow for flexibility, adaptation and evolution of the urban environment through the construction, modification and fine-tuning of local environments by local communities.

References and further reading

Bak, P. 1997, *How Nature Works: The Science of Self-organized Criticality*, Oxford University Press, Oxford.

Benjamin, A., ed, 1995, *Complexity: Architecture, Art, Philosophy*, Academy Group, London.

Castells, M. and Hall, P. 1994, *Technopoles of the World: The Making of the 21st Century Industrial Complexes*, Routledge, New York.

Raberg, PG., ed, 1997, *The Life Region: The Social and Cultural Ecology of Sustainable Development*, Routledge, London, New York.

Eco, U. 1987, *Travels in Hyperreality*, Picador, London.

Kauffman, S.A. 1993, *The Origins of Order: Self Organisation and Selection in Evolution*, Oxford University Press, New York.

Levi, S. 1992, *Artificial Life: The Quest for a New Creation*, Penguin, London, UK.

Roe, E. 1998, *Taking Complexity Seriously: Policy Analysis, Triangulation, and Sustainable Development*, Kluwer Academic Publishers, Boston, MA.

Rushkoff, D. 1996, *Playing the Future: How Kids Culture can Teach us to Thrive in an Age of Chaos*, HarperCollins, New York.

Rutherford H., Platt, R.H., Rowntree, R.A. and Muick, P.C. 1994, *The Ecological City: Preserving and Restoring Urban Biodiversity*, University of Massachusetts Press, MA.

Waldrop, M.M. 1992, *Complexity, The Emerging Science at the Edge of Order and Chaos*, Penguin, London.

Questions

1. Discuss how urban planning has changed in your region over the past decade in response to changes in knowledge structures (eg more regulatory or participatory? or more rigid or flexible?).

2. Chapter 28 of Agenda 21 states that local authorities in each country should undertake a consultative process with their populations and achieve a consensus on a local Agenda 21 plan for the community? Have you seen evidence of a shift in responsibilities for the environment from the national to local level?

3. What do you think are the roles of government and the community respectively in developing strategies for sustainable development at a local level?

4. 'Order can only emanate from a structured response to the difficult issues we are currently facing in our urban environment around the world.' Discuss.

5. 'North American popular culture, in a globalised economic environment, threatens both local cultures and local environments.' Discuss.

6. Debate: 'To remain viable socially, economically and environmentally, cities will need to rely on partnerships between industry, community and government.'

Projects

1. Find out what processes are used in your local government area to bring the community into the decision-making process related to urban planning, development and management. Make a list of what you consider the strengths and weaknesses of these processes. Based on your findings, develop recommendations to improve the process and present these to the local government authorities.

2. Prepare a poster that communicates the idea of 'bottom up', participatory planning that is advocated in this chapter. What would a 'top up' form of participation be?

Vanda Rounsefell

Many current global and local problems have arisen from the denial that our habitat is thoroughly embedded in nature's complex network of ecosystems, and shared with a host of other living beings on whom we also depend. Human ecologists recommend that we should 'align with nature' in our design work, and encourage inclusive and socially participatory processes. To do so, we need to understand complexity and complex systems better. This chapter introduces a tool to help organise complex design information and generate ideas.

Complex systems are not simple

Science has often attempted to approach complex systems by pretending they were simple. Control strategies are still used, such as misleading simplification, linear models, treating a colourful world as if it were black and white, smoothing away surprising experimental findings, leaving out important variables, giving simplified aggregate figures and 'standardising' experimental conditions – which means the findings only apply to 'ideal' situations.

Problems also arise when science approaches living systems as if they obeyed the rules for machines. With machines, movements are regular and predictable; the parts are replaceable. It is easy to see the connection between cause and effect. With complex systems, such as ecosystems and social systems, there is often no clear cause for an event. Many fields of influence are grouped together, and the combined result of their interaction is often hard to predict or see until it is too late. The impacts are seen long after and far away from initial sources.

Conventional human **habitat** design makes little ecological sense. We use ecologically damaging technologies to 'tame' nature and help humans live more comfortably. We remove the constraints which ecosystems rely on to keep them in balance; for instance, cars, roadways and stormwater systems have radically changed local water regimes, and carved up natural habitats. Most housing and site design have ensured that energy and water use are extremely wasteful. Importing companion animals, lawns, and exotic trees and shrubs has displaced entire populations of native animals, birds and plants.

It is easy to see patterns from the air where humans have been, because they simplify the complexity of nature with straight lines (roads, fences, dams), low-diversity suburbs with rows of similar houses, and **monocultures** (ie crops with only one plant type instead of the diverse mixture seen in healthy bushland). Cities have impacts which extend around the planet. Building materials, appliances and food have often taken world trips to reach our cities, adding tonnes of greenhouse gases to the global burden in the transport process. Most aspects of modern urban design and lifestyle are only sustained by pilfering the carrying capacity of other places, especially that of the less developed countries. We should build and live in ways that use as many local resources and local talents as possible, although this is in direct conflict with present processes of globalisation as encouraged by most governments.

Designers need to be as familiar with the ecological and environmental context as they are with the building itself. A holistic approach to site evaluation, planning and design for both ecosystem and human needs (including psychological and social needs) is increasingly expected in 'best practice' design. Architects often lead project teams, but ecological experts are often left out of this process. Design specialists also need to be informed generalists, especially at small scales of work where clients cannot afford to hire other experts. Thus the connection between design decisions for individual projects and global ecological threats (eg loss of **biodiversity** and major climate change), needs to be clearly understood and respected by each practitioner. Otherwise the **tyranny of small decisions** will continue. Hence decision aids are needed to assess what information to collect and to assist in organising it for purposes of reporting and for generating ideas.

Design metaphors

Over the years, society has had numerous design **metaphors** which have moulded the interpretation of reality and influenced the design of cities and buildings. Over time, patterns of social order and relationships (spiritual, interpersonal, community, dominance and so on) have been formalised into cultural norms, laws and regulations. Since religion was a major life focus in early centuries, it was often a determinant of cities and buildings. Thus, early cities often had geometric or highly symbolic designs, which have been referred to as a 'crystal' metaphor (Lynch 1981, p. 667). With the industrial revolution, people started to think of cities as machines with smoothly operating, replaceable parts and clearly separated functions (as in a factory). Our modern zoning systems are remnants of this approach.

Cities have also been seen as organisms with pathologies, organs (heart, lungs), metabolism, circulatory, respiratory and waste systems – a medical model. Later came the ecosystem model (also called urban metabolism), which mainly addressed eco-cycles, the tracing of matter (resources) and energy processes through the system and between the city and hinterland.

With the advent of communications technology, another metaphor has emerged: the web or network. Terms like 'multi-function', 'multi-disciplinary', 'inter-departmental', 'integrative strategies', 'multi-cultural', 'business network' and 'global village' have gained mainstream currency. These flag the arrival of a new appreciation of the social as well as functional complexity of the modern scene, and the theme of meeting challenges through partnership rather than conflict.

At the same time, market ideology has introduced a satisfier model: the advertising industry has argued for short-term satisfaction of every possible whim, with maximum choice for each individual. Cities are now increasingly being designed to stimulate the senses: we look at paintings, movies and crowd spectacles, listen to concerts, eat and drink in endless variety, socialise, share social drugs (eg caffeine, tea, nicotine, marijuana, ecstasy) – every perceptual channel is impacted.

There is a tendency to drop old metaphors; however, metaphors remain useful in design, because they provide multiple ways of understanding. When dealing with complex systems, it is useful to have many metaphors to help take multiple 'snapshots' of the reality before us. At the same time, there is a need to mentally categorise information, so as not to be overwhelmed by detail.

The 'ecosystem' metaphor is a complex systems metaphor that can address all the metaphors mentioned above. It inherently supports habitat and biodiversity, representing life and life-forms, or **biotics**. Unified Human Community Ecology offers a tool to think through design work in a way that aligns with an ecosystem metaphor, and provides mental 'hooks' from which to hang data [**Box 10**].

Unified Human Community Ecology

Unified Ecology is based on a complex systems theory and was designed to assist ecologists to communicate better (Allen and Hoekstra 1992, pp. 259–262). It looks at an ecological subject from a series of different perspectives and studies the relationships between them. The different views or 'Criteria of Observation' which Allen and Hoekstra chose, represent the work of different sub-groups of ecologists. These categories are: Landscape, Ecosystem, **Biome**, Population, Community and Organism.

These different ways of understanding the same complex reality are similar to several of the metaphors mentioned above, and also apply quite well to human ecology. They can be reinterpreted for Human Ecology as: Eco-cycles, Landscape, Biotics, Population, Community, Organism, Elements, **Genius Loci**, **Connectivity** (**Connectance**), Time and Catalysts. Together they describe the human settlement/ecosystem complex. Catalysts are elements which enable and facilitate change or implementation, such as money (funding and finance), marketing, business, media or other influence or social connections, ownership, contracts, licences, and shared vision. They can also be seen as the positive (amplifying) and negative feedbacks (balancing constraints) of a complex system.

The scales for Human Community Ecology could be: microscopic (micro-organisms), individual entity (eg human, animal, plant, furniture), room, house, housing cluster or neighbourhood, town/city subsection/suburb or bio-region, city region (often bio-region), state or province, nation, major political region (sometimes biome), global (international/ biosphere).

Design process

The Unified Human Community (or Human Settlement) Ecology Criteria can be used to form headings for data searches, to check for missed aspects, for documentation and for tracing linkages.

The designer must choose and use the range required and may well need to deal with them all at once. For instance,

Landscape concerns the patterns of natural and built elements on maps. At decreasing scales this becomes the city or neighbourhood pattern related to site, pattern of arrangements within the site plan, and below that, a floor plan for a specific structure, the arrangement of furniture in each room, the arrangement of items within furniture ... it is up to the designer to choose and use the range of scales required. This process is called 'scaling' or 'scoping'.

The first step in any design process is, of course, to visit the site and experience it personally, emotionally and intuitively. Once this is done, the project is considered from each criterion, and data collected until a working knowledge is gained in each area, noticing how the details change as one moves up or down the scales. The types of questions related to the different criteria are provided below.

The process is to keep mentally walking around the design task, viewing it from each position in turn. After that, a matrix can be drawn which invites thinking about each criterion in relationship to each other. This is laborious at one level, but helps to avoid missing much of the ecological importance, and it is especially helpful for large sites (which are complex anyway). The design, as it emerges, should be rechecked to ensure that the different aspects are accounted for.

Some concepts and strategies which are useful in ecological design work include:

- An ecological landscape is the dynamic pattern that emerges from an interaction between the growth and expansion of living entities and the natural constraints of their environment (including natural and human impacts). A design is one of those impacts. A design provides a supportive **backcloth** which will attract or support a traffic, such as a building, people, vehicles, living things – and hopefully continue as an agent supporting nature and human health.

- Have an information collecting period, then leave it for a few days. This allows for analysis and integration time. Design ideas often emerge if the problem is shelved for a brief time: some can access creative processes by having the project in mind as they fall asleep. But as time pressure is destructive, an appropriate pace and schedule can also be important.

- **SWOT Analysis** is a business technique that assists objective analysis: a project and design can be considered under the headings of 'Strengths', 'Weaknesses', 'Opportunities', 'Threats' (Criterion Catalysts). An early map of site constraints is also helpful.

Conclusion

In a world of specialised professions, we often forget that everything we do has impacts on our local and distant environments, which are well outside of our normal professional areas of concern. We cannot improve upon nature nor impose buildings upon it without impacting our ecology. Our impacts are time bombs; the further we shift from working with nature, the more difficulties we face in the longer term.

Understanding the underlying connectedness and vulnerability of ecosystems at all scales should support the choices we make about things like site design, building layouts and construction materials. We need to be as familiar with the ecological and social context as we are with the building itself. This is, in essence, a problem of redesign, because so much of our lifestyle is set in concrete, bricks and asphalt, and few clients have an ecological vision.

Designers need to be conscious of all scales of design and all criteria at once. To do so, we need a personal repertoire of strategies, built up over years of training and experience, with conscious commitment to learning, innovation and experiment, user feedback and good literature (see Mollison 1988; Walter et al 1992). The student of design can add to the following check list over time, improving upon and personalising its structure.

References and further reading

Allen, T.F.H. and Hoekstra, T.W. 1992, *Toward A Unified Ecology*, Columbia University Press, New York.

Begon, M., Harper, J.L. et al 1990, *Ecology: Individuals, Populations and Communities*, 2nd edition, Blackwell Scientific Publications, Boston, MA

Berg, Per G. 1996, 'Sustainable Exchange of Nutrients Between Townscapes and Landscapes', in M. Rolen, ed, *Urban Development in an Ecocycles Adapted Industrial Society*, Swedish Council for Planning and Coordination of Research, Stockholm, Sweden.

Lynch, K. 1981, *Good City Form*, MIT Press, Cambridge, MA.

Mollison, B. 1988, *Permaculture: A Designers' Manual*, Tagari Publications, Tyalgum, Australia.

Walter, B. and Arkin, L. et al, eds, 1992, *Sustainable Cities: Strategies and Concepts for Eco-City Development*, Eco-Home Media EHM, Los Angeles, CA.

Questions

1. What features of the city or region where you live give it a special character? Describe the 'spirit' of your place. Are these features mostly natural (eg rivers, hills) or built (eg towers, monuments)?

2. What differences would you expect between the landscapes (patterns) of human-affected areas and unaffected wilderness (eg linear, monocultural, organic)?

3. What are the design factors that make our neighbourhoods safe and pleasant or unhealthy and dangerous?

4. Imagine a city as some kind of animal (an organism). How might we tell if it is a healthy animal or not? What would constitute 'illness' in an urban area?

5. Debate: 'Designers need not understand complex systems in relation to societies and nature.'

6. What ecological and social advantages could arise from having a local procurement policy for the design and implementation of a project? Is it more important to obtain new ideas from other regions and countries?

Projects

1. Take each of the Unified Human Settlement Ecology Criteria in turn and, using the table of Criteria, discuss its potential application to cities, to neighbourhoods and to houses. Notice the differences which emerge at the different scales for each criterion. Practise the strategy of taking the subject (a house, a neighbourhood or a city), and mentally walking around it, getting the feel for the different criteria as lenses on reality.

2. Visit two neighbourhoods that are noted for greatly differing crime rates. Identify all the built environment design differences (eg street activity, safe places). Are these differences a result of social factors like poverty and crime, or did some of these design factors precede and perhaps contribute to the social problems? Discuss.

Box 10   Human Ecology Design Checklist

Vanda Rounsefell

Criteria	Essential qualities	Questions to ask about site or project
Genius loci	The spirit of place Meaning Sensory quality Voice of the land Local history	What meaning does this place have and for whom? for what? What memorable events happened here in the past? Geological? Indigenous? What are the soft voices here? What sorts of 'vibes' do we pick up here? What are the energies? How does it look from a distance? From high up? From all sides? From its lowest points? Colour? Sounds? Odours? Texture? Does our design want to align with this spirit? replace it?
Landscape	Patterns of spatial relationship Locations of elements on maps and plans	Where is it on the map? What landscape and built features are there already? What patterns are there? Where and how might our design fit in?
Elements	Physical features Climate and weather	**Earth**: What are the characteristics of the soil?, geology? Slope? Seismology? Engineering issues? **Water**: What water bodies are here and what are their flow patterns? How much rain? Ice or snow? What extremes? How does water drain? Does it leave the site? Where are the water tables? Where does the water supply come from? **Fire**: Where is the sun through the year? What angles? What temperature ranges are there through the seasons? What extremes? Is solar access a problem? How well would solar power or hot water generation do here? Where is the grid supply from and how generated? **Air**: What are the prevailing winds? How strong are they and when? How would wind power do here? Are there any air quality issues? Odours coming from nearby of on the wind? Salty air from the sea? Temperature issues? Cold air drainage? Frost pockets? **Climate**: What sort of climate is it? Is there a special micro-climate? What happens seasonally?
Biotics	Life and its support systems Animals, plants, microbes (Biota) Habitats Toxins	**Habitats**: What habitats are here (large and small)? Are they connected or fragmented? How do they fit into the bio-region? The larger scales? Are they healthy? Is there any significant contamination? What is the local history of chemical and other toxin use? **Biodiversity**: What animals and plants live here? What used to live here? Should or could they be restored? What algae, bacteria, moulds, fungi, viruses and parasites are supported here? What is the ferals and weeds situation? Are there migratory birds?
Community	Relationship Power Human–Nature relationships Social control Group and community processes Institutions	**Relationships between different human groups**: What do the people here believe in? Making money? Following a religion? Having peace and quiet? Having fun? Who has the power around here? Who is disempowered? Who are the stakeholders? Does everyone have a voice? How can we involve the local community? The community of users? Community leaders? Any conflicts? Can we get them talking to each other? Can we run a charrette or a round table to get some understanding? Do we have allies? Enemies? What educational opportunities are available? **Relationships between humans and biota**: How much space can Nature have here? Can we make it more visible or accessible? Is a healing relationship called for? Stewardship? How can we prevent damage? How do companion animals fit in?

Box 10 continued

Criteria	Essential qualities	Questions to ask about site or project
		Should they be banned or controlled? Could we grow food here? Could there be any health issues with water? sewage? air? **Formal relationships in society**: How is this place managed or governed? What laws or regulations may impact on what we want to do here? Who owns the land? Are there any covenants on it? Who owns next-door? What are ALL the strategic plans for this area?
Population	Numbers of a species present	How many humans come here? What attracts them? What repels them? Where do they come from? How many can the place cope with? Is there another species or group of biota to protect or discourage here? Who or what do we want to attract here? What do we need to know about their special needs? How can we support that in our design? Whom or what are we satisfying?
Organism	Individual living or non-living entities Health and function issues, basic needs	For which individual species (including human) do we need to know the basic needs here? Is health of humans, animals or plants an issue here? Allergies? Disabled? What are our standards? What are the relevant regulations? How does/will this site function as a whole? What do the separate non-living parts (eg paths, recreation areas, specific rooms in buildings) need for optimal function internally and integration externally?
Eco-cycles	Processing cycles of matter (materials, resources, information) and energy Embodied energy, efficiency, technology Pollution	What processing is going on around this site? What enters? What leaves? Can any of the wastes be reused? Can we design this in? Stormwater? Green organics? Energy? Personal effort? How do we deal with building wastes during construction? What are the ecological costs and life cycle of materials used? Can they be reused easily? Are they toxic? Polluting? What can we do locally instead of importing? How can we minimise resource use? Could we use renewable energy? Local materials? Local sewage treatment? Water strategies? Local people? What are we relying on Nature for here? elsewhere? At higher or lower scales? Are we destroying nature's processing capacity? Are we adding unnecessarily to the ecological burden? To greenhouse gases? To long-term energy use?
Connectivity	Linkage and access Communications Services Transport: people and goods	How is this site connected to the rest of the city or settlement? Power? Water? Information technology? Roads, traffic patterns, parking? Public transport, access, timetabling, support facilities? Pedestrians? Cyclists, bike parking, cyclist facilities? Emergency vehicles? Deliveries? How is the project connected internally? Are there any areas we should disconnect (eg wildlife breeding areas)?
Time	Change over time Life cycles Evolution Learning systems Continuous improvement	What change has this site seen before? What are our future goals? How will we measure progress? Has a learning structure been agreed on (bench-marking, evaluation, response to improve)? Have we allowed space for evolution and change over time? How do all other criteria change over time? What are our staging plans? What long-term maintenance is needed? By whom?
Catalysts	Positive & negative feedback Ownership Implementation	Who owns this project? Do we have an agreed, focused vision we can present? Who owns the land? Is it financially feasible? What non-financial help do we need? How could the Government help? What promotion do we need? SWOT analysis & constraint map.
Unspecified	Any special project theme(s)	Check theme(s) against all other criteria to ensure taken care of. Examples: Aboriginal, feminist, minority group, educational purpose.

4.3   The Bionic Method in Industrial Design

Gowrie Waterhouse

The branch of industrial design known as bionics begins with an examination of natural systems, particularly the many bio-mechanical characteristics one observes in nature. The rationale for this approach is that what is perceived as appropriate for a given life form could also provide a precedent for products which are sympathetic to the natural environment. This chapter discusses the bionic method in conjunction with computer modelling as an alternative design tool.

Introduction

The study of life forms as a basis for design inspiration dates back as far as the earliest civilisations. The **bionic** method today seems specifically oriented towards applied science and tends to be grounded upon the general claim that exploring design through biology yields a superior result, particularly as measured against environmental criteria. In regard to the relationship between the environment and product design, one can turn to Victor Papanek's *Design for the Real World* (1984). Papanek warned in his opening sentence: 'There are professions more harmful than industrial design, but only a very few of them' (p. ix).

Of course, he was not just responding to spurious objects like the electric hairbrush or rhinestone covered shoe horns, or more seriously, to unsafe cars. He was also commenting on the creation of permanent waste in and from major European and North American cities, and the environmentally unsound manufacturing processes of the day. Most ominous of all was his view that 'industrial design, as *we have come to know it*, should cease to exist' (p. x).

Design educators like Carmelo di Bartolo (Instituto Europo di Design in Milan) took notice of such statements, and urged a restructuring of the industrial design process that would better take into account environmental concerns. Di Bartolo claimed that 'our alienation with the environment leads us to live badly and [from a designer's point of view] propose badly' (1991, p. 3).

Reflecting a late modernist concern, he went on to say that

all too frequently, objects lacked any coherence between form, function and material. This, he felt, led to poorly resolved design solutions. Let us turn to nature, he proposed, because 'nature builds with a great deal of experience, and it continues to improve' (1991, p.3). He argued that natural structures like snail's shells or bird's feathers, embody a form–function–material equilibrium that could surely provide a starting point for thinking about restructuring industrial design itself.

Di Bartolo, among many others in Europe and elsewhere (Otto 1972, 1985; Bombardelli 1991), began to explore what benefits might be gained from combining biology with design. This return to 'nature' (in the narrow, biological sense) was, and is, demonstrated in at least two ways which can be called the inductive and deductive approaches. The **inductive approach** begins with an observation of living nature, which is then documented, pending some application of the principles abstracted from the natural subject matter. The **deductive approach** is a reversal of this and begins with a design problem or design brief before extending to a search through nature for a solution or an appropriate response.

Two case studies

Two brief case studies, drawn from the University of Canberra and the Instituto Europo di Design industrial design courses, illustrate the characteristics of the two approaches.

The inductive approach

The inductive approach begins with the very broad theme of 'locomotion', and explores the caridoid escape reaction exhibited by crayfish, lobsters and yabbies. To begin, a particular yabby, *Cherax destructor*, was researched and cursory information was brought together from the various zoologically based sources as shown in Figure 4.3.1.

The next step in the process was to abstract the bio-mechanical principles, identifying lever-arms, fulcrum locations and moments, thereby producing some representation of the relationship between them. This provides an overall picture of how this particular mechanism functions in terms of the organism's locomotion (Figure 4.3.2).

Figure 4.3.1: Basic physiological examination of the abdomen of *Cherax destructor*

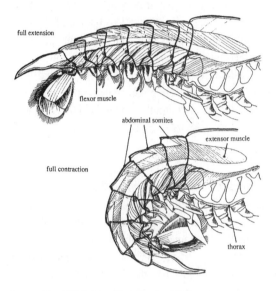

Source: Yee 1993 (adapted from Huxley 1880)

Figure 4.3.2: Basic bio-mechanical principles of the caridoid escape reaction of *Cherax destructor*

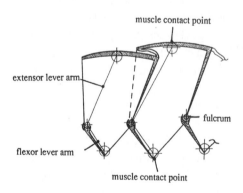

Source: Yee 1993

Generally at this stage, the bionic designer has the choice either to archive this information and await some later application, or to use the principles as an immediate guide towards the creation of a material object. In this undergraduate project, the student proceeded to create a multi-function gripping and cutting tool, based on the bio-mechanics of *Cherax destructor* (Figure 4.3.3). This

prototype had three different cutting or grasping jaws, and force from the hand can be directed to the specific jaws required for a certain task. The overall form of the tool is not dissimilar from the natural precedent.

As genuinely interesting as the result might be, however, this product may not actually represent the specific kind of form–function–material relationship anticipated by di Bartolo, given the totality of different requirements of the yabby's rapid escape response in water and the requirements for a successful hand-tool.

Figure 4.3.3: Hand-tool based upon *Cherax destructor*

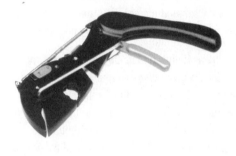

Source: Yee 1993

The deductive approach

The deductive approach example begins with a given brief, namely to design a more efficient clasping hand-tool. While the example of an inductive approach described above concluded in the development of a hand-tool *without* this outcome being specified at the beginning of the process, this deductive case was much more explicit in terms of the desired result. Students searched through the biology literature, deliberately looking for the various ways gripping and grasping is achieved in living nature. The search quickly narrowed down to an investigation of beaks, jaws and claws. Individual species were further investigated if they seemed likely to provide useful information that could directly inform the designer.

Figure 4.3.4: Pliers based upon the bio-mechanics of the human jaw

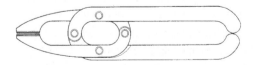

Source: Carson 1988

Figure 4.3.4 is an indication of the sort of hand-tool that can be developed from a study of the bio-mechanical principles underlying the jaw structure of *Homo sapiens*. Ultimately, however, it was concluded that none of the hand-tools so derived, including the one above, was any more successful than those currently available.

Discussion

It is the results suggested by these case studies that gives the bionic method minimal appeal for industries related to industrial design. To an evolutionary biologist, however, this would probably come as no great surprise. The basic criticism of these bionic approaches can be simply put: if a bird's beak is not the same as a crab's claw, then why should either be a satisfactory guiding principle for a hand-tool?

Clearly, what is absent is any effective understanding of the complex interactions between a species and its environment and the role of these interactions in the development of any biophysical structure. For these approaches to have been more applicable, one would also need to search nature to find some useful similarity between environmental conditions experienced by the subject organism and those environmental conditions experienced by humans. Were this possible, one might expect to be able to abstract valuable principles from the bionic method.

It makes sense to build from basic principles found in natural structures. Building upwards to the final material object is, however, the necessary essential departure from the natural precedent. It is at this point where the equilibrium of form–function–material need not, or should not, strictly follow that of any other organism because it is vital that other fundamentally human-based concerns be considered. To retain the biological precedent, attention must shift from the evidence of form-function-material balances to the natural processes themselves. In this sense the question becomes: (assuming some distant ancestral genetic similarity), how has the bird's beak or crab's claw evolved to become these distinct, seemingly appropriate, features that clearly play a part in their respective survival?

Darwin's (1859) concept of natural selection has been with us for about 140 years and if it, or its subsequent revisions, are correct, natural selection for fitness has been occurring from the moment the inanimate compounds in suspension became a biotic soup. Over millions of years, a type of probability-based search of possible alternatives, with selection pressures at work, offered up the form–function–

material relationships observable in nature. What then is the similarity that might be seen between natural selection and design? The word *selection* offers a cue for a potentially useful similarity, since designers also *select* from a range of alternatives.

Selection in design can be complex, with a range of impinging considerations requiring a network of dependent decisions. The number of considerations the industrial designer must take into account is increasing, not decreasing. Furthermore, the criteria themselves are complex. It seems reasonable, then, to investigate what further useful analogies there might be between selection in nature and selection in design that might help the designer navigate through the maze of possibilities.

Genetic algorithms

Recently, computer-based **genetic algorithms** have provided an interesting array of results, addressing highly complex relationships among competing variables (Holland 1975; Goldberg 1989). It is a model of natural selection at the level of genes. Paralleling nature, they form a computer-based genotype. In other words, they encode information necessary to build an entity, which in this case might be a certain product or design.

With genetic algorithms, one begins with a random population of entities. What these entities are depends on what one wants to develop. They might be floorplans for a house or designs for a hand-tool. In any case, these entities are strings of binary digits (just as anything in a computer is only comprised of ones and zeros). Each of these entities (known as *schema*) is tested against whatever the desired criteria for fitness might be. In the initial population, some entities are bound to be fitter or more desirable than others. These entities are preferentially selected and, in a computer-oriented sense that attempts to model sexual reproduction, 'bred' together. Simply put, this means that parts of two selected binary strings are joined together to produce an 'offspring' string. The new offspring entities form a new digital population, together with some of the other first generation entities. These then make up the second generation, which is again tested against the criteria, and again selectively bred according to how well they respond to the criteria. This **iterative** process also includes an element of random mutation, so as to represent some fidelity with nature's evolutionary processes. The procedure is stopped after a given number of generations or when an entity is bred which satisfies the criteria. (In nature there are no 'preset criteria' of course – the complex interactions between species create the selective processes driving evolutionary processes.)

There has been a credible attempt to apply genetic algorithms in architecture, especially in space layout planning and in numerous engineering fields and robotics (Davidor 1992). It is still unclear whether genetic programming can be successfully brought into industrial design. Research into producing novel furniture designs by computer **morphing** the images of chairs using a type of evolutionary algorithm (Graf 1995) has generated visually curious results but no more than this. Still at issue is whether other criteria typically considered by the industrial designer can be transcribed into a computer-based language effectively. However, there are a number of reasons to believe that an attempt to do so is worthwhile.

Firstly, the emphasis would shift from the finished object (often marked by questionable product differentiation, and an over-emphasis on the aesthetic) towards a careful, deliberate analysis of design criteria. At this level, the design act becomes much more input-oriented rather than output-oriented since the process demands that the inputs be clearly articulated by the designer. The design output or result is directly a function of the computer-based program, leaving the designer with more time at the start of a project to become involved with all the complex, competing inputs which characterise environmentally sound design. This reversal of emphasis from outputs to inputs should help to reinforce the designer's responsibilities with respect to broader social and environmental concerns.

Secondly and accordingly, this approach could facilitate productive cross-disciplinary design efforts. It can be argued that the success of design teams is precisely 'related to' the breadth of criteria brought to the design table (Edmonds et al 1994). In essence, teamwork denotes an enrichment in the number and character of inputs and success here only underscores the importance of these inputs as primary constituents of the design process. The genetic algorithm approach, being capable of balancing competing inputs, seems an appropriate method for producing designs based on team deliberations.

Conclusion

In this last sense, one can envisage the mathematician, the biologist, the computer scientist, the manufacturer, the environmentalist, the end-users and the industrial designer all working together on a series of criteria for a given product, and having these embodied within a computer model of natural selection. Though there appears to be no evidence of any such endeavour being applied to industrial design, the method seems sufficiently encompassing that one might reasonably expect the results of this approach to exhibit the form–function–material equilibrium witnessed in nature.

References

Bombardelli, C. 1991, *How a Bionic Product is Born*, trans, Aldo Udovisi, Faculty of Environmental Design, University of Canberra, Canberra, ACT.

Carson, D. 1988, *Bionic Research Specific Application*, Centro Ricerche Instituto Europo di Design, Milan.

Darwin, C. 1859 (reprint, 1968), *The Origin of Species by Means of Natural Selection or the Preservation of Favoured Races in the Struggle For Life*, Penguin, Great Britain.

Davidor, Y. 1992, 'Genetic Algorithms in Robotics' in B. Soucek et al, eds, *Dynamic, Genetic and Chaotic Programming: The Sixth Generation* (Sixth Generation Computer Technology Series), Wiley and Sons, New York.

di Bartolo, C. 1991, *Natural Structures and Bionic Models*, trans Aldo Udovisi, Faculty of Environmental Design, University of Canberra, Canberra, ACT.

Edmonds, E. et al 1994, 'Support for Collaborative Design: Agents and Emergence', *Communications of the ACM*, 37(7) pp. 41–46.

Graf, J. 1995, 'Interactive Evolutionary Algorithms in Design' in D.W. Pearson et al, eds, *Artificial Neural Nets and Genetic Algorithms*, *Proceedings of the International Conference in Ales, France, 1995*, Springer-Verlag, Wien, New York.

Goldberg, D. 1989, *Genetic Algorithms in Search, Optimisation, and Machine Learning*, Addison-Wesley, Boston, MA.

Holland, J. 1975, *Adaptation in Natural and Artificial Systems*, University of Michigan Press, Ann Abor, MI.

Huxley, T.H. 1980, *The Crayfish: An Introduction to the Study of Zoology*, C.K. Paul, London.

Otto, F. 1972, 'Il and Biology', *Il 6*.

Otto, F. 1983, 'Lightweight Structures in Architecture and Nature', *Il 32*.

Papanek, V. 1984, *Design for the Real World: Human Ecology and Social Change* 2nd edn, Thames and Hudson, London.

Yee, A. 1993, 'Yabby', in *Bionic Study of Locomotion in Australian Fauna* (student project prepared by the University of Canberra's Industrial Design Department, Canberra, ACT).

Questions

1. Some designers regard organisms as excellent examples of what di Bartolo called the 'form–function–material equilibrium'? Is it possible for industrial designers and product designers to match this equilibrium in the designs they create? What might prevent them from doing so?

2. What are the similarities between Darwinian evolution through natural selection and the creative process in design? Do you think the design process can be wholly described by the principles underlying natural evolution? Note that the Gothic cathedral evolved through trial and error to be taller and thinner in structure; many collapsed.

3. What are the possible benefits of employing the bionic method to design problems? The industrial design profession seems slow to accept the bionic approach as a productive one. Why?

4. The idea of evolving an object has been explored using computers to simulate natural evolution; that is, using 'generations' of designs instead of organisms as the subjects in question. This has worked well for more theoretical engineering problems, but it is less clear whether it works well for industrial or product design matters. Why?

5. What objects or designs that you know of are based on a living organism? Do these designs speak of an affinity with nature or make the beholder, user or occupant feel closer to nature?

6. What implications does the bionic method have on the sorts of people that might get involved in the design process?

Projects

1. Find a diagram from the literature on biology showing an organism's physiology, particularly indicating the bio-mechanics of the body parts used for gripping or holding (it can be any organism). On the basis of these diagrams, sketch a design for a pair of pliers. Present results and discuss the success, or otherwise, of the approach.

2. Bring in a pair of pliers (or some other object used for gripping) from home. The idea is to evolve a design for a pair of pliers. In groups, examine each pair of pliers on the basis of criteria such as function, ergonomic characteristics, material selection and overall quality. Afterwards, take the characteristics agreed on by each group as the best from all the individual pliers and combine these qualities together in a sketch design for the next generation of pliers. Discuss whether this exercise reflects the way designs are actually arrived at, and whether the metaphor of natural selection applies to design.

4.4   Green Theory in the Construction Fields

Kathleen Henderson

Over the last 25 years, increasing recognition of the environmental impact of buildings has stimulated efforts to develop assessment and management tools for improving their environmental performance. Debate has evolved into a more integrated discussion of all aspects of the life span of a building and its components. However, the research literature remains focused on building design, overlooking the role that the construction process can play in reducing the environmental impact of constructing, refurbishing, utilising and demolishing buildings. This chapter calls for the integration of eco-logical design and project management principles in the construction process.

Introduction

Until recently, construction industry project managers perceived that the challenge in every project was to 'execute the tasks to meet the required quality standards, while expending minimum possible time, cost and resource' (Burke 1992). A resource in this case is understood as being 'a commodity that is required to complete a task ... labour, machinery, material and financial funds' (Burke 1992). In this context, resource analysis is directed towards forecasting and planning resource requirements and achieving full resource utilisation. The focus is therefore on maximising economic efficiency.

As the concept of sustainability has seeped into the public consciousness, construction managers find themselves at the hub of a much more complex cycle of decision making. They are now required to achieve, not only economic efficiencies, but a plethora of requirements that address the sustainability of natural resources. New requirements being placed on the construction industry stem from both the internal and external **stakeholders**. That is, more firms are acknowledging that pursuing sustainability must be part of their overall strategic approach, and this commitment is further reinforced by extrinsic forces such as resource management law and client requirements. The complexities facing construction managers may lead to new foci, such as a general awareness of the environmental impact of

construction, and more specific targets such as eco-efficiencies.

Such requirements should not necessarily be viewed as 'negative constraints'. For example, **ecological modernisation** can be seen as is a positive approach to environmental policy. Hajer (1995) proposes that environmental improvement does not have to be secured within the constraints of a capitalist market logic (which would be a negative argument). The recognition of the ecological crisis actually constitutes a positive challenge for business. Not only does it open up new markets and create new demands but, if well executed, has the capacity to stimulate innovation in methods of production, industrial organisation, and in consumer goods.

In this sense the discourse of ecological modernisation puts the meaning of the **environmental problematique** upside down: 'what first appeared to be a threat to the system now has become a vehicle for its very innovation' (Hajer 1995). Indeed, activities that have developed from concepts in sustainability, such as new 'environmentally friendly' products, have themselves become big business, a part of all the forces that produce the 'fundamental impulse that sets and keeps the capitalist engine in motion' (Hajer 1995).

Concept of sustainability

Sustainability did not appear as a catchphrase in the construction literature until 1985. Research since 1990 has moved towards more 'whole building' and life span energy use assessments. A milestone for addressing sustainability in building research was the *First International Conference of Sustainable Construction* (CIB TG16) supported by CIB W92 in 1994. A variety of research papers was bought together under this single theme which evoked the sustainability ethic. A large number of papers were theoretically based, establishing principles and discussing the application of sustainability to the construction industry.

The *Second International Conference of Buildings and the Environment* (CIB TG8 1997) provided a forum for the publication of the most recent building research. In addition to assessment methods for the indoor environment, there is considerable debate within the literature on the appropriate methodology for assessment and the utility of management tools for the life cycle analysis of buildings. Aspects of building design, materials, maintenance, reuse and demolition are included in the LCA.

Environmental impact assessment tools

The development of tools to measure the environmental impact of buildings is an ongoing and evolving process [11.4]. The assessment tools being developed tend to have the following elements in common:

- They measure the environmental impact over the full life cycle of the building and generally use a Life Cycle Analysis approach.
- They recognise that, ideally, tools should measure the environmental impact of the total building rather than that of the individual parts.
- They use a hierarchical modelling approach to collect data on materials and individual components and aggregate that data into elemental and then whole-building analyses.
- They currently utilise methodologies with a combination of relatively coarse quantitative measures and some subjective judgements.

Optimal decisions

Preferred outcomes are most likely to be achieved when environmental analysts and building economists are able to work together with building designers and construction managers. In this relationship, buildings will be designed which optimise the interplay of cost, benefit and environmental impact, in a manner that also accords with the building owners, value system (Henderson and Boon 1998). However, within the field of building economics, a consensus appears to have been reached that it is not possible to formally optimise a property development project in terms of cost and economic benefit. The best that can be achieved is a satisficed position (Newton 1990). Satisficed is a term coined by Simon (1975) to describe the position reached when the debate has been continued and the options explored until the parties are satisfied that a 'good enough' outcome has been achieved. If this is the case when consideration is given only to economic matters, the additional complexities of environmental impact will clearly not assist in solving the problem of optimisation.

Very little research is being done that goes beyond design and into the process of building construction, certainly none that looks at 'greening' construction processes. This begs the question: what are the disincentives to such research, and what might be incentives for it to begin? Disincentives are likely to include:

- Regulations that specify particular materials and methods (which are unsustainable) [11.1], and industry and client reluctance to meet the costs involved in proposing and investigating alternatives.
- Commercial factors such as a commitment to the promotion of existing materials in order to recoup the capital costs of development and production facilities (capital and R&D costs far outweigh production costs).
- Lack of expertise, in that tradespeople and professionals do what they have been trained to do, and what they know will produce the result within a given time and price structure.
- Most tradespeople and professionals look for ways to cut costs, not increase sustainability.

Possible incentives to change might be:

- A broadening and deepening public concern and awareness, such that customers form a commitment to 'being part of a solution rather than part of a problem', and create demand for 'green' or sustainable processes.
- Economic incentives, given the analogy of many examples of cost savings in cleaner production methods adopted by (among others) US military and heavy industry.
- New regulations that demand more sustainable methods in the construction process.

Figure 4.4.1: Construction organisation systems

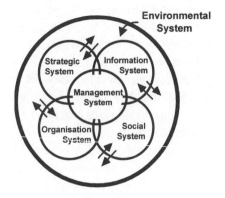

Source: Newcombe et al 1994

Complex systems

Newcombe et al (1994) advocate systems theory as a powerful tool for analysing construction organisations. A systems approach may be utilised to develop construction processes that integrate the ecological dimension. This is illustrated by a series of inter-linked spheres, each relating to the other and with the environment (Figure 4.4.1). Each of these systems may be evaluated in terms of labour management, materials management, plant management and financial management (Figure 4.4.2). The **synergy** of these inputs is the construction process.

Figure 4.4.2: Input–conversion–output model

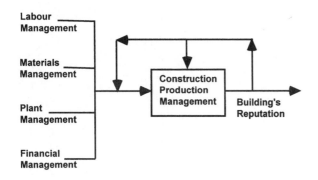

Source: Newcombe et al 1994

Conclusion

It is possible (and necessary) to fully integrate environmentally conscious design and project management principles into the building process. Political and social discourse increasingly reflects a preference for anticipatory and integrated approaches to using the natural environment. The challenge is to stimulate individuals within the environmental and building policy areas, and those charged with the planning and design of buildings, into systems thinking that accepts and values both principles and methods for ecologically sensitive solutions. Environmentally-friendly construction processes are an essential step to developing sustainability.

References and further reading

Burke, R. 1992, *Project Management Planning and Control*, Cape Town Press, Cape Town.

CIB TG8 1997, *Proceedings of the Second International Conference of Buildings and the Environment*, CIB (Conseil International du Batiment), Task Group 8, Paris.

CIB TG16 1994, *Proceedings of the First International Conference of Sustainable Construction*, CIB (Conseil International du Batiment), Task Group 16 Gainsville, FL.

Hajer, M. 1995, *The Politics of Environmental Discourse*, Clarendon Press, Oxford.

Henderson, K. and Boon, J. 1998, 'Green Building Economics', *Proceedings of the New Zealand Institute of Quantity Surveyors and Pacific Association of Quantity Surveyors Conference*, Queenstown, NZ.

Henderson, K. 1997, 'Ecological Modernisation and Sustainable Development in the Urban Environment', *Proceedings of the XI Ecopolitics Conference*, 4–5 October, Melbourne University, VIC.

Meadows, D. 1972, *The Limits to Growth: A report for the Club of Rome's Project on the Predicament of Mankind*, Potomac Associates, London.

Newcombe, R., Langford, D. and Fellows, R. 1994, *Construction Management 2, Management Systems*, B.T. Batsford, London.

Newton, S. 1990, 'Formal Optimisation and Informal Design', in V. Ireland, H. Giritli, C. Roberts and M. Skitmore, eds, *Proceedings of CIB 90 Syposium on Building Economics and Construction Management*.

Petherbridge, P., Milbank, N. and Harrington-Lynn, J. 1988, *Environmental Design Manual*, BRE Watford Building Research Station, Garston, NZ.

Shand, D. 1996, 'Life Since UNCED', *Planning Quarterly*, June, Wellington, NZ.

Simon, H. 1975, 'Style in Design in Spatial Synthesis', in *Computer Aided Building Design*, C.M. Eastman, ed, John Wiley, New York.

1. What are the blockages to sustainability becoming a top priority in building design and construction professions? List means to address these blockages.

2. Should governments require that buildings be constructed in an eco-friendly manner? Should inspectors be private or government agents? Can regulation be overseen or implemented by professional bodies, such as Master Builder Associations?

3. What are some of the commercial factors resisting the development of new eco-building products or systems? How can these be addressed? Do patents always encourage innovation and technology transfer?

4. Do you think the systems theory approach to analysing construction organisations can have practical value? Is it too complex? Explain.

5. Describe the relationships between the environmental system and each of the sub-systems illustrated in Figure 4.4.1. 'Fill out' the diagram so that it provides more information on these relationships.

6. The green movement has adopted, as a symbol, the picture of the Earth as viewed from space. Can you recall any cases in the media where an association between some negative symbol and the green movement has been attempted (eg the swastika)?

1. This chapter suggests that there are changing trends in building research. Is this true of built environment design fields as well? Find some examples in the literature in your area of interest (eg landscape architecture, industrial design) that support or contest this hypothesis.

2. Is complexity theory merely applied superficially to academic fields as a metaphor to describe new systems approaches, or does it reflect a deeper understanding? Find an article in your field of interest that uses complexity theory and determine whether it is being used to develop a deeper analysis or just to describe systems relationships; that is, does it have heuristic value?

Box 11   Eco-design Considerations for Urban Buildings

Janis Birkeland

Broader social and environmental context

- Consider including public uses like childcare facilities, galleries and restaurants.
- If appropriate, reflect traditional design elements that characterise the region.
- Reinstate diversity through facade articulation, increased 'edge' and **vertical gardens**.
- Design for allowable envelopes of adjacent buildings to ensure future solar access.
- Minimise dependency on urban infrastructure (water, gas, electricity, sewers).
- Consider embodied energy, life cycle and material flows analysis in all design stages.
- Reduce existing urban wind tunnels through building form.
- Consider 'design for crime prevention' strategies through people-friendly design.
- Provide for public environmental education tours of building if appropriate.

Transportation and global warming

- Avoid contributing to congestion (eg location of vehicle entry and loading bays).
- Encourage tele-commuting policies where feasible to reduce transport.
- Ensure building is sited to reduce regional transport requirements.
- Select products and materials that minimise ozone depleting or greenhouse gases.
- Accommodate public transport (eg by convenient and safe bus or tram access).
- Use locally sourced construction materials and products.
- Use local subcontractors and labour force in construction where feasible.

Contact with nature in urban areas

- Provide outdoor open space, seating, plazas for employees and/or the general public.
- Ensure possibility of integrated food production on site (eg roofs, balconies, atria).
- Provide worm farm facilities in restaurants and tea rooms for on-site gardens.
- Create micro-habitats for flora and fauna (eg nests on solar screens and balconies).
- Design building forms to provide areas for indoor plants, ponds and fountains.
- Use solar landscaping (eg trees for shading and ponds/ fountains for cooling).
- Allow private and public areas for gardening (eg roof gardens, balconies and atria).

Floor planning and layout

- Locate services (wires, ducts) in the floor for easy access and upgrading.
- Consider business trends such as hot-desking or tele-commuting in floor planning.
- Locate heating loads like office equipment and machines to minimise impact.
- Screen the sun in hot areas with services (eg storage, lifts, corridors to east and west).
- Ensure that movable partitions cannot disrupt air vents.
- Optimise open plan and private workspace opportunities for longevity.
- Maximise individual access to green spaces and windows in buildings.
- Ensure lighting fixtures are easy to access for maintenance.

Daylighting and employee comfort

- Integrate facade with passive solar systems (eg light shelves, trombe walls, trellises).
- Organise direct user participation in planning and design, as well as user surveys.
- Maximise natural lighting in interior (eg light shelves, atriums, skylights, mirrors).
- Use shallow floorplates (eg 12m max) for cross-ventilation and daylighting.
- Design ceiling for both acoustics and absorption of heat from lights.
- Avoid glare and heat from windows (eg by orientation, screening, smart windows).
- Vary facade design and window treatment according to solar orientation, wind, etc.

Air quality and health

- Optimise natural ventilation using solar stack technology on facades and roofs.
- Reduce or avoid air conditioning by cool air intake (over water, underground, etc).

- Use atria and building mass to moderate climate extremes.
- Avoid hazardous materials (eg VOCs) in furniture, walls and carpeting.
- Reduce noise amplification through wall and ceiling articulation, materials, etc.
- Assess local air quality (eg openable windows in polluted or high crime areas).
- Make windows operable by users (except where dirty air is significant).
- Ensure air intake is not near kitchens, loading docks, congested streets or garbage areas.

Resource and materials conservation

- Use products having low embodied energy in manufacturing and operation.
- Design for the capture, storage and reuse of rainwater from roofs.
- Develop a system for collecting, storing and distributing surface water run-off.
- Treat greywater on site with low-maintenance organic systems (eg Living Machines).
- Consider dedicating basement space to local organic waste treatment plant.
- Consider retrofitting existing building stock in lieu of new construction.
- Where feasible, reuse materials of any buildings to be demolished nearby.
- Use replaceable parts and design for disassembly.
- Design for durability (reusable or recyclable parts and components).
- Design for long life and 'loose fit' (flexibility of future use).

Timber usage

- Avoid rain-forest timbers and, where possible, native forest timbers.
- Specify sustainably managed plantation wood products, where timber is appropriate.
- Specify timber products with low gaseous emissions during manufacturing.
- Use 'woodless' timbers (eg from hemp, bamboo) and engineered timber alternatives.
- In specifications, minimise timber waste (off-cuts and residues) due to generic sizes.
- Plant trees to replace those used in the construction.

Energy and heat conservation

- Design for local climate – wind, humidity, 'worst case' conditions.
- Consider co-generation (heat from a process used to power/heat another function).
- Use passive solar heating and cooling technologies throughout.
- Consider (partially or totally) underground building for energy conservation.
- Specify green lights, products and appliances in fit-out.
- Ensure high-efficiency electrical office equipment is used.
- Ensure structural air-tightness and avoid thermal bridging (breaks in insulation).
- Use optimum insulation serving multi-functions (eg noise and heat control).
- Reduce temperature swings with exposed thermal mass (eg floor slabs, walls).
- Optimise low embodied energy, thermal storage capacity of building form itself.

Technology

- Ensure flexibility, expansion and adaptability for new technology in plan layout.
- Avoid technical complexity to reduce risks of failure and avoid maintenance costs.
- Consider testing experimental green technologies (where economic risk is low).
- Design for future upgrading and downsizing of mechanical equipment.
- Ensure back-up mechanical equipment (where required) is not over-specified.
- Consider automatic windows operated for night-time chilling of the structure.
- Consider smart windows that shade automatically, and generate electricity.
- Use photovoltaic cells that are integral to the roof or walls to generate electricity.

Construction process

- Demand minimal packaging of materials and products that are delivered to the site.
- Evaluate relative eco-efficiency of on-site/off-site assembly of building components.
- Use performance-based contracting systems to provide incentives for eco-solutions.
- Ensure that construction processes, as well as the building's operation, are eco-efficient.
- Develop a comprehensive waste management plan for the construction process.
- Ensure a construction safety plan is developed and implemented.
- Ensure energy conservation measures are checked and fine-tuned after use.
- Conduct post-occupancy evaluation to ensure equipment operates properly.

Section 5: Permaculture and Landscape Design

5.1 Permaculture and Design Education

Angela Hirst

Permaculture has been defined as the harmonious integration of landscape and people, providing their food, energy, shelter, and other material and non-material needs in a sustainable way (Mollison 1996, p. ix). Yet permaculture, as a paradigm, has potential significance beyond sustainable food production. Based on a feminist analysis, it is argued that permaculture can be used as a method of design, and a vehicle for improving environmental design education.

Introduction

One implicit assumption found in urban landscaping is that edible landscapes have no place in cities: trees should not bear fruit, groundcovers should not be edible, and shrubs should not be vegetables. The role of city landscapes is 'ornamentation', with similar bounds being placed on country, suburban and wilderness landscapes (see Willers 1999). This tacit premise in landscape planning is in conflict with sustainability: a significant part of the global environmental crisis is due to society's current agricultural practices and transport to provide food for urban dwellers.

This ideology of unproductive urban landscaping is reinforced through environmental design education. Leslie Weisman argues that design education marginalises social and environmental responsibility and is therefore in danger of becoming 'anachronistic and irrelevant' (1996, p. 273). First, the teaching of environmental design underplays the importance of creating an ecological architecture. Although students may be encouraged to think environmentally, buildings are still being constructed that show no consideration of sustainability (Mackenzie 1997, p. 8). Second, cooperation and teamwork, which are essential qualities for architects, are generally not being taught. Third, the users of architecture are often not included in the design process at all. Thus nature, collaboration and user participation are still undervalued in design education.

Feminist theory delves into the reasons for this marginalisation of people and nature in environmental design. Feminists such as Wilshire (1989) have explained

how physical and social space are shaped by dichotomies in Western thought. Mind, reason, spirit, order, public and permanence have been considered masculine, while ignorance (the occult), body, emotion, chaos, private and change have been considered feminine. These dichotomies justify the repression of any subject on the feminine side, as these attributes are deemed inferior in Western patriarchal culture (Table 5.1.1). This repression works by making the inferior subject, such as 'nature', conform to its relevant masculine subject, in this case 'culture' (Warren 1997; Mies and Shiva 1993). Ecofeminist theory has explained how this mental backcloth has contributed to the exploitation of nature and the repression of humans (Gaard 1993). This construction, called **hierarchical dualism**, offers insights into basic assumptions underlying the enculturation of architects.

Weisman relates two major aspects of this ecofeminist analysis to architectural education. First, she questions *what* architecture students should be taught. In education, the marginalisation of certain forms of knowledge occurs through an androcentric (male-centred) process of indoctrination – subtle decisions are made about what is and is not important to teach students. For example, design is often taught in isolation of its social and ecological impacts, giving students the message that the responsibility of the designer ends with function and aesthetics (Mackenzie 1997, p. 8). Weisman argues that it is narrow-minded and 'morally irresponsible' to educate students about aesthetics, building performances and cost without also teaching students to consider social and environmental factors (1996, p. 281). When environmental architecture is taught, it tends to deal with a simplified form of sustainability that focuses on environmental factors devoid of their social context. Consequently, 'green' architecture – as well as the dominant architectural ideologies – can perpetuate patriarchal norms (Birkeland 1994).

Second, Weisman questions *how* students should be taught. Hierarchical dualisms such as expert/client and theory/practice, have contributed to the absence of community participation from architectural education. Generally, architectural education still captures the enthusiasm of students by encouraging the 'solo virtuoso designer' (Weisman 1996, p. 280). Max Bond points out the futility of this method: 'In the profession and practice of architecture, it is increasingly rare to find buildings of any significance being done by one individual, yet we maintain the myth that individuals design buildings' (Dutton 1999a, p. 87).

Social/environmental responsibility and community participation, then, are marginalised in architectural education, because of the influence of patriarchal values. These relationships, which prevent social and environmental issues from being taken seriously in architectural education, must be deconstructed if architecture is to make a contribution to the creation of a sustainable society [Box 1].

Table 5.1.1: Hierarchical dualisms of Western thought

CULTURE / MALE		NATURE / FEMALE
reason (the rational)	—vs—	emotion (the irrational)
knowledge	—vs—	ignorance
(accepted wisdom)	—vs—	(the occult)
higher (up)	—vs—	lower (down)
good, positive	—vs—	negative, bad
mind (ideas), mind	—vs—	body (flesh), womb
spirit	—vs—	nature (earth)
order	—vs—	chaos
control	—vs—	letting be, spontaneity
objective (outside)	—vs—	subjective (inside)
literal truth, fact	—vs—	poetic truth, metaphor
goals	—vs—	process
light	—vs—	darkness
written text, logic	—vs—	oral tradition, myth
public sphere	—vs—	private sphere
seeing, detached	—vs—	listening, attached
secular	—vs—	holy and sacred
linear	—vs—	cyclical
permanence, ideal forms	—vs—	change, fluctuations
independent, individual	—vs—	dependent, social
isolated	—vs—	integrated
hard	—vs—	soft
dualistic	—vs—	whole

Source: Wilshire 1989

Educational principles

Weisman proposes that this happens through four educational principles, each of which has responsibility for a contemporary issue in the architecture discipline at large:

'Employ collaborative learning', 'Share authority and knowledge', 'Eliminate false dichotomies' and 'Emphasise ethical values and Interconnectedness' (pp. 280–281). These principles define a strategy for learning which, according to Weisman, would empower and inspire students to seek alternatives to the present. While Weisman does not specifically describe these principles as 'ecofeminist', they challenge the hierarchical dualisms that characterise patriarchal thought which have been linked to environmental and social injustice by ecofeminist theory.

1. **'Employ collaborative learning'** questions the view that architectural expertise is superior to other lay knowledge. Weisman identifies the importance of having team problem solving over the usually competitive individual design methods currently favoured by most design studios. In this way, the boundaries of the problem to be solved become the determinant of who will be involved in the design process (p. 281).

2. **'Share authority and knowledge'** challenges the view that gives an educator's knowledge authority over a student's knowledge. If collaborative learning is to be employed during the design process, the roles of all people involved must be dramatically reworked. Education for participatory design requires that students learn to pursue other disciplines and knowledge bases for solutions independently. For this to occur, teachers must surrender their exclusive possession of knowledge and, in so doing, compromise their own authority (p. 281).

3. **'Eliminate false dichotomies'** suggests that a more realistic and socially responsible relationship between theory and practice must be constructed. However, making links between theory and practice is not enough because, as Weisman suggests, 'although architecture has always been a service profession, it has traditionally served only those who can afford to pay it' (p. 281).

4. **'Emphasise ethical values and interconnectedness'** calls for eliminating the hierarchical dualism that places 'culture' over 'nature' (pp. 280–281). It is quite common today for architectural education to emphasise the metaphor of 'touching-the-earth-lightly'. However, as ecological architects Brenda and Robert Vale explain, the ecological meaning of this phrase is often confused with its common use as visual metaphor: 'A building that guzzles energy, creates pollution and alienates its users does not "touch-this-earth-lightly"' (Vale and Vale 1991, p. 139).

In essence, Weisman has identified the need to re-evaluate the concepts underlying conventional architectural education and decision-making practices to incorporate an ecologically sustainable ethic. But how can this be implemented on the ground? It is suggested here that the model for a more participatory, and more environmentally and socially responsible architectural education may be found in permaculture. This potential is demonstrated by drawing connections between permaculture's design philosophy and Weisman's four educational principles.

Permaculture as an educational tool

Permaculture addresses the high-energy costs of modern monocultural agriculture. Permaculture takes these human controlled, energy demanding, artificially designed landscapes, and arranges them so that they work to conserve energy or even generate more energy than they consume. Second, permaculture places food production where most people live: the city.

But permaculture is also a comprehensive design system that provides a practice that gives physical expression to ecofeminist or 'green' philosophy by challenging the 'hierarchical dualisms' of contemporary landscapes (nature/culture, chaos/order, country/city, artistic/practical). For example, permaculture helps eliminate hierarchical dualisms by integrating useful landscapes into urban environments so that urban dwellers have more contact with nature and live more integrated lives.

Permaculture encourages cooperation: Permaculture achieves sustainable landscapes by designing the connections between components in a system. To do this, it borrows whatever information it needs from different disciplines. Due to the complex nature of this interdisciplinary approach, collaborative learning should produce a more comprehensive outcome. Such a learning process allows a more extensive knowledge base to be achieved, provides a space for more lateral problem-solving techniques, and allows design to occur at a more intricate scale within normal time restraints.

Permaculture encourages authority to be shared: Because permaculture involves new design processes and knowledge resources, it is not possible for educators to teach permaculture in a top-down way. Instead, it requires a collective process of searching for answers. By including permaculture in architectural projects, educators would, in effect, become involved in a new learning process. Thus, the integration of permaculture into architectural education

should lead to the sharing of knowledge and authority.

Permaculture requires implementation: Permaculture helps eliminate dichotomies such as theory/ practice because it is 'design in landscape, social, and conceptual systems; and design in space and time' (Mollison 1996, p. 9). For example, permaculture design is a process that cannot be understood in terms of finite drawings. Judgement of its success depends on more complex and changing issues rather than form and structure, which dominate architectural education now. The success of a permaculture design depends on its sustainability as a system, and on how it contributes to social interaction and inclusivity over time. Through its implementation, a permaculture project becomes a demonstration of action research and design. If the built environment were perceived in the same way, permaculture would contribute to the environmental and social relevancy of the urban environment.

The fundamental directive of permaculture is ethical: Mollison feels that it is the acknowledgment of how interconnected our survival is to each other and to the survival of nature that leads to the evolution of sustainable and sensible behaviour. 'We will either survive together, or none of us will survive' (1996, p. 1). The ethical implications of permaculture design and the focus on interconnectedness as a permaculture design objective encourages students to examine and formulate value systems that are linked with their design practice.

Conclusion

'Aesthetics' in architecture design education has inhibited the formation of environmental ethics because it has been associated with controlling nature's messiness. Aesthetics has created 'monocultures' of design. The self-organising systems in permaculture, in contrast, allow nature to follow its own evolution. Nature can flourish within an initially 'constructed' but supportive landscape. Permaculture design could be a point of departure in a broader search for an 'environmental aesthetic' for built environment design that emphasises ethical values and interconnectedness.

As these four examples illustrate, many hierarchical dualisms can be deconstructed by students and educators through a permaculture discourse. In this sense, permaculture could be seen as, in part, the practice of ecofeminist theory. This compatibility makes permaculture a model for architectural education. Permaculture's focus has been on reducing the impacts of food production and building a more sustainable culture. However, as a model for architectural education, permaculture could change the way architecture students learn, and therefore influence the practice of building and landscape architecture.

References and further reading

Birkeland, J. 1994, *Eco-feminism and the Built Environment*, Paper presented at the Architecture and the Environment Conference, Pomona, CA.

Dutton, T.A. 1991a, 'Architectural Education and Society: An Interview with J. Max Bond, Jr.', in T.A. Dutton, ed, *Voices in Architectural Education: Cultural Politics and Pedagogy,* 1st edn, pp. 83–95, Bergin and Garvey, New York.

Dutton, T. A. 1991b, 'Introduction: Architectural Education, Postmodernism, and Critical Pedagogy', in T.A. Dutton, ed, *Voices in Architectural Education: Cultural Politics and Pedagogy,* 1st edn, pp. xv–xxix, Bergin and Garvey, New York.

Gaard, G., ed, 1993, *Ecofeminism: Women, Animals, Nature*, Temple University Press, Philadelphia, PA.

Holmgren, D. 2000, *Permaculture Principles and Other Ideas*, Holmgren Design Service, Hepburn, VIC.

Macarthur, J. 1998, *Image as Material*, Unpublished Seminar Paper, The University of Queensland, Brisbane, Qld.

Mackenzie, D. 1997, *Green Design: Design for the Environment*, Laurence King Publishing, London.

Mars, R. 1996, *The Basics of Permaculture Design*, Candlelight Trust, Hovea, WA.

Mies, M. and Shiva, V., 1993, *Ecofeminism*, Zed, London.

Mollison, B. 1996, *Permaculture: A Designers' Manual*, 5th edn, Tagari Publications, Tyalgum, NSW.

Vale, R. and Vale, B., 1994, *Towards a Green Architecture*, RIBA Publications, London.

Warren, K.J. 1997, *Ecofeminism: Women, Culture, Nature*, Indian University Press, Bloomington.

Weisman, L.K. 1996, 'Diversity by Design: Feminist Reflections on the Future of Architectural Education and Practice', in D. Agrest, P. Conway, and L. Weisman, eds, *The Sex of Architecture*, Harry N. Abrams, New York.

Willers, B. 1999, *Unmanaged Landscapes: Voices for Untamed Nature*, Island Press, Washington, DC.

Wilshire, D. 1989, 'The Uses of Myth, Image and the Female Body in Re-visioning Knowledge', in A. Jaggar and S. Bordo, eds, *Gender/ Body/Knowledge*, Rutgers University Press, London.

Zimmerman, M. 1994, *Contesting Earth's Future: Radical Ecology and Postmodernity*, University of California Press, Berkeley.

Questions

1. How can buildings be designed to provide their own ecosystem services? List some ideas.

2. Why do you think architecture students design predominantly non-edible landscapes around their buildings?

3. How can Weisman's four feminist principles of architecture education be applied to the relationship between professionals in the built environment (eg planners, landscape and building architects)?

4. Under what circumstances can you imagine students having a equal 'power relationship' with their teachers? Would there be any detrimental outcomes from such a situation?

5. Analyse the landscapes that create a context for the designs in a popular landscape or architecture journal. Critique the landscapes and the relationship they have to the buildings on the basis of their sustainability and usefulness.

6. Can you identify any conflicts between your values and those that underly conventional landscape design practice?

Projects

1. Write a brief for an environmental design studio assignment that would incorporate the principles expressed in this chapter; then develop a set of criteria by which to evaluate the project.

2. Examine your local professional design organisation's education policy. Critique it and develop a new framework using Weisman's principles. Submit it to the organisation and examine its response to the proposal.

5.2   The Sustainable Landscape

Paul Osmond

Designed landscapes are frequently ecologically unsustainable, and issues of landscape sustainability are usually abdicated to the field of environmental management, which is not equipped for the task. Ecological landscape design requires a radical shift in thinking from the linear and reductionist to the lateral and holistic. This chapter uses the case of rooftop greening to illustrate the idea that landscape eco-design can play a catalytic role in the achievement of ecological sustainability.

Introduction

The designed landscape is pivotal to the discourse of sustainability. From the individual site to the city or region, the landscape – intentionally altered (designed) by humans – is the ground upon which the production/construction/consumption system takes shape. Landscapes can be seen as the matrix within which the structures and processes of modernity and postmodernity operate, and a potential form-giver and catalyst for a paradigm of sustainability. Yet, except for agricultural landscapes, landscape design is conventionally approached more as 'exterior decoration'.

Although it is widely held that modernism tended to ignore the landscape except as backdrop to the grand architectural statement, it might be more accurate to say that it intensified pre-existing tendencies towards **banality** in Western landscape design. The overwhelming impression of the Western (or Westernised) urban exterior is of islands of corporate 'blandscape' in a sea of fragmented and car-dominated leftover space.

Where creative and delightful landscapes have emerged, too often their appeal relies on a superficial order, constructed and maintained through massive inputs of resources and energy. Examples of outstanding design which are at the same time ecologically sustainable are rare indeed.

At the same time, sustainability in relation to the land and its ecosystems is perceived as primarily an environmental management problem. The adverse impacts of unsustainable design practices, within a conventional

management perspective, are simply not understood as requiring *prevention* through sustainable design in the first place. Hence the sustainable but design-free and decontextualised landscapes which frequently result from ecological restoration projects. The best 'urban bushland' projects express the dynamic contrast between the vegetation and the surrounding urban form. However, when the same concept is replicated without regard to the contextual relationships between the living and constructed elements of the environment, that vitality is lost.

'Design for sustainability' incorporates a number of generic concepts such as a holistic perspective, reduction of material and energy inputs and outputs, responsibility and respect for context which establish a dialogue between design and ecology (Riley and Gertsakis 1992). Landscape design, whose resources explicitly encompass living entities and systems, has a potentially unique integrative role across the eco-design spectrum. The case of rooftop greening can be used to illustrate a landscape design framework which integrates the principles of ecological sustainability in the context of place and time, function and meaning.

Design for the sustainable landscape

Landscape design may be regarded as a process of structuring relationships between humans and nature. The concept of 'nature' itself is a social construct, a function of the changing relationship between humans and the external world. New holistic perspectives emerging from fields as diverse as physics, economics and philosophy provide useful insights and methodologies through which the relationship between people and nature may be restructured [4.2]. A series of landscape eco-design principles evolved from new insights into the relationship between humans and the external world, and a toolkit of methodologies and techniques derived from a variety of disciplines, can provide both conceptual guidance and practical delivery.

Sustainability tools: Landscape design is interdisciplinary by nature and has long been represented (if not always taught or practised) as an integration of art and science liberated from the constraints of 'style' (Eckbo 1950).

Therefore, landscape design, like the other environmental design fields, should draw upon and adapt a toolkit of sustainability methodologies. These include permaculture [Box 12], bionic design [4.3], environmental impact assessment [12.4], ecological accounting measures [Box 6], material accounting tools [Box 31], embodied energy analysis [11.4], life cycle analysis (LCA) and environmental management systems (EMS) [12.3].

Computer tools: To complement methodologies adapted from a range of disciplines are computerised tools which themselves have a synergistic relationship with both the outcomes and process of design, eg CAD and computer visualisation, geographic information systems (GIS) and environmental systems modelling. Digital techniques may be treated as simply a profit-driven method of improving 'efficiency', as a way of enhancing presentation and facilitating client or community involvement: an approach which computer-literate designers prefer (eg 'Technology Feature' 1998), or – still too rarely – as a means to creatively explore and extend the boundaries of design.

Organisational tools: Traditionally, design has been viewed as a linear progression – survey, analyse, design. Sustainable outcomes require a new, inclusive and iterative design process, which reflects the non-linearity of natural processes and also recognises and incorporates ongoing management as a design element. **Parameter analysis** (Jansson et al 1992) provides a useful model for a non-linear design process, an iterative cycle which must include evaluation. Among the techniques now available to the landscape designer to facilitate participatory and multi-disciplinary design is a plethora of organisational tools, from **community visioning** to **force field analysis** (ICLEI 1997).

Conventional design tools: There is no reason either why techniques of the modernist, postmodern or other traditions – eg metaphor and **analogy, deconstruction** (Norris and Benjamin 1988), **pattern analysis** (Alexander 1977) – cannot also be drawn on to address the needs of sustainable design. Ecological principles can provide conceptual (metaphor, pattern etc) as well as practical guidance.

Principles for sustainable landscape design

Pursuing the above approach engenders a number of eco-logical principles which, with creativity in application, can extend the designer's scope well beyond the boundaries of the conventional and banal. The 'ecological' and the 'aesthetic'

are deliberately mixed in the following framework, as the aim is to evolve an *ecological aesthetic*.

Return to original sources of inspiration, whether nature or culture, is regarded as a fundamental concept of eco-design, avoiding introspective and self-referential perspectives which ignore reality (Papanek 1984).

Respond to the site, designing in harmony with its distinctive character to enable the unfolding of the landscape's ecological potential over time. This may involve:

- creating connections and themes (functional and perceptual as well as spatial) within and across sites while defining and delineating boundaries;
- transforming site constraints into environmental opportunities;
- minimising negative environmental impacts (including sensory as well as physical pollution);
- maximising positive impacts, off-site as well as internally.

Landscape design has a key role here in enhancing the sustainability of building design (eg through modifying microclimate and reducing heating/cooling demand).

Minimise inputs of materials and energy and maximise outputs of renewable and reusable resources – from initial concept to final construction. This includes design for long life, durability, energy efficiency and recyclability of hard landscape elements, and represents a way in which landscape design can catalyse eco-logical advances in other design areas.

Maximise resilience and dynamic stability in the landscape such that each element fulfils several functions and each function is undertaken by several elements. Two additional principles adapted from permaculture are:

- maximising the diversity of landscape elements and the diversity of relationships between elements;
- creating opportunities for the emergence of self-sustaining and self-regulating systems in the landscape.

Create 'place' as distinct from merely manipulating space, such that the design maximises the potential for user interaction with the environment. This involves designing for all the senses – touch, taste, smell, hearing and movement – not just vision.

Make systems visible means making environmental processes apparent and celebrating them – a specific application of the broader principle of featuring contrasting processes (dynamic contrast) as well as the use of contrasting static elements in a synthesis of art and ecology.

Minimise maintenance and maintain to enable full expression of design, acknowledging that ongoing management is itself an aspect of design, to ensure the continuity of sustainable outcomes.

Practice – rooftop greening

Greening the city's roof (and walls) is a concept which provides ample opportunities to integrate and implement many of the aesthetic and physical design principles outlined above. However, this certainly does not imply that all roof gardens are sustainable – in this respect they are subject to similar criteria as gardens at ground level. The use of vegetated (sod) roofs dates back to prehistory, reflecting the value of soil and turf as shelter from heat, cold and rain. However, the value of green roofs can stretch far beyond simple energy conservation (City of Port Phillip 1999).

Rainwater retention: Rain falling on pervious surfaces soaks into the soil and is slowly released through evapo-transpiration, or percolates to the water table. However, on impervious urban surfaces some 15–20% of incident rainfall evaporates and the rest is lost to stormwater drains. Green roofs retain a significant proportion (40–70%) of rainwater, depending on season, soil depth and slope, partially restoring the natural water cycle.

Creation of green open space: Market forces and policies to combat urban sprawl continue to drive redevelopment of inner suburbs, increasing population density and concentration of built form, and reducing public and private ground-level open space. Extensive and intensive greening of roofs, terraces and balconies provides an opportunity to mitigate some of the negative impacts of higher density development. 'Extensive' roof gardens rely on shallow growing media and hardy groundcover plants able to survive on incident rainfall to create a green veneer of (usually indigenous) vegetation over low load-bearing, inaccessible roofs. 'Intensive' roof gardens may include groundcovers, shrubs and trees and a range of hard landscape elements constructed on purpose-built slab roofs – essentially conventional, accessible gardens installed on structure.

Urban character: Observed from above, rooftop greening adds a constantly changing natural element to the predominantly artificial 'viewscapes' of city dwellers. From below, vegetated rooftops, terraces and balconies provide character and interest to the buildings of which they are a feature, and add variety and richness to an urban precinct.

Habitat restoration: As land is more closely developed, remnant native plant species face local extinction. Low indigenous rooftop planting, designed for habitat and visual interest, provide the potential to restore the distinctive groundcover flora of the region and in time its dependent insect and bird populations, while conventional (intensive) roof gardens can help to conserve local tree and shrub species.

Microclimate modification: Green roofs provide a source of natural evaporative cooling. As warm air above hard surfaces rises it is replaced by cooler air from above the vegetated roofs, creating an urban 'sea breeze'. In contrast, concrete and asphalt surfaces absorb summer heat by day and release it to the atmosphere at night (the 'urban heat island').

Improved air quality: Augmenting the city's stock of vegetation, roof gardens can help improve air quality by producing oxygen and assimilating excess carbon dioxide produced by city traffic and industry. Vegetation can also relieve respiratory problems by trapping airborne particulates on leaf surfaces. Tree-lined streets have been found to contain only 10–15% of the dust found on similar streets without trees.

Insulation: Buildings with roof gardens lose about one third less heat during cool temperate zone winters. Thermal insulation (and soundproofing) from soil and vegetation are supplemented by the air spaces within the drainage layer, which together can deliver substantial savings in energy consumption and heating/cooling costs.

Economic benefits: Green roofs generally last longer than exposed roofs because the multiple layers of waterproofing, drainage, soil and vegetation protect roofing materials from temperature extremes and ultraviolet light. While intensive roof gardens may be expensive to establish, life cycle costing indicates an extensive greened roof can actually be cheaper than a standard roof when depreciation is factored in.

Social benefits: Gardening, or even simply experiencing a green environment has been shown to lower blood pressure, relieve stress, and enhance recovery from illness (Relf 1992). Buildings designed to provide a mix of public and private, rooftop, terrace and balcony 'gardens in the sky' can provide the physical basis for both improved health and a renewed sense of community.

Urban agriculture: Since the Industrial Revolution the trend to separate cities from their sources of nutrition has both spatially and psychologically distanced urban dwellers from the land which supports them. Urban agriculture is currently experiencing a resurgence (largely in response to economic necessity) and is the focus of rooftop greening projects from St Petersburg Russia, where rooftop food production to supplement prison rations has been under way since 1995, to Chicago USA, where Lutheran church workers grow vegetables on city roofs for distribution to the poor and homeless.

Vertical gardening

A variant on rooftop greening is 'vertical gardening'. A green wall project which encapsulates the principle of single element, multiple functions, is the 'vertical wetland' incorporated in a Berlin apartment block. The exterior wall is fitted with a cascade of terracotta basins, filled with gravel and planted with reeds. Greywater trickles through the basins, removing pollutants through filtration, settlement and active uptake by roots and bacteria (Seidlich 1992).

A more high-tech approach to vertical greening is the 'Breathing Wall' at the Canada Life Assurance building in Toronto, a collaboration between research scientists, architects and industry. The focus has been on developing an ecologically complex and stable plant/microbial community, utilising hydroponic growing media, to improve indoor air quality – an interface between natural process and the building's HVAC system.

Conclusion

Eco-logical landscape design is in a unique position to catalyse a more general shift towards sustainability through:

- Integrating art and ecology across a range of parameters from the hydrological cycle to urban agriculture.

- Mitigating negative environmental impacts and creating positive ones.

- Enabling opportunities for green products and services both upstream (supply) and downstream (disposal) of the design project.

- Facilitating a multi-disciplinary, participatory and empowering design framework based on 'placemaking' (landscape plus architecture).

References and further reading

Alexander, C. 1977, *A Pattern Language*, Oxford University Press, New York.

Benson, J.F. and Roe, M.H., eds, 2000, *Landscape and Sustainability*, Spon Press, New York.

City of Port Phillip 1999, *Rooftop Greening Design Guidelines,* VIC.

Eckbo, G. 1950, *Landscape for Living*, F.W. Dodge, New York.

ICLEI (International Council for Local Environmental Initiatives) 1997, *Local Agenda 21 Planning Guide*, Melbourne, VIC.

Jansson, D.G., Condoor, S.S. and Brock, H.R. 1992, 'Cognition in Design: Viewing the Hidden Side of the Design Process', *Environment and Planning B: Planning and Design* 19, pp. 257–271.

Mars, R. 1996, *The Basics of Permaculture Design*, Candlelight Trust, Hovea, WA.

Mollison, B. 1988, *Permaculture, a Designer's Manual*, Tagari Publications, Tyalgum, NSW.

Norris, C. and Benjamin, A. 1988, 'What is Deconstruction?', *Academy Editions*, London.

Papanek, V. 1984, *Design for the Real World*, Thames and Hudson, London.

Relf, D., ed, 1992, *The Role of Horticulture in Human Well-Being and Social Development*, Timber Press, Virginia.

Riley, T. and Gertsakis, J., eds, 1992, 'Sustainability through Design', *Ecodesign 1 Conference Proceedings*, RMIT, Melbourne, Vic.

Seidlich, B. 1992, 'Landscape Architecture: The Integral Design for a New Ecology', in T. Riley and J. Gertsakis, eds, *Sustainability through Design, Ecodesign 1 Conference Proceedings*, RMIT, Melbourne, VIC.

'Technology Feature', 1998, *Landscape Australia* 2, pp. 111–133.

Thompson, J.W. and Sorvig, K. 2000, *Sustainable Landscape Construction: A Guide to Green Building Outdoors*, Kogan Page, London.

Whitefield, P. 1993, *Permaculture in a Nutshell*, Permanent Publications, UK.

Questions

1. Identify some of the 'unsustainable' elements of a park or other urban landscape you are familiar with, and state why they are unsustainable. Why do you think the site was designed in this way?

2. Investigate an urban bush or woodland regeneration project. What are your initial impressions about the 'fit' between the site and the surrounding urban form upon first visiting the site? Do your feelings about the site and its context change after examining something of its history?

3. Debate: 'New urban buildings should be required to carry the weight of significant landscaping on their roofs.' (Note: There has been significant development of lightweight soils for rooftop use.)

4. Explain the difference between a linear and an iterative design process. What comparisons can be made between iterative design and the 'continual improvement cycle' of environmental management systems (EMS)?

5. This chapter identifies a range of benefits from rooftop and vertical greening. What are some of the potential *negative* environmental impacts, for example, in terms of resource consumption, embodied energy and so on?

6. Do you think there is likely to be significant resistance and/or inertia towards widespread adoption of sustainable, but unconventional, landscape architecture such as roof gardens? If so why?

Projects

1. Following on from Question 6, identify potential barriers to the achievement of sustainability in the urban landscape. Analyse the major issues, identify the key individuals/organisations which need to be engaged in the process of change, and develop an outline strategy for overcoming the hurdles.

2. The central thesis of this chapter is that eco-logical landscape design can play an integrative and catalytic role with respect to sustainability in general, and the different design disciplines in particular. With reference to the (re)design of a specific site, explore specific ways in which this may occur.

Box 12 Permaculture: 'Functional Analysis of the Chicken'

From Bill Mollison with Reny Mia Slay, *Introduction to Permaculture*, Tagari, 1991

The chicken demonstrates the process of **relative location**.

First, we list the innate characteristics of the chicken: its colour, size and weight, heat and cold tolerances, ability to rear its own young, etc.

Chickens have different breed characteristics: light-coloured chickens tolerate heat better than dark-coloured ones; heavy breeds cannot fly as high as light breeds (which means fencing height requirements are different); some breeds are better mothers, others are better layers.

We also look at the behaviour of the chicken: what is its 'personality'? We see that all chickens scratch for food, walk, fly, roost in trees or perches at night, form flocks, and lay eggs.

Secondly we list basic needs of the chicken: Chickens need shelter, water, a dust bath to deter lice, a protected roosting area, and next boxes. They need a source of shell grit to grind food around in their crops and they like to be with other chickens. A solitary chicken is a pretty sad affair – best to give it a few companions. That's all easy enough to provide and wouldn't take us more than a few days to set up.

Chickens also need food, and that's where we start to make connections to the other elements in our system, because we want to put the chicken in a place and situation where it will scratch for its own living. Any time we stop the chicken from behaving naturally – ie foraging – we've got to do the work for it. Both work and pollution are the result of incorrect design or unnatural systems.

Lastly, we list the products or outputs of the chicken: It provides meat, eggs, feathers, feather dust, manure, carbon dioxide (from breathing), sound, heat, and methane. We will want to place the chicken in such a position that its products are used by other elements in the system. Unless we use these outputs to aid some other part of our system, we are faced with more work and pollution.

Sketch plan of the chicken run: Now we have all the information needed to sketch a plan of the chicken run, to decide where fences, shelters, nests, trees, seed and green crops, ponds, greenhouses, and processing centre will go relative to the chicken. Thus:

The house needs food, cooking fuel, heat in cold weather, hot water, lights, etc. It gives shelter and warmth for people. The chicken can supply some of these needs (food, feathers, methane). It also consumes most food wastes coming from the house.

The garden needs fertiliser, mulch, water. It gives leaves, seeds, vegetables. The chicken provides manures and eats surplus garden products. Chicken-pens close to the garden ensure easy collection of manures and a throw-over-the-fence feeding system. Chickens can be let into the garden, but only under controlled circumstances.

The greenhouse needs carbon dioxide for plants, methane for germination, manure, heat, and water. It gives heat by day, and food for people, with some crop wastes for chickens. The chicken can obviously supply many of these needs, and utilise most of the wastes. It can also supply high heat to the greenhouse in the form of body heat if we place the chicken-house adjoining it.

The orchard needs weeding pest control, manure, and some pruning. It gives food (fruit and nuts), and provides insects for chicken forage. Thus, the orchard and the chicken can interact beneficially if chickens are allowed in from time to time.

The wood lot needs management, fire control, perhaps pest control, some manure. It gives solid fuel, berries, seeds, insects, shelter, and some warmth. Chickens can roost in the trees, feed upon insect larvae, and assist in fire control by scratching or grazing fuels such as grasses.

The cropland needs ploughing, manuring, seeding, harvesting, and storage of crop. It gives food for chickens and people. Chickens have a part to play as manure providers and cultivators (a large number of chickens on a small area will effectively clear all vegetation and turn the soil over by scratching).

The pasture needs croppings, manuring, and storage of hay or silage. It gives food for animals (worms and insects included).

The pond needs some manure. It yields fish, water plants as food, and can reflect light and absorb heat.

Simply by letting chickens behave naturally and range where they are of benefit, we get a lot of 'work' out of them. Using the information above, we place the chicken near the (fenced) garden, and probably backing onto the greenhouse. Gates are opened at appropriate times into the orchard, pasture, and wood lot so that chickens forage for fallen fruit, seeds, and insects, scratching our weeds and leaving behind manures.

Pamela Kaufman

Understanding the values of local residents and community groups allows planning and heritage professionals to conserve and create environments that have meaning and identity, and may help planners to reduce potential conflict and increase resident satisfaction. While planning professionals generally believe that they consider the values of local residents in planning decisions, residents often disagree. When planning authorities disregard community values, they do not obtain adequate information to be able to make decisions affecting cultural landscapes.

The concept of place

> *'Before it can ever be a repose for the senses, landscape is the work of the mind. Its scenery is built up as much from strata of memory as from layers of rock'.*
> (Schama 1996, pp. 6–7).

A cultural landscape may be defined as ' ... an expression of human attitudes, values and interactions with the environment' (State of the Environment Advisory Council 1996, pp. 9–20). This inter-relatedness of natural and human forces in shaping the environment has its theoretical roots in the 'humanist approach', adopted by cultural and human geographers of the late 19th and early 20th Centuries (Jacques 1995). The humanist approach has played a major role in the evolution of our understanding of **cultural landscapes** by introducing the concept of meaning of place. **Meaning of place**, in this context, may be described as the 'thoughts, feelings, memories, and interpretations evoked by a landscape' (Schroeder 1991). These are the intangible elements that contribute to the social and spiritual nature of places.

Understanding the social and spiritual dimensions of place is required before planners can make informed decisions about cultural landscapes. However, the planning profession has been slow to adopt the theoretical concept of landscape 'meaning' to their practice. Rather, the physical fabric of place continues to be the focus of conservation, management and planning (Pearson and Sullivan 1995, p. 311). This stems from difficulties in identifying and assessing

community values, the perspectives and attitudes of planning professionals, and the highly structured, top-down process of traditional planning practice.

Community value

Local residents and community groups do not tend to distinguish between different types of values when explaining why a place is important to them. More often, their values for a place are interwoven into feelings of reverence, belonging and sense of place (Pearson and Sullivan 1995, p. 18). This overall value that a community has for a place is referred to here as **community value**. However, planners and heritage practitioners often attempt to tease out formally recognised values such as social, aesthetic, historic and amenity values. This enables practitioners to assess the individual significance of values when determining conservation decisions.

Social value is a significant component of community value and, due to its intangible and subjective nature, is difficult to identify and assess. According to Australia ICOMOS, social value is said to 'embrace the qualities for which a place has become a focus of spiritual, political, national or other cultural sentiment to a majority or minority group' (1992, p. 73). Thus, social value plays a key role in establishing and maintaining a community, sense of place, identity and belonging (Pearson and Sullivan 1995, p. 21).

However, social value has tended to be used as a 'catch-all' for those values expressed by the community which fall outside the current framework of professional heritage practice. One reason for this tendency is that current heritage assessment practices are too narrow and fail to reflect the breadth and depth of interest present in society (Johnston 1994, p. 4).

Differing perspectives

Perspectives about community values and the significance of local places often differ between the planning professional and local residents. 'Social values are inherently about people's values, not those that arise out of a detached professional view' (Beck 1996, p. 7). Social construct theory suggests that a professional's or expert's mental construct of a locality is based on a broad range of experiences which can relate to many different contexts (Ganis 1995). These experiences, however, may not be relevant to the way local residents perceive place. Furthermore, planners tend to rely on general principles of planning and development that are context-independent and consist of 'conceptual knowledge which is often abstract, "top-down" information' (Ganis 1995, pp. 3–4).

On the other hand, local knowledge tends to be detailed and place specific, usually derived from direct experience in a particular locality (Ganis 1995, p. 4). Local residents often have an intimate knowledge of their community and its functions. Residents can often provide valuable information about their environment. However, local knowledge is often perceived by professionals as being secondary to expert knowledge in terms of decision making. These perspectives may arise from professional training that encourages structure, control and objectivity (Beck 1994).

Community involvement

'[Citizen participation] implies an interactive process between members of the public, individually or in groups, and representatives of a government agency, with the aim of giving citizens a direct voice in decisions that affect them'. (Munro-Clark 1992, p. 13)

Statutory consultation processes are usually required prior to approval of certain planning decisions including **development applications**, planning policies, master plans and design guidelines. Through a variety of public meetings, exhibitions and written notification, the public is provided with information and invited to comment and make submissions. Residents often express their concern that this type of consultation is perfunctory, only to fulfil a requirement for community input. In some situations, public involvement may be used as a way of defusing opposition, managing conflict or spreading responsibility (Munro-Clark 1992, p. 17). Therefore, a distinction should be made between consultation and participation.

In 1969, Sherry Arnstein published 'A Ladder of Citizen Participation' as a model for the different levels of citizen involvement in government, ranging from token forms of consultation through to 'true' participation that involves a real transfer of power. In an ideal situation, each individual member of a decision-making body, including the public, would have equal power to determine the outcome of

decisions (Pateman 1970, p. 71). However, this situation rarely occurs. More often, through consultation, the public is asked to comment on expert data already collected, such as planning proposals, or development applications.

Alternatively, participation aims to actively involve the community, including its knowledge and values, in decision making (Beck 1996, p. 7). Planners often justify unilateral decision making with 'expert' knowledge, regional planning goals and arguments for the 'public good'. However, politics, development pressures and economic rationalisation often determine planning outcomes. Planning practitioners also view public involvement as time consuming and costly, and it is particularly difficult to justify scarce resources when its value is not explicit.

There are times, however, when planners decide that more involved consultation and information gathering is required. This usually involves non-statutory methods including consultative committees, focus group meetings, workshops and surveys. These processes may result in a greater depth of understanding about community values and needs. They may also offer opportunities for representatives of community groups to enter into discussion with decision makers. Discussion is essential to the process of negotiation, in which trade-offs and compromises may be made.

The case of Interim Park

The case of former Interim Park, in Ultimo-Pyrmont, Sydney, illustrates the differences in perspectives and expectations among planners, heritage practitioners and local resident groups. The park was established in 1991 on a half hectare of land that had lain vacant for 20 years near Pyrmont Point. Redevelopment of the Ultimo-Pyrmont area began in 1991, with the vision to create a medium-density, mixed-use urban environment. Interim Park was meant to be a temporary measure, providing community open space during the extensive redevelopment phase. Residents of the Pyrmont community developed the park themselves incorporating used stone, timber kerbs and a variety of shrubs and perennials. The result was an intimate community park, different in character from other more formal public parks in the vicinity.

Long after Interim Park was cleared (August 1997) to make way for development, there continued to be an emotional and committed fight by the creators of the park for its re-establishment. However, there was another faction of the resident community that argued against retention of the park. This group felt the park was not well used by the majority of local residents and was not of significant community meaning or value. Despite these conflicting views the Australian Heritage Commission (AHC) made an official statement of cultural significance for Interim Park and placed it on the Interim List of the Register of the National Estate (AHC 1997). Of social significance was the fact that Interim Park was created by the community without government intervention, and the value of the park to the local and wider community who 'sympathise with the actions of people who challenge major developments that override community aspirations' (AHC 1997, pp. 1–2). The case of Interim Park demonstrates the subjective nature of the social values and the need for wider recognition and assessment of these values in planning.

Where to from here?

Methods commonly used to obtain information on values and perspectives are problematic. Public meetings frequently have low attendance rates and are not designed for discussion and negotiation. Meetings may also be intimidating to some, particularly when held in formal council chambers and dominated by 'experts'. Information provided by planners and designers is often presented in abstract, technical formats, making it difficult to understand for those with little or no experience in planning or design. There needs to be a move away from such top-down approaches that rely largely on expert knowledge, to methods of participation that recognise local knowledge and allow opportunities for negotiation.

Neighbourhood or **community learning networks** may present a means for community values to gain recognition by planners. Residents in one area can learn from the way those in other areas have fought for retention of places important to them. Through information sharing, members of local community groups can acquire the knowledge and expertise required to respond to development applications and proposals, lobby government and discover how best to communicate their needs. As part of their role, planners could provide support for these initiatives.

While diversity of meanings and values may present a challenge for planners, the understanding of these is essential to the management of lively, interesting places. Through a process where all parts of the community have a voice, trade-offs and compromises can be made that result in the best possible solution for conserving the meanings and values of places.

Conclusion

What happens before, during and after the community consultation process requires reassessment. Practitioners must question whether existing processes truly elicit community meanings and values. Important considerations include the type of information provided, the way that information is communicated, who is involved (or more importantly who is not involved), and appropriate follow-up. Finally, understanding the concept of place and community values, and respecting the different perspectives of professional planners and residents, may help to increase satisfaction of planning outcomes by revealing common goals and visions, thereby bridging the gap between the formal process of planning and the informal processes of community and place.

References and further reading

AHC (Australian Heritage Commission) 1997, *Register of the National Estate Database Report,* RR No: 100002, Item 1.

Arnstein, S. 1969, 'A Ladder of Citizen Participation', *Journal of the American Institute of Planners* 35(4), pp. 216–224.

Beatley, T. and Manning, K. 1997, *The Ecology of Place: Planning for Environment, Economy and Community*, Island Press, Washington, DC.

Beck, H. 1994, 'Social Value: Where to From Here?' in *Assessing Social Values: Communities and Experts*, Australia ICOMOS Workshop, December 1994, pp. 6–7.

Ganis, M. 1995, 'The 'Sense of Place' in Urban Design: The Impact of Development in Professional and Lay Constructs of a Locality', *People and the Physical Environment Research* 47, pp. 3–6.

ICOMOS (Australian) 1992, *The Illustrated Burra Charter*, in P. Marquis-Kyle and M. Walker, eds, Australia ICOMOS, Sydney.

Jacques, D. 1995, 'The Rise of Cultural Landscapes', *International Journal of Heritage Studies* 1(2), pp. 91–101.

Johnston, C. 1994, 'What is Social Value?', *Australian Heritage Commission Technical Publications series* no. 3, AGPS, Canberra, ACT.

Munro-Clark, M. 1992, 'Introduction: Citizen Participation – an Overview', in M. Munro-Clark, ed, *Citizen Participation in Government*, Hale and Iremonger Pty Ltd, Marrickville, NSW.

Pateman, C. 1970, *Participation and Democratic Theory*, Cambridge University Press, Cambridge.

Pearson, M.I. and Sullivan, S. 1995, *Looking after Heritage Places: The basics of Heritage Planning for Managers, Landowners and Administrators*, Melbourne University Press, VIC.

Raberg, P.G., ed, 1997, *The Life Region: The Social and Cultural Ecology of Sustainable Development*, Routledge, London and New York.

Schama, S. 1996, *Landscape and Memory*, HarperCollins, London.

Schroeder, H.W. 1991, 'Preference and Meaning of Arboretum Landscapes: Combining Quantitative and Qualitative Data', *Journal of Environmental Psychology* 11(3), pp. 231–248.

State of the Environment Advisory Council 1996, *Australia: State of the Environment*, CSIRO, Canberra.

Questions

1. Why are cultural landscapes important? Can they be in conflict with ecosystems? If so, how can such conflicts be resolved without trade-offs?

2. How do heritage and planning practitioners generally define social value? What other values may people have for places? Is the concept of 'social value' anthropocentric?

3. What are some frequent differences in perspectives between planning professionals and local residents? Can you think of instances where local residents have been more supportive of proposed developments than government planners?

4. What are the possible implications of different values among residents and planning professionals? Where local residents oppose new developments, should they take their objections to the developers or planners? What factors should be considered in deciding how to support or oppose a development?

5. What are some of the main ways in which planners can learn to better understand community meanings and values?

6. Do you think there is a difference between consultation and participation? Explain.

7. What are some of the ways in which community involvement may be improved?

Projects

1. Choose one place which is familiar to all group members. Have each member describe the types of values that they consider significant for the place. Discuss these different values, and attempt to rank these different values by their significance. Do group values determine the ranking?

2. A developer applies for rezoning of a 'People's Park' for a casino that will, he claims, attract much needed revenue for the town. It is now occupied by homeless people, community garden plots and a 'flea market'. What would be the concerns of the various parties? Have each group member take on the role of one 'community of interest' in the decision-making process (ie planner, long-term resident, new resident, developer, local business person). Discuss these different perspectives and consider what expectations they have in common. What solutions or 'win–win' compromises can be reached to keep all parties happy?

Janis Birkeland

'Playgardens' integrate structures designed to facilitate exploratory, imaginative, and interactive play with plants, trees, and the natural features of the site. This encourages children to develop positive early experiences in nature, even though they may be confined to congested urban environments. It is suggested that playgardens can help to encourage the appreciation of, and a caring attitude toward, nature.

Introduction

Most people who have been involved in implementing community-based playground projects know that an inordinate amount of time and energy can be spent in overcoming the opposition of local 'knockers', council bureaucrats and officious meddlers. But why would anyone object to something so inexpensive and cost-effective in contributing to the quality of community life as a family play environment? It could *not* be for the reasons generally stated, such as money and safety issues, as these arguments do not stand to reason (see Birkeland 1994).

In my experience, the people who oppose having money spent on things like play environments have been among those that support expenditures on casinos, stadiums, racetracks or engineering extravaganzas – playgrounds for grown-ups. While such mega-projects may satisfy the entertainment preferences of grown decision makers, this 'double standard' may come from a deeper place. Such activities represent risk taking and high stakes; they may even be seen as altars to a kind of 20th Century version of a warrior cult.

Children's play environments represent diametrically opposed values to those which such grandiose projects symbolise. It is contended that the values embodied in play environments, and community involvement in designing and building them, are inherently subversive to this value system. Just as David's sling-shot brought down the mighty Goliath, so too creative play environments undermine the hierarchical structures and values of the 'old boys club'. But before outlining this argument, we need to understand what a playgarden is.

Types of play environments

We can distinguish four types of play environments: conventional playgrounds, multi-functional playgrounds, creative play environments, and playgardens.

Playgrounds: The general term playgrounds is associated with the traditional collection of slides, swings, log forts, and commercial equipment which are found in many lonely little parks and schoolyards around the world. The equipment is usually composed of pipes or treated pine logs at a scale often unsuited for children. The basic model was designed in the late 19th Century to 'keep children off the streets' or to occupy children, rather than to foster social and physical development. Today these generally come in commercial varieties, which tend to be materials and transport intensive, and generate little local employment.

Multi-functional playgrounds: The so-called 'multi-functional' playground refers to complex structures that allow continuous movement from one piece of equipment to another. However, these are usually little more than the traditional playground concept with a slight modification: a structure connects the different items of traditional equipment onto one framework. Thus, the activity itself is not integrated but sequential. Commercial versions of multi-functional play structures generally only facilitate physical development, and are usually very costly. Officials like them though, because they can be purchased off-the-shelf and installed by grounds staff, and they seldom generate local opposition, let alone attention.

Creative play environments: 'Creative play environments' include all outdoor play areas designed to facilitate 'free' play (that is, exploratory, representational and imaginative play). Their designers usually attempt to address issues like social interaction and communication, rather than just providing a structure for physical exercise. Also, some offer other functions in addition to play value. For example, they may serve as a tourist attraction or community focal point, which increases their usage and user security. They can be small, inexpensive structures designed to enhance a limited space, or big ones designed to create a total environment for families.

Playgardens: 'Playgardens' are one type of creative play environment. Here the natural features of the site, flora and fauna are employed to facilitate children's explorations of nature and of their capabilities in relation to the environment. Where there is little pre-existing vegetation, a garden can be created which is totally integrated with the play equipment. These gardens involve the use of structures, but these structures serve as inconspicuous props to enhance child development. Because organic playgardens are functionally integrated with the landscape and vegetation, they may be difficult to see.

Playgardens reintroduce the idea of nature as being an integral part of human life. They are botanical 'exploratoriums' that bring nature back into the human habitat, they situate child development in a more 'natural' environment, where before there may have only been paving or left-over urban space. The complex of structures, spaces and plant life also creates an efficient use of land (which is increasingly scarce in developed areas). Playgardens are a small symbol of what a human settlement could be – one physically and aesthetically integrated with the living environment. They stand in stark contrast to traditional playgrounds which mould children (like the corporate system moulds society) into relationships that are competitive, non-self reliant, and disconnected from nature.

Benefits of playgardens

Some other benefits of playgardens that result from design are as follows:

Social: The objective of most recreation planning by the private sector is to divide the market, and this often works to divide families in space and time. Unlike most toys and commercial recreation, playgardens can bring whole families and different age groups together (especially where the play environment is within the neighbourhood itself). Because playgardens are botanically complex, they are interesting enough for adults to explore too. By 'inviting' parents to play with children, playgardens not only bring families together, but encourage maximum usage, activity, and security (see Sutton 1991).

Personal: Today, ever more specialised recreational equipment and accessories are marketed, usually by associating athletic achievement with sexual or social

success. However, only the few most physically assertive children can excel in a particular event. In contrast, when we provide play environments for children, we are telling them they are important for being who they are, not for how they perform. Playgardens also lend themselves to children making 'cubbies' among the plants or engaging in quiet social play with other children.

Intellectual: Research of brain development in primates and other animals indicates that brain size is correlated with the amount of play engaged in by the young of the species. Further, contrary to earlier assumptions, there is little evidence that play in animals is practice for adult skills. Some researchers have suggested that spontaneous play (as opposed to organised sport) may actually increase the cognitive processes and connectedness of the 'wiring' of the brain, and enhance creativity (Furlow 2001).

Aesthetic: Sometimes residents oppose playgrounds in their immediate vicinity because they are unsightly and attract vandals. While such views may seem petty, this position should be respected, as most traditional playgrounds are ugly and tend to detract visually from the surrounding natural and built environments. Playgardens, on the other hand, do not conflict with the surrounding architectural setting because they blend into the (formal or informal) landscaping and thus complement the built environment.

Safety: Experts agree that the accident rate in traditional playgrounds is unacceptable. Risk taking is an inevitable part of physical development, yet falling on a 'hard' surface can cause serious injury. Playgardens, in contrast, provide positive outlets for physical challenge with far less risk. Bushes and natural ground cover in thick mulch generally prevent serious injury to children, while the plants usually recover without trauma. Also, vegetation can be placed strategically to slow children down and therefore reduce speed and collisions.

Physical: In a conventional playground, the 'passive' equipment, like roundabouts or swings, require parents to do most of the work. When the children use the traditional slide, the parent must first check it for cuts in the sheet metal, then stand underneath while the children climb up a dangerous ladder protruding from a concrete footing, and then run to catch them before they land in the mud puddle at the bottom. One wonders if the children enjoy the slide as much as watching their exasperated parents. In a playgarden, the equipment is designed for the children to do the physical exercise.

Design failure

Given our appreciation of the importance of play in child development today, and the extensive criticism of playground design over the past several decades, why has playground design not substantially improved over the last century?

Because the developmental and social aspects of play were undervalued, design for play was not taken seriously. Hence little thought, money, or energy was invested in the proper design of play environments (see Figure 5.4.1). Poor design in turn meant that playgrounds were under-utilised and, as a result, they were not considered good value. When play gradually came to be appreciated by child development specialists, this knowledge was not translated into design, because playgrounds had been stereotyped as a mere 'collection of swings and slides'. Hence, the initial design assumptions were not re-examined. Another problem is that children's outdoor areas seldom receive a share of maintenance budgets, while ample expenditures are devoted to outdoor tools, vehicles and flower gardens.

Figure 5.4.1: Playground design failure

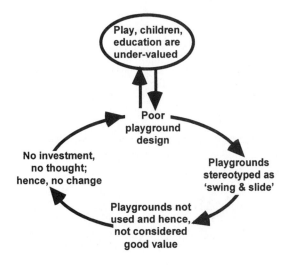

Attitudes toward nature

Children's emotional security and affinity with the natural environment is perhaps more important in shaping their disposition towards nature than their intellectual understanding of the environmental crisis. Most of the time, children are confined in artificial, highly structured environments which constrain their natural curiosity and movement. When children are denied meaningful early experiences in nature, it is arguably crippling to their personal development – comparable to being deprived of physical affection early in life.

No amount of intellectual or metaphysical teaching can inculcate a caring identification with nature: it must be felt. This is why many adults understand the environmental crisis intellectually, but do nothing. There is apparently no direct correlation between comprehending a problem and acting to resolve it. But while there may be no direct link between *knowing* and acting, there is a link between *caring* and acting. Research has established a link between the child's early experience of the natural environment and a caring and responsible attitude toward nature (Chawla 1988).

Challenging values

How do playgardens challenge patriarchal values and power structures?

First, at the political level, the process of overcoming barriers to implementing local, self-help, participatory projects serves to educate, politicise, and empower those who – if only by virtue of being new parents – are concerned with family, community building, and other non-commercial values. They begin to question why some who oppose creative play environments on grounds of *safety* do not hesitate to spend much more on soccer fields – which are less safe and more expensive, although made only of grass and dirt. They begin to question why some say there is no *money* for creative play environments on grounds that play is trivial and unimportant, but then turn around and spend millions on racetracks and casinos.

Also, the implementation of playgarden projects creates a vehicle for face-to-face relationships between parents and those in the power structure. They see first hand the hypocrisy of some bureaucrats who would rather protect their little 'turfdoms' than meet local community needs by working on an equal basis with ordinary citizens. Home-grown playgarden projects can empower parents while encouraging cooperative work, communal attitudes and self-reliance.

Community-built play environments challenge patriarchal values as well as structures and processes. In fact, they represent everything that is devalued in a capitalist society. They speak to women's and children's non-material needs; unstructured learning and unsupervised play; shared public open space and a sense of community; and art and nature that is not partitioned off from community life. Playgardens resist the categorisation of gender roles, and create a model of a society where nature, people, play, living, and working are spontaneous and integrated.

Conclusion

In challenging patriarchal values, structures, and processes, home-grown playgardens can be a form of direct action that can have as much potency and depth as 'radical' demonstrations or marches. While playgarden projects do not make sensational media events the process can enter deep into the fabric of the community. Thus, playgardens are a visual metaphor for both green values and eco-logical design.

References and further reading

Bengtsson, A. 1974, *The Child's Right to Play*, International Playground Association, Sheffield, UK.

Birkeland, J. 1985, 'Playground Design: Cliches and Common Sense', *Architecture Australia*, pp. 40–45 (reprinted in 1987, 'Playground Design', *Australian Parks & Recreation*, pp. 38–42).

Birkeland, J. 1994, 'Ecofeminist Playgardens: A Guide to Growing Greenies Organically', *International Play Journal* 2, pp. 49–59.

Cass, J. 1971, *The Significance of Children's Play*, Batsford, London.

Chawla, L. 1988, 'Children's Concern for the Natural Environment', *Children's Environments Quarterly* 6(3), pp. 13–20.

Dockett, S. and Lambert, P. 1996, *The Importance of Play*, Board of Studies, North Sydney, NSW.

Furlow, B. 2001, 'Play's the Thing', *New Scientist*, June, pp. 29–31.

Haagen, C. for the National Museum of Australia 1994, *Bush Toys: Aboriginal Children at Play*, Aboriginal Studies Press, Australian Institute of Aboriginal and Torres Strait Islander Studies, Canberra, ACT.

Hart R.A. with Espinosa, M.F., Iltus, S.R. and Lorenzo, R. 1997, *Children's Participation: The Theory and Practice of Involving Young Citizens in Community Development and Environmental Care*, Earthscan, London, UNICEF, New York.

Hughes, F.P. 1991, *Children, Play, and Development*, Allyn and Bacon, Boston, MA.

Huizinga, J. 1970, *Homo Ludens: A Study of the Play Element in Culture*, Temple Smith, London.

Johnson, J.E., Christie, J.F. and Yawkey, T.D. 1999, *Play and Early Childhood Development*, 2nd edn, Longman, New York.

Reilly, M., ed, 1974, *Play as Exploratory Learning: Studies of Curiosity Behavior*, Sage Publications, Beverly Hills, CA.

Rosebury, E.D., ed, 1998, *Child's Play: Revisiting Play in Early Childhood Settings*, MacLennan and Petty, NSW.

Smith, P.K., ed, 1986, *Children's Play: Research Developments and Practical Applications*, Gordon and Breach, New York.

Sutton, S. 1991, 'Creating a Safe Space in Which to Grow' in *Architecture! Back ... to ... Life*, Association of Collegiate Schools of Architecture, ACSA, Washington, DC.

Questions

1. Debate: 'Playgardens cannot effect children's attitude toward nature.'

2. Write a paragraph interpreting the phrase 'a few blades of grass can do as much to move concrete as a thousand marching feet' (in relation to points made in the chapter).

3. It was suggested that there is a correlation between caring and acting, but not between knowing and acting. Does this correspond with your own experience? Discuss.

4. Debate: 'Playgrounds are for kids, so the views of adults on aesthetic issues are not important.'

5. If children have been hurt falling from swings when they 'jumped off because they were bored', what is the cause of the injury: the design of the equipment or the child? What are some solutions?

6. In your memory, which play environments were the most significant to you as a child? Compare with the memories of others in the group. Are there any similarities?

Projects

1. Spend at least an hour at a designed play environment and at a traditional playground. Draw a sketch plan of the playground and chart the movements of children on the equipment and in relation to each other. Observe and compare how children play. Which appears to be the best design? Why?

2. Arrange for a classroom of young children to take notes and examine their school playground for possible safety defects. Ask them if they know of children that have been hurt on the playground and, if so, how they were injured. Find out if anything was done to correct the defects, and if not, why?

Box 13 Pros and Cons of Design Charrettes

Wendy Sarkissian, Andrea Cook and Kelvin Walsh

The charrette is a type of 'design-in'. It is a short and intensive planning/design action that attempts to reduce the length, cost and antagonistic nature of many planning processes. It brings together major stakeholders in a collaborative design exercise to produce concept plans and strategic documents/principles for major projects. Charrettes can be used to test new public policies or ideas on real sites, to engender responses to initiatives from government or neighbourhood groups or to identify opportunities which arise out of specific sites.

The process lasts between five and seven consecutive days. Aspects of a typical charrette include an initial public meeting, site visits, presentations from and consultation with stakeholders, intense facilitated design sessions and a final public meeting or meetings to present the results. A charrette may be appropriate where: (a) the project is an inherently legitimate one; (b) all major stakeholders are included in shaping outcomes; (c) an independent team exists with appropriate design, facilitation and technical skills, and (d) the client is committed to accepting the outcomes of the process.

It can be a valuable component in some consultation processes, but may not be suitable, for example, in large-scale projects such as districts, where people may not share concerns with others living at long distances. It may not ideal to begin a participatory process with such an event, however. Its values and limitations should be examined first:

Potentials

- Broadens horizons for local people to imagine and visualise and analyse a problem holistically.
- Graphics to depict ideas or decisions helps people envisage possibilities.
- Assists proponents to understand how proposals appear to the community.
- Identifies problems and differing attitudes and preferences of stakeholders to aid conflict resolution and consensus building.
- Multi-disciplinary teams can energise community participation by introducing new insights.
- The **transparent process** can give voice to all participants, even those who may be less self-assured and confident.
- The intensity of the process can stimulate community momentum and support for change.
- The promise of immediate feedback can encourage people to become actively involved.
- Community education can result through good facilitation and extensive community contact.
- The community can have input at a number of points in the process.
- Opportunities for later public review increase accountability.

Possible problems

- The compressed time period may limit participation by some who need more time to reflect and absorb the implications.
- Skilled use of graphics may cause some to feel the design is a 'fait accompli'.
- Only a limited number of people can work effectively in one place at one time.
- The compilation of base information and raising of community awareness of the process is costly.
- A developer or local interest group could manipulate or 'railroad' the process.
- Unrealistic expectations that outcomes will be quickly implemented could turn to cynicism later.
- Studio sessions that require ability to draw while interacting with others may be difficult for some.
- Geo-technical, socio-economic and environmental impact studies may not yet be well developed.
- Current processes have not included participation of teenagers or marginalised groups.
- The emphasis on present stakeholders' views may limit wider representation.
- If another statutory public consultation phase is required, duplication may occur.

6.1   Urban Forms and the Dominant Paradigm

Janis Birkeland

Different values and ethics flow from the philosophical foundations of the 'dominant paradigm' as opposed to that of an ecological or systems view. These values, in turn, lead to different approaches to planning, managing and designing the built environment and, as such, are reflected in the design of buildings, spaces and products. The relevance of theory becomes more apparent when we see how designers have unconsciously expressed elements of the dominant paradigm in the design of the built environment.

The dominant paradigm

The cultural, philosophical and structural roots of our unsustainable systems of development have been traced by various scholars to deeply rooted philosophical premises dating back thousands of years. However, the more immediate origins of the Western model of development and urban systems are found in the Industrial Revolution, as articulated in the work of Newton, Descartes and Bacon.

> *'Bacon developed methods and goals for science that involved (and involve) the domination and control of nature; Descartes insisted that even the organic world (plants, animals, etc) was merely an extension of the general mechanical nature of the universe; and Newton held that the workings of this machine-universe could be understood by reducing it to a collection of "solid, massy, hard, impenetrable, moveable particles"'.* (Dobson 1990, p. 38)

This way of understanding the world, which we can call the Newtonian–Cartesian–Baconian complex, became an integral part of the environmental management professions, institutions and decision-making systems [1.3]. It is generally not recognised, however, that these concepts are also manifested in the design of structures, products, landscapes and urban form. The elements of this complex are defined as follows (Box 6.1.1).

Elements of the Newtonian–Cartesian–Baconian complex are often found in critiques of the dominant paradigm. As a

whole, they are sometimes referred to as 'patriarchal' (see Table 5.1.1). While this world view and value system is now being challenged and is rapidly changing, the built environment still perpetuates these values, because conventional design has largely reflected culture. The following describes how the elements of this complex are reflected in the built environment.

The dominant paradigm and urban form

Linear progress: Before the industrial revolution in Europe, life was generally conceived of as a cyclical process, like the seasons. This was replaced by a concept of social 'progress' that implied a one-way, linear progression out of an earlier state of emersion in nature (Merchant 1980). Humanity was destined to strive to escape the chaos and uncertainty of life by controlling nature through technology. Progress gradually became an ultimate goal of human existence and was associated with freedom from natural constraints. Today, buildings are still celebrated as triumphs of human achievement for their technical mastery and control over nature. The urban environment has extirpated all but artificial and formalistic representations of Earth and Nature, in the apparent conviction that humans do not need contact with the natural environment. Urban form expresses a denial of human dependency on social and ecological support systems, and manifests the belief that we can ignore the ecological consequences of development with impunity. The architecture, landscape and urban design fields have, in effect, worked to reinforce the alienation of humans from the larger web of life.

Individual autonomy: Just as society was meant to strive for progress, or independence from natural constraints, the human (at least the male human) was meant to strive for 'freedom' or independence from social control. Human self-realisation meant becoming independent and autonomous, rather than submerged in community and nature, as was the case of most pre-industrial communities. Society, over time, came to be viewed more as a collection of individuals than as a whole community (a reductionist, atomistic conception of society known in political science as **liberalism**). These concepts of freedom and independence from society (as well as from nature) led to extreme ideologies, such as economic rationalism. This competitive egotism is to be found in the aesthetics of the urban environment. Most major buildings are attention seeking and often give deliberate visual expression to individualism, autonomy and competition. Ironically, this has led to a certain 'sameness' or monotony, such that few can identify different cities by their architecture.

Box 6.1.1: Newtonian–Cartesian–Baconian complex

- **Linear progress**: humanity is destined to transcend nature through technology and social control.

- **Individual autonomy**: people (at least elite white males) are meant to be independent, competitive and freedom seeking.

- **Essentialism**: the idea that humans have an 'essential nature', meaning that the ideal characteristics and values attributed to the (white male) elite are presumed to apply to humanity as a whole.

- **Reductionism**: the world can be understood as a composite of separate elements or entities, and problems are best solved by specialisation, simplification and abstraction.

- **Mechanism**: for most purposes, plants and animals are considered little more than (soulless) mechanisms, and engineering can substitute for natural processes.

- **Instrumentalism**: nature has value to the extent it is 'useful' and should therefore be harnessed in the service of humanity.

- **Hierarchical dualism**: the world can be understood as sets of opposites or dualisms, and one side (reason, power, control, masculinity) is given more value (see Table 5.1.1).

- **Anthropocentrism**: humans are considered the centre of life; therefore, the interests of animals and ecosystems are given little weight, and are largely viewed instrumentally as resources.

- **Linear causality**: consequences and impacts are seen to be linked to specific causes through linear (cause and effect) relationships and can thus be predicted and controlled.

Essentialism: The belief in progress, a kind of manifest destiny to be realised through technology, entailed a particular 'essentialist' notion of the nature of humankind. The human (white male archetype) was meant to be rational, authoritative and independent. This 'essentialist' view of 'man' became a fundamental – if often unspoken – premise of sociological, political and economic theories (Birkeland 1997). Office buildings in particular have been designed to fit this archetypal 'manikin'. That is, modernist buildings, like automotive design, could be said to honour this essential masculine ideal (rather than, say, celebrating life or nature). Similarly, much design is still misconceived as the autonomous creation of an autonomous designer when they are a product of large teams. 'Collaboration has not been a defining characteristic of "good" architecture even though it lies at the very foundation of design, development and construction' (Kingsley 1991). Design has been plagued by the 'star syndrome' where buildings, like clothing fashions, are judged by the prestige and individualism of the designer, as much as by that of the design.

Reductionism: The technological mastery of nature was associated with reductionist science (the belief that natural systems could be understood by focusing only on their basic elements). The success of early science and technology owed much to the practice of reducing problems to their parts and focusing on small understandable bits, such as forces and particles. Today, science can reproduce nature by cloning mice and sheep, but as some have observed, cannot yet create a successful biosphere. Because science and design have been dichotomised, (and design devalued) some design theorists try to emulate the (old) scientific method (perhaps to tap into some of its prestige) and attempt to reduce design to linear, formulistic processes. Similarly, many designers, like technicians, still work detached from the site. It is common practice to design from a bird's eye view and base complex development schemes on reductionist design concepts (like basing a whole design on public–private space distinctions or floor plan requirements). This leads to quite different results than would design that facilitates social diversity and interaction with the natural environment.

Mechanism: Early scientific discoveries and technical advances supported the presumption that nature is ordered, stable and hierarchically structured, or 'mechanistic', and thus replaceable by machines. This mechanistic notion is still reflected in biotechnology (Ho 1999), and the implicit view that parts of natural systems can be traded-off (that a plantation can replace a native forest, a water treatment plant can replace a watershed). Buildings have replaced natural systems with artificial heating, cooling, lighting and sewage systems, which have proven too costly in resources and energy. Mechanical systems are invariably less efficient and ecologically sustainable than natural systems. Moreover, people have been expected to accommodate the 'rational' designs of modernism. The failure to recognise humans as complex biological, emotional and social beings has contributed to sick building syndrome and lower employee productivity due to mechanical air conditioning, synthetic building and furniture materials and chemical pest control [7.3, 7.4]. Projections into the future are even more bleak: futuristic environments are usually portrayed to look like space ports on Mars, devoid of 'unruly' plants and 'dirty' animals.

Instrumentalism: The idea that nature can be reduced to simplistic processes and substituted by machines, reinforces the 'instrumentalist' view that nature is merely a resource for human needs and desires. Nature is 'used' for purposes of physical comfort and efficiency, or aesthetic pleasure and spirituality. When designs are described as 'working with nature', it usually means that nature provides a picture for windows to frame, a source of heat, light and air, protection from bugs, vermin and the forces of sun, wind, rain, or a backdrop against which to photograph buildings. This instrumental view also describes the 20th Century designer's regard for the users of buildings and products. In many ways, the built environment is still designed as if humans were mice in a maze – having only simple physical needs and senses. When designers concern themselves with the emotional needs of users, it is often to use those needs to manipulate people to behave in certain ways – like gambling or spending money (Birkeland 1995).

Heirarchical dualism: Modern architecture often reflects the dualisms of Western thought structures, where mind, culture and spirit are deemed of a higher order than the 'mundane' sphere of body, feelings and earth (Table 5.1.1). These dualisms are gendered and unbalanced, as the left side of each rung of the ladder is considered higher than the other. Nature and society are seen as separate spheres, while indigenous peoples and women (as a caste) have been devalued as being more emersed in nature, or less transcendent and autonomous. Design has been denigrated by its association with the feminine side of our lobotomised culture (as subjective, emotional, sensual) and ordinary craft has been marginalised as routine production or meaningless

ornamentation (Table 6.1.1). On the other hand, 'high art' is elevated by association with the masculine sphere of culture (transcendent, cerebral, spiritual). Artistic endeavours are often regarded as a 'higher' order, as if transcendent and apolitical. Yet ironically, 'high' art is very political: buildings and products (such as prestige cars and boats) have been designed in a way that projects status or power at the expense of ecological efficiency, public health and social responsibility.

Anthropocentrism: The nature–culture division in Western thought is a fundamental dualism reflected in our anthropocentric (human-centred) values. The growing realisation that culture and nature exist in an inseparable and reciprocal relationship has not found real expression in building design, let alone urban form. Most buildings are still designed as introverted boxes, which turn their back on nature as if nature were the opposite of civilisation. While educated designers are beginning to employ environmental management tools and life cycle analysis in design decisions [12.3], the buildings themselves still look much as before. Sustainable design 'has insufficiently considered how people derive a host of intellectual and emotional, as well as physical and material, benefits from connections with natural process and diversity' (Kellert 1999, p. 40).

Even suburban developments, which promise an escape to garden lifestyles, are little more than boxes in green moats symbolically protecting people from neighbors and untamed nature [6.2]. Housing models such as 'New Urbanism' 'unself-consciously help reinforce the injustices of environmental discrimination and trivialise ecological planning as a luxury item, analogous to organically grown produce in the grocery store' (Ingersoll 1996, p. 150). Seldom does community design represent a restructuring, or even a questioning, of the human's antagonistic relationship with nature. Traditional zoo design, for example, manifests a profound disregard for the life qualify of animals (see Polakowski 1987).

Linear causality: Because science has simplified things in order to understand them, there is a tendency to see problems as a result of single causes. Recently, an Australian city official declared that many road accidents were being caused by 'killer trees' that therefore needed to be removed from the sides of roads – not the alcohol or testosterone levels of drivers, not cars, not roads, but natural elements that get in the way. In a complex environment, such linear thinking has often led to solutions that have become problems in themselves. For example, a jail addition in Melbourne was designed to be vandal proof, but had to be dismantled a few years after construction (see Bessant et al 1995).

Environmental controls have been added on to traditional building forms that were dictated by structural and practical limitations that are no longer valid constraints. These controls such as mechanical heating and ventilating systems, have in turn created problems of air quality, noise and heat. Design must recognise and deal with complex and wide-open systems not by sterilising the natural environment, but by naturalising the built environment.

Table 6.1.2: Design paradigms

Pyramidal design *values*	Pyramidal design *devalues*
Linear	Cyclical
Hierarchical	Lateral
Mechanistic	Organic
Quantitative	Qualitative
Objective	Subjective
Reductionist	Holistic

Eco-logical design would represent a rebalancing of these two value systems

Conclusion

Art and architecture historians have examined the embodied values and concepts of buildings and artefacts for decades, but have paid little attention to how these creations reinforce the alienation of humans from the larger web of life. Human constructions create new environments or contexts (as well as artefacts) which alter existing social and natural relationships and provide both new opportunities for, and constraints upon, human and biotic communities. By analogy, useless vehicles are sometimes reused by placing them strategically in the ocean to help reefs to re-establish themselves and restore the aquatic environment. These artificial reefs can be seen as metaphors for eco-logical urban design, in that they create a means for diverse creatures to reproduce themselves and their environments, recreate communities and regenerate damaged ecosystems.

References and further reading

Bessant, J., Carrington, K. and Cook, S. 1995, *Cultures of Crime and Violence: The Australian Experience*, La Trobe University Press, Vic.

Birkeland, J. 1995, 'Ecophilosophy and the Built Environment', in *Pacific Visions: Ka Tirohaka o Te Moana-Nui-A-Kiwa, Ecopolitics VIII Conference*, Centre for Resource Management, Lincoln University, Canterbury, NZ, 8–9 July.

Birkeland, J. 1997, 'Values and Ethics', *Human Ecology, Human Economy*, Allen and Unwin, Sydney, NSW.

Dobson, A. 1990, *Green Political Thought*, Unwin Hyman, London.

Gaard, G., ed, 1993, *Ecofeminism: Women, Animals, Nature*, Temple University Press, Philadelphia, PA.

Ho, M.W. 1999, *Genetic Engineering: Dream or Nightmare?*, Gateway Books, Bath.

Ingersoll, R. 1996, 'Second Nature: On the Social Bond of Ecology and Architecture', in T. Dutton and L. Mann, eds, *Reconstructing Architecture: Critical Discourses and Social Practices*, University of Minnesota Press, Minneapolis, MN.

Keller, S.R. 1999, 'Ecological Challenge, Human Values of Nature and Sustainability in the Built Environment', in C.J. Kibert, ed, *Reshaping the Built Environment: Ecology, Ethics and Economics*, Island Press, Washington, DC.

Kingsley, K. 1991, 'Rethinking Architectural History from a Gender Perspetive', in T. Dutton and L. Mann, eds, *Reconstructing Architecture: Critical Discourses and Social Practices*, University of Minnesota Press, Minneapolis, MN.

Polakowski, K.J. 1987, *Zoo Design: The Reality of Wild Illusions*, University of Michigan, Ann Arbor, MI.

Merchant, C. 1980, *The Death of Nature: Women, Ecology, and the Scientific Revolution*, Harper and Row, New York.

Questions

1. Think back to your favourite environments in your childhood (tree house, garden, lake, bay window, class room, beach, TV room). Describe how it made you feel and why. Compare these adjectives to the list in the chapter.

2. How many ways can gardens and moving water be integrated into 'modern' office buildings to improve air quality and other amenities (eg atria)? Use sketches or diagrams.

3. List some of the possible reasons that Western culture has a tradition of 'great artists', whereas in some indigenous cultures everyone was an artist: eg the patronage of kings? the division of crafts and high culture? the money and power involved in contemporary architecture?

4. 'Architecture defines the barrier between humans and nature.' Discuss. How can the barrier be challenged through design?

5. Describe the design appeal of the motorcycle in terms of (so-called 'masculine') attributes and metaphors discussed in the chapter.

6. Debate: 'The built environment shapes our experiences with the natural environment and hence our attitudes towards nature.'

Projects

1. Look through recent architecture magazines and try to find buildings that exemplify each of the elements described as the 'Newtonian–Cartesian–Baconian complex'.

2. Many high-rise housing projects constructed in the 1960s were later torn down because they were being vandalised and destroyed by some of their occupants. Can this phenomenon (antagonism towards the built environment) be related to the elements described as 'Newtonian–Cartesian–Baconian complex'? Discuss.

Liz James and Janis Birkeland

Ecological housing initially referred to housing that conserved energy through passive solar design, and gradually included the use of low-impact materials and closed-loop water and waste systems. More recently, it has sometimes been suggested that ecological housing, by fostering the psychological health and well-being of its occupants, will also lead to enhanced care for the environment. However, in the context of social divisions and extremes of poverty and wealth, just how sustainable are these new, often expensive, ecological homes?

Introduction

Shelter is a fundamental human need, but how this need is satisfied in developed nations is largely culturally determined. As the design of habitats tends to reflect the social order, designers need to be aware of the role that housing plays in maintaining a sometimes materialistic, competitive and power-based society. Even 'green' housing designs are seldom responsive to wider social justice imperatives, such as **environmental space** [people's fair share of the Earth's resources]. Though many new ecological homes reduce pollution and embodied energy per unit of material or energy used, they are nonetheless resource and energy intensive per capita. Further, both housing design and settlement patterns can reinforce gendered and inequitable power relationships (Roberts 1991; Weisman 1992; Wajcman 1991). As a template, ecological homes do little to challenge conventional (suburban) settlement patterns: they segregate the rich from poor, home from work, and individuals from community and nature.

As inequitable social structures are incompatible with ecological sustainability and environmental justice, it follows that the current model of suburban housing arguably impedes social transformation. If this is case, an entirely new conception of housing may be a necessary part of the transformation to a sustainable society. This new form of housing must not only be eco-efficient, but foster cultural and biological diversity, assist dematerialisation and ecological restoration, promote health and well-being, discourage consumerism and contribute to community

building. The following evaluates two basic models of eco-housing against criteria that are derived from (predominantly feminist) critiques of housing.

The home and culture

Before examining ecological homes, it is necessary to provide a capsule overview of some of the studies of the home in its social, political and historical context.

Housing design and settlement patterns have responded, broadly speaking, to social imperatives, even when mediated by formal planning and public policy. One such fundamental imperative was the Industrial Revolution, which was facilitated by the '... new sexual and social division of labour, the division between production and reproduction, production and consumption, work and life' (Mies and Shiva 1993, p. 146). These gendered dualisms served the needs of a new social order: women became increasingly depicted as weak, dependent and sentimental, while rationality, autonomy and individualism were celebrated as the achievement of male maturity (Table 5.1.1, p. 96). Just as the female role was seen as dependent but supportive (Gilligan 1982, p. 23), the 'home' was sentimentalised as a 'feminine' refuge from the labours of the masculine public sphere; a haven to which the modern man could escape to renew himself.

The noise, dirt and pollution of industrialisation led to the further spatial segregation of home and work, deemed necessary to maintain social morals and healthy living conditions (Davison 1993, pp. 3–4). The home also came to represent a moral counterpoint to the world of economics and politics (which became reified as the 'real' world of male exploits). The depiction of women as the soft, moral and caring gender belonging to the private sphere (in contrast with a supposedly 'hard', pragmatic and decisive gender), rationalised the abdication of an ethic of care and nurture in the (masculinised) public sphere. This has tended to relieve decision makers in the public arena of the responsibility for not just personal care, but for the more basic necessities of life.

Feminists have argued that the concept of 'home' itself became an embodiment of Western patriarchal culture. The public/private, work/home divisions meant that human dependency on both home and nature – the bases of sustenance, maintenance and reproduction – was obscured. In turn, a domestic idyll developed which contributed to the conception of women as a resource or support base, subservient to Man's needs in a valorised public sphere. This further devalued the 'feminine' by association with domesticity.

The growing division between work/home and the public/ private spheres was later reinforced by the early 20th Century concept of technical rationality, which encouraged an even 'more strictly defined and specialised division of sexual labour' (Greig 1995, p. 124). The notion of scientific motherhood emphasised clinical standards of hygiene, and the 'moral and caring' woman was transformed by the new home economics into the 'efficient' housewife that was glamourised in advertising of the 1940s. The domestic science and modern childcare movements contributed further to the growing disassociation of people from natural processes and human necessity (Roberts 1991).

The devaluation of the values of intimacy and nurturing associated with the home was also compounded by the emergence of the **Fordist** regime of accumulation and mass production after the First World War. The suburban home was integral to the success of such a divided production/ consumption system, and it became a container for the accumulation of new consumer items. Advertising rose to a central role in encouraging domestic consumption. By targeting the idealised notion of the home and the ideal of the modern housewife, advertising campaigns reinforced these 'domestic' stereotypes. In the process, advertising trivialised and marginalised women and what are considered 'feminine' values in a patriarchal society.

Suburban conformity, by backgrounding the domestic support system and denying its diversity, further reinforced women's lower status as a caste. The 'suburban imperative', as an expression of individual autonomy, has also substantially contributed to the demise of the concept of community (Greig 1995). The insularity and uniformity of the suburban home reinforces a false sense of autonomy, where the market – rather than the community – is seen to provide for basic needs. In fact, suburban housing could be seen as a manifestation of market relationships. With a growing sense of anonymity, social interactions have

increasingly become based on instrumental, exchange relationships (Ife 1996). This has culminated in a trend towards walled suburbs and a 'domestic fortress mentality' (especially those suburbs surrounded by major traffic thoroughfares).

Themes in housing literature

There are several implicit and interrelated themes that emerge from the above snapshots of the literature. These can be used to create criteria against which to examine the current models of eco-housing:

1. **Hierarchical dualisms:** A devaluation of the domestic sphere and women where both are defined as subservient to the dominant public, 'masculine' culture. This devaluation of the activities of the home and homemakers represents a denial of dependency on the basis of reproduction and sustenance – nature.

2. **Groundedness:** The public-private dualism separates the morality of home (necessity, maintenance and responsibility for others) from that of work (power seeking, independence and competition). Further, those well placed in the public sphere are impacted less directly by the environmental consequences of their decisions.

3. **Interdependence:** The marginalisation of community through the creation of introverted suburbs and atomistic domiciles undermines the sense of interdependency, awareness of the effect one's actions have on others, and the possibility of positive, symbiotic relationships among humans, or between humans and nature.

4. **Consumerism:** The repetition of homes in islands of grass surrounded by pavement duplicates services, appliances, products, furnishings and fixtures – wasting space, materials and energy. Such duplication also fosters competition, materialism and conspicuous consumption.

5. **Social divisions:** The above four themes indicate how our contemporary models of housing – whether eco-efficient or not – reflect power relations that militate against environmental justice and hence sustainability. Also, the permanent allocation of land (essentially on a first-come, first-served basis) has meant that much real wealth is attributable to capital and wealth accumulation (and inflation) across generations, rather than to personal effort.

Since the 1960s, various models of eco-housing have been developed by both professional and 'lay' people interested in appropriate technology and alternative ways of living – although mainstream society has largely ignored such initiatives. While there may be substantial overlaps, eco-housing divides easily into two fundamental approaches to sustainability – technical ('nuts and bolts') and organic ('nuts and berries'). How do these approaches to ecological housing measure up against the above five criteria?

The 'nuts and bolts' model

The more technical, 'nuts and bolts' approach developed in response to the recognition of the limits to fossil fuel resources, and has perhaps been the most influential. Often called passive solar or bioclimatic design, it addresses sustainability primarily through the efficient use of energy (Vale and Vale 1991). With a growing awareness of the environmental impacts of building materials, this response has been extended to encompass a more comprehensive approach based on life cycle analysis. The following paragraphs assess this style of ecological housing against the above five criteria.

Hierarchical dualisms: This technical approach relies on science and technology to provide discrete solutions to narrowly defined problems (Ife 1996), such as the development of solar cells for domestic power generation. As such, it does not challenge the devaluation of what patriarchal society has defined as 'feminine' values, or the imbalance toward linear, reductionist 'rationality'. Consequently, such homes often have a cold, cubist, mechanistic aesthetic that excludes natural elements and plants.

Groundedness: As passive solar homes do not rely on mechanical heating and cooling, occupants must participate in the operation of passive systems. In making adjustments to features like ventilation and shading devices, the users (theoretically) become more attuned to diurnal and seasonal changes. While this may be a disincentive to their use, it fosters awareness of human dependence upon natural processes and weather.

Interdependence: Proponents of this model often aim for physical 'resource autonomy', seeking to draw all water and energy from the site. This form of independence from community infrastructure (ie pipeless, wireless housing) is perhaps a prerequisite of sustainable housing. However, most examples of eco-housing do not challenge the atomistic residential settlement pattern – with its duplication of products and created demand for private transport (see Mobbs 1989).

Consumerism: This tradition values efficiency, but its advocates have generally tried to sway the public by promising greater material standards of living through eco-efficiency. The duplication of products (lawn mowers, hair dryers, washing machines) are seldom addressed, which counteracts efficiencies achieved by eco-logical design features.

Social divisions: These technologically advanced homes are generally only available to elites. As status symbols, their market price can escalate out of the reach of average citizens, even when they cost less to build than traditional homes. However, this is gradually being remedied by legislated energy standards that apply to all homes, not just new ones.

The 'nuts and berries' model

Disenchantment with capitalist values in the 1960s and early 1970s prompted an 'alternative lifestyle' movement in Western nations. This led to the establishment of many intentional communities that practiced more self-sufficient and integrated ways of living. Housing associated with this alternative movement, the 'nuts and berries' approach, addresses sustainability through more 'natural' lifestyles and personal transformation, to '... heal ourselves and, in the process, heal the planet' (Pearson 1989, p. 8). This model of eco-housing often entails a spiritual dimension which has affinities with the **deep ecology** movement (Kanuka-Fuche 1991, pp. 7–16; Pearson 1989, p. 28; Baggs and Baggs 1996, pp. 14–15). The proponents of this approach suggest that the design of the home should embody principles such as those set out in the Gaia House Charter – design for the health of the body, for the peace, for the spirit, and for harmony with the planet (Pearson 1989, pp. 40–41). Does this style stand up better against the above five criteria?

Hierarchical dualisms: The emphasis on the home as the centre of a 'new awareness' indicates a revaluation of the domestic realm, even if the home is still seen as a personal and spiritual haven. By offering an integrated 'good life', it should help to heal the split morality of the public–private division (though work and home may remain physically separate for many occupants).

Groundedness: Natural materials and environmental controls, and the engagement of all the human senses (and sometimes **Feng Shui** principles), are employed to create a spiritual connection to nature. This is considered to provide '... direct pathways towards the goal of caring for the earth' (Baggs and Baggs 1996, p. 14). Once we learn to 'optimise health, beauty and conservation of the Earth's resources, the practices we institute can be extrapolated to society at large' (p. 16). But while proponents of this method advocate a moral perspective, it is entirely unclear how this will affect the lives of the disadvantaged to any measurable extent.

Interdependence: The nurturing of a 'sense of place', integral to this organic approach, does promote attachment to the particular, and a feeling of connection. Also, the house is often portrayed as an ecosystem or recycling system by advocates of this model. However, it is still generally designed as an autonomous physical and social unit, and dependency on community is de-emphasised. The family is still a tribe that potentially competes for status or wealth.

Consumerism: Living 'as one with nature' is largely only in spirit, as many of these model ecological homes express materialism, elitism and ample leisure time. Regardless of how little energy these may consume, the Earth cannot support this amount of consumption and space for everyone (with the exception, perhaps, of very low-impact 'hippy' versions).

Social divisions: In this model, change relies on transformation at an individual level (rather than at the social and institutional level). Encouraging people to live the good life while tending only to their own gardens can reinforce the concept that they are only responsible for their own direct impacts. The concept of personal change through identification with the larger whole of nature, or Gaia, could also be said to reflect '... the familiar masculine urge to transcend the concrete world of particularity in preference for something more enduring and abstract' (Kheel 1990, p. 136) — and thus excuse one from the hard work of communication and social change. Those living the good life must take affirmative action to change the system which prevents others from enjoying such elegant living.

Conclusion

These two basic models of ecological housing are admirable, but they have not yet achieved their transformative potential. These designs do not address the power structures and resultant spatial patterns that perpetuate poverty, social alienation and environmental inequities. Further, their design seldom challenges the tradition of architecture as a barrier between human and natural environments. If human demands are to respect the limits of nature, a fundamental shift in living patterns is required. The home can play a pivotal role in the transformation towards

sustainability, through the development of self-sufficient lifestyles, community building and the fostering of non-patriarchal values (White 1990; Plant 1990). However, in order to create transformative homes and settlements, designers will need to undertake more rigorous intellectual work. This will include rethinking the concepts of domestic life, work, reproduction, the division of labour, and the private/public, nature/culture, mind/body dualisms and other vestiges of the dominant paradigm that are still manifested in even eco-housing design.

References and further reading

Baggs, S. and Baggs, J. 1996, *The Healthy House*, HarperCollins, Sydney, NSW.

Davison, G. 1993, *The Past and Future of the Australian Suburb*, Urban Research Program, Research School of Social Sciences, ANU, Canberra, ACT.

Gilligan, C. 1982, *In a Different Voice: Psychological Theory and Women's Development*, Harvard University Press, Cambridge, MA.

Greig, A. 1995, *The Stuff Dreams are Made of: Housing Provision in Australia 1945–1960*, Melbourne University Press, Carlton, Vic.

Ife, J. 1996, *Community Development: Creating Community Alternatives – Vision, Analysis and Practice*, Addison Wesley Longman, Melbourne, Vic.

Kanuka-Fuche, R. 1991, 'Building Biology and Bio Harmonic Architecture – Healthy, Harmonious and Ecologically Sound', in R. Kanuka-Fuche, ed, *Building Biology and Ecology New Zealand 6: Bio harmonic design*.

Kheel, M. 1990, 'Ecofeminism and Deep Ecology: Reflections on Identity and Difference' in I. Diamond and G.F. Orenstein, eds, *Reweaving the World: the Emergence of Ecofeminism*, Sierra Club Books, San Francisco, CA.

Mies, M. and Shiva, V. 1993, *Ecofeminism*, Spinifex, Melbourne, VIC.

Mobbs, M., 1998, *Sustainable House*, Choice Book, Sydney, NSW.

Pearson, D. 1989, *The Natural House Book*, HarperCollins, Sydney, NSW.

Plant, J. 1990, 'Searching for Common Ground: Ecofeminism and Bioregionalism' in I. Diamond and G.F. Orenstein, eds, *Reweaving the World: the Emergence of Ecofeminism*, Sierra Club Books, San Francisco, CA.

Roberts, M. 1991, *Living in a Man-Made World: Gender Assumptions in Modern Housing Design*, Routledge, London.

Vale, B. and Vale, R. 1991, *Green Architecture*, Thames and Hudson, London.

Wajcman, J. 1991, *Feminism Confronts Technology*, Allen & Unwin, Sydney, NSW.

Weisman, L. 1992, *Discrimination by Design*, University of Illinois Press, Urbana, IL.

White, D. 1990, 'Bringing the Point Home', in K. Dyer and J. Young, eds, *Changing Directions, The Proceedings of Ecopolitics* IV, University of Adelaide, SA.

Questions

1. Can a new model of housing foster greater ecological awareness? How?

2. Discuss the following quote in relation to housing: 'The rich should live simply so that the poor may simply live' (Trainer).

3. 'Passive' solar homes are said to require 'active' occupants. Why?

4. Some people criticise the suburbs, but many also prefer suburban living. What factors could explain this dichotomy? Do you think that most people who were raised in suburban home environments are happy and comfortable living in the suburbs when they grow up?

5. Typical housing plans have changed over the years. One notable change is the increased size of kitchens, which are often linked to family rooms. What factors might have contributed to this: TV? The feminist movement? Increasing affluence? Discuss.

6. 'The design of suburbs isolates and disempowers home makers.' Is this statement as true today as it may have been a few decades ago? What factors could influence the social impacts of suburbs on home makers.

Projects

1. Some greens favour urban decentralisation while others favour consolidation (also called compact cities) [8.3, 8.4]. The apparent contradiction is explained by different assumptions about how these two strategies would be designed, developed and implemented. Set out the basic factors in each case that would ensure each strategy were ecologically sound.

2. In small groups, come up with design ideas that can integrate plants, natural lighting and outdoor access for medium-density urban housing. Use diagrams and sketches to convey these ideas to other groups.

Box 14   Adaptable Housing

Robert Moore

Adaptable housing is that which can accommodate anyone over time; that is, it allows for diverse needs, lifestyles and ages in the future as well as the present. The provision for future changes to the house plan are incorporated into the design, so that changes or additions can be made at a later date without costly structural alterations. Adaptable housing will require a fundamental shift in the thinking of developers, builders and designers, who generally focus on the current preferences of the immediate user groups or clients.

Adaptable housing should not be considered an added requirement, cost, or tax on the construction industry because, through good design, it should be cost-neutral – or even profitable. There is a minimal cost outlay involved in incorporating principles of adaptable housing with a potentially high financial return. This is due to an increasing demand for flexible design as awareness grows about the costs of having to relocate to more suitable accommodation as one's family and life circumstances change.

When people think of adaptable housing, they generally think of issues like unimpeded access and circulation spaces for people with disabilities, or the provision of handrails in bathrooms and toilets for the elderly. However, these considerations should be provided in all housing – as standard practice. In fact, the principles that apply to design for such special groups usually apply to other people as well, such as:

- Providing for privacy, security and safety.
- Ensuring good lighting where required.
- Creating thermal comfort through natural means, such as solar access, wind protection, and natural ventilation.
- Providing for the supervision requirements of parents or carers.
- Maximising the relationship between the internal and (natural) external environment.

- Recommended operating controls and fixtures.
- The provision for personal space.
- Ensuring the entire house and site are accessible by the disabled.
- Adaptability – the provision to incorporate future modifications at minimum cost.

The above criteria (which are only a representative sampling) generally need to be applied at the initial planning concept stage. What becomes immediately evident is the importance of planning for intended future modifications, which could be thought of as 'reverse construction'. The following is one example of planning for adaptability:

- The wall between the bathroom and the WC should not support any structural load, nor should it contain any electrical or plumbing services. It is preferable to add this wall as a removable partition after the floor, walls and ceiling have been finished, complete with relevant cornices and skirtings.

- During construction it is advisable to add wall sheeting (12mm plywood) behind the conventional sheeting for walls that may require future grab-rails or a shower seat.

- P traps to toilet pans are recommended because they permit easier relocation of the pan further out from the wall, if required for a wheelchair user. Decomposting toilets need to be at ground level.

- The bathroom floor should be waterproofed for a horizontal distance of 1.5m from the shower rose, irrespective of any shower screen. This allows removal of the screen (and hob) for a possible future wheelchair shower area.

- The kitchen cupboards should be constructed after the floor surfacing has been finished right through to the walls. The units should then be assembled to allow sections to be removed below the bench top for wheelchair and for the height adjustment of the bench tops.

Sam Davidson

Mass market toys are often criticised for the values and behaviours they encourage in young children, including consumerism, violence and gender typecasting. Given the power of design to influence preferences, designers need to continually question their own attitudes and motivations. Designers also need to consider effects on user groups for whom products are designed, and accept responsibility as contributors to children's social development.

Criticisms of toys

Toy design has been subject to criticism on several counts. For example, it has been alleged that toys actively promote consumerism, individualism, and gender-stereotyped role play. It has also been argued that they encourage domineering relationships and violence among children. Some of these criticisms are canvassed below, before considering the extent to which design influences children's preferences.

Consumerism

Some researchers contend that children's play has become 'commoditised', such that children are encouraged to own ever more toys. The toy industry and the media have been intimately associated for mutual commercial benefit. Children's television serves the marketing functions of introducing new heroes or personalities into children's culture and then leading children to use those characters in play (Kline 1993, p. 280). Consumerism is also encouraged by the cross-promotion of toys, such as 'Beenie Babies' or figurines, which advertise McDonald's, Pizza Hut or other chain stores which, in turn, promote the toys (Varney 1997).

Toys inspire a certain type of play and, in cases of over-structured toys, the avenues for play are narrowed (Varney 1997). As diversity of use in play is diminished through over-specialisation, more toys and accessories are required to maintain the child's interest. Toys that rely heavily on props, such as accessories and other characters in the same line, are a popular method by which designers increase the commercial potential of a range of products. Further, it is argued, a toy's lack of creative play value 'encourages an acquisitive, throwaway mentality' (Stern and Schoenhaus 1990).

Some toys, such as the 'Let's go shopping? Barbie' and the 'Mall Madness' game promote gratifying behaviour that makes 'an extravagantly wasteful and consumerist society seem natural' (Varney 1997, p. 10). The promotion of vanity, fashion and shopping is common in girls' toys such as the Barbie range by Mattel, where activities include beautification and preening, hairdressing, bedroom socialising and baby care (Varney 1997, p. 12). Identification with the fashion industry ideology is nurtured by the content of Barbie magazine, with pre-pubescent girls modelling the latest in clothing trends. This encouragement of materialistic ambitions in the young arguably undermines hope for a change in future consumption patterns (see Rosenblatt 1999).

Gender stereotyping

Toys are often targeted at separate markets defined by gender, and their designs encourage behaviour associated with traditional gender roles or stereotypes. These gender stereotypes associate masculinity with action, assertiveness and outdoor activity, and associate femininity with passivity, self-reflexiveness, and concern with an interior, decorative world (Buckley 1996; Whiteley 1993). Gender stereotypes in design are strikingly apparent in toy stores where, for example, toys for boys involve the use of tools for construction, while doll-houses for girls feature a mother/daughter picture on the packaging and boast 'no assembly required'.

The popular Lego range (and Duplo for younger children up to five years) are widely considered as 'unisex' products; however, the play-sets portray females as nurses, rather than doctors, or as engaged in activities such as ironing, vacuuming, child care and beautification. A particular Lego product aimed at girls (through pink packaging) features an outdoor refreshment bar where a female serves a male on his return from a bike ride.

A new rival for Barbie, named Sailor Moon, has been introduced via an associated television cartoon series. Considered to be a major improvement on Barbie in the area of intelligence, Sailor Moon still portrays an unrealistic and questionable feminine image of anorexic proportions (Molitorisz 1997, p. 11). While Action Man has up to 20 movable joints, and some versions have even included (anatomically impossible) movable biceps, Barbie usually only has joints where the head and limbs meet the body (Attfield 1996, p. 84). Exceptions to this convention were introduced when Barbie began to play golf and tennis; however, Attfield notes that these additions only enhance Barbie's ability to pose for which she was designed.

Individualism

Toys are considered by some researchers to encourage a shift in the focus of children's play from the development of relationships with others to relationships with the toy. Due to the market-oriented approach to toy design, 'toys are reshaping play towards less imaginative and more solitary activity' (Varney 1997, p. 13). Such toys discourage the development of social interaction skills such as cooperation. Varney argues that to the extent toys become a substitute friend and teacher of social roles, this may work against the development of an understanding of interdependency and cooperative relationships with others through interactive social play (p. 10). It could be said that children are being taught to communicate with products (toys) in place of people. Further gender specific toys commonly discourage children of different sexes from playing together, fostering a trend towards individualised play.

Violence

Another frequent criticism is that 'war toys' targeted at boys may encourage aggressive behaviour (MacNaughton 1996). Researchers have observed that play associated with these toys often involves repetition of the story-lines of related television shows that feature violence (Levin and Carlsson-Paige 1995). The deregulation of children's broadcasting in the US has made it possible for manufacturers to make television programs directly related to toys (Levin and Carlsson-Paige 1995, p. 68). Further, toys that encourage violent play are usually very specialised or over-structured, in that their visual appearance is so detailed that they foster play specific to their obvious use, rather than more imaginative interpretations (Levin and Carlsson-Paige 1995).

The toy industry is aware of the above criticisms about how toys play a part in child development. A typical response is: 'We are not in the business of setting values for children. It's a question of giving them what they want, so long as it's not illegal, harmful or unwholesome' (Bullivant 1993, p. 25). In any case, the solution may not be as simple as placing responsible toys on the shelves, as toy design for the mass market is always subservient to its marketability (Varney 1997). Often, toys that have been introduced as a result of concerns raised by parents have not met with commercial success (Attfield 1996). This may be partly because children often select their own toys, and parental values and concerns are undermined by advertising. Often, the media bypasses parents through the direct targeting of pre-school age children in television advertising. Advertisers realise that children are consumers with considerable purchasing power, due to their persuasiveness within the family, and thus target children with direct advertising from a very young age (Hendershot 1996).

The position of the industry suggests that it is not enough to design toys that promote good values; the determinants of children's preferences must also be considered by designers.

Toy design and children's preferences

Designers of products for children need to familiarise themselves with the research into how children's preferences are formed, and how the development of children's values is influenced by socialisation from external influences such as parents, peers, toys and the media (Almquist 1994). The jury is out, but it would appear that toys are accepted as being an integral part of children's socialisation. While the literature on the formation of children's preferences cannot be summarised completely here, some views are canvassed below.

Parents: The influence of parents on a child's toy preferences and understandings of appropriate gender behaviour is widely believed to be most significant factor. Parents, for example, may wish to select sex-neutral toys on principle; however, their own values are influenced by gender and other social norms and advertising as well (Almquist 1994). Studies suggest that boys are more often discouraged from playing with cross-gender toys by parents than girls. This may partly explain a tendency for boys to favour more sex-specific toys than girls (Almquist 1994). In a study by McGuire (1982), it was found that 'fathers held clearly delineated ideas about which toys and activities were suitable for either sex child', and that '... girls often experienced the kind of situations which accentuated male power over them, with fairly firm guidelines about how they should behave' (Butterworth 1991).

Figure 6.3.1: Circularity of influences

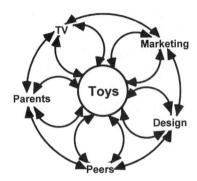

Gender identity: Regardless of the sources of gender identity, gender identity is reinforced through play itself. '... play is assumed to be the prime scenario where children portray their conceptions of male and female roles in society, as well as their own gender identity and understanding of sex-role behaviours; not least through their toy choices and play patterns' (Almquist 1994, p. 62). According to Almquist, children's toy preferences are usually sex-typical throughout childhood: children usually prioritise their choice of toy around sex-appropriateness, rather than characteristics such as the activity level and type of play involved (1994, p. 70). Taking a somewhat different view, Kline surmises from the results of studies conducted with children that they do not base their preferences on perceived differences between the sexes. Today, they believe it is 'all right' to play with cross-gender toys; however, they simply prefer not to (Kline 1993, p. 342). But while it is difficult to determine exactly why children prefer toys 'suited' for their own gender, it seems that most toys available to children are associated with one gender only. This limited choice is a result of designers' decisions.

Packaging: Toy catalogues and packaging designs flag which gender the toy is intended for. Packaging is an extension of gender-specific design, and probably serves to bolster children's existing sex-typed preferences (Almquist 1994). Gender-specific images and the use of strong contrasts in colour range – such as pinks and pastels for girls, and strong red, black and blue for boys – enforce unmistakable messages of gender appropriateness. Boys and girls are rarely pictured playing together. Kline suggests that toy designers and advertisers are well aware that children are

less concerned with the particular attributes of a toy, or the type of play it will involve, than its image or symbolic design content (1993). If so, then designers have scope for design decisions in packaging and advertising that avoid sex stereotyping in their use of image and symbolism.

Conclusion

It would appear from the above views that the issue of children's preferences is circuitous and complex (Figure 6.3.1). Toys have become increasingly dominant in child's play, and toy design has been shown to influence the nature of play and socialisation. Considering the complex nature of children's relationships with parents, peers, TV and the market, however, one cannot regard children as passive recipients of the values communicated by designers (Hendershot 1996, p. 8). Given the many factors in children's preference formation, it might seem reasonable for designers to feel that constructive design intervention will have little impact.

Conversely, this complex range of influences could also be taken to mean that designers have even more opportunities for influencing the market. If designers view their role in society more broadly, they cannot claim to be innocent victims of market forces. Designers can work collectively to create public awareness and bring their influence to bear – as parents, consumers and citizens, as well as designers. To be 'passive' about how design influences social values and relationships is to be actively complicit in the existing problem. For a start, the design profession can challenge the toy industry's failure to acknowledge and accept responsibility for its influence on children's socialisation and toy preferences.

References and further reading

Almquist, B. 1994, *Approaching the Culture of Toys in Swedish Child Care*, Stockholm, Sweden.

Attfield, J. 1996, 'Barbie and Action Man: Adult Toys for Girls and Boys 1959–93', in J. Attfield and P. Kirkham, eds, *The Gendered Object*, Manchester University Press, Manchester, pp. 80–89.

Buckley, C. 1996, 'Children's Clothes: Design and Promotion', in J. Attfield and P. Kirkham, eds, *The Gendered Object*, Manchester University Press, Manchester, pp. 103–111.

Bullivant, L. 1993, 'Playing to Win', *Design*, June, pp. 23–25.

Butterworth, D. 1991, 'Gender Equity in Early Childhood: The State of Play', *Australian Journal of Early Childhood* 16(4), pp.3–8.

Hendershot, H. 1996, 'Dolls, Odour, Disgust, Femininity and Toy

Design', in J. Attfield and P. Kirkham, eds, *The Gendered Object*, Manchester University Press, Manchester, pp. 90–102.

Kline, S. 1993, *Out of the Garden: Toys, TV and Children's Culture in the Age of Marketing*, Verso, London.

Levin, D. and Carlsson-Paige, N. 1995, 'The Mighty Morphin Power Rangers: Teachers Voice Concerns', *Young Children*, September, pp. 67–72.

MacNaughton, G. 1996, 'Is Barbie to Blame? Recognising how Children Learn Gender', *Australian Journal of Early Childhood*, 21(4), pp. 18–24.

Molitorisz, S. 1997, 'Turning Japanese', *Good Weekend*, May 17, p. 11.

Rosenblatt, R. 1999, *Consuming Desires: Consumption, Culture and the Pursuit of Happiness*, Island Press, Washington, DC.

Stern, S. and Schoenhaus, T. 1990, in S. Kline, ed, 1993, *Out of the Garden: Toys, TV and Children's Culture in the Age of Marketing*, Verso, London, p. 316.

Varney, W. 1997, 'Toys and Participation', in B. Martin, ed, 1999, *Participation and Technology*, Technology and Public Participation, University of Wollongong, NSW.

Video Classroom 1992, in G. MacNaughton, 1996, 'Is Barbie to Blame? Recognising How Children Learn Gender', *Australian Journal of Early Childhood* 21(4), p. 19.

Whiteley, N. 1993, *Design for Society*, Reaktion Book, London.

Questions

1. List and describe your favourite toys that you had as a child. Did your preferences reflect gender identification? If you played 'cowboy or Indians', did you prefer to play a cowboy or an Indian? Discuss.

2. Debate: 'Children will unthinkingly soak up all the gender messages implied in the product's design.'

3. How can the design of children's toys continue to influence consumerist behaviour when they become adults?

4. Should the advertising of toys on children's TV programs be allowed? Why or why not?

5. List reasons for and against an independent Design Review Board for children's toys.

6. Specify criteria that a Design Review Board would use in assessing toys.

Projects

1. Design and make a toy that you think is gender neutral. Arrange to have it displayed at a childcare centre, or appropriate school level, and determine whether girls or boys prefer it equally. If there is a difference in preference by gender, try to determine why.

2. If you were going to design a toy that incorporated positive social values, how would you ascertain children's preferences? Work individually to develop a method. Compare and critique strategies. Based on this evaluation, develop a strategy for determining preferences.

Box 15   The Rebound Effect

David Harrison, with Ann Marie Chalkley, Eric Billett

Designers need to think about the rebound effect: if people save money using a more efficient product, what is to prevent them from spending the savings on more products?

A key method to reduce environmental impact of a product is to make it more energy or resource efficient. However, the improved efficiencies are often partially negated by increased use of the product. For example, up to 20% of potential energy savings from improved fuel economy in cars is lost in increased travel.

The rebound effect has been discussed by a number of authors, including Radermacher, who defines it as 'the subsequent erosion of the positive potential of technological innovation by increases in overall activities, and the concomitant increase in consumption of material and energy'. The effect is particularly clear in products that have been made 'greener' by reducing their energy consumption during use: by reducing energy consumption, pollution and natural resource use is often also reduced, but the resulting lower running costs may encourage greater use of the product. Further, if a user reduces costs by using a more energy efficient product, it is likely that as well as increasing their use of that product, they will spend the saved money on other products or services which themselves may be significant users of energy. Thus the net effect of the more energy efficient product on the total consumption of energy may be limited.

Although the *local* rebound effect within a product has been described and quantified, there has been little investigation of the *global* rebound effect in which benefits gained by improvements to one product or service are, in part, negated by increased use of another. A case study below examines the extent of this effect in the sphere of consumer products.

Condensing boiler case study

Comparing gas bills from a house before and after a standard boiler (seasonal efficiency of 70%) was replaced by a condensing type boiler (seasonal efficiency 92%), it is possible to calculate the fuel savings.

Annual cost of fuel for standard boiler = £301.24

Annual cost of fuel for condensing boiler = £190.86

Assuming the boilers are in use for ten years, the total fuel use and amount of CO_2 released during the boilers use can be calculated.

Fuel cost saving over lifetime = £1103.76

CO_2 released by standard boiler = 42,562kg

CO_2 release, condensing boiler = 26,967kg

CO_2 saving over ten years = 15,595kg

On average, the purchase price of a condensing boiler is £400 more than standard model, so the overall cash saving = £1103.76 - £400 = £703.76, which is the cost of a return flight to Sydney. Each passenger causes the release of 3150kg of CO_2 per return trip, or 20% of the 15,595kg of CO_2 saved.

Conclusions

Although the global rebound effect is 20% of the CO_2 originally saved, resource efficiency still saves resources per unit of service provided – while allowing more service to be provided from fewer resources. In this case study, the additional service is the enriching experience of travel to Australia – and 80% of the original CO_2 saving still stands.

An strategy could be to encourage consumers to spend surplus money on products with high perceived value, but little environmental impact due to their low resource intensity; for example art, sport, information products, learning circles, or antiques. The concept of low-cost, but high perceived-value products is well known to product designers, but they should be made develop this further as an environmental as well as financial strategy.

Karen Yevenes

'Messages' instilled in product designs indicate how they should be used and who should use them. Product semantics is the study of such meanings, as communicated through manufactured objects using a visual alphabet of signs and symbols made up of colour, shape, form, and texture (Giard 1990). Without an awareness of product semantics, designers may inadvertently fail to appreciate some of the wider social implications of their designs and product semantics.

Introduction

A designer's **tacit knowledge** affects their design decisions and is shaped by their unique backgrounds and sociological influences, including gender (Whiteley 1993). Similarly, the consumer's subjective response to a product depends on how the codes, metaphors, or symbols embodied in the design correspond to their own backgrounds and influences. For example, this hidden 'visual language' can reinforce gender stereotypes. Further, problems can arise when the visual elements (colour, shape, form, and texture) of a product are assumed to be appropriate for particular consumer groups, such as women.

Gender in design

Designers can create objects that are gender exclusive through the decisions they make – consciously and unconsciously. Products are often designated an appropriate owner or operator through their shape or form. For example, products are encoded with design elements that suggest which gender is expected to use them. Thus, products intended to be used by men often have large, bulky features, restricting their use by women and reinforcing the position that only men or strong people can perform the task (or vice versa). Obvious examples are hand-drills and similar workshop tools.

Gender-exclusive design does not mean, of course, that women design differently than men. After all, women study design under the same conditions as their male counterparts, and the profession does not really allow women to design

differently. For example, at a 'design crit', a male representative from the commercial design field told a student, with disapproval, that her coffee pot 'looked too maternal' (she had not intended to design a 'maternal-looking' product). The work was immediately dismissed as a design that did not reflect what the consumer wants: the 'contemporary', 'modern', 'slick', 'executive' design that she was meant to aim for.

Likewise, **gender identification** does not mean that male designers design only for men. Designers create objects for all consumers according to what they believe to be marketable and aesthetically correct. However, men have dominated the design profession and therefore, some believe, a 'masculine aesthetic' has evolved that is perceived to be correct. Elements such as sharp lines, stark materials, and bold colours are some qualities associated with the contemporary masculine aesthetic that dominates the profession.

Penny Sparke analyses what she considers the well-established masculinist 'canons of taste' and aesthetic in an historical analysis of design principles. She attributes much of this to 'modernism' with its conception of social, cultural and economic order. The impact of improved metals technology, assembly lines, production techniques, and plastics technology has fostered the design of products that express this industrial technology and aesthetic.

> *'The shift from a world in which the female consumer played a central role to one in which rationally conceived, standardised mass production began to dictate a new aesthetic and role for the domestic object, came with the marriage of technological and economic modernity to cultural modernism.'* (Sparke 1995, p. 10)

Sparke argues further that post-modern design has now allowed 'feminine taste to be legitimised'. However, given the gender imbalance in the profession, one wonders if objects represent feminine taste, a new male aesthetic, or simply continue to demonstrate what designers perceive to be feminine taste.

'Women's cultural codes are produced within the context of patriarchy. Their expectations, needs and desires as both designers and consumers are constructed within a patriarchy which prescribes a subservient and dependent role to women, [and also] ... that the codes of design, as used by the designer, are produced within patriarchy to express the needs of the dominant group. They are, therefore, male codes.'
(Buckley 1989, p. 260)

If both men and women designers feel they must produce designs which reflect a male-defined aesthetic, the creation of an alternative aesthetic based on women's tacit knowledge may be impeded (Whitely 1993, p. 146).

Gender-blind design

The semantic decisions of designers go largely unchallenged during the design process, since the designer's colleagues are mostly male, and deviation from established product semantics is considered too risky in a global marketplace. Research into consumer needs, tastes and desires is not common. According to Giard, designers feel that they have the skills to make the correct visual statements, and therefore invest little time in understanding and evaluating possible user responses. Designers assume that consumers embrace certain well-established 'canons of taste', and they lack time and financial support for market research (Giard 1990, p. 5).

As a consequence, products commonly used by women often suffer from inappropriate semantic definitions, such as lack of sufficient attention to female proportions and physical capabilities. For example, various screwdriver sets have interchangeable heads, whereas a set providing interchangeable handles as well would allow smaller women to perform a wider range of workshop tasks. This is despite the fact that research detailing female size and strength parameters is widely available in the **ergonomic** literature **[Box 16]**. On the other hand, objects for cleaning and cooking are encoded with stereotypical features that suggest women should perform those tasks. This arguably reinforces the association of women's work with what are usually considered routine, menial, or custodial tasks.

The application of functionalist concepts like 'utility' and 'usefulness', commonly applied by designers, can also be problematic (Partington 1995, p. 213). What are considered 'universal' criteria usually have a gendered (masculine) quality. Crozier's research into meaning and design found that men demonstrated instrumental, activity-related,

functional and self-oriented concerns – whereas women placed importance on relational, symbolic and emotion related categories (Crozier 1994). Ironically, functionalism, without an awareness of gender difference can lead to dysfunctional design.

'Male designers applaud other male designers and award prizes for their formalistically breathtaking, but often functionally mind-numbing, objects of desire. An iron ... may be aesthetically pleasing and visually sophisticated by the standards of a classical aesthetic, but it may still be poor at coping with the "fiddly" bits of a sleeve.' (Whiteley 1993, p. 146)

Conversely, the idea of 'women's tastes' is often reduced to a set of universalised needs in the dominant (patriarchal) design process. For example, some designers assume that all women like pink products and floral motifs, and want to be personified as the care-giver or housewife. Sparke devotes much of her text, *As Long as its Pink: The Sexual Politics of Taste* (1995) to this phenomenon. During the 1950s, a wide range of pink shades were used throughout domestic interiors, epitomising what was believed to be 'feminine taste'. Exactly how 'pink' became associated with 'the feminine' is uncertain. Sparke attributes its widespread use during the 1950s to its connections with the past; it was used extensively in combinations with gold, mimicking 18th Century interiors.

While colour decisions in contemporary design have become less gender exclusive, current appliance catalogues are still saturated with colour stereotyping. For example, paint strippers and hair dryers are two objects that are comparable in size. Both perform similar functions – to expel hot air – yet they are strikingly different in terms of shape and colour coding.

Conclusion

What can designers do to avoid the conflicting effects of tacit knowledge, gender biases and user stereotyping in Western culture? Some of the literature which addresses the relationship between semantics and patriarchy proposes that objects should be more 'androgynous'; that is, less gender specific. Yet, as consumers have grown accustomed to feminine- and masculine-looking products, many enjoy this particular quality in their objects. Furthermore, gender neutrality may be a false concept in our culture since, as suggested above, 'non-gendered' objects are designed within the dominant masculine paradigm in accordance with a masculine aesthetic. Nonetheless, the above discussion suggests at least three areas where the design process can be improved.

Designers: Given that stereotypes exist, the extent of their influence has much to do with designers and *their* perceptions of society and women. Designers need to be more open to issues of gender and to be more self-reflective generally. They must also be more aware of the social implications of the symbols they use when designing objects.

Design education: Affirmative action in industrial design schools and the profession could aid in identifying gender issues and in providing consumers with products that meet the needs of more subcultures in the community. Also, while it is difficult to change the patriarchal weave of society, the inclusion of women in a greater range of product design teams could add different perspectives.

Consumer research: Designers must ensure that the objects are in fact accurate representations of peoples' tastes, desires, and needs, and therefore appropriate for a wider range of users. The profession can examine the latent perceptions it has with regard to designing for women and cultural minorities through extensive product research. Greater research into women's actual needs at the elementary stages of product development could result in less gender exclusive designs and, therefore, better products.

References and further reading

Buckley, C. 1989, 'Made in Patriarchy: Toward a Feminist Analysis of Women and Design', *Design Discourse*, in V. Margolin, ed, The University of Chicago Press, Chicago, IL.

Crozier, R. 1994, *Manufactured Pleasures: Psychological Responses to Design*, Manchester University Press, Manchester.

Giard, J. 1990, 'Product Semantics and Communication', *Semantic Visions in Design*, S. Vihma, ed, University of Industrial Arts UIAH, Helsinki, Finland.

Kramarae, C. 1988, *Technology and Women's Voices*, Routledge and Kegan Paul, London.

Norman, D. 1988, *The Design of Everyday Things*, Currency Doubleday, New York.

Partington, A. 1995, 'The Designer Housewife in the 1950s', in J. Attfield and P. Kirkham, eds, *A View From the Interior: Women and Design*, The Women's Press Ltd, London.

Sparke, P. 1995, *As Long as it's Pink: The Sexual Politics of Taste*, HarperCollins, London.

Whiteley, N. 1993, *Design for Society*, Reaktion Books, London.

Questions

1. Debate: 'Objects should be designed to be gender specific, not androgynous.'

2. Why do some tape and video recorders have many (often redundant) knobs with very small labels which most elderly could not read without magnifying glasses?

3. Why are many chairs not ergonomically designed, despite the fact that industrial designers are aware of such criteria?

4. List sme of the social and environmental impacts of lawn mowers. What are some design solutions for this? Investigate native grasses or ground covers that do not require mowing.

5. Apply the concepts of this chapter on gender to an ethnic minority of which you have some familiarity. Can you think of any product designs that are insensitive to cultural differences?

6. Have 'feminine' interiors (eg use of pink, floral patterns, etc) disappeared because of wider life style choices for women brought about by the women's movement – or because men now have more control in the 'home territory' due to men's liberation. Discuss.

Projects

1. Obtain a large catalogue and cut out the individual pictures of the hair dryers, power drills, coffee makers, irons or other such appliances. Each member of the group should select their own preferred items from each set of pictures. Do any patterns emerge among the choices? Are there discernible differences in gender preferences?

2. Set design criteria for a stove top. Consider: (a) safety, convenience, ease of cleaning, and how to let the user know which control goes with which burners; (b) needs of different users, such as children, blind, one-armed, elderly, non-English speaking; (c) costs of manufacture. What else must be considered? (For an answer, see Donald Norman, 1988, *The Design of Everyday Things*).

Box 16   Ergonomics or Human-centred Design

Bill Green

As defined by the Ergonomics Society of Australia, **ergonomics** is the matching of products, activities and environments with the needs of people. It is based on the ancient human notion of 'fitness for purpose', but is relatively new in scientific terms, the name having been coined in the late 1940s (from the Greek, ergon = work and nomos = laws or norms). It should be the fundamental basis for human-centred design, but ergonomic data are frequently inadequate, or are ignored, or are presented in ways which are inaccessible to designers. In the past 50-plus years, ergonomists, along with physiologists, psychologists and others have gathered huge amounts of data on human characteristics, such as their size, strength, endurance, vision, hearing, reaction times and diurnal rhythms. Recently, however, the focus has shifted to an emphasis from what people are, to what they actually do.

Boundary conditions: There is a seductive and scientifically supportable path available to the ergonomist in measuring human beings. Hard physical data can be generated, analysed, generalised and confidently presented; hence what might be termed the 'boundary conditions' of product and environment use have been specified. We can say, for example, that a doorway 2m high will admit around 98% of the world's population (Kroemer 1997); that a normal adult chair with a 420mm seat height will, when placed in a school classroom, leave 100% of eight-year-olds with their feet dangling above the floor (Steenbekkers 1993); and that prolonged maintenance of certain muscular tensions can eventually result in musculo-skeletal problems. We also know quite a lot about the way our physiological systems work, and have some general notions about the behavioural patterns of some populations. By observation and experiment, relationships emerge between certain product entities and what people do with them. For example, there is a general expectation that turning a knob clockwise will result in some increase of output, and that turning a steering wheel to the right will result in a corresponding vehicle movement.

Human interaction with the product: What we do not know much about is actual individual behaviour in specific situations. We can easily make a chair which is possible for 95% of all people to sit on, but we do not know exactly how they will then use it. Maybe to stand on to change a light bulb? We know that ordinary people are sometimes tired, angry, distracted, excited and so on, and that these emotions affect much of our interaction with our products, systems and environments. These conditions, together with age, physical decline, handicap, etc are those which push so-called 'normal' populations towards, and over, the boundary conditions set by human characteristics data.

The future of ergonomic research: Ergonomics is at an important stage in its development as a discipline. It is clear that the gathering of characteristics data must go on, as populations shift and change, but such data are no longer seen as adequate predictive bases for human-centred design. While much of the ergonomics profession remains (properly) concerned with scientific probity, a movement is gathering pace which recognises the need to understand the emotive connections we make with our products and environments. Emotional satisfaction comes from a complex mix of safety, useability, efficiency and joy. This is notoriously difficult to research, and is the future challenge of ergonomics in the real world.

Kroemer, K.H.E and E. Grandjean 1997, *Fitting the task to the Human*, Taylor and Francis, London.

Steenbekkers, L.P.A. 1993, *Child Development; Design Implications and Accident Prevention*, PhD thesis, T.U. Delft Press, The Netherlands.

Section 7:   Design for Community Building and Health

7.1   ESD and 'Sense of Community'

Graham Meltzer

The Western model of urban development is associated with a gradual loss of community, typically manifested in relationship breakdowns and social alienation. There is sociological literature which suggests that the kind of human relationships associated with a 'sense of community' engender greater awareness of the consequences of one's actions for others and the environment – such that excessive personal consumption is recognised and reduced. This chapter explores the link between a group's 'sense of community' and the environmental values and practices of its members.

How has 'community' changed?

Borgatta (1992) notes a preoccupation among social scientists since the 19th Century with what he calls the 'decline of community debate'. Sociologists since Ferdinand Tonnies have contrasted two kinds of human association: one based on intimacy, stability and interdependence (*gemeinschaft*); the other on self-interest, derived benefit and passing acquaintance (*gesellschaft*). Some theorists have suggested that society is slowly moving from once being broadly based on the former toward a predominance of the later under the influence of industrialisation, urbanisation and the hegemony of free market economics. Others have suggested that the trend is neither linear nor inevitable but more complex, perhaps being one of fragmentation and/or polarisation, such that concentrations of both relationship types constantly relocate, shift and evolve.

In any case, the weight of opinion, if not the evidence, supports the notion of a gradual loss in the 20th Century of the qualities of relationship previously associated with close community life (Yankelovich 1981). In *A Nation of Strangers*, Packard (1972) convincingly correlates increased mobility with a decline in levels of satisfactory human association, noting that rootlessness is associated with reduced companionship, trust and psychological security. Peter Buchanan suggests that the meaning derived from close human relationships has been all but lost from post-industrial society:

'So the deep and demanding relationships with the immediate community, whose members were inescapably encountered throughout one's life and daily activities, have been exchanged for the freedom of relative anonymity in more circumscribed relationships and superficial role playing.' (Buchanan 1985, p. 23)

Are 'community' and consumption linked?

The environmental movement has been effective in opposing singular acts of destruction of wilderness and rainforest, but far less successful in addressing endemic lifestyle issues which may ultimately reek greater havoc. What discussion there has been of broader ESD (ecologically sustainable development) concerns, has been circumscribed by matters of housing affordability, transportation, residential density, and land-use (Bamford 1995). Issues of human social and psychological dysfunction, which may be equally linked to environmental degradation, have generally been placed in the too-hard basket.

Excessive resource consumption within developed countries is clearly a root cause of environmental degradation (Erlich and Pirages 1974). However, considerable evidence has shown that despite the imperative, few people readily reduce personal or household consumption. People tend not to associate their local consuming and polluting activities with wider environmental degradation.

In his exploration the psycho-social dimensions of consumption, Packard (1972) surmises that an absence of community in our lives contributes to a personal sense of powerlessness and insignificance. In support, Buchanan (1985) suggests that,

'... an experience of community is arguably necessary to any profound understanding of one's self and the world; to real maturity and a sense of responsible engagement with that world.' (Buchanan 1985, p. 24)

Box 7.1.1: What is 'community'?

The definition of **community** has always been problematic (Borgatta 1992). Based on content analysis of 94 sociological definitions, Hillery (1955) identified three common characteristics: social interaction, shared ties and common geographical location. Contemporary conceptions of community have broadened to include abstract association (eg the scientific community) and to accommodate late 20th Century phenomena such as increased mobility and the influence of electronic communication. Participants in an internet discussion group, for example, may consider themselves a 'community' yet they share no territory or location other than cyberspace.

'Community' in this sense refers to the first two of the above three characteristics, namely, the nature of their social interaction and their *shared ties* or bondedness. We 'sense' community through appreciation of the same phenomena. A 'sense of community' evokes in the individual the feeling that 'these are my people, I care for them, they care for me, I am a part of them, I know what they expect from me and I from them, they share my concerns' (Yankelovich 1981, p. 227). This quality or depth of human relationship will serve, for present purpose, as *the* definitive characteristic of 'community'.

Without the meaning derived from a 'sense of community', people may subconsciously seek compensation through excessive self-gratification. Contentment is identified with the acquisition of newer and 'better' consumer goods. Material consumption becomes a psychic substitute for the satisfying social interaction that a sense of community engenders. The converse is also likely. Excessive preoccupation with material well-being is destructive to 'community'. Yankelovich (1981) associates the seeking of material well-being with what he calls the 'me-first, satisfy-all-my-desires attitude', and notes:

'In modern industrial society we often purchase our material well-being at a high human cost, the chief symptom of which is the destruction of community.' (Yankelovich 1981, p. 251)

The process is viciously cyclical, as Buchanan observes of our 'compulsive consumption that feeds on and masks frustration, unhappiness and alienation' (1990, p. 37).

The consequence, he suggests, is a poor or distorted sense of self and the absence of a dignified, responsible role in society.

There seems to be a connection, therefore, between quality or depth of social interaction and awareness of surrounding disorder and discontent; between psycho-social well-being and consciousness of community problems (Packard 1972). Such awareness, and the motivation to act upon it, is the basis of genuine and enduring ecological thought and action. Environmental attitudes and practices are intrinsically linked to matters of personal relationship, social interaction and a 'sense of community'. Thus any decline in the role of, or allegiance to, 'community' in our lives may carry serious implications for the environment.

A resurgence of 'community'

Fortunately, there is fledgling resistance to the omnipresence of that prime consumer item, the detached suburban dwelling, and greater emphasis being given to quality of life, as opposed to standard of living. Whether or not there has been an overall decline in levels of community, there appears to be a growing appreciation of the qualities of relationship associated with it. Yankelovich (1981) identifies a recognition among many Americans of the need for closer personal relations. Increasingly, people are seeking closer ties with others. One third (32%) of Americans whom Yankelovich surveyed in 1973 felt an intense need to compensate for the impersonal and threatening aspects of modern life by seeking mutual identification with others. By the beginning of the 1980s, the proportion had grown to almost half (47%).

Indicators such as these need to be viewed with caution, as the value people place upon social ties depends upon a range of life cycle and situational concerns (Hummon 1990; Richards 1990). Nevertheless, enough evidence exists to indicate that, over the last three decades, there has been a resurgence of shared and cooperative endeavour loosely associated with a 'sense of community'. In addition to the growth in broad-based community activity, there has been an increase in the number of cooperative and communal residential groups commonly known as **intentional communities**. They range in size, type and location from small, urban, shared houses to large rural communes. Of particular, relevance is **cohousing**. The central purpose of cohousing communities is the building of more meaningful social relations amongst residents. Members collaborate to build socially responsive housing and a stronger sense of community, but unlike most other intentional communities, they do so without necessarily sharing any other explicit values or ideologies (McCamant and Durrett 1994)[8.4].

Cohousing and sustainable development

The value of the cohousing model in regard to social *and* environmental sustainability is its recognition of, and attempt to address, some of the failings of late 20th Century society: the breakdown of community, alienation of the individual, and the neglect of disadvantaged groups such as single parents, the elderly and the young. It addresses these issues via the hardware of site layout, building design and shared resources as well as, and perhaps more importantly, the software of participatory process, shared decision making and an interactive social agenda (Meltzer 1999). A modern sense of community is engendered through:

- Extensive shared visioning and participatory planning leading to the early bonding and socialisation of group members.

- Well-defined decision making arrangements based on open, representative and fair processes – usually consensus of one kind or another.

- Diverse populations with a mix of young and old, owners and renters, families and singles – all sharing a common purpose and providing mutual support.

- The implementation of architectural design in facilitating informal social contact through well-considered public space planning and public/private zoning.

- Organised shared stewardship of the physical environment through work-groups where participation is as much as possible, made flexible, balanced and mutually advantageous.

- The sharing of common facilities, resources and spaces: typically, a common house, workshop, guest accommodation, laundry, tools, gardens, childcare, etc.

- A rich social agenda of regular shared meals, celebrations, workshops and other activities.

Conclusion

The cohousing phenomenon would have little relevance for the sustainability debate if it had no impact upon urban development as a whole. The proportion of people living in cohousing will never be high. However, cohousing innovation may well influence conventional housing provision. Following its remarkable popularity in Denmark, cohousing features that encourage and facilitate social and environmental sustainability have been incorporated into mainstream public and private housing. These include the provision of shared social spaces and facilities enabling smaller private dwellings, cooperative formal and informal childcare arrangements, an increased range of housing options for non-nuclear households, the integration of workplace, residential and recreational functions, and increased social opportunity for marginalised groups (such as the elderly, disabled and those with low incomes).

The dearth of non-standard housing models, which might encourage and inspire further innovation in both the public and private sector, is being redressed by grass roots initiatives in many countries. These encouraging developments indicate the readiness for settlement patterns previously thought to be inappropriate in the highly individualistic and privatised cultural landscape.

References and further reading

Bamford, G. 1995, 'Sustainability, Social Organisation and the Australian Suburb', in J. Birkeland, ed, *Rethinking the Built Environment: Proceedings of Catalyst '95 Conference*, University of Canberra, pp. 49–57

Bookchin, M. 1982, *The Ecology of Freedom*, Cheshire Books, Palo Alto, CA.

Borgatta, E.F., ed, 1992, *The Encyclopedia of Sociology*, Macmillan, Toronto, Canada.

Buchanan, P. 1985, 'Community', *The Architectural Review*, April, pp. 23–26.

Buchanan, P. 1990, 'Green Architecture', *The Architectural Review*, September, pp. 37–38.

Erlich, P. and Pirages, D. 1974, *Ark II: Social Response to Environmental Imperatives*, W.H. Freeman and Co., San Francisco, CA.

Hillery, G.A. 1955, 'Definitions of Community: Areas of Agreement', *Rural Sociology* 20, pp. 111–123.

Hummon, D.M. 1990, *Commonplaces: Community Ideology and Identity in American Culture*, State University of New York Press, New York.

McCamant, K. and Durrett, C. 1994, *CoHousing: A Contemporary Approach to Housing Ourselves*, Habitat Press, Berkeley, CA.

Meltzer, G. 1999, 'Cohousing: Verifying the Importance of Community in the Application of Environmentalism', *Journal of Architecture and Planning Research* (in press).

Packard, V. 1972, *A Nation of Strangers*, David McKay Company, New York.

Richards, L. 1990, *Nobody's Home*, Oxford University Press, Melbourne, VIC.

Sandhill, L. 1997, 'Snapshot of a Moving Target: The Communities Movement', *Communities: Journal of Cooperative Living* 97, Winter, pp. 5–7.

Yankelovich, D. 1981, *New Rules: Searching for Self-fulfilment in a World Turned Upside Down*, Random House, New York.

Questions

1. 'The confluence of social and ecological crises is such that we can no longer afford to be unimaginative: we can no longer afford to do without utopian thinking' (Bookchin 1982, p. 40). Discuss.

2. Why is it suggested that a universal definition of 'community' is problematic? List reasons.

3. Discuss the 'sense of community' existing in your town or suburb, and how it is manifested? Do you think it has strengthened or declined over time?

4. Social concerns are an important aspect of the ESD debate? Give examples of particular social issues pertaining to the suburbs that affect sustainability.

5. Do you agree that material consumption has become a substitute for psychological well-being and/or social satisfaction? Do you believe that material consumption is becoming less important – that there is 'greater emphasis being given to quality of life as opposed to standard of living'? On what evidence do you base your answer?

6. Would urban consolidation policies be more beneficial than retrofitting individual existing suburban houses? What information is necessary to know in order to make that determination?

Projects

1. Make a list of the household items that you commonly share with your neighbours or friends. Make another list of those items you think could appropriately and easily be shared with neighbours. Discuss the impediments to greater sharing and cooperation within current housing patterns. Develop a strategy to overcome these. What problems have you experiences in group living? List some conflict prevention/resolution strategies.

2. Imagine that your group is in the process of developing its own cohousing project. Discuss your aspirations for such a project and list the common facilities and resources you would wish to share. What similarities among your group could influence the results? Can you imagine yourself living in a cohousing development? If so, under what conditions and circumstances? Why?

Helen Ross

Traditional Aboriginal dwellings were very low-impact from an ecological perspective, yet they accommodated complex cultural systems and relationships. Modern housing provided for Aboriginal communities often fails to meet either of these criterion. This chapter compares traditional and contemporary Australian Aboriginal housing (policy, administration, funding, construction, and management and maintenance) in terms of sustainability. The case of Aboriginal housing demonstrates that sustainable design requires an integration of economic, social and environmental factors.

How sustainable were traditional camps?

Traditional camp dwellings were built afresh each time an Aboriginal group moved, although occasionally old dwellings were renewed when areas were revisited. All were built using locally available plant materials, in most cases using methods of construction which enabled the shelter to be ready within a few hours at most. In Tasmania and Victoria, permanent dwellings included sod and stone. Different styles of dwelling were built for different seasons or shelter needs, with specialised forms for shelter from wind, sun, rain and mosquitoes [Box 17]. The placement of fires in relation to the windbreak or walls assisted warmth.

In physical environmental terms, then, traditional dwellings were highly sustainable in terms of their use of materials and energy. They were also extremely efficient in terms of labour requirements, even though constructed each time the people moved. As Aboriginal people began to use discarded European materials in their dwellings, the efficiency of material use was continued. The hybrid form of the 'humpy' uses scrap metals and canvas in dwellings which are little different in form and function to those of the past.

Socially, traditional camps were very sophisticated (see Heppell 1979; Memmott 1991, p. 41–45). The manipulation of spatial relationships is a key method for maintaining social harmony in these camps (Heppell 1979). The arrangement of dwellings within a camp closely reflects the social relationships among the members at any particular time. People shift camp whenever these relationships change, as well as for many other reasons. People do not live in their camp dwellings so much as around them; the dwellings are used primarily for storage, and only as required for shelter.

Overall, traditional camps and dwellings represent a comfortable integration of the social, economic (labour) and environmental dimensions of sustainability, involving minimal use of environmental resources, and eventual return of materials to the environment from which they came.

How sustainable is contemporary housing?

The current Aboriginal demography reflects the appropriation of Aboriginal land and domination of Aboriginal peoples over the past 210 years. This has influenced where people live and how their social groupings are composed. In the history of government housing policy, in fact, housing has also been a vehicle of broader anti-Aboriginal policies, especially the **assimilation** policy extending from the 1930s to the end of the 1960s.

Environmental aspects

Contemporary houses for Aborigines are seldom built from local materials. In fact, experiments in mud brick houses in the Kimberley in the 1970s proved to contradict Aboriginal expectations about the amount of labour that should be expended in constructing a house. Most are built from materials brought into communities, fabricated wall panel materials, corrugated iron (formerly) or baked enamel roof materials, concrete, sometimes bricks (usually large concrete or mixed-material blocks), and glass or perspex windows, wooden or panel doors (fittings are also brought in). On top of the energy embodied in the creation of these materials, we must add the embodied energy (and economic) costs of transporting these materials long distances into remote communities. So even basic modern designs require extensive resource and energy output.

Many contemporary houses for Aborigines perform poorly in energy terms. Few are designed by professional designers in consultation with the prospective occupants. The majority are designed for mass delivery at the minimum possible cost per unit, so as to stretch public funding as far as possible. Unfortunately, short-term cost minimisation has led to poor design for thermal performance, and neglect of insulation. Residents use a combination of traditional means (outdoor fires and shade) and a few electrical appliances to keep warm and cool. The environmental cost of providing electricity in remote areas, usually by diesel generation, is high both in ecological and economic terms, and the cost of buying and running the appliances is borne by the occupants. Thus, government cost-cutting shifts the economic burden to the occupants while increasing the environmental costs.

In remote areas (remote from major service centres), much Aboriginal housing is designed for a high degree of dependency on environmental services such as water and fuel; these often strain local capacity. Wood for fuel is removed for miles around each community, contributing to a dearth of shade, and a dust problem which affects health. Many of the houses are designed to consume water at metropolitan rates. The water (usually groundwater) is not necessarily sufficient, especially as the housed populations grow.

Water saving technology has been slow to come in the Aboriginal housing sector, and in some cases meets Aboriginal resistance, as they expect the same types of houses and fittings as they see in major towns. Water is easily wasted when people lack the skills to fix a dripping tap, the community lacks the management infrastructure to check maintenance requirements regularly, and it is costly to bring a technician from town. Aboriginal houses in remote areas also deteriorate rapidly owing to poor construction and materials, wear and tear and neglect of maintenance. More environmental costs are incurred each time houses need renovation. In short, contemporary housing for Aborigines is largely a drain on local and global environments and largely inappropriate.

Economic aspects

The history of Aboriginal housing provision is one of the policy *trade-offs* between houses which are cheap in capital cost but poor in design, and houses which are intensive in consultation, design and materials, and thus cost more. The policy debates about the cost of housing have focused almost entirely on the capital cost of the house, and very little on the

cost of occupancy, repairs and maintenance of houses and fittings (Morel and Ross 1993; Pholeros et al 1993). Burns (in ATSIC 1993) advocates life cycle costing for Aboriginal housing, including the costs involved in bringing externally based technicians in for repairs and maintenance.

Another economic dimension important to the sustainability of housing is Aboriginal employment in the construction and maintenance of housing. This may be more expensive than hiring contractors because of a training element involved, but brings social benefits and keeps more of the housing budget within the community. The financing of the majority of the houses is such that an unnecessary burden of operating and maintenance costs is imposed on the tenants and community housing associations, which have to cover their own operating costs from rents (an expectation which does not apply to state government rental houses for Aborigines). These costs require a level of rental which can exceed the ability of tenants to pay, or what is reasonable given the condition of some of the houses.

Social aspects

The provision of contemporary housing is particularly challenging in social terms. In camps, the ability to reorganise spatial relations was frequently used to regulate social relations, particularly in times of stress, conflict or death. Contemporary houses are fixed to permanent sites and are too expensive to abandon for long. Further, contemporary settlements are often laid out according to non-Aboriginal spatial norms (straight streets, and more recently cul-de-sacs), which are irrelevant and sometimes destructive to Aboriginal social relationships. The houses are usually too close together for Aboriginal social norms. Some argue that allowing greater distances between houses would be too costly in terms of water and sewerage, although the potential for alternate technologies to allow a different spacing has barely been explored.

The layout of housing is also extremely important because Aboriginal people treat their outdoor areas as an integral and active part of their living space. People need space to sleep, cook and rest outside, without being too close to neighbours doing the same. Inappropriate spacing and town layouts cause great stress, often manifested in drinking and violence. People then expect the design of the houses to provide security from violent people. This conflicts with climatic requirements for open designs to foster cooling breezes.

These stresses are serious enough when people are able to

choose the sites of their houses. When they are located among non-kin, the social opportunities of mutual support and socialisation of young people by a range of elders are further reduced. Dispersal of kin among other language-speaking groups or non-Aborigines also makes the maintenance of Aboriginal languages much more difficult. Personal mobility, either moving in with others in the same community or visiting other communities for extended periods, is the only solution to being unable to move the dwellings. Householders doing so, have to keep paying rent in their absence, and over a long period can risk losing their house.

These social-spatial factors apply to varying extents throughout the country. However, people enjoy the higher standard of living provided in contemporary houses, especially in cooler climates, and adapt to the altered social arrangements. Aspirations are also changing rapidly, as the first generation of 'household heads' is supplanted by younger people with different aspirations and greater experience of housing.

Self-determination

The allocation of space within each house, like Aboriginal patterns of settlement space, also differs from non-Aboriginal patterns, all around Australia. In northern and central Australia, a common pattern in extended family households is for each nuclear family unit to be allocated a bedroom, or for the women and children to have bedrooms while the men – even married men – sleep in the living rooms or outside (Ross 1987, p. 85). The bedrooms and living rooms thus become multiple purpose living spaces, used day and night as required. In southern and eastern Australia, these patterns or ones more similar to non-Aboriginal ones may be found. The patterns also vary over time, as people's housing and other aspirations change. For instance, the arrival of television in Halls Creek, WA, in 1980 brought many people indoors in the evenings, who would otherwise have been outdoors.

Aboriginal people are very efficient in the amount of indoor space they use per person, and hence in the capital cost and materials of each house on a 'per person' basis. The reasons include the tendency towards outdoor living, having little furniture to take up space, extended family living, and the notorious shortage of housing nation-wide which obliges families to cohabit and to take in homeless and visiting relatives. However, indoor space, including ceiling height, is also important for natural cooling. Dense living conditions can come at a health cost, in terms of high rates of infection, stress, and pressure on the 'health hardware' of ablutions facilities (Pholeros et al 1993, 23–30). Hence, there is certainly a need to provide people with more housing to relieve forced conditions of high density living, and to design houses in ways more suited to extended family living.

The design of the house affects the sustainability of social characteristics of Aboriginal life. Where the nature of houses conflicts with social norms, some adaptation is necessary, either on the part of the people or the way they use the house (Ross 1987; Reser 1979). Thus, Aboriginal people have had to work out new ways of handling death and of maintaining avoidance behaviours (in many societies people in certain relationships are required to avoid one another, for instance mothers and their sons-in-law). They must also use housing space and handle household economics in ways which are as consistent as possible with traditional social norms.

Social issues in the delivery and management of housing include consultation and self-determination (Ross 1987; Morel and Ross 1993; Memmott 1991). **Self-determination** enables Aboriginal people, through their organisations, to have more choice about how they will live, and more control over the housing process. Local control, if suitably supported with funding and access to advice, should afford the best opportunities for Aboriginal people to acquire and maintain sustainable housing.

Conclusion

The economic aspects of Aboriginal housing are poorly integrated with environmental and social aspects. Sustainable Aboriginal housing requires the *integration* of social, economic and environmental analysis and design. The suppliers and occupants of contemporary Aboriginal housing are far from finding a new integration that reflects traditional camp systems. Any new integration cannot be the same as non-Aboriginal patterns for living. If any integration is possible, there is sure to be more than one solution, given the diversity of environments in which Aboriginal people live, and the diversity of local societies and their aspirations. This matter needs to be explored locally, through Aboriginal participation in, and/or control of, the design project.

References and further reading

ATSIC (Aboriginal and Torres Strait Islander Commission) 1993, *Proceedings of the Indigenous Australians Shelter Conference*, ATSIC, Canberra, ACT.

Heppell, M., ed,1979, *A Black reality: Aboriginal Camps and Housing in Remote Australia*, Australian Institute of Aboriginal Studies, Canberra, ACT.

Memmott, P. 1991, *Humpy, House and Tin Shed: Aboriginals Settlement History on the Darling River*, Ian Buchan Fell Research Centre, University of Sydney, Sydney, NSW.

Morel, P. and Ross, H. 1993, *Housing Design Assessment for Bush Communities*, Department of Lands and Housing and Tangentyere Council, Alice Springs, NT.

Pholeros, P., Rainow, S. and Torzillo, P. 1993, *Housing for Health: Towards a Healthy Living Environment for Aboriginal Australia*, Health Habitat, Newport Beach, Sydney, NSW.

Reser, J. 1979, 'A Matter of Control' In M. Heppell, ed, *A Black Reality: Aboriginal Camps and Housing in Remote Australia*, Australian Institute of Aboriginal Studies, Canberra, ACT.

Ross, H. 1987, *Just for Living: Aboriginal Perceptions of Housing in Northwest Australia*, Aboriginal Studies Press, Canberra, ACT.

Questions

1. If there are any ethnic or Aboriginal groups in your region, list differences between their needs and that of the mainstream.

2. What are some of the contrasts between traditional and contemporary forms of housing for Aborigines? How could modern houses incorporate these traditional social values?

3. List ways in which a better integration could be achieved between the social, economic and physical aspects of contemporary Aboriginal housing, or that of a distinct ethnic group in your region.

4. List some alternative technologies relevant to Aboriginal housing needs. What potentials are there for using alternate technologies in Aboriginal housing to improve sustainability? What are the impediments?

5. What town planning considerations are important in the design of Aboriginal or ethnic communities?

6. How has housing design contributed to assimilation? Is this desirable?

Projects

1. Form two teams. Team A represents members of an Aboriginal community (in a dry, monsoonal climate) that are to be consulted about a new housing project to replace their town camp. Nominate each member to represent different community members (with gender and age variations, different household compositions and incomes), or community office bearers such as council members, housing association staff, and health workers.

Team B represents a government team sent to consult the people, and then to supply the housing (the community is allocated a budget, which it may then use to contract your department or a private supplier to build the houses). Nominate members of the group to play a designer, a person who handles town planning aspects, engineering staff to consider sewerage, a budget manager, and Aboriginal members of the state government's Aboriginal Housing Board.

Your budget is US$500,000, sufficient to build six basic modern houses. You have 15 households on your waiting list in this community. Meet as separate teams to consider your favoured approaches, then meet together to negotiate the most sustainable possible solution.

2. Create an integrated list of design criteria for a sustainable Aboriginal house for one of the following locations:

- a coastal town in a warm, humid region;
- a remote community in hot dry region;
- a remote community in a tropical region;
- a metropolitan suburb in a large city.

Describe how Aboriginal people could contribute to creating this list. Compare the lists created for different locations.

Box 17   Aboriginal Dwellings

Helen Ross

The following show some of the Australian Aboriginal's adaptation of customary dwelling forms using introduced materials.

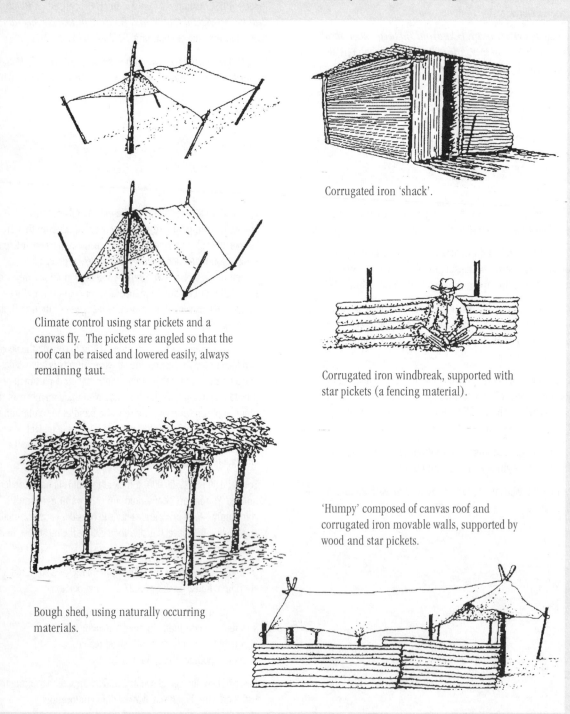

Corrugated iron 'shack'.

Climate control using star pickets and a canvas fly. The pickets are angled so that the roof can be raised and lowered easily, always remaining taut.

Corrugated iron windbreak, supported with star pickets (a fencing material).

'Humpy' composed of canvas roof and corrugated iron movable walls, supported by wood and star pickets.

Bough shed, using naturally occurring materials.

Alison Terry

Human health is greatly affected by indoor air quality (IAQ) as we spend much of our time indoors. Despite variances in construction practices, climatic conditions and life styles, industrialised countries throughout the world are facing similar IAQ problems, unique to modern building technology. One third of users in new or refurbished buildings complain of a perception of 'bad air' and disturbed well-being. This chapter focuses on domestic indoor air quality research and some research biases in this field.

The 'new' health problem

The quality, duration and effects of indoor pollutants have long been overlooked and undervalued (Maroni et al 1995). The indoor environment can be up to ten times more polluted than the exterior, and contain a greater range and concentration of contaminants. Compounding this, people now spend a greater percentage of time indoors (around 90% or more), the majority of which is spent in the domestic environment (Brown 1997). Indoor pollutants include a number of contaminants, but the two which have been identified as the most problematic are volatile chemicals and, particularly for the domestic environment, allergens and the house dust mite.

Research has focused on commercial buildings where the cost of lost productivity, directly due to poor indoor air quality (IAQ), is now higher than the remedial costs (Maroni et al 1995). Safe air quality standards in the workplace are often mandatory. Occupational exposure limits (OEL) for contaminants, allergens, and especially chemicals, have been established, which limit exposures quantities and time frames. However, these standards do not calculate the additive effect of exposure to multiple chemicals, or acknowledge that exposures may extend beyond the normal time frames (eight hours a day, five days a week). Additionally, OELs are set for healthy adults, which are too high for those with allergies, chemical sensitivities or ill health (Crowther 1994).

While safe parameters are enforceable for public outdoor spaces and the workplace, these OEL's serve merely as guidelines, if at all, in the domestic setting. The unregulated domestic environment is coming under closer scrutiny as chronic, low-level exposure to chemicals, contaminants and allergens are precipitating health problems more commonly seen in the workplace. Poor IAQ is particularly problematic for a sensitive subgroup of individuals, many of whom must spend much of their time inside.

The common diseases of industrialised countries are now chronic, degenerative disorders which have multiple environmental (rather than pathogenic) origins. Building-related research has traditionally supported safety and health issues around minimum building standards and pathogen exclusion (Haglund et al 1991), reinforced by building codes and regulations. While the built environment can 'design out' disease causes, current medical research on building design is not adequately assessed or passed onto building professionals (Crowther 1994). This lack of communication is exacerbated by limited financial resources allocated to building research, the complexity of factors contributing to poor IAQ, and the interdisciplinary nature of IAQ research. The potential negative effects of contaminants (particularly chemicals) are thus currently limited to major pollutants only, resulting in an incomplete picture of IAQ problems, particularly for the domestic environment. Additionally, the limited number of large-scale epidemiological surveys means that the evidence is not yet adequate to define unequivocally which features of poor IAQ are most detrimental (Maroni et al 1995).

Health problems associated with poor IAQ

Scientific evidence increasingly shows that poor IAQ can cause problems for the body's immune system, particularly for those with an acquired or genetic susceptibility. The health outcomes include sick building syndrome (SBS), multiple chemical sensitivity (MCS), and allergies –

predominantly asthma. Allergy, SBS and MCS are preventable or controllable. However, they are not established as legitimate 'diseases'. This is because medical **convention** requires that a disease is defined by a specific causative agent creating hallmark symptoms, diagnosable by specific tests, and responsive to a specific curative intervention, usually drugs or surgery. For example:

Allergy, which conforms most closely to the above conditions, was only accepted as a medical discipline in the United Kingdom in 1987 (Crowther 1994). The symptoms and causative agents of SBS and MCS are less readily definable as diseases; particularly MCS, which is viewed by some as a signpost of environmental decline (like the miners' canary).

SBS is considered a syndrome as opposed to a clinical disease. It is composed of non-specific symptoms often reported by inhabitants in buildings with IAQ problems. There appears to be no single causative agent for SBS; it is a combination of biological, physical and chemical factors influenced by the psychosomatic element of stress (ie observed influence of the mind on the functions of the body). The symptoms are usually relieved upon leaving the building (Maroni et al 1995).

MCS is seen as a chronic multi-system 'disorder', usually involving the central nervous system and at least one other organ. It is polysymptomatic; that is, those affected usually have food intolerances as well as other adverse reactions. Asthma has been given particular attention due to a rapid rise in its morbidity and mortality, asthma rates in Australia have risen by 50% in the last ten years).

The immune system

An individual's ability to deal with environmental contaminants is reliant on a number of predisposing factors, such as age, gender, genetic make-up and pre-existing diseases. It also relies on behavioural factors including nutrition, psychosomatic factors and stress. Immune status is also very important; normal immune function declines with age, while young children have an immature immune system. Individuals with acute or chronic disease conditions have a depressed immune status, and those with respiratory dysfunction have a weakened immune system, such as smokers with asthma (Maroni et al 1997). These individuals form what is known as a sensitive subgroup (Table 7.3.1).

MCS, SBS and allergies, if chronic, also have the capacity to compromise the immune system. All substances taken in by the body are initially metabolised in the liver. If the liver is damaged or overworked, unmetabolised substances are passed onto the immune system, damaging it and other organs. Thus the liver protects the immune system from overload. Both the liver and immune system are sensitive to chronic exposure to toxins and infections, so long-term chemical exposure can cause the liver to become ineffective at filtering out unwanted substances. An environment with a high chemical and allergen load therefore creates a two-pronged attack on the body's main defense systems, with the ultimate burden falling on the immune system.

Table 7.3.1: The sensitive subgroups with respiratory dysfunction

Sensitive subgroups	% of US population
Newborns (<1yr)	1.5
Young children (1-5yr)	7.5
Elderly (>65yr)	12.1
Heart patients	7.7
Bronchitis	4.7
Asthma	4.0
Hay fever	9.0
Emphysema	0.8
Smokers	29.9

An overlap exists between some of these groups. *Source*: Victorian EPA 1993

Gender and environmental health

Many **xenobiotic** (human-made) chemicals are difficult to process through the body. Many have long half lives and a large proportion of synthesised chemicals are fat soluble compounds, which take longer to metabolise through the liver but are readily stored in the body's fat cells; hence they are **biocumulative**. Xenobiotics compete for metabolic resources and with other metabolic functions (Crowther 1994). One of these functions is hormonal management which controls both immune and reproductive functions. Due to monthly cycles and pregnancy, women are more affected by any disruption to hormonal functions than men.

Statistics indicate that females have more allergies, MCS and SBS. While there is only a marginal, but consistent, predominance of females in allergic conditions (ABS 4102.0 1997, p. 46), 80% of MCS sufferers, and 75% of SBS sufferers are women (Crowther 1994). The limited understanding of the indirect effects of hormonal status on health is linked to the earlier practice of excluding women from studies on the basis that their hormonal fluctuations interfered with research outcomes. That is, men were considered the 'normalised' human (Bernstein 1993).

Additionally, health statistics treat men and women as undifferentiated categories, but favour biomedical over socio-medical factors. As such, biomedical factors that are highly linked to the mortality rates of males, receive more study and health dollars than socio-medical factors, which are dominantly linked to female mortality rates. This bias suggests that women, as a vulnerable group, could be thought of as a 'sensitive subgroup'. Their presence in the domestic environment is also greater than that of most men, as they are usually the home-based carers for children, the chronically ill and frail elderly.

Design and IAQ

Increased sources of chemical toxins and allergens in the domestic environment are due largely to changes to the building envelope and contents. They include:

- The pervasive use of chemicals in building products, of which several hundred chemicals are detectable in the indoor air.
- Changes to construction techniques and building

standards that have reduced fresh air exchange (naturally or mechanically).

- Changing expectations of thermal comfort, and a greater use of soft furnishings and carpets.
- Increases in building volumes and lower ceiling heights.

Internal sources of air pollution fall mainly into two categories: those caused by human activity and those caused by building materials or furnishings. Human activity introduces chemicals, combustion by-products, respirable suspended particles (tobacco smoke and dust), carbon dioxide and humidity (see Table 7.3.2). The construction and industrial sector has reduced indoor ventilation rates in both commercial and domestic buildings to reduce energy costs and the environmental impact of fossil fuel use. However, an unintentional outcome has been to create conditions which undermine the health of building occupants.

The consensus is that poor IAQ can be tackled on two fronts – ventilation (and humidity), and materials selection (Gelder 1996). Both of these are design issues.

Ventilation: The combined effect of aluminium sliding windows, weather-stripping to exterior doors, concrete slab floors and the elimination of fixed wall vents has halved infiltration rates in Australian housing (Brown 1997). Poor

Table 7.3.2: Indoor chemical pollution sources

Source	Type	Product
OCCUPANTS:	* bio-effluents: humans, pets	carbon dioxide, VOCs (volatile organic compounds) dandruff
	personal hygiene products	VOCs
OCCUPATIONS:	human activities	tobacco, smoke (VOCs)
	* combustion by-products	carbon monoxide, sulphur dioxide, nitrogen dioxide
	cleaning materials	chlorine, air fresheners, VOCs
FIXTURES & FITTINGS:	* carpets and furnishings	adhesives, solvents, formaldehyde
	finishes	paints, primers, coatings, stains, varnishes, sealants, timber preservatives, solvents
	cupboards and furniture	adhesives, sealing, bedding and jointing material, PVC/vinyl chloride, synthetic rubber, wood dust
	other building materials	concrete additives, masonry cleaners, bitumen, formwork releasing agents, grouts, insulants, polyurethane foam insulation (if burnt), VOCs
OTHER:		weedkillers , insecticides, pollen, fungi, mould, bacteria, arthropod remains/excreta, house dust mite

(* denotes highest renewal rate, then in descending order)

Source: Crowther 1994, pp. 117–130, 154; Gelder and Onyon 1996, p. 2

ventilation can raise chemical contaminant levels, particularly volatile organic compounds (VOCs). Sources include paints and varnishes, mastics and caulks, plastics and synthetic polymers, formaldehyde treated fabrics, glued timber products and pesticide treated materials (especially timber, carpet and carpet tiling, wallpaper paste and paint). It can take up to six months for levels in new housing to fall to outdoor levels under ambient conditions (Crowther 1994). High formaldehyde levels have been reported in housing less than two years old. Chemicals are reintroduced throughout all stages of the building life cycle, through alteration, renovation and maintenance.

Furnishings: Contaminant sources from soft furnishings increase over time, as contaminants are absorbed into the material. Dust attaches to airborne chemical molecules, thereby increasing their uptake in soft furnishings with age. This **sink effect** creates a reservoir of contaminants which have a continuous exchange with the air. The greater the **fleece factor** (equivalent to the total area of carpet and soft furnishings divided by room volume), the greater the effect.

Humidity: Relative humidity (RH) increases rapidly when ventilation rates fall below threshold levels. This encourages mould growth which is considered a cause in the rise of asthma (Crowther 1994). Asthma is also triggered by ambient chemicals such as nitrogen dioxide, sulphur dioxide, cigarette smoke and VOCs (Prendergast 1991) whose volatility also rises with humidity and temperature (Crowther 1994). RH levels lower than 50% have adverse effects on health and comfort. Between 25 and 45% RH inhibits sweat production, and causes fine particles to remain airborne such as cigarette smoke, perpetuating ambient contaminant levels and the sink effect (Crowther 1994).

A high ventilation rate counters these problems and reduces low-level indoor air pollution, but this is constrained by the need to:

- Limit the ingress of outdoor pollution sources and noise.
- Limit climatic effects.
- Reduce heat loss from the interior.
- Reduce energy costs of both point source heating and mechanical ventilation (for heating, cooling or humidification).

Conclusion

Early scientific and medical research largely ignored the part that hormones play in immune and health status, thus masking health outcomes that are more detrimental to women. Defining chronic illnesses by mortality and morbidity figures has created a bias towards curing male diseases and has underplayed the psychosomatic and social influences on health – thus undermining the importance of environmental factors to health. This bias has been reinforced by health funding and research agendas. Further, IAQ parameters are created for the healthy majority, not those who most need health protection – women and sensitive subgroups. Designers need to consider the health needs of sensitive subgroups in the workplace or home, not just norms, to counter-balance those adverse health outcomes.

References and further reading

Australian Bureau of Statistics 1997, *Australian Social Trends 4102.0*, AGPS, Canberra, ACT.

Bernstein E., ed, 1993, *Medical and Health Annual*, Encyclopedia Britannica Inc., Chicago, IL.

Brown S.K. 1997, *Indoor Air Quality*, State of the Environment Technical Paper Series, Department of the Environment, Sports and Territories, Australian Federal Government.

Crowther, D. 1994, *Health Considerations in House Design*, PhD thesis, Cambridge University, Cambridge.

Crumpler, D. 1994, *Chemical Crisis: One Womans Story, Humanity's Future?*, Scribe Publications, Carlton North, VIC.

Dingle, P. 1995, *Personal Exposure to Formaldehyde*, PhD thesis, Murdock University, WA.

Gelder, J. 1996, *Reducing Chemical Risks in the Built Environment*, RAIA Environmental Design Guide, Canberra, ACT.

Gelder, J. and Onyon, L. 1996, *An Introduction to Chemical Risks in the Built Environment*, RAIA Environmental Design Guide, Canberra, ACT.

Haglund, B.J.A., Pettersson, B., Finer, D., and Tillgren, P. 1991, *The Sundsvall Handbook: 'We Can Do It!'*, 3rd International Conference on Health Promotion, Stockholm, Sweden.

Maroni, M., Seifert, B. and Lindvall, T., eds, 1995, *Indoor Air Quality: A Comprehensive Reference Book*, Elsevier Science B. V., Amsterdam.

Victorian EPA 1993, *Indoor Air Quality in Domestic Premises in Victoria, a Review*, Publication 327, September.

Questions

1. If you were to design a house which limited the use of toxic chemicals and allergens, what would be some of its key features?

2. What are volatile organic compounds? What materials are they found in and how do they affect IAQ?

3. Determine which materials in the domestic environment may be the most problematic in terms of IAQ. Categorise them into construction materials, internal fit-out materials, soft furnishings and human activity (See Table 7.3.2). Which categories cause the greatest generation of volatile organic chemicals? Which categories are the greatest source of allergens? Which categories create ventilation problems? How does human activity influence the outcomes?

4. What environmental factors precipitate asthma? Where can they be found in the domestic environment? Do the sources differ in the office environment? If so, why?

5. Who designs and builds the majority of Australian housing – architects, building designers, developers or builders? Do these professions differ in their understanding and application of IAQ?

6. Which is a priority in domestic design today: energy efficiency or IAQ? Are they necessarily in conflict? Discuss.

Projects

1. Undertake a search on the health issues discussed above – MCS, SBS and allergy. Confine the allergy search to asthma as it is the most relevant to poor IAQ. Which environmental issues are causing a rise in these health issues? Are the environmental causes of MCS, SBS and asthma well understood – if not, why not?

2. Look up the principles of sustainability as defined by Agenda 21. Do they encourage a balance between environmental impact and human health issues? Are these principles compatible with current development practice?

Anne-Marie Poirrier

Western societies have become increasingly chemically dependent since the Second World War. As a result, our planet is now heavily polluted with organo-chlorine residues throughout the food web; even arctic ice and polar bears show organo-chlorine contamination. Where organo-chlorine termiticides have been prohibited, non-chemical termite management alternatives have had to be rapidly adopted. This chapter describes some of these integrated pest management practices for new building construction, with attention to termites.

Introduction

We marvel at the beauty of a butterfly and consider a worm to be a friend, yet some creatures, such as cockroaches or spiders, are viewed as nuisances, and have acquired an unwarranted social stigma. For example, concerns often include the potential for diseases to be transported. Yet the reality is that the cockroach must travel over a surface which has disease organisms, then travel over uncovered food or the like to translocate the illness. In an average modern kitchen, this is an unlikely scenario; the common housefly coming in an unscreened window poses a much higher risk.

If a pest is an organism unwanted by humans at a particular place and time, then the solution is to take some control over that place and time. Air and light help reduce insect **infestations** and also contribute to building preservation and durability. For example, we can block the gaps under and around doors, especially external doors. Pull all appliances out from the wall to allow air flow, to reduce heat and moisture and to make cleaning easier. Use sticky traps to monitor and control low-level infestations or crawling insects. Seal cracks and crevices to limit the number of safe harbourages.

Spiders result in vast quantities of pesticide application. Spiders are usually not going to die as a result of residual chemical sprays. Often, more spiders are seen after a spray, as they are agitated and hungry. The pesticides applied to external areas are usually strong nerve and liver poisons that

will kill the micro-insects which larger spiders feed upon, only killing spiders upon direct contact. The appropriate strategy for spider control is to have a straw broom or vacuum cleaner available for direct removal of individual spiders and webs, wear shoes in the garden (especially in the summer months around dusk), and wear gloves when fossicking in rockeries or storage sheds. Adults should remove sand pit covers, and toys and shoes should not be left outside overnight.

People do not take antibiotics every day in case they get sick but rather reserve this type of treatment to combat a specific illness. Pesticides should be approached in a similar fashion. No chemical pesticide should be applied as a preventative. Chemical treatment, no matter how low the hazard, should only be resorted to after all physical and cultural options are exhausted. We should learn to live with, and appreciate, the smaller inhabitants of the region, rather than poison ourselves and environment in the vain attempt to 'eradicate' pests.

Integrated pest management

Integrated Pest Management (IPM) employs a multitude of approaches and complementary techniques (physical, cultural, biological, educational and chemical) – with a priority on non-chemical control measures – to achieve maximum effect with minimum impact. IPM is an ecologically based pest control strategy that centres around detailed assessment of pest populations and the conditions under which they proliferate. Chemical methods, where necessary, are carefully selected to minimise the hazards. Effective IPM requires ongoing monitoring and assessment of the effectiveness of control strategies. For example, when forming a strategy for protecting a building from termite attack, the approach must be to:

- Ensure there are no concealed entry points.
- Reduce the attractiveness of the surrounding area.
- Have a vigilant inspection protocol.

Termite control

Termites cause more damage to structures than storms and floods. They are insects closely related to cockroaches, not ants (although often given the misnomer of 'white ants'). A termite colony contains over 1,000,000 individuals, all dependent on a central queen or queens, much like bees. All species utilise cellulose obtained from wood and wood products (eg timber, paper, cardboard). Many structures, such as brick veneer houses, have been described as 'packaged food for termites' with expanses of edible, concealed softwoods. Termites forage for food from a central nest, up to 50m away in the most common species.

Termites can be equated with rust in a car: good maintenance and diligence will reduce, but not eliminate, the risk. Some houses may never be attacked, while others may be constantly barraged. It is essential that termite management be considered at the design stage. Minimum Termite Risk (MTR) construction includes building design and construction methods which minimise the probability of termite attack and allow easy access for inspection for early signs of infestation. MTR construction optimises the use of physical **termite barriers**, physical termite shielding and building materials for the individual structure in a holistic manner. The most important element of MTR construction is incorporating **termite resistant** foundation designs into structures. This design strategy requires effective communication between the architect, builder, termite specialist and owner.

Design strategies

By implementing some fundamental design strategies, a structure may successfully be constructed and maintained using timber and timber based products, without termite damage:

- All timbers must have full inspection access.

- Timber must not be in contact with the ground.

- Physical termite shielding must be of an appropriate material and wholly applied.

- Moisture must be reduced to the lowest possible level in and around the structure, (ie garden beds should not abut structures, wet areas must be properly waterproofed).

- Paving and pathways around structures must be below interior floor levels and slope away from the structure.

Naturally resistant timbers (NRT): Some timbers are naturally resistant to termites; however, many of these are rainforest species and their use is damaging to world forests and exploitative of developing economies. Where timbers are available from certified timber sources, it is the optimum building material. Plantation softwoods are appropriate for use in a broad range of applications where timbers are not in direct ground contact. They should be appropriately shielded and adequately maintained, via the regular application of paints.

Box 7.4.1: **MTR construction requirements for floors**

Structures can be broadly divided into two types: suspended floor and slab-on-ground.

Suspended floor: MTR requirements include:

- Clearance of 500mm (minimum).

- Isolated pier/stump foundations or fully shielded perimeter masonry walls.

- Sub-floor ventilation and incident light into sub-floor void.

- Good sub-floor ventilation in suspended floor buildings to reduce the attraction of the area for pests, lower pesticide residues, and lessen the concentration of fungal spores and decay rot. Ventilation may be achieved with brass-wire mesh-style vents, or solar-powered extraction fans.

Slab-on-ground: MTR requirements include:

- Monolithic slab construction or minimal expansion joints.

- Slow-cured slabs, sufficiently reinforced and dense to minimise the potential for cracking.

- Penetrations for service pipes able to be readily inspected, if not able to be avoided or protected by a physical barrier.

- Slab-edge detail and inspection access.

- Continuous physical termite shielding.

- Inspection access to timber wall frames

Treated timbers: Where naturally resistant timbers are not available or are inappropriate, treated timbers may be employed. Impregnated pines with arsenical or other preservatives are not necessarily hazardous within a structure; however, the production site is highly contaminated. Off-cuts and sawdust at the construction site must be dealt with as contaminated material (ie placed in a landfill, not burnt).

Termite resistant building materials: Steel and glass are both termite-resistant, and do not need to be treated. Aerated concrete blocks are light yet structurally strong with good thermal characteristics and may be shaped and cut using simple hand-tools. They are highly appropriate for steep slopes. However, it may be possible for termites to tunnel through these blocks.

Minimising termites during construction

The following guidelines should be followed by those working on construction sites:

- Remove tree stumps, root systems, loose timber fragments, cardboard, paper (or any other materials containing cellulose) from the soil on which the proposed building is due to be constructed.

- Deposit all timber, cardboard and paper waste in designated areas of the construction site. These materials should be collected periodically and disposed of, or recycled, appropriately.

- Maintain very high-quality workmanship in all aspects of construction, particularly in the creation of physical barriers (eg concrete slabs, physical termite shielding).

- Remove and appropriately dispose/recycle all temporary formwork following completion of its intended function.

- Do not incorporate materials containing cellulose (eg timber, paper, cardboard) into fill of any type.

- Remove all mortar droppings from cavities and termite shields.

- Thoroughly clear and rake all sub-floor areas in raised floor buildings (or sections of buildings) on completion of construction, to remove all building debris from soil surfaces.

A full inspection of all timber components and potential termite access points should be undertaken three months after the completion of a structure. In maintaining a termite management program, all structures should be inspected annually, with high risk structures inspected three to six monthly by a qualified termite specialist.

Physical barriers

Houses can be protected from termites by installing barriers that prevent termite access. Physical barriers may be incorporated into, or placed beneath, the structure. A range of materials have been used as physical shields through walls and over piers (ant capping) which, if adequately installed, force termites out into a detectable area. Fully joining, and not perforating, shields is essential for shield integrity. These metal shields are readily available to builders and may be installed by any trades person. Shields must be expected to last the serviceable life of the structure (approximately 50 years).

Stainless steel mesh: Stainless steel mesh can be employed as a physical termite shield as a full under-slab application, perimeter wall shield and/or penetration collar.

Graded stone: A bed of granite chips can form a barrier to termites. Particles are too large and heavy for termites to carry, too hard for termites to chew, and the spaces between the particles are too small for termites to crawl through.

Attention to detail is essential, especially for perimeter areas. If the barrier is breached by the overlaying of paving, soil, gardens or paths, termites may move undetected into the timbers of the structure. Also, building design faults can compromise the barrier.

Chemical options

Many people in the pest control industry saw the removal of organo-chlorines as a move toward 'less' toxic chemicals, such as chlorpyrifos and synthetic pyrethroids. However, these chemical options break down more rapidly, so their application is usually more frequent and at higher concentrations. This will ultimately result in significant environmental contamination. Chlorpyrifos is an organo-phosphate, and the most widely used **termiticide** by the conventional pest control industry. Synthetic pyrethroids are generally of low toxicity to mammals, but of very high toxicity to aquatic life.

The limitations of chemical soil barriers are many fold. Any or all of the following points can combine to reduce the effectiveness of a chemical termiticide barrier:

- No guarantee as to the concentration of the formulation can be made; excessive dilution will usually render the barrier ineffective and higher concentrations will be hazardous.

- Disturbance of the soil after application can open routes through treated soil. This may be as a result of plumbing, electrical, or telephone service work.

- Continuity of the chemical barrier can be affected by the geomorphology of the site, or the combination of soil type (too clayey or too sandy), insufficient organic matter for the chemical to bind to, ground and/or surface water action, rock outcroppings and depth of sub-strata.

The chemical soil barrier must be continuous (ie have no gaps which allow unrestricted access of termites to the building); however, in practice this is rarely the result.

Reticulation systems use a series of interconnecting pipes placed beneath a slab prior to pour. The concept is to allow post construction application of any emulsion (be it chlorpyrifos, a synthetic pyrethroid, an insect growth regulator or bio-control agent), while not perforating the slab or membrane. The ease of application raises concerns as to the frequency of chemical application and subsequent environmental contamination.

Repellents are botanical agents that have been observed to have extensive repellent action on insects including termites. Pepper, chilli and neem have all provided localised short-term repellency (the extract has been used to drench and kill **termite colony nests**).

Termite colony control

Termite colony nests of destructive species can be removed physically or treated in-situ with a synthetic pyrethroid dust or, where permitted, other low-hazard materials such as neem. There are also indirect forms of colony control, such as termite baiting programs, arsenic trioxide and borates. A false feeding environment can be created through the introduction of a material that is detrimental to the termite colony nest. Baits can be made with the following active ingredients: slow-acting toxicants, insect growth regulators or biological control agents such as bacteria, fungi or nematodes.

Arsenic trioxide dust in formulation with ferric/ferrous oxide is a slow-acting stomach poison, requiring 1-2g to kill a termite colony nest. The termite's sacrificial instinct can result in the initial front of workers being poisoned almost intentionally to provide a 'safe' pathway for the colony. Being slow acting, stomach poison products containing borates may result in colony control. Other forms of termite detection and control are under investigation internationally. These are invariably dependent on the skill of the termite inspector to achieve optimum efficacy and include:

Detection

- Dogs: trained dogs can locate areas of termite activity.
- Gas detectors: metabolic gases vented from concrete slab entry points can indicate termite activity.
- Acoustics: feeding sounds of termites can be detected.

Localised physical control

- Heat fumigation: termites maintained at > 120°F for a minimum of 35 minutes will die. However, it is difficult to get consistent timber heating in a structure, and heat will only kill termites in the timber, not a colony in the ground.

- Cold: use of liquid nitrogen to reduce temperature to -20°F for at least five minutes is a form of chemical treatment. The treatment area size is only small; so it kills individuals, not the ground colony.

- Microwaves: spot treatments using electromagnetic energy at microwave frequencies can be used. Localised application requires occupants to vacate and technicians to wear exposure meters and leave the treatment area while the emitter is operating.

- Nematodes: parasitoids multiply and disperse to infect and kill the majority of the termites in the colony.

References and further reading

Hadlington, P. 1996, *Australian Termites and Other Common Timber Pests*, UNSW Press, Sydney, NSW.

Olkowski, W., Daar, S. and Olkowski, H. 1993, *Common-Sense Pest Control,* 3rd edn, The Tauton Press.

Standards Australia 1993, *AS3660 – 1993, Protection of Buildings from Subterranean Termites – Prevention, Detection and Treatment of Infestation,* Standards Australia, Sydney, NSW.

Standards Australia 1995, *AS 3360.1 – 1995, Protection of Buildings from Subterranean Termites – Part 1: New Buildings*, Standards Australia, Sydney, NSW.

Total Environment Centre 1996, *A–Z of Chemicals in the Home,* 3rd edn, Choicebooks, Sydney, NSW.

Tyrrell, J. 1992, *Pest Pack*, Choicebooks, Sydney, NSW.

Verkerk, R. 1990, *Building Out Termites: An Australian Manual For Environmentally Responsible Control*, Pluto Press, Sydney, NSW.

1. Can you think of new products or services for preventing or eliminating termite infestations?

2. At what stage should MTR be considered in the design and construction process? What elements in a conventional urban structure are susceptible to termite attack and at what frequency should all elements be inspected?

3. Discuss the key design features of MTR construction in (a) suspended floor design, and (b) slab-on-ground design. What are the likely short-term and long-term cost implications?

4. List the site practices which will help lower the level of termite attraction during and after construction.

5. Discuss the limitations and concerns for health and environment issues with regard to chemical control options.

6. How can landscape architects participate in MRT construction? Industrial designers? Construction managers?

1. Following the key MTR construction design features, evaluate the building you are working in for termite risk, looking at such features as paving, garden beds and access for inspection. Do the same for your own home.

2. Having made this evaluation, look at how the building could have been built with lower termite risk. Consider the design, materials, other relevant aspects and the practical limitations of the site (eg proximity to water, slope).

Box 18 Air Quality Problems in Buildings

From Sarah Hammond Creighton, 1998, *Greening the Ivory Tower: Improving the Environmental Track Record of Universities, Colleges, and Other Institutions*, MIT Press, Cambridge, MA, pp. 82–83.

Pollutant	Sources	Potential health effects	Control measures
Combustion by-products: nitric oxide, carbon monoxide, carbon dioxide, odours, particulates	Smoking Routine odours from occupants and normal activity Unvented gases Odours coming in the air intake vents Any heating source Car exhaust	Lung cancer Asthma Breathing disorders Drowsiness Headaches Discomfort Respiratory infections	Ban indoor smoking in all spaces, including private offices Offer smoking cessation assistance Improve ventilation and/or ensure it is not blocked Ensure that ventilation meets current standards Ensure that outdoor air sources are not near parking lots or sources of fumes Reduce occupant density Relocate or reduce use of heat-generating equipment
Biological contaminants: moulds, fungi, bacteria, mildew,	Humidifiers, air-conditioners, Standing water on roofs near air intake Dust mites, rodents, cockroaches	Allergies Headaches Flu symptoms	Take steps to reduce moisture Maintain relative humidity between allergens 30% and 40%. Decrease heat losses from exterior walls (insulate) Clean air-conditioner and humidifier filters Exhaust fans in bathrooms and kitchens Integrated pest management
Asbestos	Wall and ceiling insulation (installed 1930 to 1950) Old pipe insulation Some older vinyl floor tiles Old fireproof cloth products	Skin irritation Long-term inhalation can lead to lung cancer Asbestosis (scarring of the lung tissue)	Maintenance and in situ management Avoid asbestos material Remove friable asbestos using a licensed contractor Use appropriate in-place management that contains and does not disturb the asbestos Avoid exposure
Radon (a radioactive gas naturally occurring in all soil and rock)	Soil and rock Seeps into the building from natural sources	Lung cancer	Test to determine levels Seal cracks Ventilate basement Retest
Volatile organic compounds (hydrocarbons)	Cleaning products Propellants for aerosol products Deodorisers Paints and thinners	Irritation of mucous membranes of nose Headaches Heartburn Mental confusion	Use products according to instructions, especially in correct concentrations Mix concentrated solutions centrally in a controlled manner Use products with plenty of ventilation Switch to nontoxic alternatives Store and dispose of products properly
Chemicals	Laboratory experiments Chemicals sitting in laboratories Chemical storage rooms	Eye irritation Respiratory irritation	Store chemicals properly at all times Reduce chemical use at all times Ensure that ventilation is adequate Keep storage rooms at negative pressure
Semi-volatile organics: formaldehyde (HDHO), PCBs	New carpeting (usually in the backing) Furniture Particle board Adhesives Urea formaldehyde insulation	Eye irritation Upper and lower respiratory irritation Pneumonia (sensitivity varies widely)	Remove source if identifiable Steam clean new furniture and carpets Avoid products with high levels of formaldehyde Seal particle board with varnish Ventilate

8.1 Greening the Workplace

William Browning and Joseph Romm

Energy efficient design may be one of the least expensive ways for a business to improve the 'bottom line'. Energy-efficient lighting, heating, and cooling in commercial buildings can increase worker productivity, decrease absenteeism, and/or improve the quality of work performed by reducing errors and manufacturing defects. Companies have attained significant productivity increases and energy savings through retrofits of existing buildings and new facilities.

Introduction

Energy efficiency retrofits for existing buildings, and new buildings designed for energy efficient performance, have very attractive economic returns. For example, a three-year payback, typical in lighting retrofits, is equal to an internal rate of return in excess of 30%. This return is well above the 'hurdle rate' of most financial managers. The same retrofit may also cut energy use by 50 cents or more per square foot, which has significant positive effects on the net operating income of a building.

However, these savings are minimal when compared to the cost of employees (which is usually greater than the total energy and operating costs of a building). Based on a 1990 national survey of large office buildings (BOMA 1995) electricity typically costs US$1.53 per square foot and accounts for 85% of the total energy bill, while repairs and maintenance typically add another $1.37 per square foot. Both contribute to the gross office space rent of $21 per square foot. In comparison, office workers cost $130 per square foot – 72 times as much as the energy costs (based on US Statistical Abstract 1991). Thus, an increase of 1% in worker productivity can nearly offset a company's entire annual energy cost. Worker productivity can be improved by fewer distractions from eye strain or poor thermal comfort, and similar factors (this is measured in terms of production rate, quality of production, and changes in absenteeism). The companies mentioned here based their decisions solely on projected energy and maintenance savings, rather than increases in worker productivity. The gains in productivity observed by the companies were, for the most part, unanticipated.

Retrofits

Boeing

Boeing participates in the US Environmental Protection Agency's voluntary 'Green Lights' program to promote energy efficient lighting. To date, the aircraft manufacturer has retrofitted more than 1 million of the 8 million square feet of assembly space in its hangar-sized assembly plants near Seattle. Using various efficiency measures, Boeing has reduced lighting electricity use by up to 90% in some of its plants, and the company calculates its overall return on investment in the new lighting to be 53%; thus the energy savings fully paid for the lights in just two years. Lawrence Friedman, then Boeing's conservation manager, noted that if every company adopted the lighting Boeing has installed, 'it would reduce air pollution as much as if one third of the cars on the road today never left the garage'.

However, Boeing has discovered even more interesting results from its lighting retrofit. With the new efficient lighting, employees have more control, the interior looks nicer, and glare has been reduced. One woman, who puts rivets in 30ft wing supports, had for 12 years been relying on touch with one component because she was unable to see inside due to bad lighting. Another riveter reported that with the old lighting, a rivet head would occasionally break off, fly through the air, hit one of the old fluorescent light tubes, and possibly break the lamp. The new high-efficiency metal-halide lamps have hard plastic covers that do not break when a flying rivet head hits them.

Machinists with new lighting say that they can read the calipers on their lathes and measurement tools much more easily. One of the tasks performed by machinists who produce interior sidewall panels for jets is to attach a panel to a stiffening member using numerous fasteners, which leave very small indentations in the panel. The old fluorescent lighting had poor contrast and made it difficult to tell if a fastener had been properly attached. With the new high-efficiency metal-halide lamps, the indentations left by properly attached fasteners are far easier to detect; improving workers' ability to detect imperfections in the shop by 20% (*Boeing News* 1993).

Freedman says that most of the errors in the aircraft interiors that used to slip through 'were not being picked up until installation in the airplane, where it was much more expensive to fix'. Even worse, some imperfections were found during customer walk-throughs, which was embarrassing, and costly. Although it is difficult to calculate the savings from catching errors early, a senior manager estimated that they exceed the energy savings for that building.

Pennsylvania Power and Light

In the early 1980s, Pennsylvania Power and Light became increasingly concerned about the lighting system in a 12,775sq ft room that housed its drafting engineers. According to Russell Allen, superintendent of the office complex, 'the single most serious problem was veiling reflections, a form of indirect glare that occurs when light from a source bounces off the task surface and into a worker's eyes' (Allen 1982). Veiling reflections 'wash out the contrast between the foreground and background of a task surface, making it more difficult to see'. This increases the time required to perform a task and compounds the number of errors likely to be made. According to Allen: 'low-quality seeing conditions were also causing morale problems among employees. In addition to the veiling reflections, workers were experiencing eye strain and headaches that resulted in sick leave' (1982).

After considering many suggestions, management decided to upgrade the lighting in a 2275sq ft area with high-efficiency lamps and **ballasts**. New fixtures were reconfigured and installed parallel, to reduce veiling reflections. To improve lighting quality still further, the fixtures were fitted with eight cell **parabolic louvres** – metal grids that help reduce glare. By converting from general lighting to task lighting, more light was directed specifically to work areas and less was applied to circulation areas. With veiling reflections reduced, less light was needed to provide better visibility. Finally, local controls were installed to permit more selective use of lighting during clean-up and occasional overtime hours. With multiple circuits, maintenance crews can now turn the lights on and off as they move from one area to the next.

Allen performed a detailed cost analysis, comparing the initial capital and labour costs of purchasing and installing the new lighting with the total annual operating costs, including energy consumption, replacement lamps and ballasts, fixture cleaning and lamp replacement labour. The total net cost of the changes amounted to US$8362. Lighting energy use dropped by 69%, and total annual operating costs fell 73% from US$2800 to $765. This US$2035 annual savings alone would have paid for the improvement in 4.1 years, a 24% return on investment. In addition, the new lighting lowered heat loads, and therefore space cooling costs.

Under the improved lighting, productivity also jumped by 13.2%. In the prior year, it had taken 6.93 draughting hours on average to complete one drawing. After the upgrade, it took an average of 6.15 hours. This gain was worth US$42,240 a year, reducing the simple pay-back from 4.1 years to 69 *days*. The productivity gain turned a 24% return on investment into a 540% return.

Before the upgrade, draughters in the area had used about 72 hours of sick leave a year. After the upgrade, the rate dropped 25% to 54 hours a year. The better appearance of the space, reduced eye fatigue and headaches, and the overall improvement in working conditions all helped boost morale. Finally, supervisors report that the new lighting has reduced the number of errors. Allen said: 'Personally, I would have no qualms in indicating that the value of reduced errors is at least $50,000 a year'. If this estimate were included in the calculation, the return on investment would exceed 1,000%.

New buildings

Lockheed Building 157

One of the most successful examples of daylighting in a large commercial office building is Lockheed's building 157 in Sunnyvale, California. In 1979, Lockheed Missiles and Space Company commissioned the architectural firm, Leo A. Daly, to design a new 600,000sq ft office building for 2700 engineers and support people. Daly's architects responded with a design for energy-conscious daylighting that was completed in 1983.

Daly used 15ft-high window walls with sloped ceilings to bring daylight deep into the building. Daylighting was also enhanced by a central **atrium**, or '**litetrium**', which runs top-to-bottom and has a glazed roof. Workers consider it the building's most attractive feature. Other light-enhancing features include exterior **light shelves** on the south facade. These operate as sunshades or as reflectors for bouncing light onto the interior ceiling from the high summer sun; in the winter, when the sun's angle is lower, they diffuse reflected light and reduce glare.

The overall design separates ambient and task lighting, with daylight supplying most of the ambient lighting and task lighting fixtures supplementing each work-station. Continuously dimmable fluorescent tubes with photocell sensors maintain a constant level of light automatically to save even more energy. Daly's energy efficient improvements added roughly US$2 million to the US$50 million cost of the building. The energy savings alone were worth nearly US$500,000 a year. The improvements paid for themselves in a little over four years.

Work-stations were tailored for employee needs, and included acoustic panels and chambers to block out ambient noise. Ambient noise, or **white noise**, was further controlled by sound-absorbing ceilings and speakers that introduced background white noise on each floor.

Lockheed has never published the figures concerning the improvements in absenteeism and **worker productivity**; however, according to Don Aitken, of San Jose State University, absenteeism dropped 15%. Aitken led numerous tours of Building 157 after it opened, and was told by Lockheed officials that the reduced absenteeism paid 100% of the extra cost of the building in the first year. A top Lockheed official told Aitken that they believe they won a very competitive $1.5 billion defence contract on the basis of their improved productivity – and that the profits from that contract paid for the entire building. The architect also reported that Lockheed officials told him that productivity rose 15% on the first major contract done in the building.

Wal-Mart

In June 1993, a new prototype Wal-Mart store opened in Lawrence, Kansas. Called the 'Eco-Mart', the building was an experimental foray into sustainable design by the nation's largest retailer. The project was led by Wal-Mart's Environment Committee and BSW Architects with a consulting team that included the Center for Resource Management, William McDonough Architects, and the Rocky Mountain Institute. The team focused on experimenting with a series of environmentally responsive design strategies and technologies. Elements of the experiment included:

- The use of native species for landscaping; a constructed wetlands for site water run-off and as a source for irrigation.

- A building shell design for adaptive reuse as a multi-family housing complex; a structural roof system constructed from sustainably harvested timber; an environmental education centre and a recycling centre.

- A glass arch at the entrance for daylighting, and an efficient lighting system.

- An HVAC (heating, ventilating and air conditioning) system that utilises ice storage and light-monitoring skylights developed specifically for the project.

Wal-Mart's normal construction costs are extremely low, and a building typically pays for its own construction cost in three to five years. The Eco-Mart cost about 20% higher than the average for other Wal-Mart stores because: using sustainably harvested timber added 10% to the roof cost; the integration of systems was not optimised, resulting in a more expensive cooling system; and the building included elements not found in other stores, such as a recycling centre, a McDonald's and the light-monitoring skylights. As a cost-cutting measure, Wal-Mart decided to install skylights on only half of the roof, leaving the other half without daylighting. The energy performance of the building could also have been better. The controls on the lighting systems were not compatible with the ballasts. The ice storage system leaked water, and due to the expanded hours of store operation, was not able to fully refreeze.

According to Tom Seay, Wal-Mart's vice president for real estate, register activity revealed that 'sales pressure (sales per square foot) was significantly higher for those departments located in the daylit half of the store'. Sales were also higher than for the same departments in other stores. Additionally, employees in the half without the skylights were arguing that their departments should be moved to the daylit side. Wal-Mart is now considering implementing many of the Eco-Mart measures in both new construction and existing stores.

Conclusion

The results of these case studies are compelling for two reasons. First, the measurements of productivity in most of the cases came from records that were already kept, not from a new study. Second, the gains in productivity were sustained – not just a temporary effect. Only those energy efficient designs and actions that improve visual acuity and thermal comfort seem to result in productivity gains. This speaks directly to the need for good design, a total quality approach that seeks to improve energy efficiency and improve the quality of workplaces by focusing on the end-user – the employee. This is a point that seems to have been forgotten by many designers and building owners.

For further information, see the Rocky Mountain Institute's Green Development Services [http://www.rmi.org/gds].

References and further reading

Allen, R. 1982, 'Pennsylvania Power and Light: A Lighting Case Study', *Buildings*, March, pp. 49–56; and 'Office Lighting Retrofit Will Pay Back in 69 Days', *Facilities Design of Management*, June, p. 13.

Benton, C.C. and Fountain, M.C. 1990, 'Successfully Daylighting a Large Commercial Building: A Case Study of Lockheed Building 157', *Progressive Architecture,* November, pp. 119–121.

Boeing's Weekly Newsletter 1993, *Boeing News,* 15 January, p. 5.

Brill, M. et al 1984, *Using Office Design to Increase Productivity, Vol I* , Workplace Design and Productivity, Inc., Buffalo, pp. 224–225.

BOMA (Building Owners and Managers Association) 1991, *Experience Exchange Report*, p. 95.

Friedman, L. and Cassens, S., *Boeing News* (May 10, 1991), 1992 EPA data on the Green Lights program.

Romm, J. 1994, *Lean and Clean Management: How to Increase Profits and Productivity by Reducing Pollution*, Kodansha.

Romm, J. 1999, *Cool Companies: How the Best Businesses Boost Profits and Productivity by Cutting Greenhouse-Gas Emissions*, Island Press, Washington, DC.

US. Statistical Abstract 1991, Table 678, p. 415.

Questions

1. How convincing is the argument that good lighting affects productivity? In your personal experience, what spaces do you like to study in and why?

2. Some private companies are not charging their clients directly for modernising their building's energy and lighting systems. How do they make a profit?

3. The conversion of fuel to electricity generates pollution and wastes energy as heat and friction (about a third of electricity reaches the building). Why has centralised electricity generation been used in place of solar heating and day lighting of buildings?

4. Identify the qualities that you enjoy in your study space or those in an ideal study space (eg views, fresh air, heat, background noise, lighting and so on). Prioritise these elements and compare with the criteria set by others in the group. How important are psychological issues?

5. Is the studio space provided by the design department or firm that you work in conducive to team work? Why or why not?

6. If a government builds a public building, should it insist that the energy saving design not cost more than would a 'conventional' building, or should it take the opportunity to invest in experimental energy efficient design even though it may cost more. List pro's and con's for these positions.

Projects

1. In groups, divide into designers (eg building, landscape, industrial or other designers) and corporate clients. Try to sell the idea of ecological design to the clients. Then reverse roles and repeat.

2. In groups, set criteria for, and design, a sky light that retains heat in the winter and cools the room in the summer for the region you live in. Consider (a) use of colour and materials to absorb solar heat; (b) convenience and ease of cleaning; (c) user control of the light, heat and glare through the skylight; (d) costs of manufacture and shipping; (e) minimising materials and energy used in production; (f) adaptability to different ceilings, eg raked or flat; (g) how to allow ventilation without heat loss. What else must be considered?

Robert D. M. Cotgrove

Policies of urban consolidation and public transport have failed, and people continue to use cars despite the enormous personal, social and environmental costs involved. Traditional planning has misconstrued the nature of urban travel behaviour, and has underestimated the benefits of personal motorised transport. According to the author, the answer to the problems caused by increasing personal transport in cities lies, not in a return to public transport but, in 'civilising' car travel.

Introduction

Between 1971 and 1993, urban car travel in Australia almost doubled, from 81 billion passenger-kms in 1971 to 158 billion passenger-kms in 1993 (BTCE 1996, p. 340). During the same period, despite increasing subsidies to public transport systems and continual criticism of car travel as socially and environmentally irresponsible, car travel increased its share of the total urban passenger task from 82% in 1971 to 87% in 1993.

Urban road traffic congestion has increased significantly and now represents a major problem in our larger cities. A recent study estimated the costs of road traffic congestion in Melbourne, in vehicle operating and travel time costs alone, at approximately A\$2 billion a year (Industry Commission 1994, p. 220). If other social and environmental costs are included, the total costs of urban road congestion throughout Australia may be as high as A\$10 billion a year, and rising. These trends are similar to those of other developed countries and are occurring at even faster rates in developing countries. The world car fleet of 520 million cars and 165 million commercial vehicles is expected to double within the next 25 years, with the increase of motorised travel rising faster than both population growth and car ownership rates (United Nations 1997, p. 554).

Understanding urban travel behaviour

The time–space welfare approach

According to the time–space welfare approach presented here, urban travel is an intermediate service, a means to an end, rather than an end in itself. Travel is undertaken only if the perceived benefits at the destination outweigh the anticipated costs of getting there. The costs of urban travel are measured not only in terms of money but, increasingly, in terms of time as society moves to a **post-industrial economy** characterised by flexibility and mobility. Unless activities can be reached in time, travel will not take place.

Economic welfare is about choice and opportunity. We often think that affluence equates with money: 'the more money we have, the more choices we have, and therefore the richer we are'. This approach overlooks the fact that each of us lives in a time–space realm (Hagerstrand 1970); an accessibility cocoon, or 'prism', determined by land use arrangements (*where* things are), hours of operation (*when* things are available), and useable means of transport (*mobility*). Thus, our lives are richer by having more opportunities and available choices within our personal time–space realm. Since no amount of money can buy an opportunity that lies outside our time–space realm, anything that expands it enriches our lives and increases our welfare.

We can enlarge our time–space realm by changing any of its limiting parameters. We can locate closer to the land uses we need to access by living closer to the inner city – but only by paying higher financial costs for suitable accommodation. We can expand hours of operations by taking advantage of ATMs (automatic teller machines) at banks or by lobbying for extended shopping hours – but only to the extent that changes to trading hours are politically acceptable. We can increase our mobility by lobbying for increased public transport or by improving our personal transport options – but only at the expense of increased taxation or personal expenditure.

Hagerstrand recognised that our daily activity patterns are restricted by three major types of constraints; *capability constraints* (biological and physical limits, such as the need to eat and sleep regularly, or the inability to walk beyond a certain speed); *coupling constraints* (the need to coordinate our activity patterns to interact with other individuals at work, at leisure, or for other reasons); and *authority constraints*

Box 8.2.1: Changing urban land use and travel patterns

Public transport systems developed in the late 19th Century at a time when personal transport was limited to animal power. They enabled people to live far from their places of work – leading to the formation of dormitory suburbs and the phenomenon of daily journey-to-work commuting patterns. Residential and commercial activities developed along radial, usually flat, transport corridors to produce a star-shaped land-use pattern focused strongly on the pre-existing compact central business district.

Industrial employment patterns were ideally suited to the **economies of scale** requirements of mass transportation. A daily tidal flow of predominantly male workers travelled into the city to large labour-intensive manufacturing and office workplaces in the morning and returned home to suburban houses close to train and tram tracks in the late afternoon. However, urban travel patterns have changed dramatically with the emergence of the post-industrial service economy. New flexible, irregular, and discretionary patterns of travel (reflecting changes in employment, work and leisure), are rapidly replacing the rigid, regular, and routine travel patterns of the industrial era. The current rate of growth of female employment is now double that of males, and within a few years the number of women is expected to surpass the number of men in the work forces of most **OECD** countries (Core 1994). Employment in manufacturing has shrunk significantly in favour of service sector employment, particularly in the growth of client-based, customer-focused, informational, recreational, and professional services. These new time- and space-dispersed travel patterns, and increasingly diverse lifestyles, can only be served effectively by flexible, on-demand, personal transport systems.

The development of trucks enabled manufacturing, retailing, and office employment to decentralise to new large suburban commercial centres, while increasing car ownership has enabled families to free themselves from the necessity of living close to transport corridors and to move to desirable but previously inaccessible residential locations. In Australia, the spread of low-density suburban development and dispersed travel patterns persists, despite the significant, but minor, trend for residential conversion of redundant inner city industrial land and the adoption of urban consolidation policies (O'Connor et al 1995).

(those that limit our activities to specific locations, or domains, and make other locations legally inaccessible).

The traffic engineering approach

The traditional traffic engineering approach regards urban travel as a physical exercise in logistics. People, by their actions, indicate their desires to travel and it is the role of the traffic planner or engineer to accommodate those travel demands as efficiently as possible (given the social constraints of available transport modes and publicly funded infrastructure). Some problems with this approach are:

- By considering travel behaviour as a logistical exercise, it deals only with actual trips made and not with trips unable to be made because of time–space constraints. It fails to recognise that, to the individual, unrealised (or latent) travel may be just as important as realised (or actual) travel.

- It deals with traffic flows as a series of discrete independent trips, rather than as a daily journey made up of a set of interdependent links.

- It treats time as a flow variable, valued as a generalised cost in units of dollars per period of time, and does not account for critical stocks of time when, for example, certain highly valued activities can be undertaken only if reached in a minimum amount of travel time.

- It defines efficiency in a narrow physical sense as a function of vehicle capacities and related expenditures of energy, rather than in economic terms, as gains and losses in welfare.

The concept of the time–space prism, on the other hand, enables us to understand many aspects of travel behaviour; for example, our propensity to live in urban areas where a much broader range of activities are within reach; the limitations of fixed-route, fixed-timetable, mass transit systems that constrain activities to narrow time–space 'tubes' attached to transit stations, central areas, and other limited places at limited times; and the popularity of personal travel modes, particularly the private car or truck, which considerably enlarge our activity choices.

Characteristics of public transport systems

Public transport is mass transport. To repay the high fixed costs of capital infrastructure, operating expenses, and administration overheads, vehicles and service levels need to be designed to achieve economies of scale. This is done by having multi-passenger vehicles, fixed routes, and published timetables. Public transport operates most efficiently where travel demands are concentrated in time and space.

Mass transit systems require large numbers of passengers with broadly similar activity patterns, going from similar origins to similar destinations at approximately the same time. This applies in large cities and for certain types of activities, such as the journeys to and from work of central city workers. For other types of activities, the market for viable public transport systems is steadily decreasing due to their inability to service low density, time- and space-dispersed travel demands. Collecting enough passengers to achieve economies of scale is difficult due to the long distances from homes to transit stations and long waiting times.

Public transport is further disadvantaged in that crucial decisions, such as the types and number of vehicles, levels of service and fare structures, and choice of routes and frequencies, are beyond the control of passengers. They are in the hands of those who manage and operate the systems.

Characteristics of personal transport modes

Unlike public transport systems, personal transport systems (roads and paths) are relatively ubiquitous in time and space and are available when people want to use them. Hence they are ideally suited for serving time- and space-dispersed travel demands. Increased mobility, which has seen travel demands in urban areas greatly outstrip the supply of road space, together with the motor vehicle dependence on petroleum-powered engines, has created serious problems of pollution, social disruption and congestion in major cities. Nevertheless, the welfare enhancing benefits of personal transport are so great that car travel has continued to increase regardless of the private costs, or the quality and subsidisation of local public transport systems.

Sustainable personal urban transport

Transport sustainability requires two conditions:

• That all commercial, social, and environmental

externality costs, free of subsidies and other distortions, be identified.

• That these costs be internalised using prices which broadly reflect **marginal social costs**.

Although the principles of using marginal social cost pricing mechanisms to manage urban road transport have been recognised for several decades, it is only recently that an appropriate and cheap form of electronic technology has existed to apply the principles in practice. Advances in electronic technology now make it possible to identify, differentiate, and target individual vehicles to make them pay for the construction and maintenance costs of building urban arterial roads, as well as the congestion and pollution costs caused by using them. The impending introduction of electronic road pricing, together with other valuable in-vehicle driver information, is likely to revolutionise the way future motorists use urban roads (Hills and Blythe 1990; Wherrett 1991).

Conceptually, the use of pricing mechanisms to ration scarce road space in the face of excess demand is no different to the use of parking charges to ration scarce parking spaces. According to a recent study, efficient road user charges would represent a clear 'no regrets' measure, producing an overall saving in road operating costs to the Australian society of about A$120 billion over the period from 1996 to 2015, and reducing Australia's greenhouse gas emissions during the same period by more than 90 million tonnes (BTCE 1996, p. 308).

Given other pricing mechanisms to internalise the environmental costs of vehicle emissions, pollution can be further reduced to optimum levels. Such measures would include the imposition of a carbon tax on fossil fuels and a revenue-neutral shift of taxation from vehicle ownership to vehicle use. Society would benefit if cars were cheaper to own but more expensive to use. Shifting the costs from ownership to use encourages the conversion to smaller, lighter, and more fuel-efficient cars, and could hasten the introduction of environmentally benign solar and electric powered engines.

Smart cars interacting with smart roads will not only manage congestion to socially optimum levels, but will provide the means to enable people who are mobility impaired (such as the aged, the blind, the disabled and others with infirmities) to enjoy the same degree of time–space freedom taken for granted by others. Electronic systems will also provide on-board vehicle information relating to the appropriate route choice, available parking spaces at destination, and potential bottlenecks; vehicle safety and security information; and a range of non-travel related information, such as entertainment, news services, and telecommunications services.

Box 8.2.2: The Hypercar

What will the cars of the future look like? There are physical constraints that will continue to limit a car's speed, acceleration, braking and other performance parameters. Given that cars will still need to require an engine, passenger space and a luggage compartment, they will probably not look very different from the cars of today, apart from being constructed from strong and lightweight hybrid materials '... like the new plastics ... or new alloys of steel or aluminium' (Wherrett 1991).

Such a car, combining ultralight mass, ultra-low drag, and hybrid-electric drive to obtain super efficiency performance, has been described by Amory Lovins, Director of Research at the Rocky Mountain Institute in Colorado. Named the 'Hypercar ™', the strategy is applicable to many types and classes of passenger vehicles. It is designed to weigh two to three times less than conventional vehicles, achieve four to six times better fuel economy (up to 200mpg or 2L/100km), while providing equal or better performance, safety and amenity for consumers and manufacturing advantages for automakers. [http://www.hypercar.com].

As an individual vehicle, the Hypercar concept gives the promise of a future car that is, to all intents and purposes, environmentally benign. What it does not solve, as Lovins himself admits, is social responsibility: 'Hypercars cannot solve the problem of too many people driving too many kilometres in too many cars, and could make it worse by making driving more attractive and its marginal cost approach zero.'

Solving this social problem requires the car of the future to internalise the social externality costs of congestion that it causes by the use of 'electronic road pricing' (ERP). Not only will ERP reduce car use, but will prevent traffic accidents and reduce further the need for body mass. Combined with other on-board vehicle driver information, an optimist could expect that the car of the future will be more environmentally benign and socially responsible, while achieving sustainable personal urban transport [Box 19].

Conclusion

With electronic technology and correct pricing signals based on marginal social costs, the market can encourage the development of cars which are lightweight in construction, safe to drive, and powered by non-polluting engines. Unlike heavy mass transport vehicles, personal motorised transport has the potential not only to considerably enhance human welfare and safety, but to do so in ways which are socially responsible and environmentally benign.

References and further reading

BTCE 1996, 'Transport and Greenhouse', *Report 94*, AGPS, Canberra, ACT.

Core, F. 1994, 'Women and the Restructuring of Employment', *OECD Observer* 186, pp. 5–12.

Hagerstrand, T. 1970, 'What about People in Regional Science?', *Papers of the Regional Science Association* 14, pp. 7–21.

Hills, P. and Blythe, P. 1990, 'Road Pricing: Solving the Technical Problems', *Economic Affairs,* June/July, pp. 8–10.

Industry Commission 1994, 'Urban Transport', *Report 37*, AGPS, Melbourne, VIC.

Jones, P.M. et al 1983, *Understanding Travel Behaviour*, Gower, Aldershot.

O'Connor, K., Darby, A. and Rapson, V. 1995, 'The Great Mistake: Consolidation Policy in Melbourne and Sydney', *People And Place* 3(3), pp. 40–45.

Toffler, A. 1980, *The Third Wave*, Pan, London.

United Nations 1997, *Statistical Yearbook 1995*, New York.

Washington, S. 1992, 'Women at Work', *OECD Observer* 176, pp. 28–31.

Wherrett, P. 1991, 'Smart Cars', *21C* (Summer 1990–91), pp. 14–18.

Questions

1. Discuss the differences in approach to urban travel behaviour represented by (a) the traffic engineering paradigm and (b) the time–space welfare paradigm.

2. Using examples, discuss the meaning and importance of Hagerstrand's 'capability', 'coupling', and 'authority' constraints in determining a person's time–space opportunities.

3. Debate: 'Public transport systems are inferior to motorised personal transport in satisfying urban travel demands.'

4. In nuclear families, 80% of trips made to pick up or drop off children are made by mothers. Furthermore, working women make more such trips than non-working mothers. Other studies indicate that, compared with their male partners, women make the greater proportion of shopping, social visiting and other non-work family trips. In view of this, discuss the importance of car travel for working women faced with a limited time–space budget.

5. Electronic road pricing (ERP) offers an efficient method of managing urban traffic congestion by rationing scarce road space, in ways similar to the rationing of parking space or seats at a popular concert. Describe briefly how ERP would work and discuss the likely social advantages and disadvantages of such a system.

6. What social and other factors work against the likelihood that cars of the future could be made truly environmentally benign.

Projects

1. Urban land use patterns are said to reflect dominant transportation systems. Using diagrams, describe the changing size, shape and density of cities and the spatial organisation of manufacturing, commercial and residential land uses associated with (a) the pre-industrial city, (b) the industrial city, and (c) the post-industrial city.

2. The concept of the time–space prism is best understood by constructing daily activity patterns based on personal travel diaries.

- As a tutorial exercise, record your own travel behaviour each day for the week preceding the tutorial. In a diary, list each trip you make, noting the time and location of commencement, purpose of travel, mode of transport used, time and location of destination, and duration of time spent at the destination.

- From this information show each of your daily activity patterns as a two-dimensional line graph, with time of day along the horizontal axis and spatial location on the vertical axis.

- Discuss the key features of your time–space graphs, emphasising the nature of the various constraints, the reasons for choosing different transport modes, and other important travel related decisions.

- As a group, discuss alternatives that may help expand your time-space prisms and hence improve your welfare.

Box 19 The 'Hypercar' Concept

Michael Brylawski and Rocky Mountain Institute

The automotive industry is overdue for fundamental innovation. In mid-1991, the Big Three automakers claimed that fuel economy could not improve more than 10% without making the car unmarketable. However, the Rocky Mountain Institute (RMI) argued that carefully integrating advanced technologies could make cars better in all respects, fuel efficiency, low emissions, life cycle benefits, and probably cost. Since 1991, RMI (and its Hypercar Center since 1994) has advised several dozen current and potential automakers, heightened customer expectations, and fomented market competition.

From the start, RMI gave away its Hypercar intellectual property instead of patenting it, in order to maximise the competition to exploit it. The value of an idea or artefact increases with the number of users. Thus, by giving away its Hypercar concept, RMI has increased its value by expanding the network of Hypercar advocates and potential adopters.

The Hypercar concept integrates an ultralight, ultra-low-drag vehicle platform with a hybrid-electric drive system. This combination, applicable to both cars and light trucks, can make dramatic improvements in fuel efficiency and emissions without compromising safety, amenity, performance, and probably affordability. Computer models indicate that these ultralight, low-drag, hybrid-drive Hypercars should improve fuel efficiency three- to fourfold. With near-production-ready technologies a four- to fivefold improvement is possible with a PEM fuel-cell powerplant and further refinements. Ultimately, fuel efficiencies up to about 200mpg for a four-seat car should become feasible. Emissions (ie CO, HC, and NOx) should be a tenth those of ultra-low-emission vehicle (ULEV) standards – even burning ordinary gasoline with no catalytic converter.

The prospect for widespread adoption of Hypercars may depend less on environmental regulations than on market forces. Hence, Hypercars have to be useful, fun to drive, fast, low-risk and inexpensive to produce. Hypercars promise these advantages by virtue of using fundamentally different materials and design and manufacturing methods. For instance, ultralight materials: make cars accelerate and handle better with a given drive-train; offer important safety features that offset their mass disadvantage against heavy steel cars; can improve durability and recyclability; and offer radically more compact, affordable, flexible, and agile manufacturing processes. There are two key design principles at work here:

Mass decompounding: reducing the mass of a vehicle, particularly the autobody, through lightweight materials helps other systems. Less tractive load provides the same or better performance with a smaller hybrid-drive system. That makes the car even lighter, reducing suspension and chassis loads. The lighter suspension, chassis, and drive system can reduce loads on the autobody, reducing its mass further. This cycle continues through recursive mass decompounding until stalled by diminishing returns.

Cost decompounding: for ultralight hybrids, mass decompounding can also lead to **cost decompounding**. An ultralight platform's smaller drive system produces fewer kilowatts of average and peak power, which can decrease costs for components like fuel cells. Several automotive mechanical and electrical components can also be eliminated, further reducing the cost.

The extra cost of advanced materials and drive system technologies can be roughly offset by savings from their careful integration, frugal use of materials, and, ultimately, economies in fabrication, painting, and assembly. Thus, paradoxically, costlier ultralight materials can be the key to a competitively priced car.

Chérie Hoyle and Paul Downton

Is it really possible to convert a city to an eco-city? Advocates of Eco-cities claim that we can. Cities are constantly changing and evolving in any case, with an enormous investment of energy and resources. Advocates of Eco-cities are simply saying that we must direct the course of that evolution towards particular goals (Girardet 1993). This chapter argues for denser cities and gives examples of initiatives to create models for urban living.

Introduction

Fifty years ago, things looked different, and were actually done differently. There was practically no TV, fewer cars, telephones were still a bit of a luxury, and flying certainly was. Streets were different, the houses were different. Street gangs? – where were they? There were twice as many trees on the planet and **suburban sprawl** had only just started. So how different might things be in another 50 years – when our children might be thinking back to their childhood days of hanging around in shopping malls, and watching videos because there was nowhere to go. Their memories may not be as rich or deep as ours, because the safe, natural creeks, forests and villages are mostly gone.

The future built environment is created in the present. As a rule, for instance, a typical new building in Australia is intended to last about 25 to 30 years (ie how long it takes to justify the investment required) although they often last longer. But we would do well to amortise the investment of energy and resources over a longer period and design and build as if it were going to last a century or more [2.4, 3.4].

Sprawl

For sustainable cities, the thing that most needs changing is the very shape of our city, its urban morphology (Kostof 1991). A typical sprawling metropolis in Australia or America, for instance, is not an ideal shape when the future is going to favour the compact and efficient. In the eco-city of the future we would expect to be able to get to most places just by walking. Instead of sprawling suburbs we need more

convenient, neighbourhood-oriented communities (Van der Ryn and Calthorpe 1986). As Richard Register, an eco-city activist, puts it: 'The quickest way to get from A to B is to build B next to A, or proximity planning' (Register 1987).

The city is a result of decisions taken, and trends followed from, years ago. The city is shaped by traditional planning that looked at the immediate past, extrapolated the trends on the graphs and assumed we needed more of the same. 'Real' planning would look ahead at where we would like to get to and then figure out the best ways to get there (that is how we got to the moon).

If we want to live in a future of friendly, convenient, efficient and comfortable communities, we have to start planning immediately. To get the right kind of planning regulations in place, we need the right kind of council members elected. It is not planners who make the regulations, it is our elected representatives (Engwicht 1992). Real planning draws on the collective wisdom of the citizenry (Bookchin 1995).

Our sprawling suburbs are inefficient and, although individual gardens may sometimes be very pleasant places, the huge areas of paved road that connect our suburban 'castles' are just the opposite. We need to remake the street as a healthy, attractive place to be rather than just an expensive, life-destroying track for noisy, poisonous machines. We tend to forget that the exhaust gas from a car is quite literally, deadly poison (people even commit suicide with it). Enormous road networks result in gross energy inefficiencies, and barriers between people, making it hard for spontaneous communities to work in the way that healthy towns and villages used to (Mumford 1961). The Australian/American dream of the quarter acre block has become a nightmare; petrol costs too much, the water is running out, the kids live too far from their friends and the houses are behind fences. If your neighbour drops dead you might never know about it. Suburban sprawl has killed any spontaneous sense of community (Newman at al 1992).

It is also a self-indulgence which the world will no longer allow us. Developing countries are being provided with unworkable models for city-making (Girardet 1993). Sprawling suburbs are environmentally unsustainable and there is not enough room on this planet, nor enough resources, to lead everyone up the suburban garden path. The quarter acre block is no longer an achievable dream. But there is a better way.

Private courtyards, gardens and other spaces for intimacy or leisure can be designed into any kind of housing that is no more than three to four storeys high. The public realm comes alive when urban environments have well designed and appropriate public spaces (Webb 1990). Food can be grown in greenhouses, rooftop and community gardens even in the city. Swimming pools, tennis courts and other facilities can be provided as shared resources. Transit, cycles and walkable streets can replace the near-total dependence on private cars. Attached dwellings, clusters and terraces can provide more energy efficient houses. Cohousing can provide other shared facilities like laundries and playrooms for young children [7.1].

The quarter acre block demonstrates the power of its owner; control of a large area of land speaks of dominance, control, power, success. But in a civilised society, it should be possible to find more responsible ways of demonstrating success. Cities can be good for us (Sherlock 1991). In **eco-cities**, success would be demonstrated by showing an understanding of the need to nurture nature and restore ecosystems – to stop being 'future eaters' (Flannery 1994).

Denser is better

Keeping down the size of a building's physical footprint can contribute to reducing the overall size of its ecological footprint (Rees and Wackernagel 1996). The need for greater dwelling densities suggests that eco-cities may have some high buildings, but high densities can be comfortably achieved with three or four storey housing, so except for the few childless couples or individuals who choose it, there is no need for high-rise housing (Sherlock 1991). Having people live within easy walking distance of one another facilitates spontaneous personal interactions, helping to generate a sense of community.

Urban consolidation or denser living, also called 'compact cities', would allow space for natural environments and to restore the health of the ecosystem. However, the key argument is economically based. Fewer pipes, wires and roads are needed if houses are closer together. So, provided the quality of life in denser living is as high as that in low-

density living, then the ecological, economic and social arguments favour higher densities [8.4].

We desperately need to get back in touch with reality, not to escape from it. Advocates of eco-cities offer their vision for the future on the basis that it is grounded in ecological reality and provides a socially responsible and responsive approach to design and development that evolves from education, understanding and the participation of the community. Their vision is practical and result-oriented and, being about the real ecology of life, starts and continues with a focus on people. As Fritjof Capra puts it:

> *'Reconnecting with the web of life means building and nurturing sustainable communities in which we can satisfy our needs and aspirations without diminishing the chances of future generations.'* (Capra 1996, p. 289)

Two Australian eco-city projects

Urban Ecology Australia Inc (UEA) is a non-profit education and advocacy association, working to integrate social, economic and cultural initiatives with eco-city projects as catalysts for systemic environmental improvement in cities and their bioregions.

The Halifax Eco-city Project

In Adelaide, 1991, members of UEA searched for an inner-city site for a small eco-city development. In 1993, the old Adelaide City Council (ACC) Depot was vacated and the 2.2ha site was made available for redevelopment. With Ecopolis, UEA sought to promote the development of the 'Halifax Eco-city Project' (HEP), a proposal for a car-free, mixed-use development with ecological architecture, renewable energy, water capture and reuse, and integrated on-site sewage recycling. A major goal of the project was not just to create an 'environmentally-friendly' development, but also to address social equity issues and the impact of the city on its hinterland.

After six years the HEP proposal resulted in the Adelaide City Council making a commitment to complete the remediation of the contaminated site to residential standards. This was to be an environmentally advanced redevelopment of the last major vacant site in the city.

The HEP proposal attracted international attention and won several awards. Nonetheless, in 1989 the ACC allowed a development of conventional brick veneer rowhouses and apartments set along new roads on the site.

This unfortunate experience led Urban Ecology Australia to adopt a new strategy, leading to the creation of a non-profit developer, 'Wirranendi', and building company, 'EcoCity Developments'. In 1999 Wirranendi Inc bought a small block of land near the Halifax site, called Christie Walk. A microcosm of the HEP, it shows how the Halifax site could have been developed.

Christie Walk: Christie Walk is a cohousing project initially comprising 14 dwellings and gardens at 105 Sturt Street in Adelaide. Construction is taking place in stages. Four townhouses and a strawbale cottage were completed in December 2001; stage two includes three larger strawbale cottages and six apartments; stage three will be a mixed-use building with apartments, 'green' office accommodation and community facilities.

Information about the design of the Christie Walk project is available at http://www.greenhouse.gov.au/yourhome/technical/fs73.htm

The Whyalla eco-city development

Whyalla is a working class, 'steel town' of 26,000 people, 400km north of Adelaide (by road). In 1996 Ecopolis and UEA, with the support of the University of South Australia, were commissioned to create an eco-city concept for a 15ha 'core site' in the city's centre.

A concept plan was prepared after extensive workshopping and community participation, using processes drawn from experience with the Halifax Eco-city Project. An Arid Lands Centre for Urban Ecology was set up and has been operated by local people since late 1996, providing environmental information to the region and exhibiting eco-city plans.

Construction of a Buddhist temple has begun and stage one of the new headquarters for the 'Excel' disabled services organisation. A high-mass earth construction, self-cooling, ecological Anglican church is planned to occupy a central position on the site. The council has commissioned an interpretive feature, housing sub-divisions and a variety of low/medium cost, solar eco-housing designs from Ecopolis.

Conclusion

Eco-cities are achievable in the medium to long term. They will have densities more like traditional European cities – significantly higher than those typical in present day sprawling 'suburban cities' of Australia or America. Higher density has to do with more efficient use of land and resources allied to more responsive, community-driven design and development, with social and cultural dividends that are not available in the suburban model of urbanism. Eco-cities replace machine-dominated spaces with people and green space. They do not presuppose high-rise buildings, but do require extensive and intensive green areas and a strong focus on a 'sense of place' derived from community input and regional ecological responsiveness.

References and further reading

Capra, F. 1996, *The Web of Life: A New Scientific Understanding of Living Systems*, Anchor Books, New York.

Engwicht, D. 1992, *Towards an Eco-city: Calming the Traffic*, Envirobook, Sydney, NSW.

Flannery, T. 1994, *The Future Eaters: An Ecological History of the Australasian Lands and People*, Reed Books, Auckland.

Girardet, H. 1993, *The Gaia Atlas of Cities: New Directions for Sustainable Urban Living*, Gaia Books, London.

Hough, M. 1995, *Cities and Natural Process*, Routledge, London.

Kostof, S. 1991, *The City Shaped*, Thames and Hudson, London.

Mumford, L. 1961, *The City in History*, Penguin, New York.

Newman, P., Kenworthy, J. and Robinson, L. 1992, *Winning Back the Cities*, Pluto Press, Leichhardt, NSW.

Rees, W. and Wackernagel, M. 1996, *Our Ecological Footprint: Reducing Human Impact on the Earth*, New Society Publishers, Gabriola Island, BC and Washington DC.

Register, R. 1987, *Eco-city Berkeley: Building Cities for a Healthy Future*, North Atlantic Books, Berkeley, CA.

Sherlock, H. 1991, *Cities are Good for Us*, Paladin, Boulder, CO.

Van der Ryn, S. and Calthorpe, P. 1986, *Sustainable Communities*, Sierra Club Books, San Francisco, CA.

Webb, M. 1990, *The City Square*, Thames and Hudson, London.

Williams, K., Burton, E. and Jenks, M., eds, 2000, *Achieving Sustainable Urban Form*, Spon Press, London and New York.

Questions

Debate the following propositions as (a) an eco-city advocate, and (b) a committed sub-urbanite:

1. Crime in the city would be reduced by a more community-oriented environment.

2. Cities should be responsible for preserving the countryside (in Brisbane there is already a small environmental levy of A$5 per person per quarter which the city uses to buy private bushland to preserve for future generations).

3. Private cars provide an inefficient and wasteful transport solution; therefore, ending car dominance must be a priority in all future urban planning.

4. Access to all facilities is best achieved by living close to them – moving buildings 'back to the centre' should be the ultimate goal of all city planning with all facilities within walking distance.

5. Work places should be close to home for as many people as practicable.

6. Cities should provide for biodiversity within their area as well as dense urban development.

Projects

1. Suburban shrink: If we need to progressively reverse suburban sprawl back to eco-city village/neighbourhood cores, how can we get there from here? Consider your own city or council area and try to come up with a strategy.

2. Scenario planning: Revisit Ted Trainer's chapter [2.1], and make a list of positive arguments favouring both urban consolidation and radical urban decentralisation.

Greg Bamford

In general, there is an inverse relation between the population densities of cities and their petrol consumption per capita: as densities decline, petrol consumption increases. But is our only choice between US suburban sprawl and the much higher density European city? The fixation on density, with little scrutiny of, for example, land use, site cover or social organisation, impoverishes the debate. Lower densities are not necessarily an impediment to creating cities with significant environmental virtues.

What is space for?

In spite of the problems with the suburbs that we have inherited, the relatively generous and equitable distribution of space at the household and neighbourhood level has been one of their enduringly popular characteristics (Stretton 1974, 1994). But this distribution is changing. The zoologist, Tim Flannery, has remarked that of all the environmental problems facing Sydney, 'the great sleeper' for him is 'the alienation of young Australians from their natural heritage'. He recalls that:

> *'When Sydney was smaller and less crowded, wildlife abounded. As recently as the '70s many of the city's reserves were homes to bandicoots, gliders and echidnas, as well as children's forts and cubby houses ... Now, many reserves have been turned into islands by development on all sides ... if nothing changes, Sydney will become a biological desert inhabited by more than 6 million [people] by the time I am an old man.'* (Flannery 1995, p. 11)

Australia has a rich and unique heritage of flora and fauna, and our lower urban densities have left us with more biological diversity in our cities than may otherwise have been the case. Elsewhere, Flannery notes that Black Mountain, which lies near the heart of Canberra, is inhabited by 'more species of ants ... than there are in Britain' and that his 'tiny backyard' in Sydney shelters 'seven species of skinks, while Great Britain is home to just three species of lizard' (1994, p. 75). The same goes for our native flora. How,

then, are we to weigh up the competing environmental claims on urban space and the values which shape our choices?

To highlight the issue of density, consider the relation between density and a single environmental good, namely, home-grown food production. In general, as population density increases, home-grown food production declines – the converse of the relation with petrol consumption (see Table 8.4.1).

A small city like Hobart, in Tasmania, is considerably more productive than Sydney. With barely 5% of Sydney's population (at less than two-thirds the density), Hobart produces the same quantity of home-grown poultry as Sydney does, in addition to producing more than four or five times the quantity of fruit, vegetables and nuts per capita (Division of National Mapping 1980; ABS 1993, ABS 1994). Given the structure and demands of a contemporary market economy, home-grown food production is typically a small fraction of commercial production (and it is generally greater outside the capital cities). There are, however, some notable home-grown quantities: the average fruit growing garden in Australia produces 49kg annually; for vegetables the quantity is 70kg; and at 26 million dozen eggs per annum (or just over 4 dozen eggs for every household). Home-grown egg production is almost 20% of the commercial industry. Moreover, quantities are not the only benefits – freshness, taste, convenience, recreational values and concerns about commercial pesticide use are important for growers (Bamford 1992).

The contribution that lower densities can make to the productive capacity or output, efficiency and flexibility of the household economy is substantial. Lower densities can also increase the scope and quality of domestic and neighbourhood recreational or social pursuits, and better meet changing household preferences and life circumstances. All of these have environmental implications, many of them benefits (Stretton 1974, 1991 and 1994; Bamford 1992; Troy 1992). Home-grown foodstuffs (and flowers) are simple examples of how space need not be

Table 8.4.1: Ratios of home-grown food production per capita

Australia's five largest cities in order of decreasing population density (persons per hectare – pph) and Sydney = 1 for each foodstuff.

		Vegetables	Fruit	Nuts	Eggs	Poultry	Beer
SYDNEY	(19 pph)	1	1	1	1	1	1
MELBOURNE	(16 pph)	1. 7	2. 4	3. 1	1. 6	1. 2	1. 3
ADELAIDE	(14 pph)	2. 2	5. 2	17. 0	3. 4	8. 8	2. 4
BRISBANE	(11 pph)	1. 5	3. 4	6. 8	2. 0	9. 0	2. 9
PERTH	(10. 5 pph)	1. 2	2. 5	3. 9	3. 1	12. 6	2. 0

'wasted' by lowering urban densities (Newman and Kenworthy 1992, p. 4). Whether space is wisely allocated in our cities depends on, among other things, what that space is, or can be, used for and what values are fostered by such uses.

Density is a crude instrument. For example, Brussels is more than twice as dense as Copenhagen, yet it consumes more petrol than the Danish capital (Newman and Kenworthy 1992, p. 9). Adelaide's petrol consumption is only marginally higher than Sydney's. Therefore, it might not be wise to set about rebuilding Adelaide, increasing its density by a third to match Sydney's. The first garden city, Letchworth in the UK, is similar in density to Sydney; but Letchworth could double its density by sacrificing its productive green belt for housing. Would that make Letchworth, or England, more sustainable? Density is only one or several possible indexes of the sustainability of cities; the extent of nature reserves and home-grown food production are also important.

Alternatives to high density

It is worth noting that Ted Trainer's deep green vision for the Australian city depends on low-density settlement patterns [2.1]. As part of his critique of the market-orchestrated consumption of Western societies, Trainer (1995) argues that much of the production of the goods and services which the market economy has captured or seized, should be returned to cooperative neighbourhoods and household backyards. Most goods and services which the market supplies to households come at great environmental cost. In a tradition which stretches back at least to the 19th Century and William Morris (1971), Trainer thus imagines reuniting communities with productive and stimulating neighbourhoods.

While some favour the more substantial higher density European (or North American) **urban villages** (Newman

and Kenworthy 1992), there are other European traditions that have adopted a different strategy.

Cohousing is a cooperative housing and neighbourhood type. It took shape in Denmark in the 1970s and 1980s, spreading rapidly to other Scandinavian countries, The Netherlands, and more recently the US and Canada. By 1994, more than 140 such communities had been built in Denmark (McCamant and Durrett 1994), and in the US, over 50 communities were built or under construction in 1997 (with a further 100 under development). Communities with 20 to 30 households are common, and the housing is typically compactly organised around courtyards or pedestrian streets, with cars grouped at the periphery of the site. This allows for generous communal possibilities. Schemes range in size from 6 dwelling units up to 80 or a 100 dwellings, with most having between 20 and 40 dwellings [7.1].

Communities typically have a common house where residents can cook and eat together. The common house relieves individual households of the need for their own laundry, workshop or guest room; and provides shared storage and recycling facilities, and spaces for children or teenagers. In cohousing, the neighbourhood is an intentional creation; it attempts to secure the social advantages of a more community-oriented or cooperative life in the immediate neighbourhood, without sacrificing the autonomy and privacy of individual households. Social relations are developed between households in the planning and design phase of a cohousing community, and space and facilities are organised at the community level to facilitate and maintain these inter-household relations. There are also significant environmental benefits due to shared facilities.

Overdrevet and Ottrupgård in Denmark, for example, are cohousing communities on the edge of small towns which have reused old farm buildings, established a playing field and common vegetable gardens, keep pigs or chickens, and produce substantial renewable energy (wind, solar). These communities employ medium-density housing types, but retain substantial open space on their sites, so that Overdrevet has the same density as a typical Australian suburb of detached houses and Ottrupgård is even less. It would be difficult to argue, however, that they do not exhibit an environmentally responsible use of land and resources. The sophisticated level of inter-household sharing and cooperation in cohousing is the key to its environmental possibilities. In one community in The Netherlands, for example, 14 households jointly owned one car and had a simple and workable system for its use and maintenance. Relatively few may want to live in cohousing, of course, but it is an instructive model. In Denmark, the success of cohousing has influenced the planning and design of social housing and, importantly, of new neighbourhoods.

On 55ha of 'surplus' farmland, Torsted Vest in Horsens has been planned as a mixed-use, ecological suburb with 800 to 900 dwellings. Housing is to be clustered to form sociable streets and squares, with relatively little space devoted to the movement of vehicles, enabling most of the site to be retained as open space. The site will be re-afforested, wetlands and wildlife habitats created, vegetable gardens and orchards planted, and parklands established. On-site stormwater management is planned, along with extensive reuse and recycling of wastes. (By 1995, the first stage was complete, but the project stalled with a drop in housing demand.)

15 km from the centre of Copenhagen and on the edge of a green corridor, Egebjerggard is a mixed use housing scheme of 600 to 700 dwellings on 27.5ha inspired by cohousing. The scheme has an urban feel, with generous recreational ponds (stormwater retention) and green space along the backs of housing clusters. Both projects are similar in density to those parts of Australian cities which have some townhouses or walk-up flats (Bamford 1995).

Conclusion

It is quite feasible to make existing Australian cities much more sustainable even with their current densities. And it is clear that only modest increases in overall urban densities can be expected from policies of urban consolidation (eg Stretton 1974, 1991; McLoughlin 1991; Troy 1992). Moreover, even if we did pursue a policy of substantially increased housing densities in 'urban villages', it does not

follow that we should then move to higher urban densities. Quite the reverse. We should make corresponding provisions for more open space nearby such 'villages', for a variety of environmental, as well as social and recreational, purposes. In the end, our challenge is to construct satisfying urban lifestyles which are 'more modest in their material demands [and] less destructive of the physical environment' in an economy and a society moving in the opposite direction (Coombs 1990, p. 165). How we might do this is still very much open to debate.

References and further reading

ABS (Australian Bureau of Statistics) 1993, *Year Book Australia 1994*, Canberra, ACT.

ABS 1994, *Home Production of Selected Foodstuffs, Australia, Year Ended April 1992*, Canberra, ACT.

Bamford, G. 1992, 'Density, Equity and the Green Suburb', in Ronnie Harding, ed, *Ecopolitics V: Proceedings of Ecopolitics V Conference, University of NSW, Sydney, 4–7 April, 1991*, University of New South Wales Centre for Liberal and General Studies: Kensington, NSW, pp. 661–666.

Bamford, G. 1995, 'Sustainability, Social Organization and the Australian Suburb', in J. Birkeland, ed, *Rethinking the Built Environment: Proceedings of Catalyst '95 Conference*, Belconnen, ACT, University of Canberra, Centre for Environmental Philosophy, Planning and Design, ACT, pp. 49–57.

Coombs, H. C. 1990, *The Return of Scarcity: Strategies for an Economic Future*, Cambridge University Press, Cambridge.

Division of National Mapping, Canberra 1980, *Population* 2, *Atlas of Australian Resources*, 3rd series.

Flannery, T. 1994, *The Future Eaters*, Reed Books, Port Melbourne, VIC.

Flannery, T. 1995, 'Blueprints for Sydney', *The Sydney Morning Herald*, 22 August, p. 11.

McCamant, K. and Durrett, C. 1994, *Cohousing: A Contemporary Approach to Housing Ourselves*, rev edn, Ten Speed Press, Berkeley, CA.

McLoughlin, B. 1991, 'Urban Consolidation and Urban Sprawl: A Question of Density', *Urban Policy and Research* 9, September, pp. 148–156.

Meltzer, G. 2000, 'Cohousing: Verifying the Importance of Community in the Application of Environmentalism', *Journal of Architecture and Planning Research* 17, Summer, pp. 110–132.

Morris, W. 1971, 'How Shall We Live Then?', in P. Meier, 'An Unpublished Lecture by William Morris', *International Review Of Social History* 16, pp. 217–40.

Newman, P. and Kenworthy, J. with Robinson, L. 1992, *Winning Back the Cities,* Australian Consumers' Association, Marrickville, NSW, and Pluto Press, Leichhardt, NSW.

Stretton, H. 1974, *Housing and Government: 1974 Boyer Lectures*, Australian Broadcasting Commission, Sydney, NSW.

Stretton, H. 1991, 'The Consolidation Problem', *Architecture Australia* 80, March, pp. 27–29.

Stretton, H. 1994, 'Transport and the Structure of Australian Cities', *Australian Planner* 31(3), pp. 131–136.

Trainer, E. 1995, *The Conserver Society: Alternatives for Sustainability*, Zed Books, London.

Troy, P. 1992, 'The New Feudalism', *Urban Futures: Issues for Australian Cities* 2, July, pp. 36–44.

Questions

1. Is the idea of relatively self-reliant or strong local communities in cities important to sustainability, or is this merely nostalgia for some imagined rural past? Discuss.

2. Suppose the urban village does introduce significant reductions in personal car use. Will consumption previously associated with car use simply be displaced by such things as 'weekend escape packages' to distant places? Discuss.

3. Debate: 'Urban consolidation is the key to producing a change of attitude in society toward sustainability.'

4. Can lower-density cities be (re)structured so that cars are less necessary, or is this just wishful thinking (especially in low-density cities like Canberra)?

5. How could existing neighbourhoods benefit socially and environmentally from the lessons of cohousing?

6. 'Low-density cities can provide more flexibility for responding to environmental challenges: more opportunities exist for a greater mix of higher and lower-density housing options and for the use of open space within such cities.' Develop a list of pros and cons for this position.

Projects

1. Work in pairs to monitor and list what each person produces and consumes in one day. Compare notes and consider how space, resources, and production and consumption patterns could be arranged to reduce these demands on the environment.

2. In two groups, select a small neighbourhood and prepare a plan or an inventory of the building types and open spaces. Carefully consider how these spaces and facilities are used by *all* concerned. How could you improve the life sustaining and enriching capacities of these locations? For example, housing densities might be varied without increasing site cover while creating more pleasant and useful spaces; a local shopping centre might benefit from the addition of some social housing above ground for those without cars, and a car park might be converted to a shady park, which still accommodates cars but only when the main shops are open.

Box 20   ESD and Urban Transport Infrastructure

Peter Newman

Cities, cars and sustainability: For cities to be characterised as being more sustainable, they must simultaneously reduce their input of resources, reduce their output of wastes and increase their livability (the Extended Metabolism Model). However, our data indicates that the biggest culprit preventing the achievement of this trifecta of goals is the car. Despite their appeal as symbols of status and freedom, cars are the globe's largest consumer of energy and contributor to greenhouse gases. They cause more deaths than wars and famines. They cause smog and sprawl and the loss of community so endemic to 'modern' cities.

Losers: Our data shows that the more car-oriented a city is, the more total transport costs there are. Car-dependent cities like those in the US and Australia need to work an extra day a week to pay for their cities' obsession compared to cities with more balanced opportunities for travel. Sadly, the newly developing Asian cities like Bangkok, Jakarta and Manila, are putting large proportions of their wealth into car-based infrastructure and, as a result, have even higher transport costs.

Model cities: There are cities which have committed themselves to a less car-dependent future and are already gaining the benefits. These cities all had major freeway plans in the 1960s – like every city in the world – but either did not build or stopped building them. They instead developed infrastructure for fast, effective rail systems integrated with local buses, and created dense walkable mixed-use sub-centres with, in some cases, substantial bicycle infrastructure. Cities that have chosen a more sustainable transport infrastructure are among the most wealthy (eg Singapore, Tokyo, Copenhagen, Stockholm and Zurich). Others like Boulder and Portland in the US or Vancouver and Toronto in Canada are reversing patterns of car dependence and making demonstrable gains in life quality and economy.

Urban ecology: The Urban Ecology agenda is to green the city through closing material, water and energy loops, providing more parks and permaculture. Our research has shown that this is best done through a community association. Car-based suburbs are the least active in urban ecology as they do not foster community. Cities can create denser, walkable nodes of activity so vital to a good transit system while introducing urban ecology initiatives throughout the city by, for example, varying density to allow restoration of natural creeks and wetlands. However, studies reveal that the most active examples of urban ecology are in denser parts of car-restricted cities like Copenhagen.

New urbanism: Building community in cities is a major part of the rationale for the New Urbanism, as well as being fundamental to the sustainability agenda. If this is to be achieved, however, there is much that needs to be changed in the manuals of professional practice for town planning, transport planning, traffic engineering, water engineering and community development. As long as cars receive the lion's share of infrastructure funding, then community and sustainability will not be realised in this model.

Community building: 'Building community' means respecting the organic processes of cities in their built heritage and culture; using development to heal community through new sub-centres where local jobs and services can be provided viably rather than scattering them; fostering community art and the spiritual values of hope; and generating opportunities for people to see a better, more sustainable world for their children. The 'privatism' of modern technology undermines this social infrastructure – the most potent force for privatism being the car and car-dependent land uses. All elements of sustainability in cities are threatened unless car dependence is overcome.

See Newman, P. and Kenworth, J. 1999, *Sustainability and Cities: Overcoming Automobile dependence*, Harcourt Brace/Island Press, Sydney/Washington.

Section 9: Design with Less Energy, Materials and Waste

9.1 Living Technologies

Nancy and John Todd

Ideally, water pollution should be prevented through the redesign of industry such that the water discharged from a process is of as high or higher quality than that primarily used. Where pollution is unavoidable, however, it should be treated at the source, before it can escape into the environment. The 'Living Machine', a technology developed for water treatment by John Todd, is essentially solar powered microbe-based ecosystems that purify and recycle waste, turning it into a resource.

Introduction

The quality of water in many ways determines the quality of life. Yet water is becoming contaminated throughout the world, spreading disease and carcinogens. Currently, the wastewater treatment industry is itself a major polluter. Conventional facilities produce sludges that are often toxic and difficult to dispose of. They use hazardous compounds in the treatment process, such as chlorine or aluminium salts, which end up in the natural environment. Moreover, they are not cost-effective in monetary terms, as they require massive federal subsidies while failing to produce useful by-products.

In contrast, **Living Machines**™ are self-contained networks of ecological systems powered by the sun and designed to accomplish specific chemical functions. They are designed along the same principles evolved by the natural world in building and regulating such ecologies as forests, lakes, prairies and estuaries. These miniaturised ecosystems are usually housed in a casing of lightweight materials to create a series of holding tanks, that may be contained in greenhouse structures where the climate needs moderating.

While conventional technologies are often reliant on fossil fuels, the **primary energy** source of Living Machines is sunlight. Instead of resource and capital intensive hardware and/or hazardous chemicals, they contain a diverse corps of living organisms, such as bacteria, algae, microscopic animals, snails, fish, flowers and even trees, that break down and digest pollutants. Thus, the focus is on diversity of interaction between plants, animals and micro-organisms.

Background

The first experimental water treatment plant was developed in 1987 for a ski resort, where the peak demand for sewage treatment in winter meant freezing temperatures and little sunlight. Even under these difficult conditions, a range of food chains that feed upon the waste stream eventually established themselves (partly by trial and error) producing fish, flowers and clean water. Having achieved this, the next challenge for this system of natural water purification was to attempt the treatment of **septage**, the highly concentrated sewage pumped from septic tanks.

At the test site on a Cape Cod septage lagoon, 21 translucent cylinders (each 5ft high) were aligned, each aerated and connected by plastic tubes and topped with a raft of floating plants. The septage entered the uphill end and passed through each tank in turn, a process taking about ten days. At the halfway point, the flow was diverted to drain through a large wooden trough that contained a simulated marsh and was then pumped back into the tanks. The tanks removed nearly all the ammonia, phosphorous, and nitrate levels, and also heavy metals, fats and grease. The fish in the downstream end of the system were found to be free of contaminants.

Since these early experiments, many projects have been completed which address a range of pollution problems on many scales (see www.livingmachines.com). Current applications include:

- Pre-treatment of industrial waste to eliminate sewer surcharges.
- Advanced treatment to recycle wastewater for irrigation, aquaculture, toilet flushing, truck washing and other uses.
- Treatment for municipalities, developments, resorts and industrial parks.
- On-site sludge treatment.

Ecological engineering

H.T. Odum, the father of ecological engineering, articulated the need to view species, nature and technology in a radically new way. He stated: 'The inventory of species of the earth is really an immense bin of parts available to the ecological engineer. A species evolved to play one role may be used for a different purpose in a different kind of network as long as its maintenance flows are satisfied' (Odum 1971). Ecological technologies apply a wide range of selected life forms in their design which, in new settings, have the ability to co-design with the engineer.

Living Machines, then, represent an emerging synthesis of industrial design and natural systems. These systems had to wait for the development of cost-effective, energy efficient and environmentally responsive materials. This is because the containment vessels needed to be fabricated from lightweight, light transmitting, flexible materials that could be bonded and waterproofed, and that were capable of withstanding high pressures and ultraviolet radiation.

To create a Living Machine, organisms are collected and reassembled in unique ways depending on the chemical requirements of the project. The components can come from almost any region of the planet and be recombined in any number of ways to create a unique constellation of organisms in a relatively closed system. The characteristics of the pollution determine the selection of organisms and the ratio of each set to the other. Balance may be achieved through trial and error, removing some species and replacing them with others and making other biological and mechanical adjustments to optimise the system. The initial system is 'artificial' – in the sense that the original toxins and array of organisms result from human actions – but with care and attentiveness, an environment with ecological integrity is gradually established.

The potential exists to design Living Machines that not only treat wastes, but produce food or fuels, purify air and regulate climates in buildings. They can, for example, be used in the manufacture of materials ranging from paper products to advanced composite construction materials. Ecological technologies can be integrated with built environment design and applied at all scales: homes, commercial buildings, industrial plants, urban systems and even the restoration of damaged bioregions. Ecological engineers are conceiving, designing and engineering 'zero' emission industrial zones in a number of cities.

In the future, Living Machines could also make it possible to feed large numbers of people, particularly in urban areas, and become part of a strategy for addressing issues of inequity between peoples and regions. By miniaturising the production of essential human services, Living Machines would reduce ecological footprints, and allow wilderness areas – our repositories of biological diversity – to be restored and protected from human interference.

Box 9.2.1: Differences between Living Machines and conventional machines

1. The vast majority of a Living Machine's working parts are live organisms, hundreds of species ranging from bacteria to higher plants and vertebrates such as fish and amphibians.

2. Living Machines have the ability to self-design. The engineer provides the containment vessels that enclose the Living Machine and then seeds them with diverse organisms from specific environments. Within the Living Machines the organisms self-design the internal ecology in relation to their prescribed tasks and the energy and nutrients streams to which they are exposed.

3. Living Machines have the ability to self-repair when damaged by a toxic shock or an interruption of an energy or nutrient sources. The self-repair ability enables Living Machines to be quite robust and capable of dealing with unexpected and unpredictable events.

4. Living Machines have the ability to self-replicate through reproduction by the vast majority of organisms within the system. This means that, in theory at least, Living Machines can be designed to operate for centuries or even millennia. In Living Machines the intelligence of nature is reapplied to human ends. They are both garden and machine.

Source: Todd, J. 1999, 'Ecological Design, Living Machines, and the Purification of Waters', in C. Kibert, ed, *Reshaping the Built Environment*, Island Press, Washington, DC.

Advantages of Living Machines

Some of the advantages of Living Machines are that:

- They enable owners to recycle treated water or discharge it to the environment, realising significant annual cost savings by eliminating service surcharges, minimising sludge disposal costs and reducing water purchases.

- They are biologically diverse and can treat a wide variety of waste streams. They are naturally resistant to drastic changes or 'shock loads' in the waste stream. Operators enjoy ease of operation and highly reliable treatment performance.

- Sludge handling and disposal expenses are significantly lower than for conventional technologies. Sludge is consumed in the process, greatly reducing sludge quantity compared with conventional biological treatment. Optional on-site sludge composting with reed beds virtually eliminates sludge handling costs altogether.

- For high-strength waste streams that require treatment to attain reuse standards, Living Machines have lower initial capital costs and lower annual operating costs compared to conventional alternatives. They can also be designed to accommodate expansion in future years. This allows owners to match capital outlays with the growth of a business or community, because the system is more flexible.

Complexity

In the last few years, there has been a cross-fertilisation between practitioners of ecological technology and those in fields studying complexity and chaos dynamics. Kauffman provided research into how self-organisation, generated in nature, explains why Living Machines work, and why it is possible to use these attributes in technological settings (Kauffman 1993). His theory of criticality posits that organic forms may reach a state of supracriticality, and in that state they literally invent new molecular combinations or species arrangements. Diverse ecosystems may have this property of supracriticality, whereas subcritical systems lack adaptiveness because they lack the critical diversity or ability to support this diversity. The question posed by complexity theory for ecological designers is how living technologies can be developed that are supracritical, capable of self-design, self-regulation and invention, and carry out specific functions.

Conclusion

Whereas the phrase 'design with nature' is usually used only metaphorically, Living Machines represent quite literally designing with nature. Environmentalists rightly honour nature and struggle to protect the pristine natural places that remain, but the survival of our civilisation equally may require another fundamental step. It may be essential for us to find ways of decoding the natural world and using its teachings to reshape and redefine our tools and technologies.

Successful farmers and gardeners have long had this kind of relationship with nature. With the unfolding and application of the ecology, it is possible to extend this relationship into a new dimension. Ironically, the greatest hindrance to the widespread adoption of living technologies arises from the very problem they are intended to solve – the estrangement of cultures from the natural world.

References and further reading

Bak, P. 1997, *How Nature Works: The Science of Self-organized Criticality*, Oxford University Press, Oxford.

Dent, J.M. 1993, *Complexity: Life at the Edge of Chaos*, Roger Lewin, London.

Gardner, G. 1997, *Recycling Organic Waste: From Urban Pollutant to Farm Resource*, Worldwatch Institute, Washington, DC.

Kauffman, S.A. 1993, *The Origins of Order: Self Organisation and Selection in Evolution*, Oxford University Press, New York.

Odum, H.T. 1971, *Environment, Power and Society*, Wiley Interscience, New York.

Shulman, S. 1999, *Owning the Future*, Houghton Mifflin, Boston, MA.

Todd, J. and Todd, J.J. 1994, *From Eco-Cities to Living Machines: Principles of Ecological Design*, North Atlantic Books, Berkeley, CA.

Todd, J. and Josephson, B. 1996, 'The Design of Living Technologies for Waste Treatment', *Ecological Engineering* 6, pp. 109–136.

Todd J. 1999, 'Ecological Design, Living Machines, and the Purification of Waters', in C. Kibert, ed, *Reshaping the Built Environment*, Island Press, Washington, DC.

Waldrop, M.M. 1994, *Complexity: the Emerging Science at the Edge of Order and Chaos*, Penguin, VIC.

www.livingmachines.com

Questions

1. List the ways that 'living technologies' could reduce urban impacts on wilderness areas, both upstream and downstream. Is the connection too remote?

2. Could living technologies make it possible to feed large numbers of people in urban areas? Is this unrealistic? What factors need to be considered?

3. If specialist organisms are imported to attack specific chemicals, what are some of the 'checks and balances' on the escape of such 'feral' organisms into the surrounding environment where they might do damage to the local ecology?

4. Could Living Machines make become part of a strategy for addressing issues of inequity between peoples and regions? Discuss.

5. Living Machines are 'high tech' because they use cost effective and energy efficient materials. How else could they be said to represent a 'higher' form of technology?

6. Debate: 'The greatest hindrance to the widespread adoption of living technologies arises from the estrangement of cultures from the natural world.'

Projects

1. Visit your local waste management agency and ask what studies or experiments they are undertaking in the area of living technologies for treating water. If none are yet under way, make it happen.

2. In your school, design and set up a simple version of an experimental living technology for greywater treatment.

Garry Kerans

Many ecological impacts originate from the management of individual household water/wastewater cycles. A genuine ecologically sustainable settlement would have no imports of energy or resources from 'outside' the boundaries or range of that settlement, and no environmental effects downstream from the site. This chapter explores the potentials of a closed system approach to the design of a single household with regard to water usage.

Introduction

It does not make environmental, financial or social sense to persist in building new dams, new and larger sewage treatment plants and more complex buried pipe infrastructure systems to deal with the world's increasing demands. The costs outweigh the benefits. Resource recovery systems will need to become more eco-efficient. Ecologically sustainable development requires using the minimum area feasible to support a population long term, and minimising the impacts of the development upstream and downstream.

Similarly, each individual household must be environmentally and financially sound, because if the costs and impacts do not work for the smallest unit of the human ecosystem, then the system cannot perform well as a whole. In residential developments the same basic stipulations apply as in urban-scale solid waste management practice: reduce demand, reuse whenever possible, and recycle if necessary within a small geographical distance.

Domestic sewage systems

Distance is a crucial design element because, for example, the cost of transporting water has a great bearing on the net energy and resource costs: pipelines require energy to fabricate, construct, and maintain. To save the sizeable cost of the pipeline and pumping costs in dense urban areas, a more localised catchment management practice is advisable. Generally, the smaller the reuse cycles are (geographically), the more sustainable the solution. Household-sized systems

are ideal in some respects because there is a one-to-one maintenance relationship between the operational responsibility for the system and the user. If any part of the system breaks down, the user will be directly affected and will seek a solution. The user will also be more likely to ensure the ongoing functioning of each system.

The main contribution to recycled, treated greywater is from the bathroom and laundry. Kitchen waste is excluded because of the clogging effects it has on the lint pre-filters. Urine can be safely added to the greywater system at any stage of its production; it is a sterile liquid with high nitrogen levels which is valuable to the surface layer of a garden. In composting toilets, urine can be broken down into ammonia by a bacteria, called *micrococcus ureae*. This has four undesirable characteristics:

- Ammonia smells.
- Ammonia is detrimental to aerobic composting bacteria.
- A valuable nitrogen fertiliser is lost.
- The remaining fertilisers are unbalanced, and hence are less useful to plants.

Many composting toilet options presently available have a small inline fan, which is necessary to establish a draught down the toilet pedestal and remove the odours from the toilet room.

Water balance

Water resource management involves the supply of clean water (catchment management), and disposal of the undesirable nutrients added to this clean water (resource cycling). External water use accounts for roughly 47% of household usage (UWRA 1994, Brisbane data). An elegant solution exists to provide the indoor water supply if one considers that the greywater produced from a household nearly equals the water required externally if **sub-surface irrigation** is utilised. If sub-surface irrigation is not used, there would either be:

- a severe shortfall in the amount of water available from the household; or

- some of the garden areas would need to dry out or be converted to a **xeriscape** (low water need) area.

There are also other benefits when networks of sub-surface forms of irrigation are used instead of surface spraying.

- Much greater areas can be kept alive by the wastewater because there are less evaporative losses.
- The nutrients are better used if they are distributed over a large area.
- There are major sewerage system savings due to the reliable nature of an extensive drainage distribution network in the soil.
- Chlorination is not required if the effluent is disposed of by sub-surface means.
- Viral and bacterial **pathogens** are readily adsorbed or inactivated in the active surface layers of the soil, the top 300mm (Farwell 1993).

Wetlands

Wetlands, a self-regulating treatment method, consist of reeds and other water plants instead of compressors to pump oxygen into the wastewater. The oxygen that is naturally supplied to the roots of the reeds enables aerobic bacteria to survive and function in the depths of the gravel bed around the roots. These type of bacteria work faster than anaerobic bacteria when it comes to breaking down wastes. Thus, oxygen in wastewater is highly beneficial. To adequately treat wastes using this more aesthetic and 'natural' method requires quite large areas of land to be set aside for this purpose in cool climates: about 10sq m per person for treatment of secondary effluent to a standard suitable for discharge into a water course, and up to 20sq m per person if reuse of the effluent is planned ('Ebb and Flow' wetland specialists UK).

Settlement basins and treatment lagoons are becoming common place for stormwater treatment, and are indispensable for proper catchment management. When all the household or community water tanks and wastewater storage are full during a wet spell, the overflows must be managed to conserve water quantity and quality. The concept of stormwater run-off as waste to be drained to the nearest large river is not desirable, especially where a community cannot supply all its summer water needs from roof tank supplies. The location of potable water supplies in dam storage sites (at a considerable distance from the demand area) is becoming ever more difficult to justify financially. In years to come, there may even be a direct relationship between density of population in a given community's bioregion and its water catchment resources (ie localised water resource use).

Dosed aerobic sand filters are very effective in the final treatment of effluent prior to storage or direct reuse. It is important that this type of biological and physical filter is designed and constructed appropriately. There are set dosing rates that need to be adhered in order to avoid the cost of digging up a sand filter if it fails in the short term.

Economics of reuse technologies

The geographical and social aspects of a community interact with sizing and infrastructure limitations of the non-potable wetland storage and reuse plant. If the population being serviced by the reuse plant is less than 150 households, then the cost per capita to maintain the treatment plant could be prohibitively high. As the household number increases above 150 households, the length and cost of the pipeline that returns the treated effluent to the homes increases, as well as the necessary size of the non-potable storage pond(s).

The topographical limitations in siting the storage of stormwater/ excess waste water becomes a critical design factor: it must be downhill from the dwellings and to the side of the zone that would be subject to periodic high volume floodings. Thus, a housing development's design layout and siting should take these elements into account and overlay these with the solar, circulation, privacy and good design aspects of the construction.

Principles for wastewater reuse

- Keep wastewater as elevated as possible, both by location of dwellings on the land and by reducing the depth of burial of wastewater pipes. Pump wells are expensive both to install and maintain.
- Consider the distribution system at the same time as the collection pipe network. A common trench saves money, but its location may be determined by the direction of the gravity falls in the collection network.
- Avoid pumps where possible by using plants to oxygenate and strip nutrients. The by-products are much more readily brought back into the food chain as mulch, and the cost of the process is less than chemical treatment supplies.
- When pumps are required, make them perform as much aeration work as possible. Air allows more efficient waste assimilating bacteria to survive and do 'work' on the

effluent, thus requiring less chemical treatment downstream.

- Separate wastewater qualities. It is necessary to retain and age wastewater effectively to attenuate pathogens. To achieve this, it is essential that short circuiting is prevented in treatment tanks, wetlands and sand filters.

- Design cleanout mechanisms and system observation locations. Someone has to be responsible for the maintenance of the treatment plant. Early observations are essential to prevent breakdowns that may be very costly to repair. For example, sand filters cannot be submerged for any length of time; a water level inspection window and/or alarm could detect a flooding problem early and save a substantial dig out task.

A practical example

In 1996, Integrated EcoVillages (IEV) designed and constructed a greywater system for 70 public housing units for ACT Housing near the centre of Canberra, Australia. The system treats the greywater from a second drainage pipe network that accepts all the laundry and bathroom wastewater from the units. Once the effluent is treated, clarified and sand filtered, it is stored in a 120 KL storage tank. A moisture-sensing irrigation computer controls a pump and distribution system which feed the treated water out to the various zones of the subsurface irrigation network on the 4500sq m site. This project was a forerunner to a more comprehensive eco-village example that has been in the planning stages for 17 years. Also IEV's SUN Village project, in Queanbeyan (near Canberra), integrates privacy aspects with best practice passive solar design, rainwater reticulation with greywater reuse, composting toilet systems with household organic waste disposal, and on-site education and employment with an active community building program.

For an example of how a homeowner retrofitted an historic inner city home to be autonomous from city services, see Mobbs (1998).

Conclusion

There are many existing alternatives for individual on site and shared water treatment systems. Governments, developers, designers and local communities need to investigate these alternatives for both new and existing housing. Localised treatment systems are much more efficient, far less damaging to the environment, and encourage personal responsibility to minimise water usage and wastage.

References

ACTEW 1994, *Wastewater Reuse Study Phase 1: Opportunities Threats and Further Actions*, ACT Electricity and Water, Canberra, ACT.

Brisbane City Council, Department of Water Supply and Sewerage 1993, *Onsite Domestic Greywater Re-use*, Urban Water Research Association of Australia.

Farwell, L. 1993, Personal Communication, Californian Department of Water Resources.

Hammer, D.A. 1989, *Constructed Wetlands for Wastewater Treatment: Municipal, Industrial and Agricultural*, Lewis Publishers, University of Michigan, MI.

Jeppesen, B. and Solley, D. 1994, 'Domestic Greywater Reuse: Overseas Practice and its Applicability to Australia', Report 73, Urban Water Research Association of Australia, Melbourne, VIC.

Knight, R.L. 1996, *Treatment Wetland*, CRC Press, Lewis Publishers, University of Michigan.

Ludwig, A. 1998, *Create an Oasis with Greywater: Your Complete Guide to Managing Greywater in the Landscape,* 3rd edn, Oasis Design, Santa Barbara, CA.

McQuire, S. 1995, *Not Just Down the Drain*, Friends of the Earth, Collingwood, VIC.

Mobbs, M. 1998, *Sustainable House*, Choice Book, Sydney, NSW.

National Small Flows Clearing House 1993, 'Subsurface Flow Constructed Wetlands for Wastewater Treatment', *A Technology Assessment WWPCDM 74*, West Virginia University, WV.

National Small Flows Clearing House 1996, *Sand Filter Information Package WWPCGN* 29 West Virginia University, WV.

National Small Flows Clearing House 1996, *Sand Filters, WWBLCM08*, West Virginia University, WV.

NSW Department of Local Government 1996, *Onsite Wastewater Management Systems for Domestic Households*, NSW Health, EPA, Land and Water Conservation, Sydney, NSW.

NSW Environment Protection Authority, NSW Department of Health, NSW Department of Land and Water Conservation 1996, *Environment and Health Protection Guidelines: On-site Wastewater Management Systems for Domestic Households*, NSW.

Serageldin, I. 1995, *Toward Sustainable Management of Water Resources*, World Bank, Washington, DC.

Urban Water Research Association of Australia 1994, 'Domestic Greywater Reuse: Overseas Practice and its Applicability to Australia', *Research Report No 73*, March.

Water Authority of Western Australia 1994, *Wastewater 2040: Discussion Paper*, Water Authority, Leederville, WA.

1. At what planning stage in a development should a designer consider planning a water reuse system? Why?

2. Is it reasonable to build a new dam to service a growing city centre? What factors need to be considered? What can be done to forestall the construction of a new dam?

3. Can a sand filter be used as a primary greywater treatment process? What are some potential problems?

4. Do pumps have to be used to filter wastewater? Why?

5. Someone has to be responsible for the maintenance of a water treatment plant; how might this be organised in a small cohousing area?

6. How do reeds and other water plants replace compressors? How does this foster aerobic bacteria?

1. Research available composting toilets in your community and find out whether they are restricted by local building codes. If so, find out why this is so. Draft a letter recommending solutions to any impediments.

2. Ask your local water authority about the incentive programs it uses to encourage on-site water treatment. If it has no such program, meet with their management to explore the possibilities of doing so, as a group. Would they be willing to sponsor a prototype?

Box 21   Principles for Designing Living Machines

From Nancy and John Todd, 1994, *Eco-Cities to Living Machines*, North Atlantic Books, Berkeley, CA.

1. **Microbial communities:** The primary ecological foundations of living machines are predicated upon diverse microbial communities obtained from a wide range of aquatic (marine and freshwater) and terrestrial environments. In addition, organisms from chemically and thermally highly stressed environments are critical. Genetic engineering cannot do what constellations of natural organisms can accomplish when they work in concert.

2. **Photosynthetic communities:** Sunlight-powered photosynthesis is the primary driving force of these systems. Anaerobic phototrophic microbes, cyanobacteria, algae, and higher plants must be linked in a dynamic balance with the heterotrophic microbial communities.

3. **Linked ecosystems and the law of the minimum:** At least three distinct types of ecological systems need to be linked together to produce Living Machines that carry out self-design and self-repair through time. Such systems have the theoretical ability to span centuries and possibly millennia.

4. **Pulsed exchanges:** Nature works in short-term and long-term pulses which are both regular and irregular. This pulsing is a critical design force and helps maintain diversity and robustness. Pulses need to be intrinsic to design.

5. **Nutrient and micronutrient reservoirs:** Carbon/nitrogen/phosphorus ratios need to be regulated and maintained. A full complement of macro and trace elements need to be in the system so that complex food matrices can be established and allowed to 'explore' a variety of successional strategies over time. This will support biological diversity.

6. **Geological diversity and mineral complexity:** Living Machines can simulate a rapid ecological history by utilising minerals from a diversity of strata and ages. The geological materials can be incorporated into the sub-ecosystems relatively quickly by being introduced as ultra-fine powders which can be solubilised over short time frames.

7. **Steep gradients:** Steep gradients are required within and between the sub-elements of the system. These include redox, pH, humic materials, and ligand or metal-based gradients. These gradients help develop the high efficiencies that have been predicted for Living Machines.

8. **Phylogenetic diversity:** In a well-engineered ecosystem all phylogenetic levels from bacteria to vertebrates should be included. System regulators and internal designers are often unusual and unpredictable organisms. The development of various phyla has arisen to a large extent from the strategic exploration of the total global system over a vast period of time. Time can be compressed with the consequences of this evolution.

9. **The microcosm as a tiny mirror image of the macrocosm:** This ancient hermetic law applies to ecological design and engineering. As much as possible, global design should be miniaturised in terms of gas, mineral, and biological cycles. The big system relationships need to be maintained in the Living Machine.

Brenda and Robert Vale

Houses could be designed to be 'autonomous', in that they are able to provide their own services (water, heating, cooling, sewage, electricity) from natural sources without the need for fossil fuels and sewage treatment plants. However, autonomous houses are very rare. Arguably, 'autonomy' should be the bottom line for industrial and building designers working on residential products and structures. This chapter suggests that sustainable design is impossible without a basic understanding and use of numbers.

Introduction

Autonomous servicing means the provision of all the resources/services needed by a building must be collected from its site. In an urban setting, it might be argued that autonomous servicing is not relevant, as the 'mains' services are cheap and reliable. However, this may not be the case. Power cuts or 'blackouts' and water shortages are on the increase. As regards price, an autonomous subdivision would need (at most) only relatively cheap mains electricity supplies (for two-way exchange of solar electricity with the grid) and telephones, which are both relatively cheap to install. This suggests the importance of understanding and working with numbers, especially for designers. It is necessary to translate the concept of autonomy into numbers to demonstrate its feasibility and economic value to clients and the general public. This helps to simplify autonomous servicing into terms that are used by the general public.

Space heating

In most cities of the developed world, space heating is needed for some portion of the winter. The closer that the internal temperatures in a building can be to the outside temperatures (while maintaining comfort), the less energy will be needed to maintain the difference. Modern commercial buildings are often maintained at an internal temperature of 21°C during summer and winter, and may need heating plant operating in the winter and refrigeration plant operating in the summer. If the traditional office dress code were relaxed

so that people could wear sweaters in the winter and T-shirts in the summer, comfort temperatures would be closer to outside temperatures, and external sources of energy might be unnecessary.

The amount of heating needed can be reduced considerably by the use of insulation in the building fabric; a highly insulated building may need no additional heating other than that produced by the body heat of the occupants and the effect of the sun shining through the windows (ie passive solar). Detailed calculations can demonstrate the need for good levels of insulation, even in areas like Brisbane (considered to have a mild climate). Space heating by passive means is made easier if thermal mass is incorporated into the building (inside the insulation), to store heat from times when it is produced (ie on a sunny day) to times when it is needed (ie on a cold evening). This thermal mass could be concrete, brick, stone or water; any heavy material that can store heat. The ideal situation is to design a building that needs no heating system; an example is the Hockerton Housing Project in Nottinghamshire, UK, which makes use of superinsulation, immense thermal mass and passive solar energy to maintain satisfactory temperatures through the English winter (Field 1998).

Water and sewage

Water

An autonomous house in Southwell, UK (occupied by a family of four), receives all its water supply from the roof. Sited in a relatively dry part of the Midlands, with an average annual rainfall of 576mm per year, the total water consumption of the house is 34 litres per person per day, little more than the 'minimum supply' quoted in textbooks (Twort et al 1993). This low consumption is achieved by careful use of water in the house, a result of consideration by the occupants who know that they can run out of water if they do not use it with care. The other factor to be considered is water storage capacity. In the autonomous house in Southwell, there are 30,000 litres of water, stored in 20 interconnected cylindrical tanks, each holding 1500 litres. This storage allows the household to go for 176 days without rain, or nearly six months.

Water treatment systems can be very simple. In Australia and New Zealand, frequently no water treatment is required (a reasonable option in an area with little pollution). Recent research in the UK found that rainwater collected off a roof in the city of Nottingham (in the centre of the country, away from sea breezes) without further treatment met the World Health Organisation (WHO) standards for drinking water (Fewkes and Turton 1994)

Sewage

About a third of the water used in households is used for flushing the toilet. Waterless toilets are available which make the sewage into a garden fertiliser, but the most effective models are bulky, and need to be designed into a building. The operation of the odourless unit is limited to pumping out a few buckets of liquid (used as a garden feed) every six weeks, and to removing a few buckets of compost once a year. A diverse range of composting toilets are now entering the market.

Water heating

The energy needed for water heating will depend on the amount of water needed by the household. The Autonomous House in Southwell uses only 13lcd (litres per capita per day). The obvious way to make hot water without using electricity is to use a solar water heater. In the autonomous house, a solar water heater was not a practical option because of the poor solar radiation availability in mid-winter, but in much of the world solar water heating panels can provide hot water to meet demands for most of the year. If the user is prepared to live with varying temperatures of water and is prepared to moderate demand, a solar panel system could be the sole source of hot water in an autonomous building in most of Australia, the USA and Europe.

Lights and appliances

What is enough?

In the UK, a typical household is thought to use about 3000kWh of electricity annually for lights and appliances (Boardman et al 1995, p. 2). The autonomous house at Southwell uses 1200kWh for lights and appliances. One reason for the reduction in electricity consumption in the autonomous house is the use of low-energy appliances;

another reason is a reduced demand. The design of autonomous, sustainable buildings is not solely a technical matter, it is also a matter of making choices about lifestyle and values. Can the world as a whole sustain Western rates of appliance use? How much of a lowering of standards would it be to use cold water detergents, or to manage without a dishwasher or a freezer, or to operate the washing machine only when it was full? Personal actions can make a real difference to global effects such as global warming from carbon dioxide emissions.

Making electricity

The choices made in appliance use have a significant effect on the design of autonomously serviced buildings. If less electricity is needed, the equipment needed to produce it will tend to be less expensive. The two most common sources of renewable electricity for buildings are wind power and solar power. Solar energy is turned into electricity by the use of photovoltaic (PV) panels. To meet the 'typical' annual demand for lights and appliances (3000kWh) requires about 20sq m of PV panels. To meet the electricity demand of the autonomous house in Southwell would need only 10sq m of PV panels. Given that PV panels currently cost around AUD$1000 per square metre, there is a clear incentive to minimise the area needed.

Wind power is captured by a wind turbine, which uses a wind-driven rotor to turn a generator. The wind turbine must be mounted on a tall tower so that it is well above all surrounding obstructions. A tower of at least 20m height is necessary in a rural location, and more height would be appropriate in an urban setting; this could lead to considerable problems with planning consents. There is also the noise of the machine to take into account. Generally, except for special cases, the wind turbine is unlikely to be suitable as an energy source for an autonomous building in an urban setting.

Electricity can be stored in batteries (usually lead-acid) as direct current. It can be converted from low voltage direct current to 230/240 volt alternating current for use with appliances by means of solid state inverters, which are relatively efficient. Batteries need careful management to prolong their life, which will vary between 5 and 15 years, depending on how they are used and managed.

An alternative to the use of batteries with all their problems, expense and negative embodied energy and environmental impact (lead is a toxic material in the environment), is to connect the renewable electricity generating systems to the local electricity grid. In this case, the grid is then used as an 'electric bank account'; electricity is put in when it is generated, and withdrawn as required. This system is increasingly common with photovoltaics in Europe and the US, and were used for the houses in the Sydney Olympic Village, Australia.

Cooking

A simple and cheap option for cooking (which needs large amounts of power for short periods, making it difficult to use a battery) would be the use of a wood-burning cooker, but, this is not convenient in the summer because of the unwanted heat. Perhaps the most straight forward option is to use an ordinary electric cooker with a grid-linked renewable energy system.

Solar cookers are commercially available, or can be made quite easily. They are surprisingly effective, but require that one's cooking habits be modified to suit the weather, and to make use of the fact that the sun is at its peak at noon. A solar cooker will roast a turkey, bake bread, or slow cook a casserole, but it must be adjusted every hour or so, to aim it directly at the sun. It is not a satisfactory technology for someone who is out at work all day and wants a hot meal when they get home in the evening (see, for example, Halacy and Halacy 1992).

Transport

Autonomous systems have the potential to reduce environmental impacts in other fields, one of which is transport. Even in Auckland, a highly dispersed suburban city, the average commuting journey is only 12.6km (ARC 1996). Used for the household's daily trips, a purpose designed electric commuter car could provide all local journeys from the output of a 10sq m grid-connected photovoltaic array. The cost of the array, which is approx NZ$10,000 (Duncan 1997) and the car ($20,000 for a purpose-built electric glass fibre 2+2 seater if ordered in lots of 100 at a time) would be little more than the cost of a medium-sized petrol car (Heron 1997). This would provide zero-emissions transport, with petrol, or perhaps bio-diesel, cars being rented as necessary for occasional longer journeys.

Other considerations

Another important aspect of urban autonomy is that of food production. A household of two adults and two teenagers will eat food with an energy content of 12.8kWh per day (calculated from data in Fisher and Bender 1970). To grow the food, transport it to a processor, and then to the consumer also requires energy. Calculations show that the energy use attributable to the entire UK food supply system is five times the energy content of the food itself (Leach 1975). This would increase the energy input to a household due to food consumption to 64kWh per day, or nearly 24,000kWh per year. These values for food energy consumption are generally much greater than the energy consumption for operation of a dwelling or for the running of the family car. It may be that an important aspect of autonomy will be to provide space for the growing of food at home, and this may be the household's greatest contribution to sustainability.

Conclusion

There are few technical obstacles to the successful design and operation of autonomous buildings. However, there are obstacles which are largely social and philosophical. If people demand 'more' rather than 'enough', autonomous services will not be acceptable. The occupant of the autonomous house has to live with the levels of servicing that the environment can provide, but the ongoing services are free, and their environmental impact is minimised. In terms of capital costs, an autonomous house is likely to be more expensive than a conventional one, but the greater cost is not large. It would be feasible to build an autonomous house for the same price as a normal house by making the autonomous version about 15% smaller in terms of floor area.

The conventional house insulates its residents from the effects of their actions on the global environment, while the autonomous house requires that its residents interact with the natural world – if it is sunny they use hot water, if it is cold they wear warm clothes, if there is a drought they save water. If the effects of ozone depletion, global warming and pollution of all kinds are to be countered, people may have to learn to live more in harmony with their environment, and autonomous buildings may well be a part of this new way of living.

References and further reading

ARC 1996, *Transport Facts and Figures Data Sheet*, Auckland Regional Environment Council, Auckland, NZ.

Boardman B. et al 1995, 'Executive Summary' *DECADE Second Year Report Energy and Environment Programme*, Environmental Change Unit, University of Oxford, p. 2.

Duncan G. 1997, Personal Communication, Solar Power Waiheke, Waiheke Island, Auckland, NZ

Fewkes A. and Turton, A. 1994, 'Recovering Rainwater for WC Flushing', *Environmental Health*, February, p. 43.

Field, J. 1998, 'Open Agenda', *Building Services Journal*, February, pp. 22–24.

Fisher P. and Bender, A. 1970, *The Value of Food*, Oxford University Press, Oxford, p. 22.

Halacy B. and Halacy, D. 1992, 'Cooking with the Sun', *Morning Sun Press*, Lafayette, CA.

Heron Motor Co. 1997, Personal Communication, Rotorua, NZ.

Leach G. 1975, *Energy and Food Production*, International Institute for Environment and Development, London, p. 8.

Twort, A.C., Law, F.M., Crowley, F.W. and Ratnayaka, D.D. 1993, *Water Supply*, 4th edn, E. Arnold, London.

Questions

1. Debate: 'Autonomous servicing is not relevant, as the mains services are more cheap and reliable.'

2. A building that needs no heating system (eg using superinsulation, immense thermal mass and passive solar energy to maintain satisfactory temperatures through winter) could conflict with the requirements to reduce embodied energy. What solutions could meet both **design parameters**?

3. What are some of the problems with using rainwater collected off roofs in urban areas and what are possible solutions to these problems?

4. List examples of principles that apply to designing both low-energy appliances and low-energy houses.

5. How can a wind turbine be designed to be suitable as an energy source for an autonomous building in an urban setting?

6. List as many arguments for providing space for the growing of food at home as you can. How can space for growing plants in homes be increased?

Projects

1. Calculate how long it would take to pay off the capital cost of a 10sq m photovoltaic panel for your residence.

2. Find out the average electricity usage for houses in your area from the local electricity utility. Compare this to your own electricity usage. Examine the main energy using appliances in your house and estimate their annual energy consumption. What appliances would you be willing to go without in order to reduce your energy consumption?

Box 22   Implementing Design for Environment

From Environment Australia, 2001, *Product Innovation: The Green Advantage* Australian Department of the Environment and Heritage, Canberra ACT.

1. **Analyse opportunities:** Review products and markets.
    - Investigate the product development process within your company, and the product market and incentives for adopting Design for Environment (DfE).
    - Identify drivers behind product design (eg are product specifications driven by engineering or by marketing?).
    - Identify the roles of individuals in the product development process.
    - Research the product market and the competitive climate .
    - Identify anticipated environmental regulations (eg through industry associations or State/Territory environment protection authorities, or regulations affecting your industry in other countries).

Analyse company capacity: identify resources and capabilities.
    - Identify skills and knowledge existing within the company that will aid the implementation of DfE.
    - Identify existing programs that can provide complimentary structures and resources for a DfE (for example, environmental management and quality assurance systems).

Identify DfE opportunities: You can begin to implement DfE with a single product, component or process.
    - Find out which products may be ready for upgrading or redesign.
    - Identify new products that are being designed but have not yet moved into the production phase.
    - Identify simple changes that can be made to existing products – for example, coding plastic for recycling.

Identify potential benefits: The benefits provide a powerful incentive for adopting DfE.
    - Identify measures that cost little to implement but have the potential for significant cost savings.
    - Identify ways to comply with anticipated regulations now, to avoid future problems and allow products to compete in the global marketplace.

- Analyse your market research to determine if there are potential benefits from environmental initiatives (eg consider DfE as way of differentiating your product).
- Identify moves by your major competitors to embrace environmental approaches. It may be easier to convince your organisation to adopt DfE if competitors are also taking new initiatives.

2. **Promote DfE within the company:** Communicating the benefits of DfE is a vital step in creating a corporate culture of eco-efficiency.   Promotion should continue throughout DfE implementation.
    - Gain commitment from senior management (eg by providing success stories and identifying incentives).
    - Provide DfE information and success stories in an accessible format (eg on the company's internal communications network).
    - Talk with individuals who have an interest in DfE or an incentive to adopt it (eg a marketing manager interested in green consumer preferences) about how you can work together to implement DfE.
    - Find and support a DfE 'champion' in each business unit, including the product development teams.
    - Provide training and education for those involved with DfE.

3. **Set goals and identify strategies:** Set organisational goals and strategies first, before working at the level of specific products. These can help to gain commitment within your company and raise awareness of the scope, implementation and likely outcomes of a DfE project. It is essential that the DfE strategies and goals are closely aligned with the organisation's overall strategic direction.
    - Hold a strategy formulation session for staff at various levels who have been informed about DfE.
    - Identify realistic goals and targets for DfE implementation, environmental improvements and economic performance based on DfE initiatives.
    - Identify the resources available for implementing DfE and seek additional resources if necessary.

- Set goals for specific products, business units or divisions.
- Ensure that DfE strategies are in alignment with overall company directions.
- Develop strategies for achieving the targets.
- Identify time-oriented milestones and areas of responsibility.

4. Apply DfE tools.

Select a product: Select a suitable product for redesign or a new product for DfE.

- Build a background dossier on the product, including the market and company information gathered earlier as well as the product details (design features, production processes etc).

Find suitable tools: Explore the many different tools that can be used in DfE – ranging from complex life cycle assessment programs through to simple checklists, guidelines and scoring matrices.

- Consider the level of sophistication needed, the resources available to invest in tools, the complexity of the product and the amount of design time available.
- Determine which DfE tools are suitable, both for the tasks and the people using them.
- Evaluate tools and select the most appropriate ones.
- Start with simple DfE tools (such as checklists) and work towards more complex ones.
- Bring in external assistance and/or training if needed.

Assess the life cycle of the product: There are simple, flexible DfE tools that capture the essence of the life cycle approach. A preliminary analysis of the life cycle (rather than a detailed assessment) can reveal where the greatest environmental impacts occur and opportunities for improvement.

- Identify the stages in the product life and the inputs and outputs of each stage.
- Identify impacts through an initial simple analysis (eg by brainstorming with other staff).
- Identify 'upstream' (before your company gets involved) and 'downstream' (following your involvement) impacts and which stages your company can influence.
- Assess environmental impacts at each stage. You can use simple tools such as 'process trees' and 'impact assessment matrices'.

5. Develop the product:
Having moved through all or some of the previous stages (as appropriate for your company), you can begin designing, developing and prototyping the new product.

- Gain company agreement on specific product strategies and development directions to be pursued.
- Prepare a brief for detailed design, development and prototyping.
- Provide the production team with DfE tools and information in a format consistent with other production specifications.
- Appoint someone to evaluate the design for compliance with environmental goals.

6. Market the product:
Much of the ability of the DfE process to add value to the product will eventually come down to marketing.

- Use the DfE process to develop credible, accurate and substantiated environmental information for the consumer.
- Become involved in appropriate rating schemes (such as water efficiency ratings) that help to market environmentally preferred products.
- Find ways to inform and educate consumers about the environmental benefits of your product.
- Consider forming partnerships with retailers, local governments, environment and consumer groups to assist in marketing.

7. Evaluate and modify:
With any new process there are risks: you may find unanticipated environmental impacts or other reasons that an aspect of your DfE project may not be completely successful. However, implementing DfE is a continuous learning process and knowledge gained from the experience can improve the next product or process.

- Adopt a formal feedback process to improve the learning ability of your company. Any person involved in product development should be able to feed back both successes and problems.
- Evaluate progress against your initial goals and milestones.
- Ensure that feedback is incorporated into new designs or follow-on products.
- Regularly audit the level of implementation within each business unit and provide incentives for adoption.

Maria Elena Santana

Wood competes with other materials and products for many building applications from structural framing to cladding, because of its relatively low ecological impacts. However, excessive waste occurs at all stages of the timber resource stream: growing, extracting, transporting, processing, using and disposing. While management systems like ecoforestry can dramatically reduce timber wastage, habitat destruction and CO$_2$ emissions at the source, innovative design strategies can also achieve significant waste reduction, value adding and resource efficiency.

Footprints of timber consumption

Timber offers a variety of benefits in buildings and products due to its high strength, good thermal, acoustic and aesthetic properties, and its versatility and workability. However, environmental impacts are created at all stages of timber's life cycle. Forestry management practices, timber production methods and design applications all need considerable improvement.

Forest exploitation and wastage is often justified by the claim that timber is a 'renewable' material; however, native forest ecosystems cannot be replaced. The natural base must be respected in order to preserve the harmony and balance that maintain reciprocal relationships between species. Thus, timber may be considered a renewable resource only when managed under strict ecological parameters that ensure ecosystem sustainability and biodiversity preservation over the long term.

The amount of waste generated during the life cycle of timber is directly related to the segmented and linear organisation of the construction industry. Over-design, over-specification and over-ordering of timber could be easily avoided if an integrated system of manufacturers, designers and contractors incorporated waste reduction techniques, value adding and resource efficiency [Box 7].

Life cycle of timber building products

Life cycle assessment (LCA) is an approach for assessing the impacts of materials and their implications at every stage of their life. LCA examines the procurement of raw materials, their conversion into construction products, and their installation, operation, maintenance, eventual removal, reprocessing, reuse, recycling and disposal (De Caluwe 1997, p. 12). In theory, at least, LCA studies emphasise the range of environmental impacts of materials, such as resource depletion, ecosystem sustainability, environmental pollution and contamination, gaseous emissions, waste generation and energy consumption.

LCA provides baseline information for selecting materials according to multiple criteria, as designers can assign ratings and weightings according to specific priorities. This system can improve the quality of building products by identifying the main ecological implications of current practices and processes within total resource flows [Box 31]. LCA studies to date have been weak on transport and packaging issues, and these operations have considerable environmental implications, particularly related to toxic emissions and waste generation. Also, LCA studies have generally not looked at impacts on biodiversity at the source, as most studies reduce information to units of energy.

The life cycle of timber building products are mainly framed by four stages: timber procurement, conversion, usage and disposal. These are examined below (Figure 9.4.1).

Timber procurement

The ecological implications associated with the procurement of wood for building products are very significant, and depend primarily on the source of extraction: native forests (old growth or regrowth) or plantation forests (hardwood or softwood). **Plantations** are considered the most appropriate source for timber production (after reusing and recycling) as they reduce the impacts of industrial forestry on native forests ecosystems. Plantations must not replace native forests, however, since the ecological consequences are irreversible and the ecosystem is not recoverable. This also disturbs the sequestration of soil in the forest floor, releasing carbon into the atmosphere [Box 25]. Plantations established on previously cleared land, however, can significantly improve

Figure 9.4.1: Life cycle of timber building products

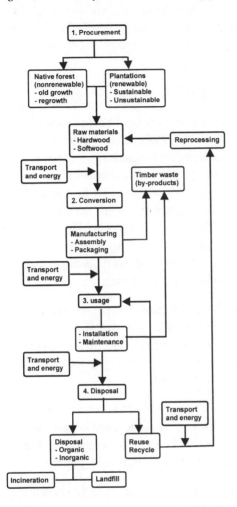

selective logging, shelterwood logging, regeneration burning and prescribed burning, as each practice generate different ecological implications (CSIRO 1996, pp. 4–11).

Timber conversion

Timber converted into building products performs relatively well in terms of energy consumption and carbon emissions, when compared with other building materials – particularly steel, aluminium and concrete. The conversion process involves embodied energy, gaseous emissions, waste generation and chemical treatment.

Embodied energy: Embodied energy is an estimation of the energy consumed in the entire manufacturing process of a particular product, starting with the conversion of the raw materials into a final consumption product. It is a significant indicator of the ecological impact, as embodied energy generates greenhouse gases and produces various wastes. The estimation of the embodied energy should include transportation between manufacturing processes, installation, operation and maintenance. The embodied energy of timber construction products during the conversion stage is far lower, compared to other alternative materials. In other words, wood generally requires the least amount of energy to process and manufacture, apart from other plant-based materials [Box 24].

Gaseous emissions: It is estimated that about 30% of the greenhouse gases emitted each year by industrialised countries are associated with buildings. These are directly related to global warming and ozone depletion (Roodman and Lenssen 1995).

Waste generation: Timber may be more efficient in terms of carbon emissions and energy consumption; however, high rates of waste generation significantly affect its benefits. Hence, waste minimisation represents a significant opportunity for the application of bio-sensitive design principles. In Tasmania, for example, most of the forest is bulldozed and, of the logs extracted, about 10% goes to sawlogs (the rest goes into woodchips for pulp). Of the 10% sawlogs, 5% to 15% ends up in a finished building product, depending on various factors such as species and manufacturing practices (Table 9.4.2). Wastage is even higher when considering roots and branches, which account for roughly 20% and 10% respectively (Jehne 1996).

Chemical treatment: The major environmental concern related to engineered timber products is the use of

soil conditions and fertility, particularly where such land has been over-grazed or over-cultivated (provided that the tree species are suitable for the location).

Growing: The procurement of timber building products involves growing and extraction. The sustainability of growth and production can be greatly affected by the use of fire, chemical fertilisers and herbicides, the removal of top soil and roads. The construction of access roads can account for up to 40% of an area to be logged (Environment Protection Authority 1993, p. 156).

Extraction: The benefits of plantations depend greatly on the agricultural practices used, and the intensity and extent of extractive operations, as these can result in significant ecological damage. For instance, the State of the Environment Report, Australia, classified the impacts of timber extraction according to the practices of **clearfelling**, formaldehyde-based adhesives, as they have high toxicity levels and very reactive compounds. However, more environmentally friendly alternatives are available, such as polyurea resin matrix adhesive (Malin 1992) or Rubinate binder, which is a moisture resistant disocyanate resin that is (unlike formaldehyde resins) unsoluble in water.

Table 9.4.2: Timber wasted in building products

Process stages	Waste rate
Sawlog	40%
Transport	6%
Sawmill	27%
Drying	5%
Retail	3%
Standard sizes	5%
Over-specification	6%
Installation	2%
Approximate wastage	**94%**

Source: Jehne 1996

Timber usage

The usage stage in the life cycle of timber building products involves installation, maintenance and chemical use.

Installation: Wastage during installation is the most significant stage where designers can minimise timber waste considerably, as it is directly related to the design process. Waste minimisation needs to be addressed in the preliminary design stage in order to avoid over-design, over-specification and over-ordering. The high waste rate attributable to over-specification may also be minimised by specifying appropriate dimensions and wood species for the required performance. Wastage at the installation stage may also be significantly reduced by demanding less packaging and by utilising modular units and prefabricated materials, which reduce off-cuts and residues.

Since timber is the largest component of the construction waste stream, such ecodesign strategies would reduce waste dramatically and thus contribute to the maintenance of forests ecosystems.

Maintenance: Durability and service requirements vary according to weather exposure and insect infestation. A selection of durable timber species and appropriate design techniques that ensure humidity protection are the best ways to prevent timber weather deterioration (NAFI 1989).

Chemical use: New technologies have been developed to replace the toxic chemicals used on termites and fungi. For instance, termites can be controlled through physical barrier systems, such as concrete slabs or stainless steel mesh, and organic pesticides [7.4].

Timber disposal

The general implications related to the disposal and recyclability of building materials are considered negligible, although there is a growing recognition of its importance. It is estimated that roughly 33% of the materials going to landfill are made up of construction waste from which 70% can be easily reduced, reused or recycled (Clark 1997). The recyclability and the recycled content of building products is a fundamental parameter to be considered in materials selection. The end of life stage of timber building materials involves disassembly, disposal and reuse.

Disassembly: Design for disassembly can enormously facilitate materials installation and salvage for reuse or recycling. For instance, bolted and grooved connections present significant advantages over riveting and welding systems (Lawson 1996, p. 64).

Disposal: Timber can be easily recycled, even timber with nails, staples or fasteners. It can be reused as second-hand wood for similar applications or recycled: chipped in flakes, fibres, or strands to form engineered lumber products.

Reuse: There is presently little incentive for the building industry to create closed loop systems. However, improved strategies that use recycled timber and off-cuts as raw material are being developed, such as glued laminated beams (Glulam), laminated veneer lumber beams (LVL) and laminated strand lumber beams (LSL).

Implications for designers

Biosensitive design can represent a paradigm shift in environmental problem solving. It is a collaborative approach that interprets design as a 'living organism' where interdependent and reciprocal relationships are always present. In other words, ecodesign concepts are based on integrative concepts instead of partial and segmented approaches. Designers and the building industry as a whole have considerable influence over the environment and the health and well-being of building occupants. However, some designers still do not incorporate new and innovative designs, appropriate technologies and materials that reduce greenhouse gases, pollution and waste. If design practitioners expect to be considered responsible professionals, ecological and health considerations must become central in materials selection and other design decisions.

Designers have a direct and significant impact on the future survival of our native forests and ecosystems. Reducing materials wastage must begin at the design stage. Designers can assist in the modernisation of the building industry by:

- supporting a shift in the construction industry toward closed loop cycles between manufacturing processes, design applications and construction techniques;

- minimising timber construction waste in the building industry to reduce pressure on native forests.

References and further reading

Adger W.N. and Brown, K. 1994, *Land Use and the Causes of Global Warming*, J. Wiley, New York.

Clark, J. 1997, *The Case for a Plantation Wood Products Industry Policy*, Centre for Resource and Environmental Studies, Australian National University, Canberra, ACT.

CSIRO 1996, *Australia: State of the Environment*, Collingwood, VIC.

De Caluwe, N. 1997, 'LCA/LCI Tools', *Ecotools Manual – A Comprehensive Review of Design for Environment Tools*. [Online] http://sun1.mpce.stu.mmu.ac.uk/pages/projects/dfe/pubs/dfe33/ecotools.htm (10 April 1998).

Environment Protection Authority 1993, *New South Wales State of the Environment*, Sydney, NSW.

Jehne, W. 1996, *Process Mapping Timber*, Canberra, ACT.

Lawson, W.R. 1996, *Timber in Building Construction: Ecological Implications*, Forest and Wood Products Research and Development Corporation, Canberra, ACT.

Malin, N. 1992, 'Formaldehyde-free Interior-grade MDF', *Environmental Building News* 1 (1). [Online] http://www.ebuild.com/Archives/Product_Reviews/Medite.html (25 February 1998).

Maser, C. 1994, *Sustainable Forestry: Philosophy, Science, and Economics*, St. Lucie Press, Boca Raton, FL.

NAFI 1989, 'Timber Species and Properties', Timber Datafile P1, *Timber Manual: Design and Specification,* National Association of Forest Industries, Canberra, ACT.

Roodman, D.M. and Lenssen, N. 1995, *A Building Revolution*, Worldwatch Paper 124, Worldwatch Institute, Washington, DC.

Willis, A.M. and Tonkin, C. 1998, *Timber in Context: A Guide to Sustainable Use*, Construction Information Systems Australia, Milsons Point, NSW.

Questions

1. List the major limitations and benefits of using timber in building construction.

2. Is all timber renewable? What about species that have very long regrowth periods?

3. What are the key considerations of life cycle assessment for timber building products?

4. How can bio-sensitive design assist timber waste minimisation?

5. What can designers do to avoid compromising native forest ecosystems?

6. List the main environmental parameters for timber-based building products and prioritise these criteria.

Projects

1. In groups, use Table 9.4.1 as a starting point to construct a flow-chart of the life cycle of timber, with specific attention to explaining how waste is likely to be caused at each stage. Brainstorm means to reduce this waste.

2. Phone or visit local construction supply stores and ascertain which engineered timber products or woodless timbers are available in your area.

Box 23   Timber Certification and Labelling

Tim Cadman

At the 1992 Rio 'Earth Summit', numerous governments, largely from the industrialised nations, accepted the need to deal with the issue of how to look after their **forests** sustainably. This was partly a response to growing concerns among consumers about forest management. Within this context, **sustainable forest management** (SFM) generally refers to forest management that is socially, economically and environmentally sustainable.

Rio led to the creation of a number of forest management protocols, including the Montreal Process. This is a reporting mechanism whereby participating governments provide information on forest management against a number of criteria (eg conservation of biological diversity). Under each criterion there are a number of indicators against which fulfilment of the criteria can be measured. These include such basics as measuring fragmentation of forest types or the area of forest land available for timber production.

While Montreal is a step in the right direction, it does not in itself either define sustainable forest management (merely commenting that all criteria taken together contribute towards SFM), nor does it provide **prescriptive** measures that will result in SFM. This is a 'passive' method of measuring progress towards sustainable forestry. There is no broader context of the debate around the sustainability of existing or alternative forest management models.

Another post-Earth Summit initiative is the International Standardisation Organisation (ISO) 14,000 series for forest managers and processors. This is an 'environmental management system' which reports on the implementation of a company's own mission and goals. This series does not address management practices in the forest, but is nevertheless useful for auditing a company's overall environmental performance, under the philosophy of 'continuous improvement'. It is not an 'eco label' however,

and should not be confused with **forest product certification**.

Independent, third party certification of forest products is acknowledged as contributing to improved forest management. The integration of environmental, social and economic factors in the development of such schemes is recognised as providing the basic platform for sustainable forest management. Certification agencies that are independent from government are essential. Their role is to verify forest management practices on the ground and establish procedures to ensure the **chain of custody** from forest to factory. The development of open and transparent consultation and participation processes that reflect the views of all key **stakeholders** – who in turn inform the development of forest management plans – differentiates third party certification from forest management driven by government policy.

By far the most commonly accepted label is that of the Forest Stewardship Council (FSC), a body that essentially certifies certifiers, according to ten 'principles and criteria' designed to result in 'well-managed' forests. Structurally, the FSC is comprised of three 'chambers' – social, environmental and economic (essentially reflecting the needs of Indigenous people, environmental NGOs and business interests); these vote on changes to the principles and criteria and endorse new certifiers. Currently there are more than 14 million hectares of FSC certified forests in over a dozen countries worldwide. In the UK and The Netherlands for example, FSC certified forest products account for more than 40% of all timber used.

Government and industry have also combined to develop their own labeling schemes. Their credibility in the marketplace will be determined by the extent to which they incorporate stakeholder aspirations, and the degree of protection offered to the forests themselves.

10.1   Earth Building

Steve Burroughs

Housing is one of the most critical issues facing the modern world. The vast majority of the population live in self-built shacks providing scarcely a few square metres of space. So often, the delivery of housing to the needy means sacrificing quality for quantity, providing minimal improvement over the existing shacks. These require excessive use of energy to maintain rudimentary comfort during cold and hot periods. This chapter argues that earth wall construction must be revisited, if we are to house the world's population sustainably.

Introduction

Household energy is required to meet basic needs such as cooking, water heating, lighting and space heating. Energy is intimately linked to health, nutrition, education, and economic prosperity. However, for local agencies and non-governmental organisations involved in housing delivery, an array of pressures and constraints mean that the energy and sustainability linkage is rarely addressed. A crucial opportunity to build sustainable, energy-efficient homes while supporting local economic development is being sacrificed with the use of 'modern' building materials and needs.

Earth wall construction (such as mud bricks, wattle and daub and rammed earth) has been used for thousands of years and has many advantages over more costly materials. Earth wall construction projects which have demonstrated energy and environmental sustainability too often exist in isolation, and are insufficiently publicised. There needs to be more monitoring of sustainable home projects and information transfer to groups delivering, legislating and facilitating the delivery of housing.

Earth wall construction

Thermal mass gives earth walls their unique properties as a building material. Thermal mass is the amount of potential heat storage capacity available in a material. Earth walls left exposed to the sun or other heat source allow this heat to travel into the core material where it is slowly released in all directions when the temperature cools. The heat absorption and releasing properties of earth walls make them a good insulator because warming and cooling temperatures rarely penetrate through their full width. When temperature changes do occur, the stored energy within the walls is released until temperature equilibrium is achieved or the earth wall begins absorbing again. The result is minimum temperature fluctuation within a building throughout the year; a cool temperature in summer, a warm temperature in winter (Department of Housing 1996).

Health, safety and cost

If thermally efficient measures are not incorporated into the design, homeowners incur high rates of energy consumption during winter. For the low-income sector in many countries, the available and affordable fuels used include wood, coal and kerosene – all highly polluting and dangerous. Further exacerbating the problem, these fuels are typically burned in inefficient stoves or refurbished oil drums, often with no flues to exhaust the smoke. Families are exposed to particulate matter, sulphur dioxide, nitrogen oxides and other respirable pollutants at levels many times above the World Health Organisation standards. One study found that black South African children are 270 times more likely to die from acute respiratory infection than children in Western Europe (von Schimding 1991). Another found that respiratory disease due to exposure to coal combustion cost South Africa approximately US$70 million per annum (van Horen 1996). There are also indirect costs such as losses in productivity and quality of life which are more difficult to quantify, but these certainly create additional economic burdens in the less developed nations.

Earth wall construction is by no means an unsatisfactory, temporary or 'second-best' expedient. Under conditions favouring its use, it has many advantages, including durability, and is worthy of being chosen on its merits. Any material in the hands of incompetent or ignorant workers can result in unstable or unsanitary structures. However, when properly constructed, earth wall constructions are as durable as other building materials. Further, low cost does not mean low quality. Earth wall homes, which incorporate passive solar design, encourage the efficient use of resources, improved indoor air quality, low energy costs, and local economic development.

Benefits of earth wall construction also flow on to the international community as emissions of greenhouse gases are reduced through good thermal performance of the dwellings. In the coal burning households of Johannesburg, South Africa, annual emission levels have been estimated as high as 13 tonnes of carbon dioxide (CO_2) per dwelling (Palmer 1995). While the average national emission levels will probably be lower, the need for housing is enormous – 5.6 million dwellings in the next two decades (ERDC 1995). The greenhouse gas savings potential is large, particularly when one considers the measures applied to these homes are expected to last the life of the dwelling, 40 years or more.

Reasonably conservative estimates of the total additional cost of a thermally efficient, passive solar home are about 6% of the total pricing of the home. If these measures were able to eliminate 50% of the household coal use identified for Johannesburg (Palmer 1995), it could prevent the release of an estimated 6.5 tonnes of CO_2 per year per home. If 10,000 homes were influenced in the process, and the savings were summed over a decade, over half a million tonnes of CO_2 could be avoided at a price of roughly US$3.3 per tonne. If these measures only reduced energy consumption by 25% due to a combination of 'take-back' or mixed fuel use, the CO_2 would still be avoided at roughly US$6.6 per tonne.

Soil criteria for earth walls

Perhaps the most important issue in connection with earth wall construction is the identification of favourable soils (Crowley 1995). Those inexperienced in earth construction are likely to choose the wrong kind of soil. As stiff clay soil becomes hard when dry, it is naturally supposed that a clay soil is most suitable for earth walls: this is not the case. In fact, only a small amount of clay is desirable, while plenty of sand or mineral aggregate is desirable. The allowable amount of clay in the soil seems to be 30%. If more than 40% clay, the soil is unfit for use. Generally, grain in sizes above 0.05mm is classified as mineral aggregate, including gravel, coarse sand, fine sand, and very fine sand; 0.05mm to 0.005 is classified as silt; 0.005 to 0.0015 is classified as very fine clay.

Information to date is that suitable soil is predominantly sand with sufficient silt and clay to serve as a binder or natural cementing agent. Without a small amount of cohesive material, such as clay, sand moisture would not be adequate. On the other hand, if the soil were predominantly clay or silt, shrinkage, swelling, and fragmenting would soon occur, resulting in the disintegration of the wall. The total **colloids** include all the clay and all of the silt, except that portion of the silt which settles in the first 15 minutes of the test and the larger grain sizes. The colloids then include all soil particles remaining in suspension.

Soils that are satisfactory for buildings can be found in situ in many parts of the world, or an economical mixture can readily be obtained by the blending of soils commonly occurring in a region (Crowley 1995). Soil to be used for earth wall construction must be of such character that, when formed into a wall, it will:

- Have sufficient strength to support the imposed loads.
- Be fairly impervious to water.
- Have minimum shrinkage upon drying.
- Offer resistance to deterioration from the weathering effect of heavy rains.
- Be reasonably non-conductive to heat.

Earth architecture in South Africa

Proper housing for the so-called 'informal' areas in South Africa is a most pressing need and presents a great challenge for the South African Government. The Durban Self-Help Housing Project was established to create a demonstration project, provide training in earth architecture and construction, and provide low-income families with access to an alternative form of housing delivery which could also generate business opportunities in housing and construction. The following factors were key issues:

- The affordability to the degree that long-term funding was not necessary. In fact, the acquisition cost was to be within the range of the government subsidy, a one-off cash payment of 15,000 Rand.

- The building structures were to be desirable and seen as conventional in appearance. Perceptions of quality were not to differ over the price range – prices must essentially be related to size, and houses were to be easily extendable.

- Non-skilled labourers were to be able to construct the homes with minimal technical support. Conventional building industry methods with typical labour, management and financial costs represent as much as 80% of the total building costs. These methods are unable to provide a solution to the housing crisis in South Africa.

The main thrust of the earth architecture construction approach has been:

- The creation of rapid building procedures that largely eliminate the need for trade skills, relying mainly on the common sense and physical ability of local people.
- A great reduction of the multiplicity of operations and procedures typical of conventional building methods, to a few simple and well-developed steps.

By these methods, labour and management costs as low as 10% of those typical of conventional building industry methods, were possible. In providing for the need of the poorest peoples of South Africa, the earth architectural option provided or arranged:

- Suitable training procedures and resident local builders.
- Standard housing plans and promotional materials.
- Standard plan price lists and costing procedures.
- Materials ordered on a group basis so as to achieve economies of scale.
- Local, provincial and federal building authority approvals.
- Assistance in the financing of earth homes.

Outcomes: This received a favourable response from a wide range of people involved in housing delivery. It soon became apparent that communities were willing to accept the technology and the concept of self-help as a delivery mechanism for housing. The development of a 'Best Practices Guide' for earth building in conjunction with the CSIR (Pretoria South Africa), went a long way to eliminating the problems of acceptability normally encountered when new technologies are presented to communities and local authorities.

In response to the favourable reaction and in order to promote the technology further, two additional housing components were added to the project. This enabled the establishment of a resource centre to assist beneficiaries with training and the production of mud bricks. The construction of demonstration units in Maputoland (Northern KwaZulu-Natal, South Africa) ensured the transfer of technology to people in a rural area of KwaZulu-Natal.

The full impact of the project to housing delivery in South Africa is yet to be seen. Factors that inhibited the completion of the project included the long lead-in time required for housing projects and the problems experienced with community dynamics, which often resulted in considerable delays.

Lessons: The project should have focused more on empowering people about the technical housing process and supporting them in getting to a stage where they were able to actually start construction of houses. The delivery of self-help housing at scale has never been achieved in KwaZulu-Natal and a third phase of the project could possibly have focused on this aspect. The successful implementation of self-help housing requires certain interventions, and prior to any attempt to implement such a project an assessment of the project needs to be carried out to ascertain whether or not the requisite interventions are in place to ensure the success of the project. This may require changes to national policy and the approach of local authorities to housing.

Conclusion

The concept of environmentally sustainable housing on a mass delivery basis is revolutionary, since it represents a challenge to all the professional, government officials, trade persons and clients investing in houses. Earth wall construction provides an opportunity for creating a model which could be applied in developed and developing countries, with a significant potential for reducing energy consumption in the 21st Century. At this time, when housing delivery programs are hopefully moving forward, it is essential that all the various lessons in innovative building design are shared and communicated. As earth building gains popular acceptance, the demand for specific support services will escalate. Provisions must therefore be made for skilled personnel such as engineers, architects and quantity surveyors, to be exposed to earth building technology. Through institutions such as universities, technical schools and standards authorities, earth building will find general public acceptance and be formally adopted as a sound construction option.

References

Bourdon, D. 1995, *Designing the Earth: The Human Impulse to Shape Nature*, H.N. Adams, New York.

Burroughs S., 1999, *Forum for Earth Building Technologies*, Conference Proceedings, Pretoria, South Africa.

Crowley, M. 1995, 'Homes from the Earth: Site Sourcing of Building Materials', in J. Birkeland, ed, *Catalyst '95: Rethinking the Built Environment*, University of Canberra, ACT.

Department of Housing 1996, White Paper, 'A New Housing Policy and Strategy for South Africa', Pretoria.

Easton, D. 1996, *The Rammed Earth House*, Chelsea Green Publications, White River Junction, VT.

EDRC 1995, *The Need for Housing in the Next Two Decades*, Draft Report for the Energy and Development Research Centre, South African Government.

International Institute for Energy Conservation 1997, 'Housing for a Sustainable South Africa', *Proposal for Establishment of Sustainable Homes Network in South Africa*, Johannesburg.

Kanuka-Fuchs, R., Rattenbury, J. and Allen, M., eds, 1992, *Earthbuilding*, Building Biology and Ecology Institute of New Zealand, Auckland, NZ.

King, B. 1996, *Building of Earth and Straw: Structural Design for Rammed Earth and Strawbale Architecture*, Ecological Design Press, Sausalito, CA.

Palmer Group 1995, *The Potential Market for Low Smoke Coal*, Draft Report for the Department of Mineral and Energy Affairs, South African Government.

The United States Environmental Protection Agency 1997, 'Housing as if People Mattered', *United Nations Conference of the Parites III*, Washington, DC.

Van Horen 1996, *The Cost of Power: Externalities in South Africa's Energy Sector*, University of Capetown, Capetown, South Africa.

von Schimding 1991, 'Acute Respiratory Infections as an Important Cause of Childhood Deaths in South Africa', *South African Medical Journal* 8, pp. 19–82.

World Bank 1995, *World Development Report 1995: Workers in an Integrating World*, The International Bank for Reconstruction and Development (the World Bank), Oxford University Press, New York.

Questions

1. How is soil a construction material in its own right? Develop a selection process for soils used in earth wall construction.

2. How does earth wall construction comply with ESD standards?

3. Since stabilised brick construction is less expensive and environmentally damaging than fired brick, and can be made to look the same, why are fired bricks generally preferred?

4. How does earth wall construetion impact on the world's CO_2 levels? Look up and compare the CO_2 output for brick veneer and other conventional materials versus earth wall homes.

5. Your group is being sent to a third world country to help with housing. The homeless want brick homes with tiles; however, the funds available prohibit such construction. Outline a presentation to the community about what type of materials should be used and why.

6. In the same situation as above, outline a presentation to the government, which explains how the homes will meet cost and maintenance requirements.

Projects

1. As a group, invite the most senior officials with responsibility for building codes and public housing in your region to a forum to discuss their views on the benefits of, and institutional barriers to, earth wall construction.

2. Find a local builder that specialises in earthwall construction (or someone who lives in an earth wall home) and arrange to visit their homes.

10.2 Strawbale Construction

Leslie St. Jacques

Strawbale construction utilises straw for wall systems, structural support and insulation, offering the potential for a more organic and environmentally sustainable method of building shelter. Along with its environmental attributes, strawbale construction allows self-help projects and is often credited for bringing people together and creating opportunities for self-empowerment. This chapter argues for greater use of this exceptional material to meet the need for simple, comfortable, accessible and environmentally responsible housing.

Introduction

Settlers in the Sandhills area of Nebraska 120 years ago used a super-insulating, locally available and annually renewable resource to build houses – hay. The oldest documented strawbale building was built in 1886 or 1887, near Bayard, Nebraska (Steen et al 1994). Homes built of strawbales and covered with stucco are still in existence today. Of the 70 historic strawbale homes documented by Welsch, 13 were still standing and 12 still in use in 1993 (Myrhman and MacDonald 1997).

The strawbale construction revival involves a consciousness of 'less is more', and an awareness of the need to promote cooperation and equity in sharing resources. Further, it recognises that the use of straw alone does not make a house 'sustainable' – all other aspects of the house and its components need to be designed with sustainability in mind. As Myrhman writes: 'grafting a "more sustainable" technology onto the old paradigms creates only the illusion of change' (Myrhman and MacDonald 1997, p. iii).

Environmental benefits

Strawbale construction offers many environment-related benefits over current construction methods. Straw is a by-product of the production of materials such as wheat, rice and oats. 'Close to two hundred million tons of waste straw are produced in the United States each year' (Steen et al 1994, p. 28). The burning of straw contributes to global warming, producing carbon monoxide and nitrous oxides,

creating serious health problems. It has been estimated that if the unused straw in the US (after the harvest of major grains) was baled for use in house construction, 3 million 1500sq ft houses could be built every year (Myrhman and MacDonald 1997).

Load-bearing strawbale structures without wood frames save a significant amount of wood over traditional stick-frame construction. In 1990, an average single family house in Canada used approximately 10,000 board feet of lumber, roughly equivalent to one acre of softwood forest (Grady 1993, p. 99). Furthermore, should the home ever need to be taken down, the straw will decompose naturally and need not contribute to the enormous burden of construction waste already going into landfill sites. According to Grady, 'the average new house in Canada generates well over 2 tons of construction waste'. This means that the equivalent of 3500 acres of softwood forest in construction waste is dumped into landfill sites every year, from new homes built in the Toronto area alone (Grady 1993).

The high insulation value of straw also means less wood and fossil fuels are required to heat and cool the home. The R-value (resistance to heat exchange) of a strawbale wall has been tested to be R-30, though this is thought to be a conservative value (Stone 1997). Some estimates from in-field tests range between R-40 and R-60; strawbale homes are '[insulated] two to three times better than the wall system of most well-insulated homes, and often five times better than older houses' (Steen et al 1994).

Social benefits

Among strawbale construction's social benefits is the opportunity to learn new skills and engage in community building activities. Strawbale building techniques allow owner-builders to involve friends and family in building projects without previous building experience. Building with straw increases confidence for individuals while it builds community: it is not only 'look what I can do' – but 'look what we can do together'.

A strawbale house can be less expensive to build and maintain than most other forms of construction, depending on the size and features designed into the home and the amount of owner-builder and recycled materials used. Steen et al (1994) calculated the 30-year life cycle costs of different homes for comparison. The costs of construction, 20% down payment, finance, energy (heating and cooling) for a 1375sq ft, three bedroom, two bath home in a moderate climate, were the basis for the comparison. The life cycle costs over 30 years for a conventionally built home came to US$171,300. The wholly owner-built home using recycled materials and with super-efficient appliances had a 30-year life cycle cost of US$29,625. The conventional home after 100 years had a life cycle cost of US$527,340, while the owner-built strawbale home had a 100-year life cycle cost of US$29,625. The authors state that, while more detailed cost analysis is necessary, 'strawbale building would prove even more cost competitive after examining environmental impact and related costs' (1994, p. 39).

Construction methods

Strawbale construction uses baled straw for walls, and less frequently, roofs and floors. Strawbale structures include houses, barns, greenhouses, storage shelters, outdoor ovens, and children's playhouses. Accepted methods and techniques of strawbale wall construction have been discovered in historic building patents, through experimentation and by utilising techniques developed with other materials. Innovation in strawbale construction techniques continues. However, most strawbale construction uses one of three types of wall structures: load-bearing, post and beam, or in-fill. The first structural type, load-bearing, uses resources most efficiently, drawing on the strength of the bales to carry 'dead loads', such as the roof, as well as any 'live loads', such as people or snow. A second method, the most commonly used (Steen et al 1994), involves 'post and beam' in combination with load-bearing construction. Such hybrid construction systems can reduce the amount of wood by using door and window frames to share the load. In this case, the straw acts primarily as insulation. The third method utilises a wood frame with strawbales as in-fill, for their insulation value. This method requires far more structural support and timber than necessary. It also makes the construction of the strawbale wall tedious, as bales need to be notched and tailored to fit around each piece of the wood frame.

In all three methods, builders stack the bales like bricks on a building platform, slightly raised above the interior floor in case the floor ever gets wet. Clean, very dry bales (bound tightly with two or three strings of polypropylene twine) are ideal. Walls are pre-stressed or left to compress for several weeks under the weight of the roof (Chapman 1995). The strawbale walls are then covered with lath and a locally appropriate waterproof but 'breathable' mixture. Wiring for electricity can be passed through a conduit, along the wall, prior to plastering, making it easy to change if necessary. Pipes for water should not be set within the wall, as a precautionary measure. Running them through the floor, or even outside the walls, is recommended. Foundations for strawbale walls can be the same as for traditional walls.

Fire and pests

Fire and pests are common fears when people first hear of strawbale housing. Strawbale walls covered in plaster have the fire resistance of wood frame walls similarly protected (Myrhman and MacDonald 1997, p. 11). A correctly built, plastered strawbale wall lacks the oxygen to support fire. However, loose straw and exposed strawbale walls will support combustion under certain circumstances (as above, p. 18). Before plastering, building with strawbales requires caution – activities that generate sparks, such as welding or smoking, have ignited strawbale at the construction site.

Sealing the bale wall carefully with stucco or plaster will deter rodents as well. In some areas, termites are specifically evolved to tunnel through wood, which points to the need to protect the wood components of the building. If the house is in an area with a grass-eating termite problem, or a severe problem with other varieties of termite, a metal termite shield should be used [7.4].

Building codes

Potential owner-builders can be deterred by stories about the difficulty of gaining approval from their building department to build with strawbale. However, guides to negotiating with building officials are available. Determination and perseverance in pursuing approval, financing and insurance are key. Some councils have already written strawbale housing into the code, simplifying the process for builders. David Eisenberg led a successful effort to have strawbale construction written into the building code in Tuscon and Pima County, Arizona, and has inspired others to work with local building officials to do the same [11.3].

Moisture

The biggest threat to the structural integrity of the strawbale wall is moisture. Bales that get wet before or after parging are subject to deterioration, rot and molding – requiring removal of the affected bales from a finished structure. There are cases where straw has become wet before completion, requiring deconstruction of the project. Bales must not have a chance to get wet; they must be baled dry, arrive at the site dry, and stay dry until protected with stucco. Bales can be stacked in small pyramids raised off the ground if rain threatens, and covered with the thick waterproof tarps. Builders are strongly advised to keep waterproof – not merely water-resistant – tarps handy. In wet climates, designs typically feature a roof (or wrap-around porches) that overhangs the wall to a good distance, to minimise the amount of rain hitting the wall. The ground should slope away from the wall outside.

Conclusion

The use of strawbales as structural support and insulation can reduce the negative environmental impacts of a structure, and supports a socially responsible building process. Strawbale construction requires caution with respect to potential fires and water reaching exposed straw. Gaining approval from building officials and mortgagors may require perseverance and discussion. However, the super-insulated strawbale wall made with locally available and annually renewable materials, deserves attention as a key sustainable building component.

References

Anink, D., Boonstra, C. and Mak, J. 1996, *Handbook of Sustainable Building: An Environmental Preference Method for Selection of Materials for Use in Construction and Refurbishment*, James & James, London.

Chapman, L., Fibrehouse Limited and Scanada Consultants Ltd. 1995, *Developing and Proof-testing the 'Prestressed Nebraska' Method for Improved Production of Baled Fibre Housing*, Canada Mortgage and Housing Corporation.

Grady, W. 1993, *Green Home: Planning and Building the Environmentally-Advanced House*, Camden House Publishing, Camden East, Charlotte, VT.

King, B. 1996, *Buildings of Earth and Straw: Structural Design for Rammed Earth and Straw-bale Architecture*, Ecological Design Press, Sausalito, CA.

Lorenz, D. 1995, *A New Industry Emerges: Making Construction Materials from Cellulosic Wastes*, Institute for Local Self-Reliance, Washington, DC.

Myrhman, M. and MacDonald, S.O. 1997, *Build It With Bales, Version 2 Out On Bale,* Tucson, AZ.

Steen, A., Steen, B. and Bainbridge, D. with Eisenberg, D. 1994, *The Strawbale House*, Chelsea Green Publishing Company, White River Junction, VT.

Stone, N. I. 1997, *California Energy Commission tests of Strawbale Wall R-values,* California Energy Commission, Sacramento, CA.

Questions

1. Why would strawbale construction be characterised as sustainable? Why is it so rare?

2. How would the roof of a strawbale home be constructed differently in a warm, dry climate, than in an area with heavy rainfall?

3. What are some of the social impediments to strawbale construction? Decide whether they can be characterised as administrative, legal, practical and so on.

4. What activities should never take place on a strawbale construction site? What type of activities require extreme caution on the site?

5. Do strawbale homes require special measures for plumbing or electrical work?

6. Compare earth wall and strawbale wall construction. List advantages and disadvantages of each.

Projects

1. Contact the local government housing department and discuss the possible construction of a strawbale demonstration house in your community. List the relevant requirements under the local council regulations and building codes. Can these be overcome?

2. List the basic design requirements for a simple 1200sq ft strawbale home for your climate. List the materials used, and calculate the total cost of materials.

Box 24   A Carbohydrate Economy

David Morris

Almost 20 years ago I coined the term 'carbohydrate economy' to describe an industrial system with two distinctive features:

- Carbohydrates replace hydrocarbons. We rely on vegetables, not minerals, to supply not only our stomachs, but our factories.

- Cultivators and their surrounding regions capture a significant portion of the revenue generated from converting plants into products.

A carbohydrate economy would fundamentally improve not only our raw materials foundation, but the structure of our manufacturing sector as well.

Today, the first leg of the carbohydrate economy – the vision of 'replacing drilling with tilling' – is rapidly gaining adherents and visibility. A bipartisan effort is underway to promote what the federal government calls a **bio-based economy** and the US Congress has enacted major legislation to implement this policy. The media are beginning to pick up stories about companies making plastics from corn, lubricants from vegetable oils, car bodies from **hemp**, paper and construction products from straw and bagasse (see ILSR's website, www.carbohydrateeconomy.org).

However, the second leg of a carbohydrate economy – structural change – has been largely ignored. As we encourage a shift from minerals to vegetables, we must also encourage a shift away from the vertically integrated, absentee ownership structure of the mineral industry toward a more democratic and locally based industrial structure. This could reverse the trend for rural economies – that once boasted a diversified agricultural base – to be decimated.

The US, at the time of writing, is about to endorse a national policy of cultivating and harvesting 1–1.5 billion tonnes of plant matter destined for US industrial and fuel markets. This would more than double the amount of plant matter currently used for all purposes. This national enterprise could spawn thousands of new manufacturing facilities. The high costs of transporting crops would lead most of these to locate near their raw material. The scale of biorefineries could be much smaller than fossil-fuel refineries.

Unfortunately, this proposal does not, by itself, provide for the economic security of farmers and farm communities. Some policy makers think that by simply expanding the market for plant matter, farmers will benefit. However, agricultural income has declined in the last generation, even though productivity and consumption keeps rising. The price of corn, soybeans, and other grains is near an all-time low. Those farmers who have survived are increasingly becoming captive contract producers for a handful of transnational corporations.

Public policy should favour locally owned and farmer-owned facilities. With virtually no government assistance, more than 150 farmer-owned manufacturing facilities with a capitalisation of more than US$3 billion have been created in the last 15 years. In Minnesota, in-state ethanol plants provide about 10% of all automobile transportation fuels. Two thirds of the 15 biorefineries are owned by some 8500 farmers. The so-called 'Minnesota model' was assisted by state policies that encourage in-state production by small and medium-sized facilities in which farmers own a significant share. Recently, a federation of state-based farmer-owned investment alliances met to share ideas about how to expand these numbers even more rapidly.

If in the year 2030 farmers produce their crops and livestock for Exxon, Dupont and International Paper and Ford, along with Smithfield and ADM and Cargill and General Mills, we will have missed an historical opportunity. Favouring locally owned facilities would allow us to tackle the environmental crisis, which is largely caused by the use of fossil fuels; while at the same time tackling the agricultural crisis, which is largely caused by the lack of farmer power in the marketplace. In this way we would achieve a true carbohydrate economy.

Victor Cusack and Lou Yiping

As an economical building material, bamboo's speed in developing matured harvestable timber production outstrips any other naturally growing resource. The annually renewable harvest cycle is unprecedented in any other timber producing species. The diversity of use and species available makes it possible to find a bamboo that will suit most different climates or environments. With rapidly deteriorating timber resources, the time will come when bamboo will play an important role in the Western world generally. Yet despite millions being spent on bamboo research in Asia, the Western world is not yet taking this useful plant seriously.

Bamboo in construction

The Costa Rican government has introduced an education program to build at least 3000 bamboo houses every year. Each house is designed by an architect and constructed from the South American Guadua species of bamboo, grown in plantations established only eight years ago. This species is not indigenous to Costa Rica, which meant establishing new plantations and waiting seven years for the wood to grow large enough and mature enough to harvest.

These houses were especially designed to overcome the regular death toll experienced from frequent large-scale earthquakes. Unlike Bali's elegant tropical designs, their structures are indistinguishable from conventional houses, their exterior and interior rendering is supported by the superbly strong, flexible bamboo frames that also provide superior insulation qualities.

Using bamboo columns on simple concrete post drilled foundations, the walls are fitted as prefabricated bamboo panels with both faces pre-lined with bamboo splits (attached and ready for cement rendering to form inner and outer wall surfaces). The cavity acts as a sealed inner insulating chamber. The roof trusses are extraordinarily strong, light prefabricated interlocking trusses made from machine sawn culm wall sections, assembled quickly with glue and clouts. Concrete and tiled floors in better-quality homes use large diameter bamboo culms lain side by side as reinforcing, which are then sealed forever into the concrete (Cusack

1997, 1999). Deprived of oxygen by sealing in concrete, Columbian architect Lucy Amparo Bastidas claims that bamboo undergoes a petrification process that prevents further deterioration.

Such simply constructed houses are regularly built in both Colombia and Costa Rica, with many being large homes indistinguishable from elegantly designed conventional rendered masonry houses. Some of the older Colombian buildings have been standing for more than 90 years. A Columbian architect, Simon Velez, constructs huge modern bamboo houses and buildings of breathtaking beauty, generally for wealthy clients in that country.

While temporary structures are easily built, permanent houses that comply with council standards can be constructed if the intending builder takes the trouble to study some of the necessary basic skills and procedures needed (Cusack 1997, 1999). As an example, good design involves simple bracing triangulation and load direction placement of members, together with an adequate understanding of the different joining systems available for both lightly and heavily laden columns and beams. Columns, beams and truss members need not be limited to single bamboo culms, as massively strong members can be constructed using multiple culms pinned and lashed together.

To take advantage of bamboo's high tensile strength, the joints must be designed to discourage splitting. The modern bolted, filled joint designs, such as those used by Velez, are even stronger than the traditional pinned and lashed joints developed originally by locals.

Bamboo as a building material has suffered greatly from poor species selection, inadequate material harvesting, flawed treatment systems, and inadequate preparation, and many failures due to builders' enthusiasm exceeding their knowledge. When constructing houses, the design should ensure that bamboo is never buried below ground level (irrespective of the precautions taken), and should always be used in such a way that it is protected from direct rainfall or contact with water.

If larger spans involve trusses or longer beams, it may be necessary to have a qualified engineer prepare simple calculations, and sometimes a drawing, in order to obtain council approval. Generally speaking, councils will approve bamboo structures subject to the plans being accompanied by an engineering drawing or specification, and an indication that the bamboo is of a suitable structural species that has been prepared in the correct manner. Design strengths of different species are now available. For example, Byron Shire in New South Wales, Australia, has recently approved two house constructions from bamboo.

Types of bamboo

Bamboos are divided into two fundamentally different forms, each with minor variations. These are the cooler climate running bamboos (with monopodial **rhizomes**), and tropical clumping bamboos (with sympodial rhizomes). Both are extremely strong and useful, but each is more suited to different areas of use as a construction material. With careful selection and design, both forms can be used for a diversity of applications. However, young 'sappy' culms harvested before maturity usually suffer excessive shrinkage and cracking, and are often quickly destroyed by the powder beetle larvae attracted by the young culms high starch level (Cusack 1997, 1999).

Monopodial or running bamboo produce long underground rhizomes that travel out to re-establish the plant in new feeding territory, and tend to be a slower growing plant because of their invasive nature and extensive underground development. Each slow developing Rhizomes can produce many culms when mature enough. Given time, they normally create a dominant monoculture forest of that species. The running bamboo species, mostly smaller in diameter and thinner walled, are very useful for value-added building materials because of their ready splitting ability. Running bamboos are harvestable from year 9, but mature-diameter culms take 13 years.

Sympodial or clumping bamboos are actually giant rainforest type plants: huge, powerful clumping grasses that send out a fine system of radial roots to acquire their food. Their clumping habit, a result of having a single culm only from each short-necked Rhizome, makes them stay where they are planted, and they generally co-exist comfortably with other species. They tend to be much faster in reaching mature size because they invest most of their energy above ground. The larger stronger clumping bamboo have commonly been used in their natural state as strong structural members in buildings, particularly in South America and Indonesia. Clumping bamboos are ready for harvest in about six to seven years, and produce an edible shoot crop after three years.

Bamboo culm strength and treatment

In Colombia and Costa Rica, bamboo is treated against powder beetle and fungus attack with the 'Boucherie' SAP displacement system of pressure injection (now installed and operating at Bamboo World, NSW). A simpler but much slower system of treatment based on leaf expiration is available if small quantities of timber are required. According to Colombian bamboo architect Oscar Hidalgo Lopez, Guadua is a resistant bamboo, but it will still be attacked by powder beetle and suffer splitting and shrinkage problems, unless harvested when mature, or unless treated for use in an environment exposed to rainfall.

While clumpers are usually superior in unit tensile strength because of a different cellular structure and longer fibres, even runners are also very high in tensile strength when compared to wood. However, the main problem with all bamboo, when compared to wood, is that it lacks medullary rays that bind the fibres together radially, or sideways. The parenchyma cells joining bamboo fibre bundles are not strong; however, they do get steadily stronger with age, so the older the culm, the harder it is to split. Runners take longer for their fibres to reach mature strength and to resist splitting so, in China, they are usually left standing for at least five years before harvesting instead of three years for clumpers (in Indonesia and China, bamboo poles are so valuable, they often get harvested too soon to be good quality). Superior structural bamboo species are usually thick walled, straight culmed, larger diameter species; plantations should use only superior species suitable for the particular environment.

Processed bamboo timber products

Using modern technology, immensely strong value-added building materials are now being produced in Asia on a major scale. Because of bamboo's longer fibre length and higher strength, they are superior on a strength to weight basis to similar wood products. Some examples of desirable bamboo products are as follows:

- Bamboo plywood: Glued in hot presses from machine split bamboo culm, usually 3-ply (but often more), and with thicknesses from a about 5mm to more than 20mm.

- Bamboo laminated floorboards: Glued in hot presses

after assembling rectangular culm sections that have been cut and pre-machined to size, these strong boards are finally machined to a standard 'tongue and groove' size and length.

- Bamboo laminated beams: Constructed in the same way as floorboards, these beams are more massive, and immensely strong.

- Bamboo woven mat plywood: Constructed using a similar hot press gluing technique to the normal plywood, but using woven split bamboo instead of straight grained splits. It is immensely strong because of the woven pattern, and highly decorative because the woven pattern remains visible.

- Bamboo particle board: Stronger than other particle boards, it is manufactured from the shattered, separated fibre sections which are press glued into a dense board, with a high-quality finish often applied.

- Bamboo chipboard: Similar to particle board and not quite as strong, made from coarser chipped pieces of culm.

- Bamboo fibre consolidated concrete board: This is a lightweight version of particle board using cement and chemical additives to bond the bamboo fibres.

All these products are being produced in various qualities, from high-grade veneers to coarse but strong concrete formwork boards, each designed for an appropriate use in the building industry. The quality of the product range is superb, but must be selected for the correct application. The Bamboo Division of the Research Institute at Fuyang, China, has played a major roll in assisting the development of these modern materials. Many are now being exported to Western countries. In some cases (laminated floor boards and beams, and woven mat plyboard being examples), fairly efficient machines have been developed for part of the manufacturing process. However, the less automated processes are highly labour-intensive. So even if bamboo was available in sufficient quantities, Western countries could not be internationally competitive.

Future potential and training

Demand for a diversity of uses for good-quality bamboo culms will increase considerably in the Western world as more superior quality bamboo timber becomes available. This is beginning to happen now because of the establishment of hundreds of hectares of plantation bamboos now taking place in Australia. For example, Bamboo World has developed its own tissue culture laboratory and is producing the correct species en masse to establish these plantations. Once established, a bamboo plantation is capable of producing 30–40 tonnes of usable materials each year. Mature bamboo plants can be harvested after seven years, which makes it a very attractive alternative to cutting down **old growth forests**.

There is a comprehensive educational and marketing program being developed by the plantation growers corporation (ACBC). Architects and engineers are showing an increasing interest in adopting some of the modern applications of bamboo as used in Balinese resorts. At present there is a shortage of carpenters with the skills to economically build bamboo structures, but the education process must be part of the growing availability of the resource. Bamboo World is also researching the feasibility of building a bamboo panel and truss factory for prefabricating components similar to the Costa Rican experience, primarily as an value added production for using the culms produced as a by product by the edible shoot plantations (currently 10–15 tonnes/yr/ha of timber).

Conclusion

In the future construction industry, bamboo will become a major contributor. Research will help by finding new ways of using the unprocessed culm material as in Costa Rica and Colombia, and in manufacturing high-grade building materials similar to those pioneered by China in recent years.

References

Cusack V. 1997, *Bamboo Rediscovered*, Earth Garden, Trentham, VIC.

Cusack, V. 1997, 'The Establishment of Commercial Bamboo Plantations in Australia', in P. Maoyi and P. Yiping, eds, *International Bamboo Workshop: Bamboo Towards the 21st Century, 7–11 September*, the Research Institute of Subtropical Forestry and the Chinese Academy of Forestry, Anji, Zhejiang, China.

Cusack V. 1999, *Bamboo World*, Simon & Schuster, East Roseville, NSW.

Contact: Bamboo World, Wadeville 2474, NSW, Australia. <bamboo@nrg.com.au>

Questions

1. Why would you choose bamboo as a building material instead of wood or earth wall? How would you convince your clients to use it?

2. What are the disadvantages of bamboo as a building material? What are the advantages of using treated bamboo culms as opposed to untreated ones?

3. Which form of bamboo makes the best building material, and why?

4. What life expectancy would be reasonable as a design criterion for bamboo exposed to the elements, as opposed to properly harvested culms used in a sheltered environment?

5. List ways in which bamboo building products could be inappropriately designed, fabricated or used in a manner that would work against sustainability.

6. How would the relative strength of laminated bamboo products compare with that of laminated wood products?

Projects

1. Research the key requirements for a plantation of bamboo (eg climate, water, sun, soil). Identify the closest area in which a bamboo plantation would be successful.

2. Find out what your local master builders' association, architect's institute and/or similar organisations are doing to promote the use of bamboo and other timber substitutes. If they do not have information on bamboo, encourage them to acquire or develop such information.

James Danenberg

Hemp is a renewable source of cellulose fibre and seed oils. Until the late 19th Century, hemp or Cannabis sativa was a vital and widespread industrial, military and strategic resource. Later marginalised for its psycho-active properties, it is now being rediscovered as an environmentally friendly material with numerous applications. Industrial hemp is now grown in over 20 countries. This chapter examines the potential of hemp in ecological architecture and the 'carbohydrate economy'.

Introduction

Henry Ford asked: 'Why use up the forests which were centuries in the making, and the mines which required ages to lay down, if we can get the equivalent of forest and mineral products in the annual growth of the fields?' (HEMPTECH website 1996).

Hemp is a natural, non-toxic, renewable and low energy material. It needs less water and fertiliser than cotton, and needs no pesticides. High in cellulose, it is four times as productive as trees for paper. Less well known is the fact that its fibrous bark and softer hemp hurds also make excellent sources of building and construction materials. Hemp seeds also provide a high-quality, edible oil with highly nutritious properties, which can be used as a raw material for biologically derived plastics, resins, paints, varnishes and shellacs.

A **carbohydrate economy** promises environmental, economic and social benefits. Harvesting annual hemp crops could reduce the need to use old growth forests for paper. Carbohydrates from plants could be used to make chemicals, with only a tiny fraction of the pollution generated by the manufacture and use of petrochemicals. Hemp could also be used to produce energy, through fermentation and conversion into ethanol, or through a more efficient chemical process called 'pyrolysis' (Pettijohn 1996). With the CO_2 cycle balanced, total greenhouse emissions would be reduced, as hydrocarbon fuels could be replaced. Air quality would also be improved, as biomass fuels do not contain sulphur or lead. Farmers could 'grow fuel' on their own farm, and end their dependence on expensive, imported, polluting and non-renewable fossil fuels.

Hemp and the carbohydrate economy

Combining economic development with ecological sustainability is one of the most crucial problems facing the world's governments. One of the most promising solutions to this dilemma is a transition towards what William Hale coined 'chemurgy' in the 1930s, and more recently termed the 'carbohydrate economy' **[Box 24]** (Morris and Ahmed 1995). Essentially, this involves using biomass from plants as an industrial raw material, instead of hydrocarbon-based petrochemical products.

At first, this may seem unrealistic, but until the turn of the last century, the raw materials for most industrial products like textiles, adhesives, inks, paints, varnishes, dyes, medicines and most other chemicals were derived from plants, or to a lesser extent, from animals that fed on plants (Morris and Ahmed 1995). In 1938, *Popular Mechanics* magazine found that over 25,000 products can be manufactured from the hemp plant, 'from cellophane to dynamite'. Celluloid, the first commercial plastic, introduced in the 1880s, was made from cotton; while Bakelite was derived from wood pulp. Cellophane and rayon, the first plastic film and synthetic fibre respectively, are still made from tree-based cellulose (Morris and Ahmed 1995).

Now, however, hydrocarbons have replaced starch, vegetable oil, and cellulose as industrial raw materials for every industrial product except paper. Up to 65% of our clothing and virtually all of our inks, paints, dyes, pharmaceuticals and plastics, are today made from oil (Morris and Ahmed 1995).

It was the US industrialist Henry Ford (the founder of assembly-line manufacturing) who first noted that practically everything that can be made of hydrocarbons can also be made of carbohydrates. He joined forces with the American Farm Bureau to develop prototypes of farm-grown and farm-fuelled cars. In 1941, Henry Ford unveiled an experimental car made of cellulose containing fibres including hemp, flax, wheat straw and sisal. Combined with resin as a binder and moulded under a hydraulic pressure of 1500 psi., Ford's prototype car had ten times the impact resistance of steel, and weighed 100lbs less than a comparable steel car (*Popular Mechanics* 1941, pp.1–3). European car makers like BMW are again testing hemp agro-composites due to pressure to meet European Commission criteria for 70% of a cars to be made from recyclable material by 2000 (Reuters 1996).

How do you build a house from hemp?

Hemp mixed with lime has been used as a building material in France at least since the time of Charlemagne (between 500 and 751 AD), and is now undergoing a worldwide renaissance (*Chènovotte Habitat* 1992). There are now hemp products commercially available that are environmentally friendly and economically feasible. These include using hemp fibres to make composite fibre products like medium density fibreboard (MDF) and other cellulose composites. Hemp hurds are very absorbent (hence their commercial use today in animal bedding in the UK and EU), and also uncommonly rich in silica, a chemical compound naturally occurring as sand or flint. When mixed with lime, hemp hurds change state from a vegetable product to a mineral, in effect 'petrifying' or turning to stone, yet weigh between one-fifth to one-seventh that of cement (Michka 1994, p. 50). Modern uses include eco-friendly floors, walls, bricks and insulation panels.

Is using hemp commercially viable?

In France, hemp hurds are now available commercially under several different brand names, '**Isochanvré**', 'Canabiote' and 'Canomose', and come in two forms: for use in construction or insulation (*Chènovotte Habitat* 1992, p. 2). To date, over 250 houses have been constructed using this material (Robertson 1996, p. 13). The processing required is similar for both types of products. The bast fibres (bark) are mechanically removed in a drying process without chemicals or the need for a retting (rotting) stage, leaving behind the interior core, or hurds. These are then 'naturally stabilised' (with borax) to make them fire and water resistant. As insulation, the product is used in a loose form, and is either poured or blown into roofing, partitions, floors or wall cavities. Isochanvré meets the norms of the French CSTB criteria (Scientific and Technical Centre for Building) and is a good insulating material (*Chènovotte Habitat* 1992, p. 2).

Unlike common insulating materials, Isochanvré also has a high thermal mass – an ability to store warmth and later give it back, due to the high proportion of silica within the plant. Thermal mass and insulative ability are usually mutually exclusive, yet empirical evidence from more than 250 houses constructed to date using Isochanvré suggest that this claim is invalid. For example, 'In autumn, owners of Isochanvré houses activate their heating systems 15 days after their neighbours'. Less heat is needed in winter and humidity is lower; and in summer, Isochanvré slabs are 3°F cooler than the ambient air temperature (*Chènovotte Habitat* 1992, p. 5).

Isochanvré is processed slightly differently for construction purposes. The product is mixed with natural lime (not cement) and water in a cement mixer. Sometimes plaster of Paris (pure gypsum) or 10% river sand is added. At this stage the compound resembles cement. It can be poured like cement, hardens and becomes mould and insect resistant (Michka 1994, p. 51). After drying, the Isochanvré is a lighter tawny colour with a texture similar to cork. It can be used in drywall construction between form work, as an interior and exterior insulation, be poured as a floor, or as an addition to the existing slab to raise the level of the floor (*Chènovotte Habitat* 1992, p. 2). The forms can be removed within a few hours, while the petrification process continues (Michka 1994, p. 51).

What are the advantages of Isochanvré?

Isochanvré makes several layers of conventional building materials superfluous. It can replace bricks or cement, a vapour barrier, insulation, and plaster board or Gyprock panelling (*Chènovotte Habitat* 1992, pp. 4–5; Michka 1994, p. 51). The only finish required on the exterior is a coat of whitewash, with or without added pigments, while the interior can retain the cork-like texture by either waxing or varnishing the finished surface (Michka 1994, p. 51). *Chènovotte Habitat* makes other claims as to advantageous qualities of Isochanvré which would make it an exceptional material, by any criteria, from an ecological, architectural, practical, or end-user's perspective. These include:

- Easy to use, flexible and crack-resistant.
- Ideal for cyclone and earthquake prone areas due to (strength/weight ratio)
- Lightness (appreciated in floor renovations).
- Excellent acoustic insulation.

- Breathes, prevents condensation.
- Self-draining and waterproof.
- Non-flammable (no toxic combustion products).
- Resistant to rodents, termites, insects, fungi and bacteria (because of silica content).
- Requires fewer finishing touches with no plaster, painting or wallpaper necessary (*Chènovotte Habitat* 1992, p. 5).

Life cycle analysis

Given the economic and environmental impact of the construction industry, it is crucial that materials minimise pollution and waste, and maximise the use of renewable sources of energy and materials. Hemp-based building products like Isochanvré fit the criteria of 'eco-products'. From its origins as an annual plant that supports agriculture (and rural areas), it provides an alternative to forest clearance for woodchipping or timber, obviates the need for mineral exploration and mining, and requires no chemical processing in the defibration or stabilisation stages.

Simple, natural materials means no pollution of air or water is caused, no waste is produced, with all sections of the plant being used and only minimal energy required to process it. Isochanvré is uniquely packaged in paper sacks made of a micro-porous material, solving the dilemma of disposal of packaging, by designing it to be incorporated into the insulation of either attics or floors. The lightweight nature of the product also reduces transport costs. The lime-based nature of Isochanvré makes it an easy and safe material to work with and it does not require any maintenance over time. In fact, the petrification process means it improves with age, and it is also biodegradable (*Chènovotte Habitat* 1992, p. 4).

Conclusion

The task of testing, evaluating, publicising and popularising the extraordinary characteristics of hemp products for the construction industry has only just begun. It is clear, though, that hemp offers an innovative and resource efficient alternative for ecological construction. Hemp can play a central role in the transition from a hydrocarbon-based economy to an ecologically sustainable carbohydrate-based economy.

References and further reading

Chènovotte Habitat 1992, 'Isochanvré – Nature as Architect', R. France, in J. Herer, 1995, *Hemp and the Marijuana Conspiracy: The Emperor Wears No Clothes*, Queen of Hearts/ HEMP publishing, Van Nuys, CA, pp. 144–151.

Herer, J. 1995, *Hemp and the Marijuana Conspiracy: The Emperor Wears No Clothes*, Queen of Hearts/ HEMP Publishing, Van Nuys, CA.

HEMPTECH 1996, Industrial Hemp Information Network Website <http://www.hemptech.org>

Michka 1994, *Building with Hemp: A Report from France*, 1 rue Pétion, 75011 Paris.

Morris, D. and Ahmed, I. 1995, *The Carbohydrate Economy: Making Chemicals and Industrial Materials from Plant Matter*, Institute for Local Self-Reliance (ILSR), Washington, DC.

Pettijohn, D.C. 1996, *The Carbohydrate Economy: Industrial Products From the Soil*, Institute for Local Self Reliance (ILSR), website <http://www.ilsr.org>, Minnesota and Washington, DC.

Popular Mechanics 1938, 'The New Billion Dollar Crop', February, pp. 238–240.

Popular Mechanics 1941, 'Auto Body Made of Plastics Resists Denting Under Hard Blows', December.

Reuters News 1996, *UK Hemp Report*, Bishop Stortford, in Hemptech website, op cit, 7 August.

Robertson, R. 1996, *The Great Book of Hemp: The Complete Guide to the Environmental, Commercial and Medicinal Uses of the World's Most Extraordinary Plant*, Park Street Press, Rochester, VT.

1. The transition to a carbohydrate economy would have social, economic and environmental consequences for our whole society, but especially for rural areas. Why?

2. How can hemp and other biomass crops be used for producing energy (heat and/or power)?

3. Who would benefit from a carbohydrate economy? Who stands to lose?

4. What are the obstacles to an emerging carbohydrate-based economy? How could these be minimised/overcome?

5. What advantages would biodegradable plastics made from hemp-derived cellulose have over conventional hydrocarbon-based, non-biodegradable plastics?

6. 'Ecologically sustainable development is a modern concept based on old practices.' Discuss this in terms of hemp and hemp products.

1. Make a list of the contents of your bag and what you're wearing. Divide your list into two sections; naturally sourced products, and synthetic or artificially produced items. Choose one item from each category and describe what it is made from, where the raw materials come from and how it is made. Is this item sustainable? If not, can you think of a sustainable alternative(s) to the product or item?

2. Make a list of environmental issues that you are concerned about, eg land clearance, soil erosion and salination, depletion of the ozone layer, the greenhouse effect, air pollution, and so on. Discuss what difference a shift to a sustainable carbohydrate-based economy would make to these issues.

Box 25   Carbon Storage

Janis Birkeland and Simon Baird

Increased atmospheric carbon dioxide (CO_2) levels and the global rise in temperature are in part due to deforestation. Because forests recapture (and store) carbon from the atmosphere as they grow, some argue that plantation forests serve as 'carbon sinks' that can be used to offset industrial activities. However, this argument has been used to support the logging of native forests and their replacement with monoculture plantations as a means to reduce global atmospheric CO_2 emissions. This debate provides a good example of the interplay of values, science and conceptual frameworks in design decisions (such as materials selection) [Box 23].

The positions: The forest industry position is that forest operations improve the balance between the amount of carbon stored in the earth and that released into the atmosphere as CO_2. Whereas young trees produce oxygen and absorb carbon, and timber products store carbon, old growth forests decay and release carbon. Therefore, some contend, old growth forests should be harvested and replaced with plantations. In contrast, greens point out that clearfelling old-growth forests is not sustainable by definition, as these forests may take 1500–2500 years to recover their original ecological structure. Most of the carbon is stored in the forest floor and soil, and industrial forestry techniques essentially 'mine' the forests, causing erosion.

We compiled a chronological history of public statements made by peak forest industry and environment organisations in Australia on the issue of CO_2 emissions and forests. Charting their responses to new information and opposing arguments enabled an analysis of the underlying assumptions and conceptual structure of their positions. Although the forestry debate concerns 'values' (eg the relative weighting that should be given to the direct economic functions of timber and forests), we also found a distinct contrast in the logic of the arguments themselves. Not surprisingly, industry took a linear–reductionist view with short time horizons; greens took a more systemic view and included a broader range of social concerns. In essence, the positions are validated by the same facts filtered through different ways of thinking.

The science: We also evaluated their 'appeals to authority' against the available scientific literature. Some of the more interesting findings in the research indicated that:

- Plantation forests, even when fully mature and ready for harvest, only contain around 1/3 of the carbon volume as native forests; there is a direct relationship between plant species diversity and carbon storage.

- Great amounts of wastage occur at the site of extraction (up to 85% in parts of Australia), most of which is burnt or left to decompose, releasing CO_2 emission; between 50–60% of timber is wasted during the initial milling process (in Australia).

- The percentage of carbon stored in the soil of native forests is substantial and is released when it is logged and/or burnt.

- Most wood products have a short life-span, and carbon storage in these products is lost when they decompose; a large percentage of timber from native forests (in Australia) is used for the pulp and paper industry, and paper products have short life spans.

- In some cases, plantations located where forests did not exist before may increase global warming (eg planting could reduce snow cover and ground reflectivity).

- The carbon storage capacity of forests are estimated by measuring the uptake of carbon by leaves; this is then scaled up to estimate the amount of carbon fixing in forests – so the figures are uncertain at best.

Thus, before we replace native forests with plantations and count plantations as carbon sinks, we need a greater understanding of forests ecosystems and the relationship of forests to global warming. Science itself does not yet have all the answers, and the policy implications depend not only on assumptions and methods, but on frameworks of thinking.

Adger, N. and Brown, K. 1994, *Land Use and the Causes of Global Warming*, J.Wiley, New York.

Atwell, B. Kriedmann, P. and Turnbull, C. 1999, *Plants in Action: Adaptation in Nature, Performance in Cultivation*, MacMillan Education Australia, Melbourne.

Janis Birkeland

Most pollution control systems are either regulatory or economic instruments which, in effect, make it cost more to damage the environment, so that firms will reduce pollution and waste to save money. In this sense, they are 'indirect' in that they create (positive or negative) incentives for industry to find solutions, but do not directly result in pollution reduction, let alone prevention. These indirect approaches can be distinguished from 'direct' environmental controls based on eco-logical design.

Introduction

The fundamental objective of pollution control should be to prevent pollution in the first place: this is achieved by incorporating less polluting systems, materials, processes, functions and building forms into the design itself. Instead, the conventional aim has been to internalise the costs of pollution, so that the price of products includes the social and environmental costs of production. By making pollution and waste more expensive, it is assumed that industry will find ways to reduce these costs on their own initiative. This indirect approach to pollution control has contributed to end-of-pipe strategies. Pollution is filtered or dispersed rather than eliminated through the redesign of systems. The conventional approach has been too slow, and therefore increasingly costly – both to the economy and environment.

Traditionally, there has been a debate over whether pollution control systems should be centred in the market economy or government domain. Pollution controls have therefore been categorised according to whether they are nominally in the private sector (market-based) or the public sector (regulatory). This conventional typology is misleading, because it is based on a false public–private sector duality. As the controversy over the Multi-lateral Agreement on Investment (MAI) has shown, for example, governments appear to be losing whatever controls they once had over transnational corporations.

In a complex society, there is always regulation, whether it is primarily in the 'visible' hands of government, or left to the 'invisible' hands of industry. Further, a complex government bureaucracy is still required to implement indirect market-based regimes. A better approach than one based on the anachronistic public–private dualism is to distinguish two basic methods of protecting the environment: *direct* design-based approaches (solutions-focused) and *indirect* market-based or regulatory approaches (incentives-focused).

Direct actions can be distinguished from incentives-based approaches that are calculated to bring about behaviour change in consumers or industry. Direct actions are those that government authorities can undertake themselves to bring about immediate outcomes in energy, materials, public health or other resource savings. Whether a strategy is direct or not, then, depends on the number of possible intervening factors between action and desired outcomes. Changes can be made to physical conditions, organisational structures, systems or behaviours that improve environmental health and sustainability. The money saved from reduced costs can be 'recycled' into more long-term systems changes, such as land use controls or incentives programs.

Indirect actions, such as incentives programs that encourage others to conserve resources, have been the standard approach with regard to environmental policy. Economic instruments (eg pricing signals, subsidies or taxes) and regulatory controls are typically 'indirect', (although they may generate immediate responses from industry and consumers) because, for example:

- other things outside local government control can intervene, like global economic forces,

- the charges, standards, fines, taxes, etc, do not internalise a large enough portion of the full costs; that is, pollution, deforestation, global warming are not 'internalised' by industry – despite the addition of unproductive transaction and regulatory costs.

- there is investment leakage (eg builder training programs or their graduates may not incorporate the new requirements), and/or

- there can be unintended results (eg the price of resources goes up, and industry responds by laying off workers rather than becoming more eco-efficient).

Both direct and indirect approaches may require action through the political process (often at a national level), which are typically slower than shifts in public awareness. However, some direct design solutions escape political processes and buy time to institute more complex systems changes that involve the cooperation, and/or behaviour change on the part of others.

Table 11.1.1: A new typology of pollution controls

INDIRECT INCENTIVES	1. Market approaches (economic incentives) - Rights based - Price based
	2. Government controls (regulatory incentives) - Prescriptive (technology forcing) - Performance-based
DIRECT SOLUTIONS	1. Systems design (preventative) - No pipe / no loop - Closed loop
	2. Innovation forcing (regulatory intervention) - Prevention (requiring systems re-design) - Mitigation (requiring systems change) (eg specifying solar energy, **bio-based materials**, etc)

Typology of environmental controls

Indirect controls include both market-based and regulatory incentives.

Market-based approaches involve the use of economic or legal instruments that make it cheaper to conserve energy and resources or to avoid pollution and waste. As firms may willingly take into account the social and environmental consequences of their decisions where these increase profits, these have usually been viewed as 'positive' incentives. Market-based or economic instruments are discussed further in Chapter 11.2. This chapter discusses regulatory and design-based approaches.

Regulatory controls generally either prescribe that certain actions be taken or certain technologies be used, or set certain 'performance criteria' through laws, codes, treaties, interstate agreements or other forms of legislation.

Standards and/or **performance-based** regulations specify a standard or criteria (eg a maximum amount of emissions, or a product 'energy rating') and allow business or industry to meet this criteria in any way they choose. These may provide an incentive to develop more efficient technologies to save costs and thus compete more effectively. These standards are generally enforced through a licensing scheme, a system of monitoring, and penalties for non-compliance. The incentives for industries to comply with standards are mostly 'negative' (eg fines, loss of licence).

The measurement of environmental quality or pollution can be based on the:

- Source of pollution (at the pipe or smokestack).
- **Ambient** levels of pollution in the air or water.
- The impact of pollution on humans, flora and fauna.

Prescriptive regulations can be technology forcing or innovation forcing. 'Technology forcing' regulations usually require that a certain pollution control technology be used (eg catalytic converters on cars), or simply require the use of the most practicable (affordable) pollution control technology. These controls have typically been end-of-pipe measures that address 'symptoms' rather than 'systems', and use the threat of penalties to enforce compliance. Regulations can also require preventative measures, such as stipulations that no waste leave the site, or that the producer take back the products for recycling at the end of life. These could be called 'innovation forcing' regulations as they encourage design solutions.

The trend has been for regulations (such as planning laws and building codes) to become less prescriptive and more performance-based [11.3], as many problems have arisen over time from imposing specific technological solutions upon a changing world. Both indirect approaches (economic and regulatory) have advantages and disadvantages, and can be appropriate in certain cases. Both are responses to a lack of awareness and responsibility on the part of business and industry – and their engineering and design consultants. Neither approach is self-implementing; ultimately they must rely upon good governance and personal responsibility (to blame environmental regulations for not working is like blaming laws for the existence of crime). The following outlines some common forms of regulatory controls.

Problems with pollution regulations

Standards setting: Standards are often set by state governments, resulting in differences in environmental quality standards. This creates competition among states to attract industries (for tax and employment benefits) by offering lower environmental standards and/or lower worker health and safety standards. The standards themselves are a result of political decisions, regardless of the scientific advice provided. And, since industry has a key role in setting standards, they will usually be at a level that minimises economic impacts on industry.

Competition: In a competitive market, those that invest in pollution control technology may (initially) experience a net loss in competitive advantage. This is because products and services that externalise their environmental costs, or are imported from countries with less stringent workplace safety regulations, will have a lower price. To cut costs, hazardous industries have moved to countries where environmental and employment standards are lower, or have even paid poorer countries to accept their toxic wastes. On the other hand, if every factory in the same industry had to conform to high environmental standards (globally), then they would compete to do so more efficiently. But at present, it appears current moves towards uniform pollution standards will be trumped by economic globalisation and free trade, which favours the lowest common denominator.

Costs: Regulations often require manufacturers to do things which cost money, such as pay licence fees, install pollution control equipment, dispose of waste properly and so on. This imposition has sometimes led firms to oppose regulation in court, which is not only costly, but anti-productive. Business often musters its ingenuity to evade regulations, yet, they are able to improve technology quickly when they have to due to competition or regulation. Regulations also impose large costs upon governments for administration, licensing and monitoring, which can be annoying to taxpayers. The costs of pollution technologies and administration are passed onto the consumer in higher prices and higher taxes, but the economic gains due to pollution reduction are often not made apparent to the consumer/taxpayer.

Enforcement: If there is a violation, the license can be withdrawn or fines can be charged, but these fines are generally less than the long-term public costs of pollution. Further, fines are charged for accidental or excessive pollution – after the fact – rather than for the activities which cause the problem. Thus, firms that take risks (eg Union Carbide and Exxon Valdez) are penalised by a small portion of the amount of damage, and only if an accident occurs, creating a fiscal incentive to gamble.

Complexity: More fundamentally, regulations have not corresponded well to the complexity of the environment. Some problems are as follows:

- **Threshold concept:** Some pollution controls set standards for air or water quality, such as 'parts per million', based on our present, limited knowledge about what are safe levels of toxins for humans or for the ecosystems upon which they depend. Yet arguably, there are no safe thresholds for many toxic substances. As we are able to measure smaller parts, we find what was once assumed to be a safe level is in fact not safe (eg parts per trillion is significant in the case of organochlorines).

- **Chemical synergy:** There is not as yet adequate knowledge about the interrelations and interactions of chemicals, ecosystems, and human health, nor how they **biocumulate** in the environment and **biota** over time. Hundreds of chemicals are released into the environment every year without any testing. Any of these could interact with other chemicals in unpredictable ways.

- **Measuring and monitoring:** Pollution is difficult to measure and monitor, as many pollutants biocumulate in air, water, soil, plants and animals over time. How the pollution is measured can affect the results. If the emissions are measured at the factory, this does not indicate how the pollution accumulates over time and causes unforeseen problems of health or biodiversity. If we measure the concentrations of pollutants in the environment, these may be dispersed by high smoke-stacks which only conceal the long-term impact. The same toxin has different impacts in different media.

Technology forcing: Rather than setting a standard or performance criteria, environmental controls can force industry to do things differently, such as to install specific pollution control technologies. This form of control has not been popular, because it is seen as paternalistic and may not suit the individual needs and circumstances of different firms.

Early technology-based controls were mostly end-of-pipe mechanisms such as scrubbers on smokestacks or filters on waste pipes, that dispersed the pollution or transferred it to other environmental mediums (air, water, soil). This at best slowed the rate of pollution. Cleaner forms of fossil fuels, such as gas instead of coal, merely reduce the impacts; they still consume non-renewable resources and, produce greenhouse gases.

Technology-forcing pollution controls have required either the **best available technology** (BAT), or **best practicable technology** to reduce pollution. The 'best available' technology could be too restrictive and beyond the means of an industry, while the 'best practicable' technology could be, in effect, the best technology that the firm believes is affordable. In either case, it is difficult for a regulatory authority to determine which technology is the best available or most affordable, as the regulated industries are the main source of information.

Technology-based controls often impose greater requirements on new industries and technologies by **grandfathering** or giving **dispensations** to existing establishments. Dispensations are, however, inequitable (though politically expedient) and reduce the effectiveness of the control.

Innovation forcing: Examples of regulations that are largely preventative and innovation forcing might include the use of certain:

- **Fuels** such as solar-heating systems or wind-generated electricity instead of electricity from coal-fired electricity plants.

- **Materials** such as bamboo or hemp-based building products instead of products made from native timbers; or materials made from natural instead of synthetic fibres.

- **Processes** such as on-site biological waste treatment (bioremediation) instead of chemical treatment plants.

- **Equipment** such as natural ventilation or solar cooling systems instead of air conditioning; or on-site rain water tanks instead of chemically-treated piped water.

- **Human behaviour** can also be regulated to prevent health problems, but this is controversial in a market society. Examples would include drinking tap water, instead of bottled or canned soft drinks, and using hemp bags for shopping.

Direct design-based systems

Design solutions prevent pollution by the use of low-impact products, component materials, and/or systems of production, as well as the form and function of the product or building itself. Rather than applying a specific technology

to a generic class of industries, products or buildings, design-based approaches generally focus on a particular case of problems within their systems context. When current technologies do not allow optimal **no loop** solutions, design-based approaches internalise pollution *physically*, by closing resource and energy loops [3.4].

Closed loop systems are where waste, heat pollution or other environmental impacts are reprocessed on the development site (city or network of industries) or used for another productive purpose [3.1, 3.2]. The most efficient examples are those that most closely emulate nature, like Living Machines [9.1].

No loop systems are where the industry, building, city or bioregion are designed (theoretically) such that virtually no pollution or waste is created by an activity in the first place. No loop systems are a theoretical design 'ideal'. Buildings constructed of organic materials, and heated, cooled and ventilated by natural systems come close to this ideal once embodied energy is discounted [Section 10].

Conclusion

Indirect approaches rely on firms that are presently profiting from pollution to find solutions. Design solutions employ technologies appropriate to the nature and scale of the particular problem. Direct approaches are more likely to be preventative and cheaper in the long run because they skip the 'middle man' or regulator, and offer the possibility of being profitable – through converting waste into a resource.

References and further reading

Barrow, C.J. 1999, *Environmental Management: Principles and Practice*, Routledge, London and New York.

Chilton, K. and Warren, M., eds, 1991, *Environmental Protection: Regulating for Results*, Westview Press, Boulder, CO.

Enmarch-Williams, H., ed, 1996, *Environmental Risks and Rewards for Business*, Wiley, New York.

Holcombe, R.G. 1995, *Public Policy and the Quality of Life: Market Incentives versus Government Planning*, Greenwood Press, Westport, CN.

Korten, D.C., 1995, *When Corporations Rule the World*, Berrett-Koehler Publishers, San Francisco, CA.

May, P. et al, eds, 1994, *Environmental Management and Governance*, Routledge, London and New York.

Sagoff, M. 1988, *The Economy of the Earth: Philosophy, Law and the Environment*, Cambridge University Press, Cambridge.

Tietenberg, T., ed, 1992, *Innovation in Environmental Policy*, Edward Elgar Publishing, New York.

Welford, R. 1995, *Environmental Strategy and Sustainable Development: The Corporate Challenge for the Twenty-first Century*, Routledge, London, New York.

Questions

1. Debate: 'Technology-forcing pollution controls are preferable to standards-based controls.'

2. Should existing factories or processes be allowed to continue without conforming to new environmental laws in order to protect jobs? Are there 'win–win' alternatives?

3. Companies have made profits on their investment in clean technology. If you are required to visit the managers of a local industry and encourage them to invest in more eco-efficient processes, how would you prepare for such a meeting?

4. The threat of media exposure is considered to be a very effective means of bringing about industry cooperation. Can you think of ways to bring about more media attention to pollution in your area?

5. Debate: 'True economic efficiency would dictate that no pollution leave the development site.'

6. Clean technology can result in lower energy and waste disposal costs, reduced future liability for cleaning up sites or from law suits, fewer brushes with regulatory agencies, lower maintenance, lower liability insurance, improved morale. How many other benefits of environmental regulations can you name?

Projects

1. Obtain the environmental policies of the political parties in your area and compare them in terms of how preventative or remedial they are in character. Create a matrix to assist in the comparison.

2. Drawing upon the above environmental policies, draft an ideal set of environmental policies. After these have been reviewed, send them to the relevant political parties and request a considered response.

Janis Birkeland

There are numerous kinds of economic instruments for internalising the costs of environmental damage, so that industry will prevent, mitigate or clean up pollution in order to increase profits. Like regulatory schemes, these instruments are 'indirect' and can also involve administrative complexities. Rather than impose a bureaucratic licensing system, however, economic instruments, or market-based 'regulation' relies on prices, taxes, charges or markets in property rights.

Introduction

Market-based approaches tend to be preferred by those who feel that government regulation is itself the problem and that the market, if left to its own devices, will find the most efficient process almost automatically. Economic instruments appear as 'positive' incentives, in that the decisions are made in the private sector and are not imposed 'from above' by governments.

If firms paid the full public costs of their activities, those that reduced the environmental consequences of their operations would ultimately prevail over competitors as their costs would be lower. However, as the economic system still subsidises environmentally harmful activities and processes market distortions continue. Even worse, public sector expenditures (like public transport) are regarded as 'subsidies', when they should be seen as 'investments' that reduce subsidies for environmentally-damaging private sector activities (like private car production and use).

There are two basic types of economic instruments: price-based and rights-based measures, discussed below.

Price-based measures

Monetary or price-based measures include charges, taxes and levies which impose a kind of tax on the public costs of production, so that it becomes cheaper to modernise or convert to cleaner processes. How this is accomplished is left up to each industry. The **polluter pays** principle means industries can pollute if they pay for it, because their rational interest in profit should lead them to adopt more eco-efficient

technologies, processes or products to reduce the costs of pollution over time. The polluter pays principle fails where there is a monopoly, however, as firms can simply raise prices. Also, the polluter may be able to make their books balance by replacing jobs with new technology, and hence lower labour costs to compensate for charges or taxes (Beder 1994).

The polluter pays principle can be distinguished from the **user pays** principle where, in general, people (or firms) who pay for public goods (eg to use a park, hunt or fish) will become more ecologically aware if they have to pay for using these resources directly. These principles fail, however, where there is an unequal distribution of wealth or power. For example, firms can exercise their political power to reduce royalties for extracting timber below cost; or rich people can pay large sums to shoot endangered 'big game' species.

Increasing the cost of energy and materials, or imposing fines for pollution are 'indirect', because they do not ensure eco-solutions. Further, they do not prevent pollution and usually only internalise a portion of the public costs. Monetary instruments are inadequate in themselves, because they attempt to fit a complex environment into a rarified, yet over-simplistic model of reality: the economic system. Instead, the economic system must be redesigned to work within ecological realities. Some of the monetary devices for increasing the cost of resource and energy consumption or pollution and waste are outlined below.

Subsidies and bounties

Subsidies can reduce the price of goods or services that are environmentally friendly, in order to encourage their sale over other products. A **bounty** is similar to a subsidy, but it is an amount paid to the producer for the goods before they reach the consumer. Where there are subsidies or bounties, industries do not actually pay the full cost of control measures because they are passed on to the taxpayer. Traditionally, subsidies were used, not to protect the environment, but to assist firms that could not afford to modernise – thereby increasing adverse environmental impacts. Tariff support for the steel industry, subsidies for fertilisers, or tax breaks for maintaining out-of-date technologies are some examples that reflect the political power of older fossil fuel-based industries.

Subsidies are often hidden. For example, a limit was set on the amount of insurance that could be claimed in case of an nuclear accident. Had the market prevailed, new plants would not have been built, due to the costs of possible damage that would have to be insured against. Merely removing 'perverse subsidies' would make a big difference. In many places, for example, recycled paper is more expensive than new paper, a logical impossibility without the subsidy of allowing native forests to be logged far below replacement cost. Removing such subsidies would make the market function more rationally.

Environmentally destructive or perverse subsidies are usually created in the name of protecting jobs; however, there are other more constructive ways to create and protect jobs. Industry retraining schemes, green business **incubator programs**, subsidies for environmental retrofits, environmental audits, and similar programs pay dividends in the long term, and can create even more employment by reducing inefficiencies.

Charges

Charges are a price paid for using or polluting the environment. The fewer resources used or less pollution produced, the less industries pay. However, the fees are usually too low, due to political pressure. If the money raised were required to be used by governments for environmental protection, it might balance out some of the losses – but instead these funds often end up in general revenue. This means that pollution is, in a sense, a fund-raiser for governments.

Charges come in many forms and can be:

- Based on the content and quantity of a firm's discharges into the air or water. If the charges are too high, however, the firm may dump illegally. (In a recent case, a company director was jailed for illegal dumping. The judge pointed out that legal disposal had been a cheaper option, thus illustrating that management behaviour is not always economically rational.)

- Tied to a resource, such as royalties on timber. If high enough, this would create an incentive to establish more plantations. For example, Australia could meet all its timber needs through plantations, but instead continues to clearfell priceless native forests – at highly subsidised rates – often for woodchips.

- Based on the provision of a service, such as fees for the collection and treatment of waste or recycling.

- Added to the price of products to encourage recycling or reduced packaging, or cover the costs of disposal. Deposit refund systems add an amount of money to the price of a product which is refundable if returned, as is sometimes the case with drink bottles.

- Based on the cost of the government control system, such as the administration of registration fees and licences.

If the charges are applied evenly and do not give anyone a competitive advantage, producers or developers have no reason to complain, as they can pass the costs onto consumers.

Taxes and grants

Taxes can be removed from labour and investment to make these less expensive, or added to environmentally harmful products or processes to make these more expensive [**Box 26**]. Tax deductions, grants and other programs can also be used to encourage environmentally responsible research and development. Programs directed at consumers can encourage energy and greenhouse gas conservation, such as tax rebates for solar collectors and rainwater tanks, grants for the poor to insulate their homes, or tree planting schemes.

A point of public controversy is the idea of a carbon tax, which exists in some countries. A tax on the carbon content of fuels encourages a shift from coal to oil and natural gas (which emit less carbon) or other alternative energy sources. Because the tax is on the combustion of fossil fuels, it is levied at the point of production or port of entry, rather than on exports. The concern is that industries highly dependent on electricity from fossil fuels (such as aluminium) may be unable to compete at the international level. An evenly applied international system of carbon taxes would ensure that countries are not put at a competitive disadvantage during the transition to more eco-efficient economies (Diesendorf and Hamilton 1997, p. 313).

A **closed loop** tax has also been suggested, where 'companies that produced more than a certain amount of pollution would pay a tax whose revenue would be recycled in a subsidy, paid on a sliding scale to those who produced less than the benchmark' (Cairncross 1995, p. 67).

Financial enforcement

Fines are indirect, negative incentives that seldom cover the full social or environmental costs of non-compliance. In fact, the fines may be lower than the profits made by non-compliance. Another problem is that the cost to the public of enforcing fines could involve costly legal action and enforcement. Performance bonds or liability insurance are two ways to avoid the costs of enforcement. **Performance bonds** are payments made in advance and refunded when it is shown that compliance is achieved. **Liability insurance** schemes can cover compensation for possible environmental damage. A firm may pay lower premiums where there is a low probability of processes or products causing damage due to their design.

Rights-based measures

Rights-based measures create artificial property rights in environmental 'goods', and in some cases allow industries to trade any unused rights to pollute. The idea is that private industry will protect and preserve its interest in what it owns. That is, if people have the right to own or use natural resources, they will take care of them and consider the longer term – much as many farmers now protect the soil upon which their future income depends.

Further, individuals will use their ingenuity to find the best means to protect the value of their private property. In Zimbabwe, local people were given property rights over animals. They auctioned quotas of animals for the highest bidders to shoot. The money earned was shared, so they had less incentive to kill the animals when they invaded their gardens. The approach used in Zimbabwe stands in marked contrast to that used in Kenya. It established a paramilitary force to combat the poachers. Interestingly, both approaches seem to have had measurable success.

Tradable pollution rights

When tradable ownership rights for an environmental good is difficult (as in the case of air), a right can still be recognised through, for instance, the right to emit specific pollutants up to a certain limit. By creating such property rights, systems for **tradable pollution rights** allow each firm to trade any unused units of allowable pollution. Each time a transaction occurs, there can be a reduction in the amount of pollution allowed. This is economically efficient, in theory, as polluters can reduce total amounts of pollutants where and how it is cheapest to do so.

Maximum allowable concentrations for specific air pollutants can also be set for each region. Then firms can still expand production either by making reductions at the original plant, or by paying for reductions from other firms or government facilities – called **offsets**. The use of this approach has not equaled the academic attention it has been given, however. Another approach is to set standards for the total emissions of the industrial complex (or an entire region) as if it had an imaginary bubble over it with one hole. This allows the industry to cut the emissions of whichever pollutant is cheapest, as only the average amount of pollution is regulated, not specific outputs.

Trading systems can also be used to allow those with 'excess carbon' (in the form of trees) to sell these 'unused rights to produce pollution' to industries in other countries. This would arguably conserve forests in developing nations, as industries from developed nations would buy and preserve forests to offset their carbon emissions. There are many difficult issues to be resolved, such as how the sale of forests in developing nations affect the poor who may depend on them, or how the sales revenue is allocated by their governments.

Problems with market-based controls

Economic instruments to reduce pollution may overcome some of the problems with government regulation but they also have their own problems.

Grant to pollute? Individual polluters may prefer to continue polluting and pay a fee, tax or charge where, for example, the resource (such as minerals or rare timbers) is running out, therefore making factory upgrading impractical. To avoid modernising to meet new standards, for example, a paint factory simply left Tasmania and built a new factory elsewhere, leaving the mess for the local taxpayers to clean up. Thus, while market-based schemes may gradually reduce overall levels, they do not necessarily create an incentive to develop better technology.

Bureaucracy? Any system for implementing and monitoring pollution reduction requires some form of government bureaucracy. The administrative costs of trading schemes are high and few industries are involved. **Emissions trading** still requires the political will to force technological modernisation through the reduction of the emissions value of the permits over time. As with standard-based systems, rights-based regulations require setting the level of emissions that individual firms will have a right to attain (under which level trading can occur): this is a function of politics and power. Also, dirty old industries may have the resources to buy up other pollution rights to increase their market share without cleaning up their production.

Democracy? Leaving decisions to the self-interest of private corporations and individuals means that the general public has little say in trade-offs between the environment and economics. The market does not take into account the relative value of the product produced, or the cost per job created. This means that market-based regulations can give a competitive advantage to a relatively anti-social product. The market can also be inequitable, as some areas are subject to more pollution than others – usually poor areas. Environmental justice has become a field of academic inquiry, but seems to offer more descriptions than solutions thus far.

The free market position

The extreme free market position holds that the air, soil, water, and other environmental goods should be owned by private individuals and firms that are free to maximise their own economic self-interests. If there were a private market for forests, for example, the invisible hand would allocate them to their 'highest' use, whether that be for logging or preservation, as people would express their valuations freely through the market. Free marketeers maintain that if entrepreneurs owned rare species, they would charge visitors to see them and therefore ensure their preservation. But would that not encourage these entrepreneurs to make their species become more rare?

Clive Hamilton has used the case of the disappearing rhino to illustrate the problem of leaving environmental preservation to private markets (Hamilton 1994). When the horn of the rhino is privatised, its value is determined by one (probably wealthy) hedonist who feels he needs an aphrodisiac. It can only be consumed once and only for his own personal benefit. However, when the horn is attached to a rhino, 'the value of the horn is determined by the sum of the valuations of all the people who value the free-roaming Rhinos' (p.75), whether they hope to see one or not.

According to the extremists among economists, of course, environmentalists can just buy all the rhinos back and

protect them from poachers, along with the land, air, and water upon which they depend. This would mean that present consumer preferences would determine the future. But what if, in the future, consumers wanted environmental preservation or the protection of endangered ecosystems or species? Would citizen groups be financially capable of outbidding corporations to buy the land and resources back? Can many disparate and disorganised individuals with low personal stakes in particular environmental issues really be expected to outbid corporations – not just once, but any and every time any corporation sets its sights on any piece of the environment?

References and further reading

Beder, S. 1994, *The Nature of Sustainable Development*, 2nd edn, Scribe, Newham, VIC.

Cairncross, F. 1995, *Green Inc. A Guide to Business and the Environment*, Island Press, Covelo, CA.

Carraro, C. and Leveque, F. 1999, *Voluntary Approaches in Environmental Policy*, Kluwer, Dordrecht, The Netherlands.

Crognale, G. 1999, *Environmental Management Strategies: The 21st Century Perspective*, Prentice Hall, Englewood Cliffs, NJ.

Diesendorf, M. and Hamilton, C. 1997, *Human Ecology, Human Economy: Ideas for an Ecologically Sustainable Future*, Allen and Unwin, Sydney, NSW.

Glasbergen, P. 1998, *Co-operative Environmental Governance: Public–Private Agreements as a Policy Strategy*, Kluwer Academic, Dordrecht, The Netherlands.

Graham, J.W. and Havlick, W.C. 1999, *Corporate Environmental Policies*, Scarecrow Press, Lanham, MD.

Hamilton, C. 1994, *The Mystic Economist*, Willow Park Press, Canberra, ACT.

Hawken, P., Lovins, H. and Lovins, A. 1999, *Natural Capitalism: Creating the Next Industrial Revolution*, Earthscan, London.

Madu, C.N. 1996, *Managing Green Technologies for Global Competitiveness*, Quorum Books, Westport, CN.

Morelli, J. 1999, *Voluntary Environmental Management: The Inevitable Future*, Lewis Pubs, CRC Press, Boca Raton, FL.

Shulman, S. 1999, *Owning the Future*, Houghton Mifflin, Boston, MA.

Tietenberg, T. and Button, K.J. 1999, *Environmental Instruments and Institutions*, Edward Elgar, New York.

Weizsäcker, E. von, Lovins, A. and Lovins, H. 1997, *Factor 4: Doubling Wealth – Halving Resource Use*, Allen and Unwin, NSW.

Questions

1. Should environmentalists be required to purchase the remaining parts of the natural environment that they wish to save (on behalf of the rest of society)?

2. Debate: 'Government regulation is preferable to the use of economic instruments as a means of reducing pollution.'

3. Do free markets in environmental decision making ensure power remains in the hands of corporations or consumers? Discuss.

4. Think of an incentive scheme to encourage homeowners to install photovoltaic cells and become independent of the electrical grid. What are some of the impediments?

5. Free marketeers believe that entrepreneurs do not 'kill the goose that lays the golden egg'. This means, for example, those who own forest or mineral rich land would not choose to denude them and move on to another source of wealth; or concessionaires running national park facilities for profit would not over-develop them. Discuss.

6. There are two relatively successful approaches to poaching animals in Africa: militias and auctioning quotas. Which do you prefer and why?

Projects

1. Make two lists, with as many problems with economic instruments and regulatory measures for reducing pollution as you can think of. Compare to the design-based approach described in chapter 3.4. Which problems does the design-based approach overcome? Where it does not appear to solve the problems of conventional controls, design some solutions that work.

2. As a group, visit your local environmental protection agency and discuss your findings from the above exercise with one of the representatives who deals with these issues.

Box 26   Environmental Taxes

Steve Hatfield-Dodds

Environmental taxes and tax concessions are two of a number of incentive-based 'economic instruments' for environmental policy, and may be defined as a tax or concession aimed at achieving environmental objectives by changing relative prices.

Their underlying logic is that people do not take full account of the environmental impact of their actions, including their purchasing decisions, because the environmental 'costs' are borne by others. Environmental taxes help redress this by providing signals to individuals and companies about the relative impact of different actions, and so can help steer behaviour towards more socially desirable outcomes. Well-designed economic instruments allow decision makers maximum flexibility in deciding how they will achieve social goals, and so involve the lowest possible costs to society as a whole. This flexibility is particularly important where costs differ across individuals or firms (such as due to different existing equipment, products, inputs, or locations). For example, a firm using the latest technology might find it very expensive to reduce their emissions, while a firm producing a different product or using old equipment might be able to reduce their emissions dramatically at a relatively modest cost.

There are three main forms of environmental taxes:

- Emissions taxes, (the least used) involves levying a tax on the actual emissions or environmental damage – requiring a legally robust means of measuring or estimating the emissions or activity to be taxed. Acid rain, for example, might be reduced by a tax on the sulphur content of coal burnt by power stations.

- Product taxes is more common, and involves taxing a good or service that is closely associated with the problem to be addressed. For example, motor fuel taxes reduce congestion, and deposit–refund systems provide an incentive to return used containers.

- The most common environmental tax incentive provides tax concessions for specific goods or types of expenditure, such as a sales tax exemption for recycled products. The main problem is that they subsidise 'good' behaviour

without addressing 'bad' behaviour, and that they are difficult to target with any precision.

Environmental taxes and concessions work best where they are comprehensive, applying to all major sources of the environmental problem, and where the tax rate is able to be differentiated according to the relative impacts of the activities. Taxes are thus often able to impact across a wider range of activities than traditional regulatory approaches, which often only apply to new projects, or require the same action from all firms regardless of differences in compliance costs. Environmental taxes also provide a continuous incentive to improve environmental performance, unlike minimum standards, which can encourage technological inertia.

Against this, taxes often face a number of political difficulties. Taxes are sometimes criticised for providing a 'licence to pollute'; however, regulatory approaches frequently provide the same 'licence' for free, and do little to encourage performance above the specified minimum standard. Taxes also often face greater industry opposition because the costs imposed are so visible, and because they effect all firms in a sector, rather than only impacting on new projects or plants that do not meet a proposed standard. Thus, taxes are often more difficult to introduce than standards, unless they can be coupled with proposals to reduce other taxes or to spend the revenue raised on particular projects.

Concessions are of course easy to introduce, but difficult to remove when no longer required or justifiable from an environmental point of view.

In practice, environmental taxes are an efficient and effective policy tool. People in countries with higher fuel taxes use more fuel efficient vehicles, and drive them less, regardless of their personal levels of environmental concern. Tobacco taxes have been central to the success of the public health war on smoking. Noise-based airport charges have encouraged quieter aircraft fleets. Money talks, and well-designed taxes provide a powerful way of integrating environmental considerations into everyday decision making.

David Eisenberg

Building codes exist to protect public health and safety. In many cases, however, building codes are actually jeopardising public health and safety by inadvertently resulting in the destruction of the planet's natural support systems. While much has been done to document the environmental, economic, and social impacts of the built environment, little has been done to reassess building codes in terms of sustainability. Designers and/or professionals have an obligation to re-invent these codes.

Codes and externalities

Ecological sustainability refers to the ability of whole systems to remain healthy and continue on indefinitely. Simply sustaining present human patterns of behaviour may not be desirable, however. We need to move beyond the target of sustainability towards restorative practices and materials in order to reach a sustainable existence.

Building codes represent the embodiment of our accumulated knowledge and understanding about materials and how to safely use them to build structures. In another sense, however, they exist as a disembodied data set – definitions, prescriptions, rules, and tables – developed and evolved through a process which has a strong internal logic. This logic ignores the externalities or consequences which fall outside the concern for the physical health and safety of people in or near individual buildings. We have not integrated an awareness of the real impacts of our design decisions into the design, construction, and regulatory processes.

While we cannot fully comprehend the enormous complexity of these broader impacts, it is another thing to ignore them. In reality, everything we do affects everything else. But the connections are often subtle and cumulative, making the majority of the consequences invisible to us and therefore unintentional. For example, if we throw a stone in the ocean, we can see the splash and a few ripples, but it affects the whole ocean eventually. At the least, we should begin to reduce the impacts of unintended consequences.

In this context, **appropriate technology** could be defined as

the lowest level of technology that will achieve sustainability, rather than the highest level of technology that we think we can afford. A good basic principle is to always act in ways that reduce the level of unintended consequences. Unfortunately, building codes have continuously evolved toward the use of higher levels of technology and, almost exclusively, industrially processed materials. This has greatly amplified the unintended health and environmental impacts of building.

Codes and regulations, and the processes for their development and modification, lack mechanisms to address these externalities, in part because the problem has not even been recognised. Though resource issues are often identified as being at the heart of developing sustainable patterns for building and development, they are totally absent from building codes. Further, buildings are often treated as though they require the same level of technological sophistication, regardless of use, location, owner preference, cost, or impact. The industrial basis for product and code development works to drive the system continually away from low-impact, local alternatives and towards high-impact, less sustainable materials and systems.

Though the consequences are enormous, building codes ignore the environmental impacts of:

- Where resources come from.
- Resource acquisition or depletion.
- Transportation of resources.
- Manufacturing processes.
- How efficiently resources are used.
- Whether they can be reused or recycled at the end of the useful life of a structure.
- Disposal after use.
- Embodied energy of materials.
- Contribution to global warming.

Implications

Only a third of the world's population currently lives and works in 'modern' buildings. If we were to apply the level of resource and waste intensity that is essentially required by modern building codes in the US, Australia or Canada to the world population, it would not be remotely possible to house that number of people in this manner, with available resources [1.1]. One way to address this would be to find ways to introduce non-manufactured, indigenous materials and alternative building systems into the codes. This requires flexibility in codes.

In many climates, the indigenous buildings are often comfortable and have far fewer negative impacts and costs than the modern buildings that have replaced them. There is a long and telling history of the battles between the building regulatory system and proponents of both traditional and improved low-cost, low-tech, and low-impact building systems. How did the indigenous, natural or low-tech materials and building systems – which have been used for thousands of years – get relegated to the status of 'alternative' materials and methods?

In most cases, these building systems have been abandoned because they are labour-intensive, not because they are inherently inferior to industrial systems. Yet the assumption persists that they were rejected based on inferior performance, while in most cases, these building systems need only incremental technical or design improvement to provide excellent performance, with greatly reduced impacts and costs, when compared to their industrial counterparts.

Additionally, in developed countries, labour is relatively expensive, and resources and technology are relatively inexpensive and amply available. In developing countries, labour, arguably one of the most renewable resources available, is typically over-abundant, while technology and resources are relatively scarce and expensive. The application of building practices and regulations from developed countries, in developing countries, often results in inappropriate buildings and heightened environmental, social and economic problems.

The resources which have the lowest impacts are generally in abundance. Our cultural bias keeps us from thinking we have anything to learn from 'primitive' building systems, though many are brilliant and elegant examples of appropriate technology. We have an obligation to manage our limited resources so that we may proceed down a sustainable course. We should not take option of 'outlawing' the most sustainable approaches to building. Yet, the lack of a larger context in code development and application has allowed this regulatory 'mismanagement' of resources to pass almost unnoticed for decades.

The issues of sustainable building include the toxicity of the processes through which materials are extracted, manufactured, and used. Only recently have the health effects of buildings themselves, rather than their failures from fire or structural flaws, been acknowledged [7.3]. The economic, social, and cultural issues can be quite profound as well. If the preservation of health and safety is the legitimate purpose of building codes, should the health and safety of a relatively small number of individuals in or around a specific building, be of a higher order of importance than the well-being of all other inhabitants of a region or the planet?

Modern building codes were initially developed by insurance interests and have been influenced heavily by the industries that produce the materials and building systems which are regulated by the codes. However, major insurance underwriters and re-insurers around the world are now taking seriously the threats posed by global warming, changing patterns in the intensity and frequency of storms, and how these relate to their exposure to risk. Potential losses resulting from rising sea levels alone are sufficient to force the insurance industry to begin to take environmental issues seriously. The preservation of capital investment in buildings, and the reduction of liability exposure for designers, engineers, manufacturers, suppliers, builders, and owners are powerful forces as well. They do not, however, represent the same sort of moral authority in building codes as the health and safety aspects do, nor should they be the dominant mission of the organisations that create, modify and enforce codes.

Some attention has been paid to the relative merits of prescriptive versus performance-based codes, the burden of increasingly complex codes in terms of the time and expense of compliance, the role of codes as impediments to innovation, the challenges of staying current with new materials, and the lessons learned from failures and natural disasters. Most encouraging, however, is the development and increased adoption of model energy codes. These codes actually represent the first step towards a basis for codes which are not strictly limited to the occupant's health and safety. Model energy codes help to preserve health and welfare of the wider community and environment. As we learn to factor this larger web of interrelationships into what we do (especially where the impact is so great), we will see large scale returns, even from incremental improvements.

Recognition of the seriousness of this crisis has already started to have an effect on the design and construction industries.

An excellent example is the process which the US Civil Engineering Research Foundation (CERF) has undertaken to incorporate sustainable development principles into the full spectrum of activities related to civil engineering. Other efforts by US federal agencies, such as the Naval Facilities Command (NAVFAC) to implement new sustainability criteria and policies for their building projects and the hiring of architectural and engineering firms, further demonstrates this growing recognition. While the challenges are of monumental proportions, designers must not be paralysed by the difficulty of the task, nor lulled into thinking that it will happen without a committed, focused, long-term effort.

Conclusion

The design professions have an obligation to:

- Seek government support for research, testing, and development of low-impact building materials and systems that lack a developed 'industry' or profit base for their development and promotion (as these cannot attract the type of investment that proprietary materials and systems do).

- Develop a process to assess codes on the basis of whether they really preserve or threaten health and safety, in the broader sense.

- Engage the general public with the fullest understanding of these issues (not just business interests in the process of development).

- Develop a process for evaluating and integrating impacts, costs, benefits, and risks into the codes in the local areas.

- Create a different kind of wisdom about building design and regulation that is based on seeking an understanding of local and global sustainability.

References

Elizabeth, L. and Adams, C., eds, 2000, *Alternative Construction: Contemporary Natural Building Methods*, J. Wiley and Sons, New York.

Kennedy, J., Smith, M. and Wanek, C., eds, 2001, *The Art of Natural Building*, New Society Publishers, Gabriola Island, BC.

Sorkin, M. 1993, *Local Code*, Princeton Architectural Press, New York.

'Sustainability and Building Codes', Feature in *Environmental Building News* (10)9, Brattleboro, Vermont, September 2001.

Building Environmental Science and Technology, http://www.energybuilder.com

Development Center for Appropriate Technology, http://www.dcat.net

Ecological Building Network, http://www.ecobuildnetwork.org/

http://www.buildinggreen.com

U.S. Green Building Council, http://www.usgbc.org

Questions

1. List the forces that may have caused building codes to evolve to favour resource-intensive and high-tech materials and design (instead of low-tech, low-impact design)?

2. Should building codes integrate the **precautionary principle**? As a conservation concept, would this favour existing (high-tech) technology or a change to low-impact technology?

3. The text lists nine environmental factors that building codes ignore. In small groups, think up ways that codes could address these factors.

4. Are prescriptive codes more likely to promote low-impact materials and technologies than performance-based codes?

5. How should building codes deal with non-industrial building materials and methods?

6. Should building codes have different criteria for owner-builders, and very small or rural buildings? Is it possible to have a 'universal building code' that is appropriate anywhere?

Projects

1. Analyse the local building code. Is it prescriptive or performance based? Can a lay person use and understand it? Does it limit the use of 'appropriate technology'? Does it allow for experiments to test new ideas for, say, composting toilets or strawbale construction? List other low-impact technologies or design features which are restricted by these building codes.

2. Which government agencies and elected representatives have influence on the construction industry in your region? Using the information in this chapter, and other sources of information, prepare and send a letter that explains the environmental significance of codes and ask each of these agencies what they are doing to contribute to the modernisation and improvement building codes in regard to sustainability.

Box 27   Environmental Quality Indicators

Janis Birkeland and Regina Lubanga

Environmental quality indicators (EQI) aim to provide both qualitative and quantitative user-friendly measures of the condition of, and trends in, the health of human and natural systems. A typical set of EQI can measure physical, chemical, biological or socio-economic conditions, such as the material per unit of product, energy consumption per unit of product, number of health cases reported, population size of threatened species and introduced weed/pest species.

'Urban sustainability indicators' vary greatly, but 50 or more is common, requiring a substantial investment of human resources in data collection, interpretation and updating. Due to their complexity, indicators are simply not used in day-to-day decision making. However, they are often used in support of other environmental management tools to meet the mandates of environmental management systems or environmental reporting requirements of local councils, government agencies or corporations.

Ideally, EQI should provide guidance on policy priorities to target public investment in eco-solutions. In practice, however, their application is retrospective and focused on measuring altered states and change agents, and monitoring adverse environmental impacts. There are also gaps between collecting environmental information and adopting appropriate strategies.

Common problems: Some (potential and actual) shortcomings of EQI that need to be avoided are that EQI:

- are expensive to develop and, because they need to be comprehensive, are often unwieldy;

- are not linked with budgetary systems, priorities and the timetables of relevant actors in government and business;

- have not been integrated adequately into environmental management plans at all levels (eg farm management plans, catchment plans and local council plans);

- generally only measure the current state of environmental conditions, and whether they have improved or not over a period of time; they do not usually convey how serious these conditions are;

- tend not to reflect all the 'real' costs of using the environment as the natural base for production; the costs to the public (externalities) seem small compared to the (relatively) high costs that sometimes beset immediate stakeholders;

- tend to measure problems only after they are manifested as environmental stresses, rather than providing an early warning system for preventative purposes;

- tend to focus on single issues, point sources, or measurable environmental impacts in separate media (air, soil, water), which can direct attention away from more fundamental system-wide causes and solutions;

- do not indicate ecosystem services lost (eg natural erosion control, pollination), or what ecosystem services would be obtainable but for the adverse impacts of development;

- focus on the capacity of the environment to respond to human actions (eg environmental resilience) – rather than on the performance of human management systems;

- are generally not designed to increase accountability in decision making, or to assess our capacity to prevent problems; they focus more on nature's resilience than on society's responses.

The role of EQI in design: EQI can assist in setting design criteria to improve every aspect of design – from conception to disposal – of buildings, landscapes or products [Box 28]. However, few if any design professionals have even considered using EQI in design decisions or in monitoring the results of their design solutions. As pressure to demonstrate environmental performance increases in all fields, the use of appropriate indicators to establish basic design parameters, goals and guidelines could provide a competitive edge for responsible designers.

Bill Lawson

Since the 'energy crises' of the early 1970s, people have become increasingly aware that energy production and consumption have serious environmental consequences – such as acid rain and photochemical smog – and that these impacts are of a global scale. In particular, the release of carbon dioxide and the associated 'greenhouse effect' will result in global warming. This chapter presents a practical tool through which designers can begin to address environmental impacts in the selection of materials and products.

Embodied energy

Initially, when the energy consumption of buildings was considered, most of the attention was on **operating energy**: the energy consumed in heating, cooling lighting and otherwise living in the building. This emphasis arose partly because of political expediency and partly because studies conducted in the 1970s and early 1980s indicated that operating energy was much more significant than embodied energy (Ballantyne 1975; Lowe and Backhouse 1981; Baird 1984). Towards the end of the 1980s, a renewed interest in embodied energy emerged due to significant changes that took place in the building industry during the intervening years. Later studies indicated that embodied energy was indeed much more significant than first thought (Connaughton 1990; McArdle 1993; Treloar 1993).

Embodied energy research was hampered by the lack of current data, both in Australia and overseas, and the fact that the available data were expressed in a manner which was more useful to building material manufacturers than to designers. In addition, the units varied widely between countries and industries, and sometimes obscured methodological issues, such as whether all energy used was converted to **primary energy**. It seemed clear that if designers were to use embodied energy data in the design process – particularly at an early stage where major material decisions are often made – then the data had to be expressed in a readily useable form.

As designers typically think in terms of major building elements such as floors, walls and roofs, this was considered to be a more useful basis for presenting embodied energy data. It was also apparent that typical building elements are composites rather than homogeneous materials. Even common building elements are quite complex composites. A brick veneer wall, for example, is comprised of bricks, mortar (itself a composite), timber frame, plasterboard lining, insulation, brick ties and other components – each with quite different embodied energies and used in quite different quantities. Embodied energy data for walls is summarised in Table 11.4.1 (For data on floors and roofs see Lawson 1996).

While reducing or minimising embodied energy (and reducing the operating energy of a building) has environmental benefits, energy consumption is only one aspect of the environmental impacts of building materials production. If the ultimate aim is ecological sustainability, this involves taking a more holistic view of the environmental impacts of building materials that extends beyond energy analysis (Forintek Canada and Trusty 1993; Yates 1994).

Sustainable natural processes (such as the nitrogen and phosphate cycles) are characterised by their cyclical nature and the production of very little waste. Likewise, the production of building materials also needs to be a cyclical process with wastes minimised. The current interest in life cycle assessment (LCA) or 'cradle to cradle' analysis, reflects the trend towards attempting to put the concept of ecological sustainability into practice (Totsch and Gaensslen 1992; Boonstra 1994; Lawson and Partridge 1994). While some studies have focussed on wastes, others have considered the life cycle of buildings and recycling of building materials, including the concept of **design for deconstruction** (Kinhill Engineers 1991; Lawson 1994).

225

Table 11.4.1: Embodied energy of some typical wall construction systems

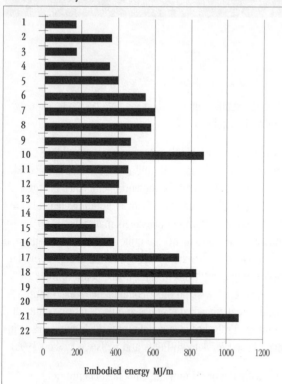

Embodied energy MJ/m

Legend

1 Timber frame, timber weatherboard wall
2 Timber frame, reconstituted timber weatherboard wall
3 Timber frame, fibre cement weatherboard wall
4 Timber frame, steel clad wall
5 Timber frame, aluminium weatherboard wall
6 Timber frame, clay brick veneer wall
7 Steel frame, clay brick veneer wall
8 Timber frame, concrete block veneer wall
9 Steel frame, concrete block veneer wall
10 Cavity clay brick wall
11 Cavity concrete block wall
12 Single skin stabilised rammed earth wall
13 Single skin autoclaved aerated concrete block (AAC) wall
14 Single skin cored concrete block wall
15 Steel frame, steel clad wall
16 Steel frame compressed fibre cement clad wall
17 Hollow-core precast concrete wall
18 Tilt-up precast concrete wall
19 Porcelain-enamelled steel curtain wall
20 Glass curtain wall
21 Steel faced sandwich panel wall
22 Aluminium curtain wall

Life cycle assessment

There are various approaches to LCA, depending on the purpose for which it is intended. For purposes such as green labelling schemes, which are aimed at the general public, a simplified LCA covering the main factors may be adequate. For more sophisticated users, a detailed and rigorous LCA is necessary. There is a trade-off between ease of use (simplification) and accuracy in each situation. This is a matter for the judgement of the designer of the assessment system. The following LCA systems have a variety of advantages and disadvantages.

A system reported in the *Green Building Digest* early in 1995 consists of a simplified LCA considering only the production and use of the product, and a five-point scale scored visually for each variable and presented in a matrix format. It is easy to assess the product under consideration and gain an impression of the 'black spots' (ie the more and larger these are, the worse the product is for the environment). How the allocation of black spots is made is not clear and the trustworthiness of the assessor is assumed. Two advantages of this system are that it provides an assessment of the supplier of the product, and attempts to assess the best value for money.

In contrast to the lack of quantified information in such systems, the Canadian Wood Council (1995) has produced an LCA of wood compared to steel framing, based on key factors such as comparative resource requirements, energy use, CO_2 emissions, manufacturing effluents, water demand and so on. The presentation of data in tables and bar graphs is supported by descriptive and explanatory notes.

Table 11.4.2: Environmental externality costs

Wood and steel stud walls – 3m x 30m

Pollutant	Cost* $/kg	Wood Wall	Steel Wall
Electricity		$ 1.46	$ 4.67
CO_2	0.15	47.00	145.65
SO_2	1.80	0.66	6.65
NO_x	4.47	4.52	7.04
Particulates	2.62	0.49	1.55
Effluents**	0.05	0.61	24.80
TOTAL		$54.74	$190.57

* *Source*: Pace University 1990 (in Canadian dollars)
** Estimated by Forintek from Pace study *Source*: Canadian Wood Council 1995

Two significant innovations in this system are the attempts to assess externality costs (Table 11.4.2) that are notoriously overlooked in conventional economics, and to link embodied energy and manufacturing concerns with operating energy and service considerations. A major disadvantage is that it provides no systematic way of putting the wealth of information together. Unfortunately, this study concludes with general and biased statements which are all too typical of assessments conducted by industry associations: 'The choice is clear. The choice is wood.'

Independent LCAs, such as those conducted by the US organisation Scientific Certification Systems, attempt to overcome the problem of bias by resorting to 'scientific objectivity', implying that it is possible to eliminate underlying bias. LCAs, of course, cannot be value free. One way of dealing with this is to make the valuing stage of the assessment clear and specific (see for example UNEP 1996).

The BES Index

The BMAS (Building Material Assessment System) was developed to provide designers with an easy to use method of assessing the environmental impacts of building materials. It was first presented at an international conference in 1994 (Lawson and Partridge). While it is based on an LCA approach in common with other assessment systems, it attempts to deal openly with values and the associated weighting of environmental issues. The original BMAS had 14 parameters defining environmental impacts along the life cycle of a material, from mining/extraction through manufacture, construction and use, to eventual demolition. Each of these was rated on a 5-point scale according to their perceived importance by a group of environmentally aware design professionals. In order to facilitate prioritisation, reflecting 'real world' choice situations, the ratings had to average 3. These ratings were then used as the general weighting for the environmental parameters.

A similar process was then undertaken by the BMAS user, assisted by the use of 'help' tables, for a specific material. These 'help' tables outlined some relevant basic information on the materials and provided a 5-point scale scoring format. It was intended that this process should be informative and encourage discussion among designers. The original paper indicates the details of how the scores were then processed according to a simple formula to give the various scores. The higher the score, the less desirable the material from an environmental point of view.

Since the original BMAS was published, there has been a continuous feedback and review process which has speeded up the process of refining the 'help' tables and led to some redefinition of the basic parameters. The parameters (expanded to 16) are now grouped to yield scores for three factors: Resource Depletion (RD), Inherent Pollution (IP) and Embodied Energy (EE). It was found necessary to make a distinction between the assessment of basic materials and products made from those materials because the way in which a material is used in a product may effect, for example, its maintenance requirements, recyclability and eventual disposal. The revised system is known as the BES Index (Building Material Ecological Sustainability Index). As with the original BMAS, it is necessary to relate scores for individual materials to scores for a given area of a typical wall, floor and roof assembly. Some relative ratings for some common building elements are presented in Table 11.4.3.

Table 11.4.3: BES indices for some common building elements

Element	RD	IP	EE*
AAC block	16.8	7.8	3.5
AAC panel	16.8	6.2	5.4
Cement render	19.5	9.2	2.0
Cement mortar	15.5	5.9	2.0
Clay brick	13.4	4.2	2.0
Clay tile	13.4	4.2	2.0
Concrete – *in situ*	15.6	6.9	2.0
Copper sheet	30.2	28.9	100.0
PVC u/g pipe	14.0	17.3	79.0
PVC floor tiles	16.0	22.1	79.0
Plasterboard	13.5	9.3	4.5
BOS steel, coated sheet	18.2	19.2	38.0
BOS steel, stud	18.2	19.5	38.0
EAF steel, reinforcing rod	8.3	9.5	19.0
Timber, softwood stud	9.2	5.7	3.5
Timber, chipboard (softwood)	9.2	7.1	8.0
Timber, hardboard (hardwood)	13.3	5.4	24.0
Timber, imported WRC frame	13.6	6.8	4.5
Timber hardwood engineered product	11.2	4.1	11.0

* Based on parameter L (PER for basic material) only.
    RD = Resource depletion
    IP = Inherent pollution
    EE = Embodied energy

Using these ratings, and knowing the quantities of materials used in a particular building assembly, ecological indices have then been calculated (see Table 11.4.4). The ratings can be seen to reflect the quantity of materials used so that a small quantity of a 'bad' material has a similar rating to a large quantity of a 'good' material. The general rule is that the less material that is used the better for the environment.

Conclusion

The assessment of the environmental impacts of building materials is complex. Various approaches of presenting this in a simplified form which is suitable for building design practitioners have been developed. The BMAS/BES Index is one approach which attempts to integrate environmental values within the assessment system. Some might argue that the accumulation of up-to-date information on the procurement of building materials is the most important outcome. Certainly, continual feedback and refinement has been an important part of the development of the BES Index to date. It also has an educational function, the benefit of which should not be underestimated.

References

Baird, G. et al 1984, *Energy Performance of Buildings*, CRC Press, FL.

Ballantyne, E.R. 1975, '*Energy Costs of Dwellings*', D.B.R. Reprint 704, CSIRO, Melbourne, VIC.

Boonstra, C. 1994, 'Method Environmental Preference for Building Materials', *Proceedings Buildings and the Environment*, BRE, Watford, 16–20 May.

Canadian Wood Council 1995, 'Environmental Effects of Building Materials', *Wood the Renewable Resource,* No.2, Ottawa.

Connaughton, J. 1990, 'Life Cycle Energy Costing', *Building Services*, October.

Forintek Canada and Trusty, W.B. 1993, *Unit Factor Estimates, Model Development and Related Studies, Phase 2 Summary Report*, Forintek Canada Corporation.

Kinhill Engineers Pty Ltd 1991, 'A Study of the Demolition Industry in the Sydney Region', *Report Prepared for the Waste Management Authority of NSW*, Ultimo, NSW.

Table 11.4.4: BES indices for some common building assemblies

Assembly		RD	IP	EE
Ground floors	Timber/clay brick piers and footings	12.0	4.9	6.1
	AAC panels/AAC block walls/ concrete footings	50.0	21.0	19.0
	Concrete raft slab	58.0	26.0	21.0
Upper floors	Timber	3.9	2.7	3.6
	150mm AAC	21.0	8.4	8.5
	150mm concrete slab	57.0	26.0	21.0
External walls	Timber frame, timber w/boards, plasterboard lining	4.1	2.6	2.0
	Timber frame, brick veneer, plasterboard lining	34.0	12.0	13.0
	Double (cavity) brick	63.0	20.0	23.0
Internal walls	AAC block with render	16.0	6.3	4.8
	Clay brick with render	36.0	13.0	13.0
	Timber studs/ plasterboard	3.6	2.4	1.6
	Steel studs/ plasterboard	2.8	2.2	3.3
	Reinforced concrete, no render	37.0	17.0	12.0
Roofs	Corrugated iron on timber framing	4.9	3.8	8.6
	Clay tiles on timber framing	13.0	5.5	5.4

Lawson, W.R. 1994, 'Design for Deconstruction', *Proceedings Buildings and the Environment*, BRE, Garston, 16–20 May.

Lawson W.R. and Partridge, H.J. 1994, 'A Method for the Quantitative Assessment of the Ecological Sustainability of Building Materials', *Proceedings Solar 94*, Sydney, NSW, November–December.

Lawson, B. 1996, *Building Materials, Energy and the Environment: Towards Ecological Sustainability,* RAIA, Canberra, ACT

Lowe, I. and Backhouse, D. 1981, 'Capital Energy Costs of Building', *Queensland Master Builder*, February.

McArdle, S.A. et al 1993, *Embodied Energy Thesis: Case Study Analysis of the Embodied Energy of Office Construction*, School of Architecture and Building, Deakin University, Geelong, VIC.

Totsch, W. and Gaensslen, H. 1992, *Polyvinylchloride – Environmental Aspects of a Common Plastic*, Elsevier, London.

Treloar, G. 1993, 'Embodied Energy Analysis of Buildings, Part 2: A Case Study', *Exedra* 4 (1).

UNEP 1996, *Life Cycle Assessment: What It Is and How To Do It, United Nations Environment Programme*, Industry and Environment, Paris.

Yates, A. 1994, 'Assessing the Environmental Impact of Buildings', *Proceedings Buildings and the Environment*, BRE, Watford, UK, 16–20 May.

Questions

1. What key changes do you think took place in the building industry during the 1970s and 1980s which led to the renewed interest in the embodied energy of buildings?

2. Why is energy consumption regarded as an important indicator of environmental impacts for materials and processes?

3. What aspects of the production of building materials may be more important than the energy used? Why? Give examples.

4. Why is recycling of building materials an important environmental strategy? Why is it commonly overlooked?

5. Debate: 'Trying to assess the environmental impacts of building materials is too difficult; it is easier to just use less materials.'

6. Can environmental assessment schemes for building materials be reduced to a single score? What are the problems and benefits of such an approach?

Projects

1. Develop environmental assessments of 3 different wall assemblies based on: (a) embodied energy alone, or (b) a broader environmental assessment. Discuss the advantages and disadvantages of each assessment approach.

2. Describe some of the methodological problems associated with the environmental assessment of building materials. Discuss possible solutions.

Box 28 Design Criteria and Indicators

Janis Birkeland and John Schooneveldt

To be useful, criteria and indicators (C&I) must be readily understood by lay people, relatively easy to measure and monitor, and reflect fundamental aspects of the underlying system dynamics. Most C&I are too detailed or too general for project planning, review and approval purposes – let alone design guidance. Moreover, they are retrospective and measure only observable changes [27]. Simpler goal-oriented sustainability C&I are needed that can be used to guide land use and development, measure cumulative impacts, and raise design standards. Sample (local and regional) indicators are suggested below.

Regional indicators: urban planning and design methods should consider the regional context from the start, rather than begin with the assumption that the city is a 'perpetual motion machine' that is independent from the bioregion and its ecosystem services (eg soil production, air and water cleaning functions, etc). Sustainability requires a balance of materials and energy flowing into a building, city or region and those leaving it [31]. In order to simplify design goals, and to enable cumulative impact assessment, it may be preferable to focus on a few key indicators that relate to underlying system dynamics. Such regional indicators for project assessment at the regional level might be:

- **Carrying capacity:** the set of functions and load that the bioregion can support. Unlike the ecological footprint concept, carrying capacity depends upon the biophysical characteristics of a specific region. Sustainability would require that all development operates within the limits of its local carrying capacity.

- **Infrastructure efficiency:** the whole systems costs involved in the built environment and transport of people, water, energy (rather than, say, cost to the driver or cost per mile). This should encourage dematerialisation, decarbonisation, and resource autonomy through closed-loop systems design.

- **Environmental space:** the total amount of energy and resources (including land, water and forests) that can be used sustainably – divided by the global population; this measures the fair share of resources for a country or individual.

- **Human resources:** the relative cost of the jobs created, the nature of the work, the social displacement entailed by a project, and alternative ways of creating jobs. 'Capacity building' is needed to increase the capability of local groups or individuals to design for sustainability or engage in green business enterprises.

- **Eco-factor:** the opposite of the economists' 'discount rate'. The discount rate used in cost–benefit analysis is based on the idea that money today is worth more than money tomorrow. Consequently, it devalues the environment over time. However, the natural environment is decreasing while appreciation of its intrinsic value is increasing.

Urban indicators: buildings and landscapes can be designed to be resource neutral or 'autonomous' by providing ecosystem services to reduce or neutralise their net environmental impact. The proposed indicators cover three basic dimensions – open space, materials, and design performance – to form core elements for project assessment at the local level:

- **Land efficiency:** the proportion of private and public urban space available for 'ecosystem services'. This would correct some fundamental biases against open space protection, such as traditional valuation (eg 'highest economic use') and density indicators (eg 'dwellings per hectare'). The equivalent ecosystems services could be provided at other locations if necessary.

- **Material reusability:** the total materials and embodied energy in structures in relation to its economic life expectancy. Ideally, all components would be completely reusable in their current form (ie bricks reused as bricks, not road material). Simplified matrices can make this determination practicable [11.4].

- **Resource autonomy:** the 'performance' of a development or refurbishment in terms of its relative independence from off-site supplies of energy, soil, sewage, water, and its indoor air quality (eg does not off-gas volatile organic compounds and provides for plants to clean the incoming air) [9.3].

Section 12: Planning and Project Assessment

12.1 Planning for Ecological Sustainability

Janis Birkeland

Conventional planning has been little more than a development control process, assessing projects to promote the best available economic use of land and to mitigate the excessive impacts of growth. The failure to distinguish 'planning as development control' and project assessment from the idea of 'planning for sustainability' is one reason for this limited reactive role. There is a need to design a 'preventative' planning system that allows society to keep options open and create a safe, secure and sustainable future.

Development control

Planning, as a future-oriented decision-making process, is an essential component of developing a sustainable society. Planning concerns the allocation and use of resources for the future. It is, by definition future-oriented: we do not plan for the past. Most definitions of ecological sustainable development (ESD) stress the idea of ensuring future generations have the same range of options and resources that we have today. An ecologically sustainable planning system is one that would be geared towards preventing environmental and social problems and designing a better future in which everyone can be healthy, happy and secure. The term 'planning', therefore, should be seen as interchangeable with the concept of ESD.

In practice, however, ESD is generally used in the limited sense of including environmental policies and indicators in traditional planning and project approval processes. Plans limit where certain commercial and industrial developments may be permitted, or specify indicators of environmental quality like particular pollutants, noise levels, residential density or set backs. Planning is therefore often equated with decision-making methods and review processes designed to assist decision makers in assessing development proposals as a basis for approving, rejecting, or modifying these initiatives. Common project review tools include **conditional use applications**, **discretionary review processes**, **social and environmental impact assessment** [12.4] and **risk–benefit analyses**.

Though usually tied to comprehensive plans, these decision aids are not environmental 'planning' activities; that is, they are essentially reactive, not proactive. It is up to the private sector to propose developments, and they seldom propose projects intended to preserve the public domain from development, protect the integrity of a bioregion, or restore the natural habitat of native flora and fauna. Decisions about the nature and shape of the future environment are made incrementally by developers based on individualistic goals such as profit. Project assessment methods cannot therefore ensure the preservation of future social options and natural resources. If considered on a case-by-case basis, development pressures would eventually eliminate all remnant nature reserves and, when necessary, lead to the overturning of legislation intended to protect these areas.

Because planning was initially concerned with developing land to its 'highest' use, our methods are designed to help us choose among development proposals, by weighing the relative costs and benefits of a development. In practice, this can simply mean assessing whether the short-term (private) economic benefits outweigh the long-term (public) environmental costs. Given that social welfare is equated with economic growth in our society, the 'no development' or environmental protection option will seldom rate high enough relative to economic considerations, to reject a project proposal. The best present use for a particular site often changes the ecosystem for all time, cuts off future choices, and reduces our chances of adapting to increasingly rapid environmental change.

Development control systems sometimes lead to mitigation measures, and may be said to slow the rate of development, at least where there is sufficient public concern or opposition. However, these review processes rarely result in projects being totally rejected by decision makers, even when they do not meet environmental standards. Everything is negotiable, and capital – especially international capital – has a lot of negotiating power.

231

Comprehensive plans

Project review systems are generally based on **comprehensive plans** which often seek to implement broad social goals like ESD. Where a master plan exists, planning is usually referred to as 'comprehensive planning'. However, such plans have traditionally been designed to accommodate predictions about population growth and market trends. Thus, master planning is more predictive than preventative – following consumer and producer trends, in lieu of guiding them. Even when a land-use decision is made in the context of ESD policies, it is in relative isolation from other decisions and their **cumulative impacts**. For example, a petrol station, fast food outlet, or branch bank application may be refused because it will destroy the quality of a neighbourhood that has a strong citizen group, but the project will be permitted elsewhere where it will have virtually the same impacts.

Today, most comprehensive plans have preambles about aiming for sustainability, but to do so they must address the kinds of basic issues that are prerequisite to achieving ESD, such as population limits, wilderness preservation and biodiversity. For example, we know that population growth is unsustainable; nonetheless, many comprehensive plans simply begin with the premise that a projected level of growth must be accommodated. Further, sustainability requires preserving future options, natural resources and amenities, but mitigation measures do little to prevent the incremental consumption of land. Planners should first determine the carrying capacity of the land, the ecological footprint, and the allowable environmental space (McLaren et al 1998). Even then, it should not be a foregone conclusion that we should exploit the environment to these limits.

In short, what we now call comprehensive planning is actually incremental decision making. **Incrementalism** means letting the market take its course (while planning picks up some of the private costs at public expense). Although incrementalism should mean the avoidance of big mistakes by taking little steps, the concept only works if we are already headed the right way to begin with. The conversion to a sustainable society requires a dramatic shift in direction. Environmental policies will be nullified if the basic ethical issues continue to be determined by 'non-decision' through the incremental actions of profiteers, politicians and technocrats – all of whom pass on the long-term costs of their actions. The environment is gradually 'traded off' because, in each case, the environmental sacrifices appear small, and the public picks up the tab for the externalities.

But, one might ask, if current planning works against sustainability by legitimising the process of incremental consumption of resources and future options, while channelling public opposition into formal processes, why plan at all?

Ethics-based planning

Unlike case-by-case development approval systems, a 'preventative' planning system would be one that enables a society to address the causes of environmental problems, not just their symptoms. This means that planning must also be able to address ethical issues, as these lie at the heart of the population explosion, species extinction, ozone depletion, wilderness destruction and other environmental problems.

Why are these fundamentally ethical issues? To take population as an example; it is a complex ethical issue. Over-population can ruin the life quality of a region for all its residents; however, if a community excludes others, through zoning or other development controls, it will be discriminating against other groups of people. Present land-use controls allocate land and resources on a first come, first served basis. In the context of increasing population, the alienation of land and resources to private parties removes land from the public domain and reduces social options. This contravenes the basic ethic of sustainability: fairness to future generations. Thus, (voluntary) limits on population are a prerequisite of sustainability.

Public debates over planning issues should involve questions as to how we as a society should live, and what constitutes our duties to other beings. However, because our basic decision-making arenas (the legal, market, planning, and political systems) are 'rights-based', they are only designed to determine who gets what, when and where. This means that, to a large extent, *power* is the determining factor: the one with the most rights wins. A planning system designed for sustainability must instead be based on an ethic of care and responsibility, not rights alone.

In a governmental or market system, competing demands for resources are settled according to the relative political clout of the immediate contenders. Planners cannot implement new objectives, principles and policies within the existing institutional framework of governance. For example, in recent years, the **precautionary principle** has been adopted in many international agreements concerning the environment, and it should be fundamental to any planning system. However, it cannot be fully realised within the existing resource allocation and planning system, which is geared towards weighing costs and benefits, or competing interests in development. Further, it cannot assure the more basic imperative of keeping options open.

If the purpose of planning were reconceived as 'to prepare for the future' or 'to design a sustainable society', our decision-making system would have to be dramatically transformed. Planning would be designed to enable us to resolve the fundamental ethical questions that underlie environmental problems. That is, it would need to be an ethics-based (as opposed to a power-based), decision-making system. Planning, then, should be thought of as a collective, future-oriented process of imagining, thinking, debating and problem solving. This requires a planning forum for people to consider basic long-term problems, which the market and political arenas are thoroughly ill-equipped to do.

In an ethics-based decision-making system, the methods, processes and structures used to guide the decision-making process would be designed from the ground up, on fundamental principles or ecological/ethical precepts. This challenges the usual approach of adding new ESD policies on top of old decision-making structures, methods and processes. Planning needs a fundamental shift. To determine what these basic precepts should be requires a community-based 'constitutional design' process. There is surprisingly much agreement on general values, because decisions are agreed before interests have vested and positions have become fixed. For example, the Earth Charter provides such a consensual basis for planning. It has received support from individuals, communities and even government authorities around the world [Box 29].

Conclusion

If we were serious about achieving ESD, we would set about to redesign our systems of environmental governance at regional, national, and global levels (Birkeland 1993). This would not be as difficult as many things we presently do as nations – like fighting wars. There are precedents: the US designed and enacted an innovative constitution based on what were then new concepts about human rights. We need to institutionalise new concepts of human responsibility and new ways of making decisions about the natural assets that affect life quality, social relationships and the life support system. An easy first step is for organisations, institutions and corporations to endorse the Earth Charter as a constitutional basis for their operations.

References and further reading

Aberley D., ed, 1994, *Futures by Design: The Practice of Ecological Planning*, Envirobook Pub., Sydney, NSW.

Allmendinger, P. and Chapman, M., eds, 1999, *Planning Beyond 2000*, J. Wiley, New York.

Beatley, T. and Manning, K. 1997, *The Ecology of Place: Planning for Environment, Economy and Community*, Island Press, Washington, DC.

Birkeland, J. 1993, 'Towards a New System of Environmental Governance', *The Environmentalist* 13(1), pp. 19–32.

Brunckhorst, D.J. 2000, *Bioregional Planning: Resource Management Beyond the New Millennium*, Harwood Academic Publications, Amsterdam.

Buckingham-Hatfield, S. and Evans, B., eds, 1996, *Environmental Planning and Sustainability*, J Wiley, New York.

Clayton A.M.H. and Radcliffe, N.J. 1996, *Sustainability: A Systems Approach*, Earthscan, London.

Cullingworth, J.B. 1997, *Planning in the USA*, Routledge, London.

Cullingworth, J.B. 1997, *Town and Country Planning in the UK*, Routledge, London.

Frey, H. 1998, *Designing the City, Towards a More Sustainable Urban Form*, Routledge, London.

Jewson, N. and MacGregor, S., eds, 1997, *Transforming Cities: New Spatial Divisions and Social Transformation*, Routledge, London.

Kenny, M. 1999, *Planning Sustainability*, Routledge, London.

Lewis, P.H. 1996, *Tomorrow by Design: A Regional Design Process for Sustainability*, J. Wiley, New York.

McLaren, D., Bullock, S. and Yousuf, N. 1998, *Tomorrow's World: Britain's Share in a Sustainable Future*, Earthscan, London.

Miller, A. 1999, *Environmental Problem Solving: Psychosocial Barriers to Adaptive Change*, Springer, New York.

Parfect, M. and Power, G. 1997, *Planning for Urban Quality: Urban Design in Towns and Cities*, Routledge, London.

Questions

1. Debate: 'The precautionary principle cannot be fully implemented within the existing form of planning.'

2. If all land is alienated to private citizens and corporations, population increases will make land become very expensive. A person's right to use and enjoy land will increasingly depend on circumstances of birth. Discuss.

3. If your local council put restrictions on the number of families that could live in the community, would you object? What are the ethical arguments for and against such a regulation?

4. Would you support a law that requires rural residential lots to be a minimum of two acres? What are the ecological costs and benefits of this subdivision restriction?

5. Debate: 'Cheap transport turns rural villages into dormitory towns' versus 'Small farms turn rural villages into dormitory towns.'

6. To be fair, people in poor nations should be given the same environmental space as people in Canada, Australia or the US. However, this is impossible, as there are not sufficient resources to raise the standard of living in poor nations to that of rich nations. What are the solutions?

Projects

1. Draft a preamble to the national Constitution to incorporate the idea of a Bill of Environmental Rights. Find existing ones and compare.

2. Attend the next hearing of the local planning commission. Make notes of the decisions made and the criteria upon which they were based. Do you agree with the criteria used to make the decisions? Have significant impacts or issues been overlooked?

Box 29 The Earth Charter

The Earth Charter

The Earth Charter is a declaration of fundamental principles for building a just, sustainable and peaceful global society in the 21st Century. It is the product of a ten year long worldwide, cross-cultural conversation about common goals and shared values, involving the most open and participatory consultation process ever conducted in connection with an international document. It can be used as a basis for codes of conduct in businesses, organisations, communities and nations, and could become the basis for an international constitution or treaty.

Principles

I. Respect and care for the community of life

1. Respect Earth and life in all its diversity.

2. Care for the community of life with understanding, compassion, and love.

3. Build democratic societies that are just, participatory, sustainable, and peaceful.

4. Secure Earth's bounty and beauty for present and future generations.

In order to fulfil these four broad commitments, it is necessary to:

II. Ecological integrity

5. Protect and restore the integrity of Earth's ecological systems, with special concern for biological diversity and the natural processes that sustain life.

6. Prevent harm as the best method of environmental protection and, when knowledge is limited, apply a precautionary approach.

7.   Adopt patterns of production, consumption, and reproduction that safeguard Earth's regenerative capacities, human rights, and community well-being.

8. Advance the study of ecological sustainability and promote the open exchange and wide application of the knowledge acquired.

III. Social and economic justice

9. Eradicate poverty as an ethical, social, and environmental imperative.

10. Ensure that economic activities and institutions at all levels promote human development in an equitable and sustainable manner.

11. Affirm gender equality and equity as prerequisites to sustainable development and ensure universal access to education, health care, and economic opportunity.

12. Uphold the right of all, without discrimination, to a natural and social environment supportive of human dignity, bodily health, and spiritual well-being, with special attention to the rights of indigenous peoples and minorities.

IV. Democracy, non-violence, and peace

13. Strengthen democratic institutions at all levels, and provide transparency and accountability in governance, inclusive participation in decision making, and access to justice.

14. Integrate into formal education and life-long learning the knowledge, values, and skills needed for a sustainable way of life.

15. Treat all living beings with respect and consideration.

16. Promote a culture of tolerance, nonviolence, and peace.

Janis Birkeland and Cam Walker

Bioregionalism is land-use planning that integrates industry, agriculture, economics and governance together with the ecology of the region. It begins from the premise that humans evolved in response to their environments, and are subject to natural laws and limits; therefore, communities should be designed to fit their bioregion. However, bioregional planning could also be designed to assist in the transition to a bio-based economy.

Introduction

Bioregionalism is an alternative movement that calls for a new form of planning process modelled upon natural systems. Bioregional planning begins at the opposite point from that of conventional planning. Conventional planning systems are processes for 'choosing between' development proposals or land uses according to the highest economic use of land. Generally, they accommodate growth or 'progress', in the sense of transforming nature (Figure 12.2.1).

Figure 12.2.1: Conventional and bioregional planning

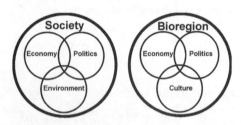

Conventional planning transforms nature   **Bioregional planning transforms society**

In contrast, bioregional planning starts from the recognition that humans are biological entities and therefore need systems for living that are designed to meet their cultural, economic, and physical needs, but in ways that foster symbiotic relationships with the complex ecological systems of the bioregion. Human cultures have co-evolved with nature, a relationship which has been integral to both human survival and biological evolution. Thus, humans are dependent on the integrity of the food chain (eg without the bacteria in our stomachs, we might be unable to live).

Therefore, lifestyles, cultures, industry and even systems of governance are rooted in, and should conform with, the natural conditions of the region.

The recent wave of bioregionalism emerged in the 1970s (Aberley 1999). Its intellectual roots, however, are attributed to Peter Kropotkin and other land reformers in the late 1800s. He in turn influenced Ebenezer Howard, initiator of the Garden City Movement at the turn of the 19th Century, and Lewis Mumford, who wrote trenchant critiques of urban planning and industrial society (Mumford 1925). In architecture, a parallel concept appears as placemaking (which implies the integration of buildings and landscape). However, the term 'bioregion' has only recently entered the vocabulary of planners, urban visionaries and mainstream environmentalists (DEST 1995).

The term bioregionalism was introduced by Allen van Newkirk in the mid-1970s (Aberley 1999). It contains the Greek word *bios* (life) and the Latin *regere* (territory), and means 'life place politics'. Peter Berg (1995) started the widespread use of the term 'reinhabitation' – the process of becoming native to the place where we live, or learning to live within the natural parameters of a particular area, in a way that restores the local ecology (Dodge 1981). Bioregionalism reintroduces the concept of 'place' to current debates and advocates a rediscovery of 'home' (a region defined by biological features rather than political jurisdictions).

Cultural dimension: While the protection of biodiversity and the maintenance of ecological processes are essential, bioregional planning systems attempt to affirm and maintain the cultural identity and **sense of place** of local residents [5.3]. Accordingly, culture is a key feature in Jim Dodge's definition of bioregionalism as:

> '... a decentralised, self-determined mode of social organisation; a culture predicated upon biological integrities and acting in respectful accord; and a society which honours and abets the spiritual development of its members'. (Dodge 1981)

Social dimension: An ecologically literate citizenry is an essential element of bioregional planning. Bioregional planners seek ways to transform society and its institutions through public education and participatory democracy, informed by knowledge of the local ecology. In a bioregional framework, residents determine their own form of bottom-up, participatory decision making, based on intimate knowledge of local areas and needs. As well as active community participation in planning, bioregionalism encourages practical self-help projects in neighbourhoods and regions, such as recycling or revegetation programs which build community while solving local problems.

Economic dimension: Conventional planning focuses on physical and functional problems driven by economics. In bioregional planning, however, the region's economic activity and means of production are tailored to local materials and resources. As resources and energy become increasingly expensive, some of this is beginning to happen of necessity rather than through planning. For example, new steel mills are now locating around the US (rather than near sources of virgin ore) where they can collect local supplies of scrap metal. Paper mills are now located near cities (rather than forests) to utilise local supplies of recycled paper (Brown 1999). This contrasts with traditional planning, whereby communities were disintegrated for the benefit of freeway projects and commercial chain stores to accommodate what were seen as economies of scales.

Kirkpatrick Sale (1985) has suggested that there are three levels of bioregional organisation, each of which fits inside the next larger one. However, this may not be the best approach [Box 30]:

- **Ecoregions:** the largest unit is the 'ecoregion', such as an island or desert region.

- **Georegion or biome:** a 'biome' is a large, well-defined ecological community, such as grasslands or wetlands. A georegion is an identifiable geological region such as a range of mountains or discrete section of coast. These regions are made up of component bioregions. In some cases, a bioregion may cross or straddle a biome/ georegional boundary.

- **Bioregion:** the smallest unit is the 'bioregion', which tends to be more catchment-based. Bioregionalists propose that communities should seek to become regionally self-sufficient in basic commodities at this level.

Issues

The value of a planning system depends on its ability to address the fundamental threats to the survival of human civilisation. Three of these are ecological ignorance (also known as **economic rationalism**), **globalisation** and rapid urbanisation.

Ecological ignorance: Ecological ignorance is destroying the scientific information base itself. Species extinctions, the genetic narrowing of major crops (monocultures), and the loss of cultural information from indigenous and rural populations (especially that of the last 50 years) could be said to be greater than all the information accumulated by science and technology in the same period. This is not solely due to the irresistible forces of capitalist development. In Australia, for example, the majority of individuals live as if they were in Europe or America. Most of its population are immigrants who came with preconceptions of large-scale agriculture and centralised urban planning and design, and did not modify their behaviour to suit the more fragile Australian landscape. A few examples are lawns of European grass watered all summer, broadacre grazing by hard-hoofed animals, rivers diverted to irrigation for non-native crops. The resulting environmental degradation has turned much of the continent into wasteland and is costing the Australian economy billions of dollars in lost revenue (Flannery 1994).

Globalisation: At the same time, globalisation of economies through institutions such as the International Monetary Fund, World Bank, and transnational corporations – aided by policies on the part of powerful governments – have eroded barriers to trade and exposed local economies to the forces of global capital. The 'economic rationalist' world view, which drives this process, has transferred technologies and created economies of scale that are inappropriate to local needs in developing nations. It has also brought the destruction of biological and cultural diversity, and led to an homogenisation of cultures and products modeled on Western consumerism and individualism. As multi-nationals control greater proportions of all business (eg supermarkets, the housing industry and the media), the diversity and responsiveness of each region deteriorates correspondingly. Along with this, the sense of community identity and self-reliance erodes (Eade 1996).

Urbanisation: With increasingly global urbanisation, the management of cities becomes increasingly fundamental to any possible solution. However, the urban management fields have traditionally viewed urban areas in isolation from the regional and global environment [3.2]. Land speculation, the perceived demand for low-density housing, the marketing infrastructure, and financial frameworks that make housing on city fringes the most affordable, has meant the loss of valuable open space and agricultural land. With rapid migration to cities and cultural homogenisation, communities lose cohesion, feeding the cycles of further alienation, dependency, and societal breakdown.

Nature cannot conform and adapt to human technology rapidly. Therefore, people must identify shared social, economic and cultural goals, and match these to the opportunities provided by the natural characteristics of the bioregion and constraints set by environmental processes (Aberley 1994, p. 167). Bioregionalists have developed some basic strategies for achieving this.

The bioregional planning process

Bioregional planning is a model which addresses the roots and results of ecological ignorance, globalisation and urban development on the natural and social environment:

- By stressing local self-reliance, participatory democracy and community building activities, it offers resistance to these centralising forces.

- By applying basic indicators of social justice, like ecological footprints and environmental space, it provides a more equitable basis for resource allocation.

- By involving the community in developing shared and positive visions for the future, it stimulates activities that restore local ecosystems and renew traditions which give communities social and ecological value.

Defining boundaries: The first step is usually to identify the bioregion. Rather than conforming planning areas to political jurisdictions, bioregional boundaries are determined by the edges between natural systems having different vegetation, climates or topography. As such, the boundaries tend to be permeable, merging into each other, and subject to re-interpretation over time as climate or other changing natural processes are modified [Box 30]. Each region offers different environments and hence different resources and constraints to which local industry and agriculture must be responsive. Gradually, the culture, economy, architecture and products become differentiated, creating distinctive regional qualities which many planners, architects and artists have also called for (Amourgis 1991).

In defining regions, a variety of criteria are used, such as watersheds or catchment areas, land forms, or elevation. Dodge has suggested six criteria which could be useful in determining place:

- Biotic shift – the percentage change in species of flora and fauna from one region to another.

- Watersheds – catchments or groupings of the catchment areas.

- Land forms – geological features and soil types.

- Elevation – different elevations support different flora and fauna.

- Cultural patterns – indigenous people have retained knowledge and practices that evolved with their bioregion.

- Spiritual places – local factors would influence the development of place-centred spirituality.

Making inventories: Once regional boundaries are defined, an inventory is created, drawing on the natural history of the region (including traditional Aboriginal knowledge). Information on flora and fauna, climate, landforms, human ecology, agricultural potential and other resources, existing settlement patterns, **demographics**, and so on, combine to create a 'directory' of the bioregion. So far, there have been few attempts to collate information about natural systems in bioregional terms, and in a way that is accessible and useful to average citizens. Geographic Information Systems (GIS) is making it possible to record changes in the spatial characteristics of biotic and abiotic resources within the region. GIS, however, is still seldom used in connection with bioregional planning (Uddin and Birkeland 1999).

Education: Local citizens may have the best knowledge of local environmental and social issues, but often lack ecological literacy. 'Studies show that the average child in the US can recognise 1300 corporate logos, but only 10 plants and animals native to the bioregion' (McGinnis 1999, p.7). Also, they lack the time and resources to think about the consequences of the present choices they are making. Material flows analysis [Box 31] can be used to show what would happen under different future scenarios due to new developments or changes in land use. GIS can assist material flows analysis in presenting information in visual form to provide the community with information about resource flows in and out of the region. This can draw attention to forms of trade or commerce that militate against regional self-sufficiency (such as the export of trees and the import of paper). Similarly, the distribution of environmental benefits and burdens among different communities and social groups within the bioregion can be mapped, to analyse environmental justice.

Carrying capacity: A fundamental issue is the need to determine how many people the region can sustain in real terms. The ecological footprint is an ecological accounting tool that translates various categories of human consumption into the areas of productive land required to provide those functions and services. From this, the area of land required to support a given group of people, with their resources and waste, can be calculated [Box 9]. The carrying capacity depends on the type of consumption, construction and manufacturing processes, and assumes that agricultural lands can be maintained at current production rates (Brown 1996).

Creating a vision: The next stage is to develop a long-term vision and plan for the bioregion. An important aspect of this vision is to identify and preserve the areas most in need of protection in core reserves. Core reserves should be, at the least, connected by nature corridors and protected by buffers from areas where some resource extraction occurs (Aberley 1994). Proper bioregional planning would regenerate degraded ecosystems, rather than just responding to population growth or attempting to protect arable lands from urban sprawl.

Bioregional planning should also identify the bio-based or carbohydrate resources that could lead to regional self-sufficiency in basic commodities, including fibre, energy, building materials and raw materials for industry [Box 24]. Early attempts at the government level to adopt bioregional planning processes has thus far merely tried to measure conventional resources, industries and processes. Further, they have:

- Treated land uses as separate functions, which reinforces monocultural (rather than permacultural) approaches to development [5.2].

- Failed to examine environmental justice issues in relation to bioregional planning (eg distribution of benefits and burdens).

- Inventoried land uses in relation to the needs of a fossil fuel economy, rather than examining potential *alternative* plant-based materials that would assist the shift to a carbohydrate-based economy.

- Failed to calculate transfers of natural capital stocks out

of the region in relation to resources flowing in, which would reveal the unsustainable nature of conventional systems of production and development.

The restoration of natural ecosystems might also require urban consolidation, but not in the form usually advocated by economic interests [8.4]. When driven by economic concerns and conventional infrastructure, consolidation can overload existing facilities (schools, sewage, water, roads), increase rental turnover and traffic congestion, and reduce open space, tree cover and natural habitats. Thus, any urban consolidation process must be guided by principles of ecological restoration, such that urban areas provide their own ecosystem services. Through various tax and zoning incentives, 'development and restoration' programs could increase population densities at selected nodes of a city, while reducing them in areas identified for restoration. In some places, for example, residents are uncovering natural streams (Register 1998).

Conclusion

By becoming aware of the ecological footprint and carrying capacity of their bioregions, communities get a better feedback mechanism on how well the land is being managed. Similarly, material flows analysis can assist in funding better means to meet community needs from resources available in the region. By placing human activity within the constraints of natural systems, urban planning, landscape architecture, product design and other design fields can begin to create whole environments for living that are diverse, varied, and rich in life quality. As communities move towards local self-sufficiency in industries, buildings and products, a countervailing force is established to the ecological ignorance (ie economic rationalism), globalisation and urbanisation that are destroying cultural and ecological diversity.

References and further reading

Aberley, D. 1999, 'Interpreting Bioregionalism: A Story From Many Voices', in M.V. McGinnis, ed, 1999, *Bioregionalism*, Routledge, London.

Aberley, D., ed, 1994, *Futures by Design: The Practice of Ecological Planning*, New Society Publishers, Philadelphia, PA.

Amourgis, S. 1991, *Critical Regionalism: The Pomona Meeting Proceedings*, Pomona, CA.

Berg, P. 1995, *Discovering your Life-Place: A First Bioregional Workbook*, Planet Drum Foundation, San Francisco, CA.

Brown, L. 1999, *Crossing the Threshold: Early Signs of an Environmental Awakening*, World Watch, Washington, DC, March/April.

Brunckhorst, D.J. 2000, *Bioregional Planning: Resource Management Beyond the New Millennium*, Harwood Academic Publications, Amsterdam.

DEST 1995, 'Approaches to Bioregional Planning Conference', *Biodiversity Series, Paper No 10*, Biodiversity Group, Department of the Environment, Sports and Territories (now Environment Australia), Melbourne, VIC.

Dodge, J. 1981, 'Living By Life: Some Bioregional Theory and Practise', *CoEvolution Quarterly* 32, pp. 6–12.

Eade, J. 1996, *Living the Global City: Globalisation as a Local Process*, Routledge, London.

Flannery, T. 1994, *The Future Eaters: An Ecological History of the Australasian Lands and People*, Reed Books.

Johnson, K.N., ed, 1999, *Bioregional Assessments: Science at the Crossroads of Management and Policy*, Island Press, Washington, DC.

McGinnis, M.V. 1999, *Bioregionalism*, Routledge, London, p. 7.

Mumford, L. 1925, 'Regions – To Live In', *Survey Geographic* 7, pp. 91–93.

Register, R. 1998, 'Strategies and Tools for Building an Ecological Civilisation', in *Proceedings of Catalyst '99*, University of Canberra, Canberra, ACT.

Sale, K. 1985, *Dwellers in the Land*, Sierra Club Books, San Francisco, CA.

Uddin, K. and Birkeland, J. 1999, 'Applications of GIS in Bioregional Planning', *GIS '99 Conference*, Vancouver BC, March.

Questions

1. What are the advantages and disadvantages of the current move towards a single global market? List these in categories such as: human rights, the environment, employment and culture.

2. How many indigenous animals in your bioregion can you name?

3. What are the key bioregional indicators for defining the region you live in?

4. Try to list as many advantages and disadvantages of a bioregional economy that you can.

5. What would be the main impediments in achieving a bioregional society? How can these be addressed?

6. Draw a diagram of the sources of water, energy and sewage systems in your bioregion.

Projects

1. Cognitive mapping (Each person needs a large piece of paper with coloured pens and pencils.)

- Draw a conceptual map of your daily life. Mark the place that is most central to your experience (home, place of work or study). Then mark the other significant places and show links between these places and the way in which you travel (eg by foot, car, train).

- Mark the boundaries of your 'home' region – the area you feel most connected to and concentrate on this area.

- Mark the natural and social features of your place: hills, mountain ranges, defining landscape features, streams, beaches, significant areas of indigenous vegetation. Mark any places especially important to you: places of inspiration, refuge, animals that signify your home place. What are the seasonal variations? What influence does the weather have on your life? Where is food grown? What seasonal variation are there in your travel patterns?

- Mark the main limits and opportunities for your home place.

- Work out who lives closest to whom. Each person should explain their own map. Are there any correlations in the maps? Discuss.

2. List all the government agencies and authorities that have decision-making powers affecting the region. Do these have conflicting mandates? What would be the best form of natural resource governance for your bioregion?

Box 30   Bioregional Boundaries

Janis Birkeland

Ecological sustainability and biodiversity protection require that agricultural, manufacturing and construction industries be transformed to function within the limits of the carrying capacity of the bioregion. Mapping material and energy flows on a bioregional basis will assist in determining the most ecologically appropriate systems of production and construction for different regions [31]. To date, bioregional analysis is impeded by a lack of existing data that can be aligned with regional boundaries. Moreover, data from different sources on stocks and flows of basic materials (such as water, wood and energy) often do not add up, due to different methods of measurement.

But perhaps a more fundamental impediment to bioregional planning is that the concept of boundaries itself does not match the realities and characteristics of ecosystems. A premise in bioregional literature is that one set of (nested) boundaries needs to be defined for all political, cultural and ecological features. First, focusing on defining regional boundaries can give a misleading view of natural systems dynamics. There are fundamental differences between fluid natural systems and rigid human-constructed boundaries. On the one hand, the range of different structures and processes that underlie natural systems often do not coincide, and are certainly not static. Natural systems are adaptive, self-organising entities, whose boundaries are constantly shifting (eg rivers move, climates change, species adapt). One the other hand, boundaries are necessary for administrative purposes, which result in rule-based and regulated management systems. Because administrative boundaries effect power relationships, they are difficult to change.

There are also problems trying to separate local and global environmental boundaries. Thinking in terms of nested regions at difference scales (georegions, ecoregions, bioregions, etc) does not take into account the influence of large-scale global forces, such as climate change, and how climate interacts with local topographical and micro-climatic variations. Natural phenomena are more like Chinese puzzles than Russian dolls. Thus, it may be better to adapt environmental mapping to the idea of overlapping and fluid boundaries, rather than hierarchical ones.

The emphasis on trying to establish boundaries that mesh different kinds of human and natural systems stems from two contradictory visions within bioregional philosophy:

- the political or transformative value of community building and creating a sense of place, versus

- the need to develop land uses, businesses and industries that fit the biophysical limitations of the region or catchment.

The desire to merge governance, culture and ecology into one bioregion is based on the notion that if people identify with a region they will understand, value and protect it. But there is no necessary connection between values and the capacity to design appropriate development.

Planning should focus on enhancing each natural system's capacity for self-organisation within the constraints of needs and parameters created by other systems. This means the data should be relevant to the particular land use or ecosystem, rather than a geographical region. In short, for purposes of research, policy making and systems design, a new environmental management framework is needed at the regional level. A better starting point might be to map critical issues (eg water, energy), or whatever are determined to be the most fundamental limiting systems in the region. Using advances in computer modelling capability, it is now possible to map these crucial systems separately and examine the overlays, conflicts and potential synergies.

The process should identify weak points in fixed and fundamental limiting systems at the regional level. By mapping the flows in the system we can then find leverage points to optimise that limited resource (eg improve water quality and distribution mechanisms). For example, in Australia, where salinisation of both land and waterways is a big problem, salt can be drawn off fields to be used in dying (colouring) materials, or salt lakes can be used to produce solar heat, and so on. That is, uses can be found for salt that removes it from the land for profitable purposes. Observing the operation of eco-innovations that improve the health of primary ecological systems while improving the economy can be as educational as learning to empathise with one's region.

John J. Todd

Environmental management tools are sometimes dismissed as 'academic', 'obvious' or 'irrelevant' by designers. However, each procedure has been very carefully structured and refined over several decades of use. They are designed to minimise the risk of oversight, highlight areas of ignorance, and facilitate appropriate interaction with clients and the community. As such, their routine application represents the bottom line of responsible design practice. Any design process that has not rigorously applied appropriate management tools for optimising environmental performance does not represent 'ecodesign'.

Introduction

There are many design tools available to assist sustainable or restorative design, such as life cycle assessment (LCA), environmental impact assessment (EIA), environmental auditing (EA), and environmental management systems (EMS). These tools serve two basic purposes. They reduce the risk of providing designs that are poor from an ecological perspective, and they reassure prospective clients that systems are in place to produce the required environmental outcome. It is therefore essential that designers understand and apply these tools as a routine part of their practice.

In making a judgement as to whether or not something is sustainable, one can either use intuition or objective assessment. When it comes to complex systems, such as ecosystems, intuitive decision making can be fraught with danger. The tools described here help achieve an objective assessment. Nonetheless optimum use of these tools still requires skill and experience.

Environmental impact assessment

Environmental impact assessment (EIA) is the first of the environmental management tools to be applied to any proposed development. It is a predictive tool. By objectively considering the environmental consequences (negative and positive) of a development early on in the planning process, it is often possible to improve the proposal so that less environmental harm occurs.

All Australian states have legislation in place that requires a formal EIA for significant developments. This means that architects working on larger developments, such as resorts, shopping centres and industrial premises, will have to comply with well-defined EIA procedures **[12.4]**. The principles are covered in many texts (eg Thomas 1996; Gilpin 1995) and the details are available from state government authorities. A list of government contact addresses is provided in Todd (1997).

Designers should not restrict their use of EIA to situations where the law requires its application because it is also a valuable tool for small projects. An environmentally conscious business should develop internal mechanisms for predicting environmental outcomes for all new projects. The following steps are important for ecodesigners:

- EIA must be done during the design stage, with the intention of improving/altering the design as the EIA process unfolds.

- The EIA process must begin with a detailed description of the environment existing before the development takes place. In the case of a new building, this straightforward. In the case of design of consumer items, it becomes less clear. A clock radio is likely to be used on a bedside table where people spend many hours in close proximity. Thus, low level electromagnetic fields become more important than for a wall-mounted clock.

- The characteristics of the development must be thoroughly documented, and then the impact of placing the development in the existing environment assessed. At this stage, improvements in design can be incorporated in an **iterative process** until adverse impacts are minimised. This notion of 'lowering' a new development into an existing environment and trying to predict how the environment will change can be quite enlightening. There are many devices available to assist in this predictive process, ranging from simple check lists to complexcomputer models.

- A clearly written statement of the existing environment,

the development characteristics and the predicted impacts must be prepared for public or critical peer review. Often, someone less familiar with a design will see issues that have been overlooked by those engrossed in the project. Writing an EIA for review by others may be seen as unproductive or 'impossible' in the inevitable tight time frame for projects. However, if this step is skipped, it is not best practice design.

- Finally there must be a mechanism and willingness to take on any valid criticism of the design, rather than brushing it aside as too late or too hard.

Life cycle assessment

Life cycle assessment (LCA): LCA aims to provide an objective method for evaluating the total environmental burden of a product or activity, by identifying all the material and energy inputs and wastes. The relative harm of each of these inputs and outputs is then assessed. Opportunities for reducing the environmental impact of the product may also be included in the LCA. LCA is a very ambitious assessment method that requires large inputs of information. However, once the pioneering studies are done, and public databases become available, LCA becomes accessible to small businesses for application to their products. LCA is the key ecodesign tool for consumer products.

For a typical consumer product, there are several stages that must be considered. Raw materials will be mined or harvested, requiring energy and creating waste, and perhaps involving land degradation and hazardous chemicals. Transporting raw materials to the next stage of the production process will require more energy and cause more releases of pollutants. At each processing stage there will be other uses of energy and materials and more waste produced. The completed product may require further energy for use (eg a light globe) or more materials (eg water use in a toilet). At the end of its useful life, the product may be recycled or simply disposed of.

The complexity of LCA means that it is important to follow an accepted method; otherwise one result cannot be directly compared with another. As with EIA, it is essential to prepare a written statement (EIS) that is subject to peer review. The Society of Environmental Toxicology and Chemistry (SETAC 1993) has developed comprehensive guidelines for LCA which, in slightly modified form, has been adopted as the international standard method (ISO 14040-43). The four main stages of LCA are:

Scoping: In keeping with moves towards greater 'transparency' in decision making and reporting, the scope should indicate the methods used, assumptions made, who is funding the LCA and what it will be used for. It must clearly indicate to the reader how much reliance can be placed on the outcome.

Inventory analysis: The inventory analysis component of LCA attempts to quantify all the inputs and outputs associated with manufacture, use and disposal of a product. This requires a sound knowledge of each step in the manufacturing process. Sometimes quite toxic materials may be released in small quantities, but the environmental impacts could be large.

Impact assessment: The list of materials identified in the inventory component must be converted into a measure of environmental harm. This is done in three steps:

- All substances are grouped into 'environmental impact categories' covering human and ecological health and resource depletion (eg climate change, human toxicant, photochemical oxidant, ecological toxicant, biotic depletion).

- Each substance within the group is characterised and given a relative weighting. For example, one unit of methane has 14 times as much global warming potential as one unit of carbon dioxide.

- The relative importance of each of the impact categories is specified. This the most subjective step. For example, the relative importance of climate change gases compared to substances causing eutrophication in waterways must be determined. Sometimes a consensus of 'experts' can lend greater objectivity. If a valuation proves impossible, the LCA might simply present the total impacts under a number of impact categories and leave it up to the user of the LCA to decide which is most important.

The aim of this impact assessment is to present, in a simple final form, a *quantitative* measure of the total environmental burden of the product or project in question.

Improvement assessment: The final component of LCA addresses the critical question of how production might be altered to reduce environmental harm. Attempts at reducing environmental harm at one point may simply increase it elsewhere. The LCA can assist in identifying means to attain an overall improvement.

Environmental audit

An environmental audit (EA): EA is an objective check on how well a business is meeting its environmental obligations. It may include assessment of management practices, emissions, use of best practice pollution control, environmental credentials of suppliers of components or raw materials, site contamination, compliance with environmental laws, and a range of other environmental features of the business. EA differs from EIA in two important respects: (a) it is not just an examination of environmental impacts, it may also be an examination of the management processes of the company doing the design work or manufacturing the product; and (b) it is a measure of actual performance, not a prediction. The *Environmental Audit Guidebook* (Brown 1993) provides a comprehensive overview of EA approaches and should be on all designers' shelves.

EA is not usually not compulsory. The trouble and expense of conducting an EA will, however, help designers convince clients that they are 'doing the right thing' by the environment. To be effective, the EA must genuinely seek out any problem areas. Sometimes, the fact that the EA is an internal document, not requiring public release, can make it easier to seek out a frank assessment from the auditors.

EA can serve another valuable role for designers. It can be applied to completed developments that went through the EIA process to see how accurate the predictions of potential environmental harm or benefit actually were. If predictions in the EIA proved incorrect, a better system for predicting impacts can then be implemented.

Environmental management systems

Linked to the notion of auditing is the question of what makes a good environmental management structure within a business. The **environmental management system** (EMS) is an approach aimed at developing best practice management. It requires a commitment to continual environmental improvement. A business must not rest on its laurels, but seek ways of improving its environmental performance all the time.

Effective EMS means a company must have:

- An environmental policy (set by top management and conveyed to employees).
- Planning (proper documentation, reporting mechanisms, clear responsibilities).

- Implementation and operation processes (adequate budgets, training, maintenance, community communication, emergency plans and training, hazard analysis).
- Checking and corrective action (monitoring, compliance checks, audits).
- Management review (regular review of the EMS).

EMS can be applied to large or small businesses, to designers running their own practice from home. It is necessary to take a set of guidelines (eg International Standard ISO 14001) and systematically run through each step as it applies to the business under investigation. A standard approach is important because it provides a clear target for businesses and government agencies that genuinely wish to achieve environmental best practice.

Businesses can have their operations independently audited and gain EMS accreditation. When dealing with other companies with EMS in place, or government agencies, accredited businesses are likely to be given preference over non-accredited businesses.

Conclusion

Designers not rigorously applying EIA, LCA and EA to all their work, and without an EMS, should be ineligible to claim that they are 'ecodesigners'. Ecodesign only means something if it requires additional effort to attain, and protects the label from less informed designers. The problem of deliberate false claims of ecodesign can only be addressed through an enforced accreditation process. Unless there is something 'concrete' to accredit, such as the environmental management tools discussed here, any accreditation process will be ineffective.

References

Brown, G.A. 1993, *Environmental Audit Guidebook*, Centre for Professional Development, South Melbourne, VIC.

Elkington, J. 1994, *Company Environmental Reporting: A Measure of the Progress of Business and Industry towards Sustainable Development*, UN Environment Programme, Industry and Environment, Paris.

Fussler C. with James, P. 1996, *Driving Eco-innovation: A Breakthrough Discipline for Innovation and Sustainability*, Pitman Publishing, London.

Gertsakis, J., Morelli, N. and Ryan, C. 1998, *Return to Sender: An Introduction to Extended Producer Responsibility*, National Centre for Design at RMIT University, Melbourne, VIC.

Gilpin, A. 1995, *Environmental Impact Assessment (EIA) Cutting Edge for the Twenty-First Century*, Cambridge University Press, Cambridge.

Marcus, P.A. and Willig, J.T., eds, 1997, *Moving ahead with ISO 14000: Improving Environmental Management and Advancing Sustainable Development*, J. Wiley, New York.

SETAC 1993, *Guidelines for Life-Cycle Assessment: A 'Code of Practice'*, Society of Environmental Toxicology and Chemistry, Pensacola, FL.

Thomas, I. 1996, *Environmental Impact Assessment in Australia: Theory and Practice*, Federation Press, Leichardt, NSW.

Todd, J.J. 1997, *Environmental Impact Assessment, Environmental Design Guide*, DES 15, Royal Australian Institute of Architects, Canberra, ACT.

Welford, R. 2000, *Corporate Environmental Management 3: Towards Sustainable Development*, Earthscan, London.

Questions

1. Develop an argument as to why it is so important to get outside experts to critically examine an EIA, LCA or EA.

2. Consider designing a typical household item, such as a refrigerator or lounge suite. What would the environmental impact statement (EIS) for such an item include?

3. Map out the main issues in LCA – scoping, inventory, impact assessment and improvement assessment – in the case of a chair and/or house.

4. Consider the environmental benefits and burdens caused by the collection of glass bottles for recycling. How would you decide if benefits outweighed the adverse effects? What needs to be measured? What is the solution?

5. A client has requested the design of an environmentally sound home. Should window frames be wood or aluminium? (eg aluminium uses far more embodied energy in production, but can reduce drafts, requires less maintenance, and lasts much longer.)

6. If you were running your own small design business, what environmental management systems would you put in place?

Projects

1. LCA requires the relative ranking of different types of environmental harm. Using the library, develop a numerical ranking for: arsenic, carbon monoxide, chlorofluorocarbons, siltation, noise, lead, carbon dioxide, methane, plutonium, and nitrogen gas.

2. As a group, conduct an environmental audit of the building you are in. Develop a list of basic improvements and provide this to the relevant officials.

Box 31   Regional Sustainability Audits

Janis Birkeland and John Schooneveldt

A significant international trend is to analyse environmental problems that result from the design of human settlements and land use systems by analogy to metabolic systems. Traditionally, metabolism is a biological concept that is now also being applied to human designed entities in the **anthroposphere** such as industrial plants, urban areas, economic zones, regions, and even whole nations. Just as biological organisms have particular inputs, outputs, regulating processes and links to the wider environment – without which they cannot survive – regions and cities take in nutrients/resources/energy, transform these into useful building blocks or products, and dispose of waste products.

Agrarian societies were characterised by circular metabolism, because nutrients from crops, animals and food wastes were deposited back in the region. Urbanisation introduced linear systems, where goods, substances and wealth moved primarily from the hinterland to the city. The export of food from fertile regions to urban areas meant a transfer of organic matter to the places where the resources were consumed. This gradually depleted surrounding regions of organic matter, often leading to the collapse of civilisations. However, the invention of chemical fertilizer in the late 1800s enabled urban expansion by reviving the fertility of tributary farmland areas.

Consequently, garbage and sewage in urban regions became 'waste' rather than soil builders. Cities produced more solid and liquid waste than the surrounding terrestrial and aquatic ecosystems could assimilate. In the long term, this linear flow of nutrients led to costly sewage disposal, drinking water contaminated with fertiliser runoff, reduced species diversity due to excess nitrogen, the suffocation of rivers and lakes with algal blooms, landfills leaching chemicals into groundwater and rivers, methane into the atmosphere and so on. Most environmental problems relate to these inputs, outputs and transformations:

- **Inputs:** At the urban scale, disruption to ecosystems result from impacts related to metabolic inputs, such as the harvesting of vegetation for food, timber and fibres (causing soil erosion, salinisation, disruption of nutrient cycles, loss of biodiversity and the progressive colonisation of the natural world).

- **Outputs:** Chemical pollution is associated mainly with metabolic outputs (causing acid rain, heavy metals, contamination of rivers with nitrogen and phosphorus, greenhouse emissions and ozone depletion and the release of an increasing number of toxic substances into the biosphere).

- **Transformation (internal metabolism):** Energy and resource consumption are particularly associated with internal metabolism in transportation systems, infrastructure and facilities, consumerism, heating and air-conditioning buildings, and recycling products.

Ecological sustainability will entail the redesign of human settlements along the lines of ecological or 'closed loop' systems, where waste is avoided or treated as a resource (ie a circular rather than a linear metabolism). To achieve this, tools for integrated approaches to **natural resource management** must be developed, that enable planners and designers to understand urban form and infrastructure, construction and agriculture, services and distribution networks as whole and interdependent systems.

Techniques are being developed for mapping the overall pattern of resource and energy consumption; that is, the inputs, outputs and transformation of energy and materials within a region or urban area. Tracing the flow of materials and calculating transfers of natural and manufactured material (resource and capital) out of an urban region, in relation to those flowing in, provides a 'sustainability audit' of a region that integrates economic, social and environmental dimensions. This audit can pinpoint where the anthroposphere is impacting on the biosphere in unsustainable ways, and enable potential problems to be diagnosed and corrected by design before they become irreversible.

Janis Birkeland

Designers should understand and integrate information from environmental impact assessments (EIA) into the design process. Designers have a responsibility to examine the planning and design implications of EIAs and, if appropriate, alert clients or their consultants to any inadequacies of the report. However, designers must also be aware that EIAs are only imperfect aids, which merely improve the information base of decisions.

Introduction

Investment and development decisions by public officials, such as selling off public land and resources, or building roads, dams or sewage systems, must take into account broader health, environment and safety considerations, or else taxpayers will be burdened with the long-term costs. From 1969, the EIA process was instituted in many states and countries to ensure that environmental factors were included in the consideration of development proposals likely to have a detrimental impact on the environment (Gilpin 1995). EIA was an important step towards integrating long-term, non-material and multi-dimensional impacts into the cost–benefit equation of development decisions.

However, because EIAs are simple analyses of development impacts occurring within complex open systems, they generally cannot provide answers, only information. Further, the process is not intended to prevent environmentally damaging projects, and public criticism of the EIA does not necessarily lead to changes. Its purpose is not to assess public opinion, but to draw decision makers' attention to environmental risks. EIA should instead be used as a proactive tool to help designers achieve greater eco-efficiencies, not just as a retroactive project assessment mechanism for officials. Accordingly, it is important that design professionals understand their limitations as well as benefits and, where appropriate, take steps to identify and overcome any project deficiencies through redesign, not impact mitigation.

Benefits of EIAs

The EIA assists public decision makers to be more disciplined,

informed and objective in making determinations on complex or contentious development issues. The EIA has doubtless also improved government evaluation of development proposals by:

- Making it easier to be consistent, objective and rational in project assessment.

- Making the basis of development decisions more transparent to the public.

- Making the values beneath government decisions more explicit, or helping to validate the views and preferences of the general public.

- Forcing consideration of alternatives.

- Integrating scientific analysis and information into decision making, while demystifying scientific expertise.

- Creating a place in government agencies for scientists and interdisciplinary professionals (thus influencing the organisational culture of these agencies).

The EIA process may result in conditions being placed on the development approval; for example, more energy-efficient design, cleaner technology, or even a better location for the project. Because of the time and costs involved in preparing EIAs, they are sometimes viewed as a burden by developers. However, EIAs can improve the financial information base of private investment decisions. Moreover, they can result in significant savings if begun at an early stage in the development process, because resource and energy reductions usually coincide with environmental impact reduction. EIAs also alert developers and owners to potential legal risks and future management costs arising from health and safety issues that could result in 'toxic tort' law suits or 'sick building syndrome' [7.3].

Some problems with the EIA process

EIA processes vary, so a representative or generic (federal) government process is used here to illustrate common criticisms and possible solutions.

Many projects are not subject to EIAs: Many large-scale

247

infrastructure and development decisions made in the private sector can escape assessment. For example, private developments are not subject to the EIA process unless some separate Commonwealth decision must be made concerning the proposed project. Where a government decision is involved, the government agency responsible may chose not to refer a project to the relevant environmental protection agency (EPA), and thus the project may escape public oversight. Logically, all major projects with potentially adverse environmental impacts should be made subject to EIA procedures, or the EPA should have discretion to trigger the assessment process (as is the case in some EIA systems). Where projects are not subject to EIAs, designers should encourage their clients to conduct mini-EIAs.

The EIA is usually separate from the design process: The choice of materials, layout, processes and components can make a big difference in the adverse impacts of a type of industry, building or other land use. In fact, environmental impacts depend largely on the way projects are designed. The current legislation does not specify when or whether the assessment should begin. If not undertaken at the same time that the project is being planned and designed, proposed changes will usually be resisted by the developers, due to their 'sunk cost' in a preferred option. Designers should consult with EPA staff before site acquisition or the development of a schematic proposal, whether this is required or not.

The process focuses on individual projects: The environmental impact of a single project often seems small in comparison to, say, the jobs that will be created. A number of such projects can have significant cumulative and regional impacts, however. For example, one needs to look at – not just the one pulp mill that is approved – but the precedent this establishes. That is, there may be pressure to approve other mills in the region because they meet the same or higher environmental standard. In such cases, designers should encourage a cumulative impact assessment to be undertaken, where major new projects are assessed as part of a revised land use plan for the region. 'Scenario planning' (which analyses the consequences of alternative futures) is a related approach to addressing this problem.

The EIA is prepared by the proponents: EIAs are often used to defend a controversial development which was already endorsed on grounds other than fiscal and environmental responsibility. Where a government department that proposes a major project is the approval authority as well, the EIA may serve more as a promotional document than as an objective study. Accountability is enhanced where an independent

assessments office, or a separate division within the EPA reviews the adequacy of, edits and approves the EIA (that is, assumes authorship). Where this is not the case, the designer should advise their clients to use EIA consultants that are independent of the agencies. All authors and assessors of EIAs, and their qualifications, should be made public.

There is a bias against the 'no development' option: A major benefit of the EIA process is in identifying and evaluating alternatives. Sometimes, however, a narrow range of alternative developments is defined by the proponents. Where this is so, EIAs cannot determine the best use of land. The 'no development option', which seldom creates jobs, does not generally compare well to a proposed development as the benefits appear to be valueless. However, the economic benefits of leaving natural ecosystems intact (such as forests and river systems) may only be valued highly enough to protect when so unique as to be unsustainable as 'natural' systems. Designers can determine the functions most needed from a bioregional perspective [12.2], and where appropriate, demonstrate how natural systems can deliver these functions.

EIAs frame the issues as 'yes or no': Under the present EIA process, the decision is often perceived as a simple 'yes or no' issue, for example, 'to dam or not to dam'. A proposal for a more ecologically sound source of energy is not seriously considered in the absence of a developer ready to invest in an alternative energy producing facility. EIAs do not usually encourage the examination of the value of a dam in relation to, say, decentralised energy structures. Therefore, an EIA may impede our ability to find the best use of public investment capital. Examining the industrial and urban metabolism of a region is one way to develop a basis for public investment and planning decisions [Box 31].

The EIA looks at quantity, not quality, of jobs: EIAs tend to evaluate the number of jobs only. For example, dam construction appears to create more jobs than the 'no dam' alternative, partly because the question is framed to disregard the relative cost of the jobs created, the nature of the work, the social displacement entailed by a short-term construction project in a remote area, and alternative ways of creating jobs. More jobs might be created, for example, by assisting small business enterprises than by borrowing overseas funds to build a dam. The EIA process does not weigh in community building activity either. Designers should therefore seek to ensure that **social impact assessment** is conducted and integrated with environmental impact assessment.

EIAs tend not to look at cradle to cradle factors: It has been widely recognised that EIAs exclude many social costs, such as cumulative pollution, medical bills, lost options, clean-up costs, and other externalities. For instance, cost–benefit analyses for nuclear plants tended not to include the costs and risks of insuring or decommissioning nuclear plants. Consequently, these costs were left for taxpayers, investors and consumers to worry about; which amount to between 50 million to 3 billion dollars per plant, and rising. Designers should alert their clients to both public and private costs and the risks to business of ignoring them. In some cases, they may have a duty to inform the public of the hidden costs and risks of a proposed development.

The future is discounted: Long-term costs seem very remote and uncertain, and tend to be neglected. Government decision makers want to appear decisive and like to fast-track major decisions. Even when indirect and remote impacts are considered, such as effects on future generations, these are 'discounted', or reduced to current values. In fact, however, environmental costs increase over time. Designers can advocate the inclusion of an 'ecological factor', in lieu of the discount rate, which recognises that people will probably value the natural environment more in the future especially as it diminishes. This would help overcome the bias towards short-term profit in favour of investment in quality.

The project is seldom monitored for compliance: Once the project approval is granted, the environmental impacts are, in effect, ratified. That is, even unforeseen environmental effects are 'approved' when the building permit is issued. Follow-up procedures can be instituted to ensure that the assumptions and claims made in the EIA were reasonably accurate. Designers can encourage their clients to conduct post EIA audits to ensure that environmental safeguards are being followed and that information on developer's and builder's compliance is verified. Performance bonds can also be required to ensure environmental standards are met or rehabilitation occurs (eg after mining).

The EIA tends to be very technical in presentation: The technical nature of the EIA report can be intimidating to lay people. This can also mean that what is represented to be a participatory process is actually obfuscatory. One remedy to this exclusionary tendency is to provide funding for community groups concerned about the impact of a proposal, so they can obtain expert advice. Another is to ensure the right to contest the adequacy of an EIA report, or the procedures followed, and the merits of a development in the courts or special tribunal. Designers should ensure their clients understand how they will benefit from lay public involvement early in the design process by avoiding such disputes down the track [4.1, 6.3].

EIAs do not consider distributional aspects: Areas with low pollution, such as farm land, are likely prospects for industry location due to ambient air quality well above minimum standards (leaving more room for pollution). In urban areas, poor people tend to bear the costs of development, because it is usually cheaper to put an industry in an area with low property values. As well as ignoring costs, decision analysts often ignore the indirect subsidies and pre-existing benefits that the developer receives from the community which make the project likely to be profitable in the first place. Many projects could not stand on their own financially without these publicly provided benefits such as the existing infrastructure of roads, grants, tax shelters, and low-cost loans. Designers should take a broader view and incorporate reciprocal benefits for the local community in planning and design.

References

Bregman, J. 1999, *Environmental Impact Statements*, CRC Press, Boca Raton, FL.

Gilpin, A. 1995, *Environmental Impact Assessment (EIA) Cutting Edge for the Twenty-First Century*, Cambridge University Press, Cambridge.

Glasson, J. 1999, *Introduction to Environmental Impact Assessment*, UCL Press, Los Angeles, CA.

Harrop, O. and Nixon, A. 1998, *Environmental Assessment in Practice*, Routledge, London and New York.

Nichols R. and Hyman, E. 1980, *A Review and Analysis of Fifteen Methodologies for Environmental Assessment*, Center for Urban and Regional Studies, University of North Carolina at Chapel Hill, NC.

Parkin, J. 1993, *Judging Plans and Projects: Analysis and Public Participation in the Evaluation Process*, Avebury, Aldershot.

Thomas, I. 1996, *Environmental Impact Assessment in Australia Theory and Practice*, Federation Press, Leichardt, NSW.

Walthern, P. 1990, *Environmental Impact Assessment: Theory and Practice*, Routledge, London.

1. Debate: 'Public funds should be provided for community groups that are concerned about the environmental impact assessment of a project.'

2. Undertake a 'sketch' scenario planning exercise by charting the range of consequences that would follow from requiring new urban office buildings to provide more parking spaces or, alternatively, restrict parking spaces to a lower amount.

3. What are some of the indirect subsidies and pre-existing benefits that a commercial building receives from the community that contributes to the profitability of the project (eg existing infrastructure, minimum wage). Should such 'remote' public contributions to a development be considered a subsidy? Should urban developers provide some form of compensation or 'exaction fee' in the form of, say, public plazas, daycare or other facilities (as exists in some places)?

4. When a developer builds a project outside the urban area, should they be required to provide their own infrastructure, such as roads, water systems and open space?

5. What should a state or provincial government do when a factory plans to leave the jurisdiction because it cannot afford to upgrade its facilities to meet new environmental standards? What if it is known that the company plans to build a more modern factory in another jurisdiction, and will leave behind a toxic site for the community to deal with? (This has happened.)

6. If industries tend to locate in areas with low property values (and low wages), some think this should create more social equity, because development creates jobs. Why then is it often stated that poor people tend to bear the costs of development? How do emissions trading systems affect this?

1. Compare your state and national EIA legislation and make a table that explains the differences.

2. Obtain an EIS and prepare a critique. How many biases and/or unstated assumptions can you find?

Box 32   Mini Debates on EIAs

Janis Birkeland

Argue each side of the following statements:

1. EIAs should be required on all major development proposals, even where the project economic benefits clearly outweigh the environmental costs.

2. EIA processes can increase the public acceptance of contentious developments without reducing impacts.

3. The EIA and appeals process should focus on the outcomes or merits of decisions, rather than on whether decision-making procedures were followed or not.

4. The EIA process should concentrate on social, cultural and health impacts, rather than on biophysical factors.

5. The EIA should be undertaken after the project is completely planned and designed to ensure accuracy of information.

6. The EIA can result in economic savings, even though EIA preparation can add significantly to the project cost.

7. Nations should not have uniform procedures for EIAs, as administrative variations allow experimentation and preserve an 'institutional gene pool'.

8. The Action agency should not have discretion to decide that an EIA process is necessary or not, as it often has little expertise in environmental issues.

9. EIAs should be made public, even where there is a need for commercial confidentiality.

10. The purpose of the EIA process is not to improve the information base of decisions, but to prevent environmentally damaging projects.

11. If the adverse impacts are significant, the Action Minister should be required to stop a proposal from proceeding, rather than just to make public the reasons for the project being permitted.

12. EIAs for new projects should be assessed as part of a revised land use plan for the region which includes the proposed project, so that cumulative impacts can be identified.

13. EIAs should be produced by consultants that are independent of government agencies, rather than by consultants paid by the proponents.

14. EIAs should consider alternative 'green' developments and not just those defined by proponents or vested (corporate or government) development interests.

15. EIAs do not encourage the public to examine the value of the industry itself and therefore may impede its ability to find the best use of land.

16. Social impact assessment cannot be integrated with environmental impact assessment due to differing methodologies.

17. Government employees have a duty to inform the public of long-term costs and risks of a proposed development.

18. An 'ecological factor' should be used in lieu of a discount rate, as people will probably value the environment more in the future.

19. Post-EIS audits can ensure that environmental safeguards are being followed by the developer.

20. Performance bonds should be required to ensure that environmental standards are met or rehabilitation occurs (eg after mining).

21. Community groups should be provided funds to review the adequacy of EIAs for projects that impact upon their community.

22. The overseas aspects and impacts of developments within a country need to be weighed in (eg imported tropical timber).

23. Judicial review of EIA decisions should be allowed by third parties.

24. An administrative appeals tribunal should be set up to examine EIA decisions on their merits and substitute its own decision where the facts do not support the government's decision.

25. The EIA process should be a design-oriented, rather than an accountancy-oriented, approach to environmental issues.

26. EIAs should put a dollar figure on all the externality costs.

Ambient: the background level of environmental pollution that exists in a particular environment, including noise.

Analogy: a reference to a similarity between things in different domains. In the design context (and in contrast to the use of metaphor), analogy facilitates a dialogue between an idea and the design problem.

Androcentrism: a value system that elevates characteristics identified as masculine attributes by the culture over those seen as feminine.

Anthropocentric: an attitude which conceives of everything in terms of human-centred values. For example, the value of animals or plants is seen to lie principally in their usefulness to human beings.

Anthroposphere: the human-made environment.

Appropriate technology: technology that is low impact and designed to serve human needs.

Assimilation: a policy of absorbing Aborigines into the dominant culture.

Atrium ('litetrium'): a light well or an interior covered courtyard providing natural lighting.

Backcloth: the supporting structure for the traffic in question: social, physical, cultural, economic; 'traffic' on the backcloth can mean cars, or any other collective entity such as a population, a disease, a building or a suburban tract development.

Ballasts: the transformer in fluorescent lights which provides the current and voltage.

Best available technology: where a particular form of environmental technology is specified by environmental legislation, to minimise environmental impacts.

Best practicable technology: legislation requiring best practicable technology allows firms to install the technology that they think most affordably meets a given standard.

Bio-based economy: another term for 'carbohydrate economy', where carbohydrates replace hydrocarbons. Plants, not minerals, supply raw materials for factories.

Bio-based materials: materials made from agricultural by-products or plants; that is, carbohydrates, not including petrochemicals.

Biocentrism: a view of reality that puts nature at the centre, or values things in terms of ecological, as opposed to human-centred, values.

Biocumulative: materials (organic or inorganic) that build up in the bodies of plants and animals over time, as the members of the food chain consume one another.

Biodiversity: the variety of all life-forms (plants, animals and micro-organisms) in an area, often considered at four levels: genetic diversity, species diversity, ecosystem diversity and landscape diversity.

Biome: a large, well-defined, ecological region characterised by a dominant vegetation or life form (eg tropical rain forest, coral reef, frost pocket); or a complex of life forms and their life support system (habitat).

Bionic method: a product design methodology which begins with an examination of natural systems, particularly bio-mechanical aspects.

Bioregion: bio-geographical region with relative ecological integrity and a recognisable functional boundary, often a river catchment and/or a socio-cultural attachment region ('place').

Bioregionalism: planning that starts from the ecology of a region, where regions are defined by biological rather than political boundaries.

Biosphere: the parts of the Earth's surface and atmosphere inhabited by living organisms.

Biota: animal and plant life forms or living entities of a region.

Biotics: body of knowledge relating to life forms or living organisms.

Black box analysis: an analysis that considers relationships between individuals, organisations or institutions, but does not examine the entities themselves.

Bounty: an amount paid to the producer for the goods before they reach the consumer.

Carbohydrate economy: an industrial system where carbohydrates replace hydrocarbons.

Carbon cycle: the cycle wherein carbon dioxide from the atmosphere is converted to fibre by plants, and then released back into the atmosphere when plants rot or burn. Some carbon also becomes part of the carboniferous strata as coal, natural gas or petroleum or limestone.

Carbon dioxide (CO_2): a natural component of air produced when animals breath, vegetables rot, or when any material containing carbon (ie fossil fuels) burns. Due to excessive production of human-caused emissions of CO_2, it is a major component of the enhanced 'greenhouse' effect.

Carrying capacity: a population or environmental impacts that a natural area can support without reducing its ability to support that species in the future. The carrying capacity of humans also depends upon the efficiency with which humans use the resources.

Certification: recognition that planning and design documentation are in accordance with regulations, codes and standards, and/or that the constructed works are in accordance with those provisions.

Chain of custody: the channel through which products are distributed from their origin in the ground to their end use.

Charges: a price paid for using resources or polluting the environment.

Circular metabolism: the reintegration of urban 'wastes' into human production and consumption activities.

Clay: a fine-grained soil produced either as a sedimentary deposit, or by the decomposition of rock. It is used as a binder, or natural cementing agent, in the construction of earth walls.

Closed-loop systems: where waste heat and other environmental impacts are reprocessed and/or used for another productive purpose (see no loop systems).

Cohousing: residential community designed to encourage social interaction, self-management, and sharing of facilities, while also reducing economic and environmental costs.

Colloids: a substance consisting of very fine particles which, when mixed with water, are too fine to settle and remain in suspension to form a gel.

Commons: public land shared by and accessible to the whole community.

Community learning networks: communication links formed within and among resident communities that facilitate sharing of information, knowledge and expertise.

Community value: the overall value, held by individuals or groups within a community, for a place. Community value may include formally recognised values, such as social, aesthetic, historic and amenity values.

Community visioning: a participatory, consensus-building exercise which involves developing a collective vision for a particular point in the future, leading to the definition of agreed goals and strategies.

Community: a group of people having shared values, social interaction and a common sense of identity.

Complexity theory: a generic term for theories derived from research into chaos and complex systems, which suggest that evolution occurs through optimal levels of interaction.

Comprehensive plan: a land use plan which seeks to implement a broad set of social goals such as ecologically sustainable development.

Conditional use: a form of planning approval where a project is permitted if it meets certain special requirements in addition to basic planning code restrictions.

Connectivity/Connectance: strength and type of connection between elements in a system. Hierarchy Theory (Allen and Starr), Q-analysis and molecular biology modellers take a particular interest in structure and dynamics of connectedness.

Conserver society: a society that lives in harmony with nature's limits. The transition from consumer society to conserver society is one of the principle goals of the environment movement.

Contextual design: design that blends in with the existing urban fabric or complements existing facades, building heights or landscapes.

Convention: a customary practice or implicit agreement on social conduct, as opposed to written rules or laws.

Creative play environment: includes all outdoor environments designed to facilitate 'free' play (that is, exploratory, representational and imaginative play) and accommodate social interaction, rather than just physical exercise.

Culm: the pole that grows from a bamboo shoot.

Cultural landscapes: those parts of the environment that have been influenced by human activity and, as such, express human attitudes and values. A cultural landscape may exist as an individual or collective memory, as well as a physical fabric.

Cumulative impacts: environmental impacts that are increased by the addition of successive environmental impacts. This can lead to specific environmental impacts growing exponentially.

Cyclic economy: an economy designed as a continuous cyclic flow of materials, rather than a linear one.

Decarbonisation: where industrialised countries move away from high carbon fuel sources such as firewood and coal, to oil and low carbon sources such as natural gas.

Deconstruction: a literary technique adapted to design which plays on conflicting logics to create contradictions in apparent structure.

Deductive approach: inference from the general to particular.

Deep ecology: a view that holds that human actions should be judged by their effect on the integrity of ecosystems. Deep ecologists have argued that we will care for the natural world if we understand it as an extension of ourselves.

Defensive expenditure: expenditure to avoid, mitigate or repair environmental impacts.

Dematerialisation: a decline in the materials and energy intensity of industrial production – a trend in industrially developed economies.

Demographics: the science of vital and social statistics of populations.

Design for disassembly: design details enabling future reuse or recycling of materials. For instance, bolted instead of nailed timber connections.

Design parameters: key factors and constraints to be accommodated by the design.

Development application: an application lodged to obtain a planning approval.

Discretionary review: a project review process that enables a project to be evaluated on policy or criteria outside the literal planning code provisions.

Dominant paradigm: a contra-ecological way of thinking that has led to an unsustainable system of development and economic growth.

Eco-cities: cities designed in response to community needs and functioning as integral parts of the biosphere.

Eco-cycle/eco-cycling: the cycle of transformation of matter and energy in an ecosystem; the nutrient and waste loop closure in human settlements; reconnecting human settlement wastes to primary production; recycling and refuse-resource coupling in industrial situations.

Eco-efficiency: product, process or service design that minimises energy, resources and waste.

Ecofeminism: a theory or paradigm that seeks to expose cultural assumptions that are used to legitimise ecological destruction. Ecofeminists have argued that the human oppression and the exploitation of nature are closely linked.

Eco-industrial park: a complex of industrial producers that create 'multi-dimensional' recycling systems or 'food webs' between companies and industries.

Eco-innovation: eco-innovation that addresses social and environmental needs while greatly reducing net resource/energy consumption or increasing positive social, economic and environmental spin-offs.

Eco-logical design: design that is ecologically and socially responsible (empowering, restorative, eco-efficient, transformative).

Ecological footprint: the equivalent land (and water) area required to support a given human population and its material standard indefinitely, including the local and global effects caused by resources used and wastes produced (ie the carrying capacity appropriated from other places).

Ecological modernisation: a discourse that recognises the structural character of environmental problems, but nonetheless assumes that existing institutions can internalise care for the environment.

Ecological rating system: a weighted score of environmental impacts to compare alternative components/materials, projects or proposals.

Ecologically sustainable development (ESD): using, conserving and enhancing the community's resources so that ecological processes are maintained, and the total quality of life, now and in the future, can be maintained or improved.

Eco-Marxism: a philosophy which considers that environmental degradation is a direct result of class society and its forces of production, and can be reversed through a classless or socialistic political system.

Economic growth: a real increase in GDP, usually in total GDP, but should be in GDP per capita.

Economies of scale: the reduction of average costs of production with increasing output, due to the sharing of fixed costs over a larger number of units; that is, the lower extra (marginal) cost of each additional unit causes the average cost per unit to fall.

Economic rationalism: the policy approach that makes traditional economic values the basis of what is deemed rational.

Ecoregion: a bioregional boundary at the largest scale – usually incorporating smaller regions.

Eco-socialism: a philosophy which identifies individualism and economic forces as the central causes of environmental destruction and calls for a more egalitarian social structure.

Ecosystem services: the role played by organisms in creating a healthy environment for human beings, from production of oxygen to soil formation and maintenance of water quality.

Ecosystem: a community of mixtures of plants, animals, and their physical, chemical, biological and atmospheric environment, functioning together as a relatively interdependent unit. It represents a complex dynamic recycling system, linking the biotic and abiotic worlds.

Edible landscapes: designed landscapes that produce food.

Efficiency: a measure of output per unit of input. Eco-efficiency means reducing resource consumption, pollution and waste.

Embodied energy analysis: the systematic study of the energy inputs and outputs of any process where numerical values are assigned to each input.

Embodied energy: the total energy required by all of the activities associated with a production process, including the proportions consumed in all processes 'upstream' (to acquire, transport, process, manufacture, and install a material or product). In relation to the full life cycle of a material or product, it would also include the energy required for maintenance and repair, as well as demolition and disposal and reuse, and the share of energy used in making equipment and in other supporting functions.

Emissions trading: a market based system that allows firms (or other entities) to buy the pollution rights of less polluting entities.

End-of-pipe controls: technologies used to minimise environmental pollution after it has been created. They are often criticised for not encouraging the prevention of pollution.

Energy intensity: the total energy embodied in one unit of a product, unless specified as the direct or indirect energy intensity.

Energy: the enthalpy of fossil fuels and derivatives, or the enthalpy of the equivalent fossil fuel source.

Entropy: a measure of the disorganisation of a system. Higher entropy means energy that is in a more ordered and useable form.

Environmental audit (EA): a means of assessing how well a business or building is meeting its environmental objectives.

Environmental cost planning: setting benchmarks against which to assess environmental impacts.

Environmental impact assessment (EIA): a predictive tool used in the early stages of the planning process to assess the environmental impacts of a proposed development (including physical, chemical, visual, and resource distribution changes).

Environmental impact statement (EIS): the written statement of an environmental impact assessment.

Environmental justice: environmental impacts and other burdens of development are not equally distributed between rich and poor in most countries and between 'North' and 'South' globally. Environmental justice is an area of research that seeks to address these issues.

Environmental management system (EMS): an approach aimed at developing best practice for a company's management of its environmental impacts.

Environmental problematique: the term recognising that environmental problems require social, economic, and political, as well as ecological responses.

Environmental services: non-marketed goods and services, such as the aesthetic and recreational services of old-growth forests or the health-sustaining properties of clean air.

Environmental space: the total amount of energy and resources (including land, water and forests) that can be used sustainably, divided by the global population. It is a means of determining the fair share of resources for a country or individual.

Ergonomics: the science of designing equipment and products so as to reduce human fatigue and discomfort (human factors engineering).

Essentialism: the belief that humans have an essential or inherent nature; the term is frequently used to misrepresent feminism.

Externalise: to pass on the environment and social costs of production and development to the public and future generations (see internalise).

Externalities/Externality costs (or benefits): the non-marketed, non-compensated negative (or positive) consequences to third parties arising from the economic actions of others (eg the cost of river pollution that results from an industry upstream).

Feng Shui: the Chinese system of arranging the built environment so that we can live more harmoniously with the environment.

Fleece factor: the total area of carpet and soft furnishings divided by the volume of the room. The fleece factor indicates the size of the reservoir of dust and chemicals which continuously exchange with the air, leading to degraded air quality in enclosed spaces.

Force field analysis: a variant of SWOT analysis which, instead of looking at 'strengths, weaknesses, opportunities and threats', identifies and assesses hindering and facilitating forces in order to develop strategies for overcoming or promoting these forces.

Fordism: the mass production system developed by Henry Ford.

Forest product certification: a process which results in a written quality statement (a certificate) attesting to the origin of the wood and its status and/or qualifications.

Fractals: things that look the same from any scale.

Gender identification: accepting the values and norms associated with a gender in a given culture as one's own (eg 'Margaret Thatcher was masculine identified').

Genetic algorithm: a computer model of natural selection at the level of genes. They contain the necessary information to build an entity.

Genius loci: the spirit or special character of a place, especially with reference to subjective and sensory associations.

Genuine progress indicator (GPI): a composite measure that adjusts GDP for a range of social and environmental factors, including income distribution, unpaid household and voluntary work, crime, pollution and resource depletion, in order to provide a better measure of progress.

Georegion: an identifiable geological region, such as a plain or range of mountains.

Globalisation: the process of colonisation by large corporations throughout the world; economies become increasingly dependent through flows of capital and trade and trans-border asset ownership.

Grandfathering: an official exemption, or release, for an existing establishment to meet new and more stringent environmental measures. This is often done in order to prevent the closure of older established industries.

Green consumerism: consumption behaviours that minimise ecological and social impacts.

Green optimum: the idea of optimising the health and well-being of the whole system in ways that do not make people worse off, or less equal, in contrast to the Pareto Optimum.

Greenhouse gas: atmospheric gases which contribute to global warming, such as carbon dioxide, CFCs, and methane.

Greens (general): an environmental movement which identifies industrial growth and ill-advised government policies as major causes of environmental destruction, and seeks social change through greater ecological understanding and more sustainable practices.

Greywater: refers to household water used for washing purposes, and not contaminated with sewage.

Gross Domestic Product (GDP): the total value of all final goods and services produced within a nation over a given period, usually a year.

Habitat: native environment or home of specific plants, animals or humans.

Hemp hurds: the inner core of the hemp or cannabis plant.

Hemp: the fibre of the cannabis plant that can substitute for many materials made from timber.

Hierarchical dualism: the understanding of the world through a binary logic where one side of each dualism is believed to more valuable than the other (eg society values reason more highly than it does caring or sentimentality).

Holism, holistic: the view which recognises an emergent character of the whole which is more than the sum of its parts, or taking account the whole to which they contribute and the relationships between all parts.

Incrementalism: the planning philosophy that believes large mistakes will be avoided by progressing towards a goal through small, rather than large, steps.

Incubator programs: programs designed to encourage new (fledgling) firms.

Indicator: measurements used to simplify, quantify and communicate trends and events.

Indigenous design: design which uses local materials and traditional methods of construction rather than industrial processes or materials.

Indirect energy: the energy consumed in the provision of inputs of goods and services to a process.

Individual autonomy: the assumption that people are meant to be independent, competitive and free from restrictive social bonds.

Inductive approach: general inference from the particular.

Industrial ecosystem: industrial systems which emulate natural ecosystems by, for example, making maximum use of recycled materials in new production, optimising use of materials and embedded energy, and using 'wastes' as raw material for other processes.

Industrial metabolism: the rate which industry uses energy and produces waste.

Infestation: massed insect attack in a particular area.

Inherent value: the idea that something has value apart from its usefulness to humans; the opposite of instrumental value.

Instrumentalism: the belief that things have value only to the extent that they contribute to human welfare.

Integrated pest management (IPM): pest management approaches that place priority on non-chemical control measures to achieve maximum effect with minimum impact.

Integration: bringing parts into a whole.

Intentional community: a group formed with the prime intention of being, or becoming, a close-knit community with shared values.

Internalise: to incorporate the broader environmental and social costs of production and development into the monetary cost of the product or development.

Isochanvré: a brand name for hemp hurds.

Iterative process: repeating a calculation after changes have been made (such as estimating environmental impacts), then changing the design to reduce the worst impacts and re-calculating environmental impacts. The process is repeated until design changes no longer produce significant environmental improvements.

LETS: a community bartering system.

Liability insurance: financial protection to an insured party who might be required to pay damages resulting from legally negligent conduct.

Liberalism: a reductionist, atomistic conception of society that views people primarily as independent beings, rather than as members of communities.

Life cycle assessment (LCA): an analysis that traces the impacts of material and non-material inputs to the product or system (eg equipment used in manufacturing and operating the system, and disposing or recycling at the end of the product's life).

Life cycle cost analysis: looks at all costs over the full life of an asset.

Life quality indicators: qualitative measures that can be used to understand and measure the health of natural and human systems.

Light shelves: reflective horizontal window panels used to increase the amount of natural light in a building or space.

Linear causality: consequences and impacts seen to be linked to specific causes through linear relationships and thus deemed capable of being predicted and controlled.

Linear metabolism: practice of allowing (urban or industrial) wastes to be created or disposed of in a manner which increases the use of resources, and in many cases does not support the functions of human and ecological systems,

Linear progress: the belief that society will transcend nature through technology and social control.

Living Machines™ : a sequence of cylinders containing ecological systems supporting micro-organisms that treat chemicals and wastes.

Material flows analysis (MFA): a whole systems approach to sustainability auditing that goes beyond simple input–output models to map the stocks and flows of materials through urban, industrial or regional areas.

Marginal social cost pricing: a price equal to the marginal social cost.

Marginal social costs: the extra (marginal) real costs (that is, the sum of the economic costs plus any environmental and/or social externality costs) of an extra unit of production.

Meaning of place: thoughts, feelings, memories, and interpretations evoked by a landscape.

Mechanistic: the view that natural processes and functions can be largely replicated or substituted by machines.

Metaphor: a figure of speech in which a descriptive term is transferred to an object which it does not literally describe in order to suggest a similarity. With metaphor, the design process focuses on the idea rather than the objective design problem.

Morphing: to incrementally change the form, shape or structure of an object to resemble another object.

Multi-functional playgrounds: structures that connect different items of play equipment to form a play circuit.

Natural capital: natural or environmental assets that can be exploited by economic activity.

Natural resource management (NRM): environmental management that focuses on regional areas as a whole, including mining, agricultural and industrial systems.

Nature/culture dualism: the idea that nature and culture are separate rather than interdependent.

No loop systems: products, industries, buildings, or cities designed such that virtually no pollution or waste is created by the activity in the first place.

OECD (Organisation for Economic Co-operation and Development): a Paris-based multi-national organisation comprised of representatives from many of the world's developed countries.

Offsets: where there are tradable pollution rights, firms are sometimes allowed to expand their production by paying for reductions in emissions from facilities to compensate (offset) their own emissions.

Old-growth forest: forest that is ecologically mature and has been subjected to negligible unnatural disturbance such as logging, mining, road building and clearing.

Open system: a system which is not self-contained or that cannot be isolated from external influences.

Operating energy: the energy consumed in heating, cooling, lighting and otherwise living in a building (excluding construction).

Parabolic louvres: metal grids that help reduce glare from artificial lighting.

Parameter analysis: an approach that divides the design process into three phases 'parameter identification' (or problem setting), 'creative synthesis' (or problem solving) and evaluation. Understanding the iterative nature of the model allows the designer the freedom to concentrate on one stage at a time.

Pareto Optimum: the objective of making individuals or firms better off without making others worse off.

Pattern analysis: a design process that uses physical and biological patterns which underlie the existing landscape and cultural patterns as the basis for the design. It is essentially an application of Alexander's *A Pattern Language* (1977) to the landscape.

Perdurable: permanent structures (the opposite of temporary or ephemeral structures).

Performance bond: an advanced payment that is refundable upon compliance with specified environmental objectives; this reduce the cost of enforcing environmental legislation.

Performance codes: standards (of energy efficiency or other measure) that a building, material component, system or design must actually achieve to allow greater flexibility and freedom in design.

Performance regulation: these specify a standard or certain criteria (eg a maximum amount of emissions or a product energy rating) and allow businesses or industries to meet these criteria in any way they choose. They can provide an incentive to develop more efficient technologies to save costs and compete more effectively.

Permaculture: a system of design for sustainable and agriculturally productive landscapes and gardens based on the symbiotic diversity of natural ecosystems.

Perverse subsidies: subsidies to industries or sectors that are hidden, which make environmentally harmful activities more economically feasible.

Physical determinism: the view that design shapes a person's values, preferences or character as opposed to, for instance, the social environment.

Plantation: treed areas lacking most of the principal characteristics and key elements of native ecosystems resulting from planting, sowing or intensive silvicultural treatments.

Playgardens: a creative play environment where the play structures are fully integrated with the landscaping to encourage children to explore nature while developing physical and social skills.

Polluter pays principle: the idea that an industry can (in effect) pollute, as long as it pays compensation for the damage (eg through emissions charges, fines, tradable pollution rights and other regulatory devices), because industry will reduce pollution in order to save money or increase profits.

Positivist science: a philosophical orientation in science based on the position that only observable, measurable phenomenon should be recognised.

Post-industrial economy: a term to describe the nature of a fundamental cultural transition from a manufacturing to an urban office-based information economy, and the range of political, social, environmental and workplace changes that have accompanied this shift.

Precautionary principle: the idea that a lack of full scientific certainty should not be used as a reason for postponing measures to prevent environmental degradation; public and private decisions should seek the lowest level of unintended consequences.

Prescriptive codes: most building codes are primarily prescriptive, in that they prescribe the materials, components, connections, finishes, systems, dimensions, methods, and so forth. The prescriptive method can limit variation and impede innovation (see performance codes).

Prescriptive regulation: these usually require that a certain technology be used rather than a standard be met.

Primary energy: the enthalpy or energy value of energy resources or flux sources in their natural state (for example, the enthalpy of raw coal or the energy value of wind or solar energy).

Primary industry: industry that utilises raw materials, like forestry, mining, energy production and agriculture.

Pyramidal design: design that externalises the social costs of extraction, conversion, distribution of resources, and tends to concentrate land, material and energy in the interests of the powerful.

Quality of life: refers to total well-being, which includes physical, mental, social and spiritual well-being (not just material).

Rebound effect: refers to the fact that a portion of the income saved through more efficient production is often spent on increased material consumption elsewhere.

Reductionism: the belief that a complex phenomenon or event can be explained by analysing and describing its individual parts.

Rhizome: the woody underground portion of the plant from which both roots and shoots grow. Clumpers (sympodial) and runners (monopodial) have very different forms of rhizomes, which accounts for their different growth habit.

Risk–benefit analysis: a commonly used project review tool which analyses the tradeoffs of risks and benefits.

Scenario planning: a methodology that tries to analyse the consequences of alternative futures.

Self-determination: the right of a people to take responsibility for setting the social agenda and controlling policy implementation.

Sense of place: a feeling of identity, belonging and attachment to a place.

Sick building syndrome: illnesses caused by buildings, such as off-gassing of chemicals from synthetic furniture and building materials, air-conditioning and so on.

Silt: a natural deposit formed from the disintegration of rock, which can be used as a binder, or natural cementing agent, in the construction of earth walls.

Sink effect: where contaminants are absorbed into the material of soft furnishings.

Social ecology: a philosophy which identifies hierarchical structures and institutional forces as the main causes of environmental destruction. Social ecology holds that environmental sustainability will come about through an anarchistic approach to social organisation.

Social impact assessment: an analysis that examines the social consequences of a proposed development.

Social sustainability: This reflects the relationship between cultural ethics, social norms and development. An activity is socially sustainable if it conforms with ethical values and social norms, or does not stretch them beyond a community's tolerance of change.

Social transformation: a fundamental shift in economic, social and environmental (whole-systems) change.

Social value: the qualities for which a place has become a focus of spiritual, political, national or other cultural sentiment to a majority or minority group.

Stagflation: the phenomenon of simultaneous inflation and recession.

Stakeholder: people with a special interest in the decision or outcome.

Standard of living: the measure of material living conditions and well-being. Standard of living is usually measured as per capita GDP, and a rising standard of living is equated with economic growth.

Subsidy: something that is in effect a money grant to support an industry or activity.

Suburban sprawl: undifferentiated, low-rise urban development, typically lacking any obvious focus except shopping centres, and highly dependent on long-distance machine transportation.

Sustainability: the ability of future generations to achieve the same level of natural, social and cultural resources enjoyed by the current generation.

Sustainable development: development that does not interfere with the functioning of critical ecological processes and life support systems.

SWOT analysis: a group planning process for identifying 'strengths, weaknesses, opportunities and threats', with the aim of developing strategies (strengths and weaknesses refer to internal factors; opportunities and threats refer to external influences).

Symbiotic: a mutually beneficial association between members of different species.

Synergy: where elements acting in combination produce an effect greater than the sum of the parts or has an unexpected or enhanced effect.

Tacit knowledge: knowledge or skill gained by experience that is not necessarily conscious or articulated.

Techno-addiction: a non-rational attraction to or reliance on technology.

Technology: all of the products of design ranging from very simple artefacts, such as toothpicks or shoes, to complex networks of equipment, such as nationwide electrical power distribution systems.

Termite barrier: a method of termite control that relies on a physical barrier, such as stainless steel mesh or graded stone that prevents termites gaining access to wooden structures.

Termite colony nest: central location of the queen and nurseries for a termite colony.

Termite resistant: able to withstand attack by termites under most conditions.

Termiticides: agents designed to kill or repel termites.

Thermal mass: the potential heat storage capacity of a material.

Thermodynamics, first law of: material conservation; a process (eg combustion) that has the same amount of materials before and after the chemical reaction.

Thermodynamics, second law of: entropy or the degradation of energy from a concentrated form to a less concentrated form.

Tradeable pollution rights: rights to trade the difference between a pollution standard and the pollution allowed by existing laws.

Transparent process: a popular term with policy makers, implying that the steps and methods used in a process are made clear to the public.

Tyranny of small decisions: the aggregate negative effect of large numbers of apparently innocuous small decisions; especially as applied to planning.

Urban consolidation: higher-density urban form achieved by 'filling in the gaps' in the existing built form; seen as an opportunity to reduce the ecological footprint of urbanisation while enhancing social interaction.

Urban decentralisation: the distribution of the population into small self-sufficient communities, as opposed to urban consolidation.

Urban metabolism: refers to the material and energy inputs needed to meet the demands of living and non-living components of urban systems, and waste material and energy outputs.

Urban village: small urban communities that are considered to reduce the environmental impact of urban development, through mixed land uses, urban design and shared facilities.

Urbanisation: the shift of population from rural to urban areas.

User pays: where the public pays a charge to use resources, such as fees to enter parks or for fishing licences.

Utilitarian: designed for function and usefulness rather than aesthetics.

Utilitarianism: a philosophy best known for the idea that public decisions should be based on the greatest good for the greatest number.

Waste: anything which, from a particular perspective and point in time, is no longer seen as useful to some set of practices. Something that might be considered waste from one perspective or at one time, may be considered useful from another perspective or time.

Western model of development: development characterised by industry and systems of production based on fossil fuels and high energy and material input (as opposed to a carbohydrate economy).

White noise: a mixture of noise of all frequencies, in the same way that white light is a mixture of all frequencies. White noise can be used to control and reduce the impact of ambient noise.

Worker productivity: the term used to identify worker output measured by things like worker absenteeism.

Xenobiotic chemical: human-made chemicals.

Simon Baird is an industrial designer and studying philosophy at the Australian National University. He is currently a research assistant with the Centre for Environmental Philosophy, Planning and Design. In recent years, he has tutored in several design for environment units at the University of Canberra.

Dr Greg Bamford teaches architectural design and people/ environment studies at the University of Queensland. He is currently researching socio-spatial aspects of cohousing and the relations between built form and social and environmental issues in Australian cities. His PhD is in philosophy and he publishes in architecture and the philosophy of science.

Nigel Bell is principle of ECO Design Architects/Consultants and 1994 Churchill Fellowship holder, and has been responsible for a range of award-winning projects involving heritage, ecotourism and place, including the national 1996 Banksia Environment Award for 'the built environment'. Nigel has written and delivered vocational training packages for the NSW Environment Protection Authority, Master Builders Association, and local council training programs.

Eric Billett holds the chair in Design at Brunel University in London. He is a Chartered Engineer and a Chartered Chemist.

Dr Janis Birkeland was an architect, lawyer and city planner in San Francisco. Her PhD is in environmental management and her research areas are architecture, ecological design, ecophilosophy, ecopolitics and planning. She lectures in the Division of Science and Design at the University of Canberra, and has taught ecological architecture, planning and environmental studies. Recently, she was the senior environmental education officer for the Australian Department of the Environment and Heritage.

William Browning is the founder of Rocky Mountain Institute's Green Development Services. He has served as a science adviser on the environment for the American Institute of Architects, was vice-chair of the ASTM's Green Building Rating Committees, and serves on the Board of Directors of the US Green Building Council, Greening America and the Roaring Fork Conservancy. He has written several books and papers on sustainable building.

Michael Brylawski is the co-founder and Vice President of Market Development for Hypercar, Inc of Basalt, Colorado. Hypercar, Inc is developing and commercialising technology solutions that will enable a new generation of advanced vehicles. Formerly Senior Research Associate at Rocky Mountain Institute, he co-developed the Hypercar concept and specialised in advanced materials, manufacturing, and economics.

Steve Burroughs has 20 years of work experience in earth wall construction and recycling of building products. He is now a consultant specialising in appropriate technologies, and has worked to implement low-income, low-impact housing in third world countries. He is completing a PhD on earth wall construction.

Tim Cadman is a founding member of the international NGO, Native Forest Network, and a Director of the New South Wales based Colong Foundation for Wilderness Ltd. He is currently working on a PhD in Applied Science at the University of Canberra, and is a research assistant for the Centre for Environmental Philosophy, Planning and Design, where he specialises in research into sustainable forest management.

Ann Marie Chalkley has a BSc in Industrial Design and is a PhD candidate in the Department of Design at Brunel University.

Andrea Cook is a strategic planning consultant, and is completing a PhD at the University of Melbourne. She has been in planning practice for ten years and has a particular interest in planning for diversity, community-based planning, participatory planning and community design for safety. She has won 11 awards for her planning work.

Bob Cotgrove lectures in environmental economics and transport economics at the University of Tasmania. He has a background in geography, political science and economics, and a Masters in transport economics and in environmental and resource economics. His research area is the changing interactions between transport systems, land use patterns and social welfare arising from the shift to a post-industrial culture.

Victor Cusack is a professional artist and proprietor of Bamboo World Botanical Garden as well as a major plantation and tissue culture laboratory for plantation species in Northern NSW, Australia. He is author of two books on bamboo.

Jamnes Danenberg is researching the use of hemp as a construction material, and its role in the transition to a carbohydrate based economy, at the University of South Australia. He was co-convenor of HEMP SA Inc and was a candidate for the SA Upper House. He is currently building a house from hemp.

Sam Davidson is an industrial designer who graduated with first class honours from the University of Canberra. He is currently working as a design engineer for a Canberra-based company that manufactures fibre-optic products for the telecommunications industry.

Paul Downton is architect of a major eco-city project in Adelaide. He has won numerous awards, including the 1992 US award for environmental journalism with Gar Smith, editor of the *Earth Island Journal*. He lectures at the University of South Australia and has authored numerous articles and papers on eco-city planning.

Dr Richard Eckersley is currently a visiting fellow at the National Centre for Epidemiology and Population Health at the Australian National University, Canberra. He has edited and contributed to two books, and is the author of several major reports for the Australian Commission for the Future and CSIRO, Australia's national research organisation.

David Eisenberg is Co-Director of the Development Center for Appropriate Technology in Tucson, Arizona. His construction experience includes the cover of Biosphere 2, houses of structural concrete, structural steel, masonry, wood, adobe, rammed earth, and straw-bale. He now leads a collaborative effort to create a sustainable context for building regulation.

Bill Green is chair of Applied Ergonomics and Design at University of Canberra. For the previous five years he was Professor of Applied Ergonomics and Design, and Head of Department of Industrial Design at TU Delft in The Netherlands. He has a professional design background, has been involved in design education in England, Australia and Europe and is a past branch chairman and Federal Secretary of the Ergonomics Society of Australia.

Dr Clive Hamilton is Executive Director of The Australia Institute, a Canberra-based public policy research centre. He is also a Visiting Fellow in the Public Policy Program at the Australian National University and an Adjunct Professor at the University of Technology, Sydney. His previous positions include Head of Research at the Federal Government's Resource Assessment Commission and Senior Economist at the Bureau of Industry Economics.

Dr David Harrison is a Senior Lecturer in the Department of Design at Brunel University in London. He has been researching environmentally sensitive design for five years. He is a Chartered Engineer, and has been a Westminster Fellow in the Parliamentary Office of Science and Technology, and written and directed for BBC Education.

Steve Hatfield-Dodds is a presently in private consulting and most recently was the Director of the Environmental Economics Unit in the Australian Department of the Environment and Heritage. He has worked previously on tax policy and structural reform issues in the Australian Treasury and Finance Canada, and taught at the Australian National University. He has published a number of papers on sustainable development, the use of environmental taxes, and the links between economic activity, environmental quality and social well-being.

Kathleen Henderson received degrees in Botany and Natural Resource Management after a career in architectural design. She now lectures in Architectural Technology at UNITEC Institute of Technology. Her primary research interest is the development of sustainable construction processes.

Dr Glen Hill has practised architecture for almost 20 years and has a particular interest in ecological architecture. He lectures in history and theory at the Department of Architecture, Planning and Allied Arts, University of Sydney. His particular research interest is the ecological implications of contemporary thought, especially that influenced by Martin Heidegger. He is currently a Director of the Eco Design Foundation.

Angela Hirst has participated in the design, regeneration and maintenance of permaculture gardens at several public and private gardens around Brisbane. She is a PhD candidate at the University of Queensland and has completed an Honours thesis in Permaculture and a certificate in permaculture design. She is currently researching urban food places at the University of Queensland, and designing an autonomous house and garden for an inner city block in Brisbane.

Cherie Hoyle is a political and ecological activist and community organiser, working in many countries. Her experience includes vice-president of the Conservation Council for SA for three years. She works with Paul Downton in the development of a major Eco-city project in South Australia.

Liz James has had a long-term interest in ecological housing, and designed and built a mud brick home for her family. She worked in the construction industry for about ten years before graduating with an honours degree in architecture, sharing the ACT Housing Academic Award. She is presently practising architecture in Coastal New South Wales, and serves on several local town planning committees.

Dr Pam Kaufman was a researcher with the Cultural Heritage Research Centre at the University of Canberra. Her major research interests include cultural landscapes, community meanings and values and public participation. Her experience includes organising and facilitating local community workshops to identify, assess and conserve places of meaning and value.

Dr Meg Keen taught urban ecology at the Australian National University. Her research interests include systems of communication and education which affect the use of environmental science in policy formation and private citizen behaviour. Currently, she works for in the Graduate Studies in Environmental Management and Development Program in the Asia Pacific School for Economics and Management, Australian National University.

Garry Kerans has trained in Engineering and Science and has been a builder for nearly 20 years. He is presently a principal of Integrated EcoVillages, a small collective proactively developing medium density urban properties as well as constructing low-energy waste water treatment plants.

Regina Lubanga is from Kenya and holds a Masters degree from New Zealand. She is presently working towards a PhD at the University of Canberra, researching environmental indicators.

Dr Bill Lawson lectures at the University of New South Wales, specialising on the environmental impacts of building materials, including embodied energy and ecological sustainability in developed countries. He recently published an important text in this area, and (with H. Partridge) developed a building material assessment system. Previously, he was a management consultant, and has also worked in development in Nepal and Papua New Guinea.

David Marsden-Ballard has been engaged in hands-on permaculture since 1978, doing his Certificate course with Bill Mollison in 1984. He has since gained four diplomas in permaculture design, a BSc in social ecology, a graduate diploma in environmental education and is working on a Doctorate in Education.

William McDonough is Dean of the School of Architecture at the University of Virginia, and has won numerous awards for his ecologically responsible architecture. In collaboration with German chemist Michael Braungart, he has also designed non-toxic shower gels, fabrics and dolls that do not contain harmful substances, biodegradable yogurt cartoons, and a recyclable Nike sneaker. His firm's buildings include a new community in Indiana called Coffee Creek Centre, which will work against suburban sprawl by establishing a compact and pleasant small town.

Dr Graham Meltzer teaches and occasionally practises architecture in Brisbane, Australia. His teaching and research focus on the architecture of environmental and social sustainability. Graham also teaches community design and collaborative design processes. He has lived extensively in 'intentional communities', including two years on a kibbutz and eight years at Tuntable Falls, Nimbin – Australia's largest residential cooperative.

Bill Mollison is the co-inventor and populariser of Permaculture along with David Holmgren, which has become a worldwide movement.

Robert Moore is currently the Manager of the Canberra Energy Advisory Service, which provides free advice on energy conservation in housing. Recently he has completed a book on adaptable housing for the Commonwealth Department of Veterans Affairs. His jobs have included building estimating, architectural draftsman, builder, senior technical officer on airports, building surveyor and he has managed his design and construction consultancy.

David Morris is Vice President of the Washington DC and Minneapolis-based Institute for Local Self-Reliance, 1313 5th St, SE Minneapolis Mn 55414, www.ilsr.org. and editor-in-chief of its journal, *The Carbohydrate Economy*. For decades he has advocated the shift to a 'carbohydrate economy', which would replace fossil fuels in fuels, oils and construction materials.

Dr Peter Newman is Professor of City Policy and Director of the Institute for Science and Technology Policy at Murdoch University, Perth, and a Visiting Professor at the University of Pennsylvania. He was an elected City Councillor for the City of Fremantle, worked with the West Australian State Government in transport planning and environmental planning roles and helped to rebuild Perth's rail system. He has worked for the Australian Government on the Ecologically Sustainable Development process, energy research priorities (NERDDC), the State of the Environment reporting process and the Better Cities program. He has also been a consultant to OECD and the World Bank on urban policy issues, and is the author of many publications and books on sustainable cities.

Paul Osmond is currently Environment Program Manager at the University of New South Wales, and previously Design Projects Officer with Port Phillip Council in Victoria. With training and work experience which cut across the traditional boundaries of ecology, environmental management and landscape design, he is interested in applying systems perspectives to the challenges of achieving 'sustainability by design'.

Anne-Marie Poirrer is an environmental science graduate from the University of New South Wales. She has been proactive in alternative pest management field for many years and is Director of Systems Pest Management, a consumers representative on the Australian Standards Committees for Termite and Inspections. She is frequently consulted by media for non-chemical solutions to urban problems, and is founder of the IPM Network.

Dr William Rees has taught at the University of British Columbia since 1969–70 and is currently Professor and Director of the University's School of Community and Regional Planning. His teaching and research emphasise human ecology and the public

policy and planning implications of human-induced global environmental trends. Much of this work falls within the domain of ecological economics. He is best known in this field for his invention of 'ecological footprint analysis'.

Dr Joseph Romm is director of the non profit Center for Energy and Climate Solutions, a one-stop shop devoted to helping businesses design customised greenhouse gas mitigation plans. He is author of *Cool Companies,* the first book to benchmark corporate best practices in climate mitigation. He led the Administration's climate technology policy formulation and was Executive Director of the Department of Energy's Pollution Prevention and Waste Minimisation Executive Board and initiated a pollution prevention program that is saving the DOE $90 million a year. He holds a PhD in physics from MIT in Massachusetts.

Dr Helen Ross is a social scientist, and Professor in the Department of Natural and Rural Systems Management, University of Queensland. Previously, she was a Fellow at the Centre for Resource and Environmental Studies, Australian National University. She is also a former public servant with the Commonwealth of Australia's Aboriginal Affairs portfolio. She has written several books on Aboriginal housing. Her other research fields are social impact assessment, and environmental management, in Australia and Thailand.

Dr Vanda Rounsefell worked in general medical practice for 25 tears and in clinical ecology since 1982. She is currently completing a PhD at the University of Adelaide, on an ecological approach to human settlement design and development. She has considerable experience in theory and practice in the fields of human settlement ecology, integrated planning and development, holistic and environmental health, and community development.

Dr Ariel Salleh is Associate Professor at the University of Western Sydney, where she specialised in globalisation, social movement ideologies, and ecofeminist ethics. Her book *Ecofeminism as Politics: Nature, Marx and the Postmodern* (1997) reflects these interests. She has also lectured in sociology at the universities of Wollongong and New South Wales, and lectured in environmental ethics in Chicago, New York and Manila. Integrating theory and practice, she has been an activist in many environmental issues, and has contributed to numerous theoretical journals as writer, editor or on editorial boards.

Maria Santana studied architecture at the America University in Bogota, Colombia and her thesis was on bamboo construction and its environmental implications. After working a few years as an architect in Colombia, she did a Masters on timber waste minimisation through bio-sensitive design at the University of Canberra. She has now returned to Bogota.

Dr Wendy Sarkissian is a planner specialising in social planning and research, housing and community participation, and has worked as a researcher and planner for governments as a private social planning consultant. She holds a Masters of Town Planning (Adelaide University) and a PhD (Murdoch University, University of Canberra). Her work focuses on community participation and the housing needs of disadvantaged groups.

Dr John Schooneveldt has qualifications in psychology, linguistics and biology, and is an independent business consultant focusing on ecologically sustainable innovation and development. When in government, he was one of the principal architects of Australia's multicultural policies and international social security arrangements. He also pioneered a range of business facilitation techniques, and is a foundation fellow of the Australian Institute of Company Directors and a founding member of the Australasian Institute of Enterprise Facilitators.

John Storey is a senior lecturer at the School of Architecture, Victoria University of Wellington, in New Zealand, where he teaches architectural design, ecological design, detail design and building construction. He is an architect and has practised in the United Kingdom, New Zealand, Finland and Hong Kong.

Leslie St. Jacques holds a Master's in Environmental Studies, Planning, from York University, Toronto, Ontario, Canada. She is a writer, strawbale enthusiast and organic farmer living in Guelph, Ontario.

Alison Terry is an interior designer with previous experience as a nurse. She has given professional development seminars on the subject of healthy building materials and has taught with the University of South Australia and RMIT.

Hardin Tibbs is a management consultant with extensive international experience. He is CEO of Synthesys Strategic Consulting, an Australian-based management consulting firm. In addition to his strategy work, he has made significant contributions on issues involving technology and environment. He consults in this field through Ecostructure, a subsidiary of Synthesys.

Dr John Todd is Head of Department of Geography and Environmental Studies, University of Tasmania. He has a physical science background, and has been teaching courses in environmental management for about 20 years. His research interests lie in the areas of energy and society, air pollution, impact assessment and environmental education. He is a member of many committees and boards dealing with environmental matters.

John Todd is presently visiting professor of ecological design at the University of Vermont. He is principal of John Todd Research and Design Inc, and director of Living Technologies, Inc, and is president of Ocean Arks International. Among his books are *Reinhabiting Cities and Towns: Designing for Sustainability* (1981) and *From Eco-Cities to Living Machines: Principles of Ecological Design* (1994).

Ted Trainer has been teaching at the University of Technology, Sydney, and writing about sustainability and alternative society themes for many years. His recent books include *The Conserver Society: Alternatives for Sustainability* (1995) and *Saving the Environment: What it will Take* (1998). He is also developing Pigface Point, an alternative lifestyle education site near Sydney.

Cam Walker has worked with Friends of the Earth for the last nine years – a grassroots, activist-based organisation which addresses environmental issues in their full social context, and seeks to offer practical solutions to environmental problems. He also edits *Inhabit*, a bioregional magazine which is generating discussion about bioregionalism and its appropriateness in Australia.

Gowrie Waterhouse began his training in forestry in the 1980s and has worked in the areas of plant biology and forest ecology before retraining in industrial design. He now lectures in industrial design at the University of Canberra. He has received awards for environmentally sustainable design. He is a PhD candidate and currently working on exploring artificial intelligence in product design.

Professor Brenda Vale and **Dr Robert Vale** have worked on the design of autonomous buildings for over 25 years, and completed the first autonomous house in the United Kingdom in 1993. Since emigrating from the UK in 1996, they have been academics at the University of Auckland, where both members of the Sustainable Design Research Centre, of which Brenda is the Director. Their books include *The Autonomous House* (1975) and *Green Architecture* (1991). They won the first Green Building of the Year Award, and have received the Global 500 Award for Environmental Achievement from the United Nations. The UK's first autonomous settlement, a group of five earth-sheltered houses designed by them, was occupied in 1998. They have just completed the design guide for the UK's first 'Zero CO_2' village in Nottinghamshire.

Sim van der Ryn is President of the Ecological Design Institute and runs an architecture practice in Sausalito, California. As a recognised authority in sustainable architecture and planning and former Professor of Architecture (Berkeley), he has created many examples of sustainable building and written several books, including *Ecological Design* (1996) with Stuart Cowan and *Sustainable Communities* (1986) with Peter Calthorpe.

Kelvin Walsh is a consulting strategic planner and urban designer with extensive experience in urban and rural strategy development, master planning, project evaluation, dispute resolution, community participation processes and developing responsive processes to ensure viable and implementable outcomes.

Kath Wellman is Associate Professor, Landscape Architecture, and Acting Director, Centre for Developing Cities at the University of Canberra. She has placed in international urban design competitions in Europe, the US and Australia. Her current interests are in the cross-sectoral relationships which shape cities, and in issues of sustainability.

Karen Yevenes has a Bachelor of Education (visual arts) and a Bachelor of Industrial Design (Hons). She has worked as a graphic designer and computer modeller in a Sydney studio, and is currently teaching design principles to tertiary students at the University of Technology Insearch. She also lectures in industrial design at the University of Western Sydney, Macarthur.

Lou Yiping is an Associate Professor in the Bamboo Research Division, Research Institute of Sub-Tropical Forestry, in the Chinese Academy of Forestry. He holds a PhD in forest ecology and silviculture in the Chinese Academy of Forestry. He has been a consultant on bamboo research and cultivation for industrial materials for the World Bank and has served as a consultant on bamboo cultivation for building materials on TCDC project in South America for Food and Agriculture Organization of the United Nations.

Index

travel behaviour 158
treatment lagoons 178

U

U curve 39
Unified Ecology 79
Unified Human Community Ecology 78–83
   criteria 79
   scales 79
unsustainable
   design practices 99
   development 114–117
urban
   agriculture 102
   car travel 158
   consolidation 165
   density 168
   density, alternatives to 169
   design 78
   development 33–35, 134–136
   development model 134
   ecological systems 58
   ecology 29, 57–60
   environment 74–76, 114
   irrigation 58
   landscaping 95
   planning 67, 74
   space 168
   sprawl 35
   traffic congestion 158
   transport 158–161, 168–172
   travel behaviour 158
   travel costs 159
   water cycle 58
urban transport infrastructure 172
urbanisation 57, 237, 246
   rate of 74, 75
usefulness 131
user pays principle 215
utilitarianism 22
utility 131

V

values, social 105
vertical gardening 102
volatile organic compounds 146

W

war toys 126
waste 43, 51, 54
   and fashion 43
   as a resource 58
   exchange system 54

generated during production 53
   landfill 58
   minimisation 188–191
   of timber during construction 188, 190
   of timber during extraction 189
   reduction 50
   treatment 173
wastewater 58–59, 177–179
   recycling 178
   treatment 173, 177
water 13
   collection of rain 182
   demand for 58
   grey 177
   in remote area Aboriginal housing 139
   pollution 173
   quality 173
   rainwater retention 101
   recycling 58, 67, 177, 178
   recycling economics 178
   resource management 177
   storm 178
   treatment 58, 178
   urban cycle 58
wealth distribution, global 34
Weisman, Leslie 95
welfare 23
   economic 159
   effects of economic growth on 38
Western patriarchal culture 120
Western thought structures 116
wetlands for water treatment 178
white ants – see termites
whole systems planning 73
Whyalla eco-city 166
women
   exclusion from health studies 145
   expectations and needs of products 131
women's status 120
women's taste 131
worker productivity 154, 156
world as a mechanism 74
World Business Council for Sustainable Development 70
World Wide Fund for Nature 40

X

xenbiotic chemicals 144